Using DataI

Walter R. Bruce III

CORPORATION

LEADING COMPUTER KNOWLEDGE

Using DataEase®

DEDICATION

To Mom and Dad

Publishing Director

Lloyd J. Short

Acquisitions Editor

Karen A. Bluestein

Product Director

David Maguiness

Production Editor

Kelly D. Dobbs

Editors

Sara Allaei
Jo Anna Arnott
Fran Blauw

Editorial Assistant

Stacie Lamborne

Indexer

Sherry Massey

Book Design and Production

Dan Armstrong   Jon Ogle
Brad Chinn   Cindy Phipps
Corinne Harmon   Joe Ramon
David Kline   Jenny Renbarger
Lori A. Lyons   Dennis Sheehan
Jennifer Matthews   Louise Shinault

Composed in Garamond and Excellent #47
by Que Corporation

ABOUT THE AUTHOR

Walter R. Bruce III

Walter R. Bruce III lives in the Washington, D.C. suburb of Springfield, Va., with his wife, two sons, and infant daughter. He is a free-lance writer and microcomputer consultant. He is the author of Que's *Using Enable/OA™* and *Using Paradox® 3* and has written several instructional texts for intermediate and advanced workshops on using popular microcomputer software packages. He also has led workshops for government and private industry clients from coast to coast.

Mr. Bruce is a licensed attorney who practiced law for three years in North Carolina and six years in the United States Air Force. For three years, he was an advisor on computer and office automation-related issues to The Judge Advocate General of the Air Force, the chief military attorney in the Air Force.

Contents at a Glance

TABLE OF CONTENTS

II   Intermediate DataEase

9   Maintaining Your Database 345

TRADEMARK ACKNOWLEDGMENTS

Que Corporation has made every effort to supply trademark information about company names, products, and services mentioned in this book. Trademarks indicated below were derived from various sources. Que Corporation cannot attest to the accuracy of this information.

1-2-3, Lotus, Symphony, and VisiCalc are registered trademarks of Lotus Development Corporation.

3+ is a trademark of 3M Company.

3Com is a registered trademark of 3Com Corporation.

Ashton-Tate, dBASE, dBASE II, dBASE III, and dBase IV are registered trademarks of Ashton-Tate Corporation.

AT&T is a registered trademark of AT&T.

Crosstalk is a registered trademark of Digital Communications Associates, Inc.

DataEase and GrafTalk are registered trademarks of DataEase International, Inc.

IBM and Personal System/2 are registered trademarks and PC XT, OS/2, and PS/2 are trademarks of International Business Machines Corporation.

MailMerge is a registered trademark of MicroPro International Corporation.

Microsoft and MS-DOS are registered trademarks of Microsoft Corporation.

Motorola is a registered trademark of Motorola, Inc.

MultiMate is a registered trademark of Multimate International, an Ashton-Tate Corporation.

NetWare and Novell are registered trademarks of Novell, Inc.

PFS is a registered trademark of Software Publishing Corporation.

ProKey is a trademark of RoseSoft, Inc.

SideKick is a registered trademark of Borland International, Inc.

WordPerfect is a trademark of Satellite Software International.

WordStar is a registered trademark of MicroPro International Corporation.

▼ ACKNOWLEDGMENTS

Thanks to the following individuals for their invaluable help in bringing this book together:

David Maguiness, Kelly Dobbs, and all the editors at Que Corporation for their outstanding work and tireless patience on this project.

The staffs of the Technical Services and Documentation departments of DataEase International for their timely assistance in providing much-appreciated technical advice.

Introduction

Welcome to *Using DataEase*. With this book as your guide, you are about to become a DataEase convert. The program's authors chose the name DataEase because they believed that the name represents a full-featured database program that is easy to learn and use. Although the concepts of "ease of use" and "ease of learning" are relative to your previous experience, after you try DataEase, you will agree that the name fits the program's capabilities.

If the program is so easy to learn and use, why do you need a book to help you? Traveling even a well-marked road for the first time is always easier if you follow someone who has been down that road before. As you journey through DataEase, this book points out the most direct route while showing you how to avoid hidden potholes and unnecessary tolls.

What Is DataEase?

DataEase is a relational database management system first released in 1983 by DataEase International, Inc.

Technical support is available to registered users through the DataEase Hotline, (voice) 203-374-2825. Registered users also can obtain assistance through the DataEase Bulletin Board. Set your modem to 2400 bps, 8 data bits, no parity, 1 stop bit and dial 203-374-6302.

DataEase is a PC-based program that enables you to collect, sort, and retrieve information on a computer and then generate reports that consolidate and/or summarize this information in virtually any order or format you choose. You even can create representations of your numeric data with color graphics by adding the optional program, DataEase GrafTalk.

1

DataEase is designed so that you can develop powerful database applications without programming. By reading the menus and using the on-line help documentation, you can learn how to use the basic features of DataEase without ever opening a book.

Don't be content with just the basics, however. This book shows you how to use DataEase to converse with your data as if you were old friends, and to create reports from your data like a seasoned mainframe programmer.

Because of its *relational* design, DataEase enables you to work with multiple database forms at once as easily as you can work with one at a time. You can create Quick Reports that generate output from your data in just a few keystrokes—output that would take hours or even days to generate by hand.

Features for the Power User and Applications Developer

For the power user and programmer, DataEase 4.0 also includes comprehensive form-design capabilities and a full procedural database application development environment called the *DataEase Query Language* (DQL). DataEase provides substantial assistance to novice developers even in the DQL. Through the Interactive mode, you can create complete programs by selecting options from menus. Even though DataEase provides this programming capability, many of DataEase's most powerful functions, such as Multiforms, lookups, and menus, are available without DQL programming.

At the time of this writing, DataEase International intends to implement a Structured Query Language (SQL) interface for DataEase. The program will act as an SQL front end that enables the use of DataEase procedures against an SQL server engine (e.g., IBM OS/2 Extended Edition and the Ashton-Tate/Microsoft/Sybase SQL server). DQL programs will be able to use SQL queries to be passed directly to an SQL server. DataEase also has announced the development of an OS/2 Presentation Manager version of DataEase.

Features New with DataEase 4.0 and DataEase 4.2

Since the introduction of DataEase, DataEase International has enhanced the program progressively, while remaining true to the original design concepts. DataEase 4.0, released in the last quarter of 1988, included over 70 enhancements not found in earlier versions of the program. DataEase 4.01, released in July 1989, fixed some of the minor problems found in

Version 4.0 and was provided free of charge to all registered users of
Version 4.0. DataEase 4.01 added no new features but made a few
cosmetic screen changes. DataEase 4.2, released in November 1989, adds
two significant enhancements—a DOS extender that supports up to
16 megabytes of extended memory (on Intel 80286- and 80386-based
IBM AT-compatible computers) and additional protection of referential
integrity when using Multiforms—but makes relatively few changes to the
appearance DataEase screens. (The screen shots used to illustrate this book
were created with Version 4.2.) The new features added in Versions 4.0
and 4.2 are summarized in table 1.1.

Table I.1
New Features in DataEase 4.0 and 4.2

Category	Enhancement
Sign On and User Interface	Descriptive database names
	Menu of database names
	Path name support
	Bar and pull-down menus
Forms and Record Entry	Multiforms
	* Referential integrity
	Table View
	Form-level security
	Suppress auto tab
	Clear form after every record
	Form-level help
	Data encryption
	Improved use of color
	Easier access to relationship definition
	Free cursor movement in field definition
	Summary functions in derived fields
	Dynamic choice fields
	Soundex "sounds like" searches
	Field dictionary
Import, Export, Convert	Convert Lotus/Symphony, dBASE, and Paradox applications
	Direct export to MultiMate and WordPerfect
Reports	Easier access to Quick Reports
	Formulas in Quick Reports
	Date and time in headers and footers of Quick Reports
	Multiform Quick Reports

Table I.1 — *continued*

Category	Enhancement
	Group totals in formulas
	Scroll screen output up and down
DQL	Increased control of system functions
	Call procedures from procedures
	Call outside programs
	Case statements
	Global variables
	Multiview on data-entry form
	Multiple data-entry forms
	Custom processing of entered records
	Custom messages to users
	List all from secondary form
	Logical control over output format
	Comments in Query Language
	Cut and paste between queries
Local Area Network	Automatic refresh of changed information
	Identify network user of locked resource
	User override of locking options
System Administration	Workstation configuration
	Database specific configuration
	Menu of available printers
	Expanded printer control
	HP LaserJet support
Capacities	DOS extender supports up to 16 megabytes of extended memory
	Two billion records per form
	Supports LIM/EMS 3.2 and 4.0
	Sorts to EMS or virtual disk
	500K RAM for called programs
	2,000 forms per database
	2,000 reports/procedures per database
	4,000 character formulas
	4,000 character help messages
Speed	Faster index update
	Faster LAN record update
	Faster sorting

Table I.1—*continued*

Category	Enhancement
International	14 languages that you can select at sign on Metric date format International currency format

DataEase 4.0, 4.01, and 4.2 are upwardly compatible with DataEase 2.12 or later and DataEase LAN 1.12. Database files and applications created in one of these earlier releases work as before. However, you must use the older version of DataEase to back up files and applications created in Version 2.53 or earlier or in DataEase LAN 1.12, and you must use Version 4.0 or higher to restore the files and applications (refer to Appendix A, "DataEase Installation and Start Up," for more information).

What Should Your System Have?

Each package of DataEase 4.2 includes two versions of the program: DataEase 640K and DataEase 16M. The 640K version of DataEase 4.2 (DataEase 640K) is essentially the same as DataEase Version 4.01 but has improved protection for referential integrity. The 16M (16 megabyte) version of DataEase (DataEase 16M), however, enables you to take advantage of the improved system memory features in Intel 80286- and 80386-based computers.

To run DataEase 640K as a single-user program, your system must be an IBM PC, XT, AT, PS/2, or compatible. The system must have at least 640K of system memory (RAM) and DOS 3.1 or higher. DataEase 4.2 can be run only from a hard disk.

The requirements for running DataEase 16M as a single-user program are more stringent than requirements for DataEase 640K. Your system must be an IBM Personal Computer AT, PS/2, or compatible equipped with an Intel 80286 or 80386 CPU (central processing unit). The system must have at least 640K of conventional memory, at least 384K of extended memory (above one megabyte), a hard disk, and DOS 3.1 or higher.

For network use, DataEase 4.2 requires a PC workstation configured as described in either of the preceding two paragraphs and connected to a network running one of the following network operating systems:

Novell Advanced Netware Version 2.0A or higher

3Com 3Plus, Version 1.2

IBM PC Local Area Network Program, Version 1.10 or higher

AT&T Starlan Network

Banyan VINES, Version 2.10 or higher

Any network that supports DOS 3.1 network functions

Performance and capacity of DataEase 640K are improved in stand-alone systems or network workstations if your system includes expanded memory (LIM/EMS or EEMS).

Who Should Read This Book?

Using DataEase is for you if you are a new DataEase user who wants to get the most out of this product. Experienced users also will find this book helpful in gaining a clear understanding of the DataEase 4.0, 4.01, and 4.2 enhancements and may learn a few new tricks along the way.

The approach of this book mirrors the approach of the DataEase software. You don't have to be a programmer to learn and use DataEase, and this book makes no assumptions about your background or experience in using PCs or database management systems. If you are a new database user, start at the beginning of the book and move at a comfortable pace. More experienced users can skim Part I, "DataEase Fundamentals," and look more closely beginning in Part II, "Intermediate DataEase." Power DataEase users may want to breeze through Parts I and II and concentrate on Part III, "Advanced DataEase Processing: Using DQL."

New DataEase 4.0, 4.01, and 4.2 features are annotated with a Version 4 icon in the margin. DataEase 2.53 owners who have not yet chosen to upgrade should skip these sections. Special considerations of interest to network users generally are addressed at the end of each chapter.

This book helps you to learn DataEase thoroughly at a comfortable pace, with a minimal amount of work. You learn how to design database forms, queries, reports, menus, and business graphs. Get to know DataEase and the program's capabilities well, and DataEase will give you everything you could want from a database management system.

What Is in *Using DataEase*?

This book is divided into three major parts. The first two parts begin with a Quick Start lesson previewing the topics to be discussed. Use the Quick Starts to get your feet wet and examine the chapters that follow for detailed explanations.

Part I, "DataEase Fundamentals"

The first part of the book covers the most fundamental aspects of creating a database with DataEase—entering data, editing data, asking questions of the data, and printing simple reports.

Chapter 1, "Navigating DataEase," explains how to use the keyboard, menus, screens, views, and prompts in DataEase.

Chapter 2, "Creating DataEase Record-Entry Forms," describes how to define and modify the DataEase forms. In DataEase, the form is the basic database building block.

Chapter 3, "Modifying and Enhancing Record-Entry Forms," builds on Chapter 2 and explains how to make changes to a form definition and how to enhance the form.

Chapter 4, "Using DataEase To Enter, Edit, and View Data," discusses the basics of entering data into a database form and how to edit and view the data after it has been entered.

Chapter 5, "Using DataEase Quick Reports," covers how to create, save, load, and run relatively simple reports using DataEase.

Part II, "Intermediate DataEase"

After you understand DataEase fundamentals, you are ready to tap the power of DataEase.

Chapter 6, "Using Related DataEase Forms," discusses in detail DataEase relational capabilities, including creating and using multiforms and creating Quick Reports with related tables and multiforms.

Chapter 7, "Building Simple Procedures with DQL," describes how to build simple DQL procedures to retrieve data for use in reports. This chapter shows you how to use DQL relational operators to analyze your data and how to save a DQL query for later use.

Chapter 8, "Customizing DataEase Reports," shows you how to select and customize the format of DataEase reports. This chapter discusses the use of standard, or built-in, formats, such as the columnar format and the record-entry format, and the use of the formatting commands to create specialized reports.

Chapter 9, "Maintaining Your Database," covers a number of DataEase features that help you administer your database. This chapter describes how to obtain status information, make back-up copies of your database, use DOS functions, and define authorized users. This chapter also explains the use of DataEase utilities to import data, transfer data between forms, copy reports and procedures between databases, convert data from other programs, rename a database, and delete a database.

Chapter 10, "Creating Custom DataEase Menus," demonstrates the easy DataEase menu-generating facility. This chapter shows you how to design a database system that can be used by choosing options from on-screen menus. (Such a database system is referred to as a *menu system*.) The menu system can make your database so simple to use that even the most computerphobic person in your office can print out reports like a pro.

Part III, "Advanced DataEase Processing: Using DQL"

The last part of *Using DataEase* introduces you to some of the more advanced capabilities and the DataEase Query Language.

Chapter 11, "Building Full-Powered Procedures with DQL," shows you how to perform calculations and change the content of database files through DataEase DQL procedures. This chapter also briefly summarizes the programming capabilities of DataEase and discusses the basic categories of programming commands available in DQL.

Appendixes

For those users who have not yet installed the program, Appendix A describes the necessary steps for installing DataEase 4.0. Appendix B briefly discusses the use of the System Configuration form to modify the video and printer configuration, default directory for temporary files, country customization, file encryption features, and other settings.

Part I

DataEase
Fundamentals

Includes

Quick Start 1:
A Typical DataEase Session

Navigating DataEase

Creating DataEase Record-Entry Forms

Modifying and Enhancing Record-Entry Forms

Using DataEase To Enter, Edit, and View Data

Using DataEase Quick Reports

A Typical DataEase Session

This Quick Start is the first of two tutorials presented in this book. Each Quick Start precedes a major division of the book and is designed to help you get a running start at DataEase. You are taken step-by-step through simple examples of techniques and concepts discussed in the following chapters. This tutorial gives you a preview of what is to come and enables you to begin using DataEase right away. Hopefully, this lesson also will encourage you to experiment as you continue throughout the book.

Quick Start 1 walks you through the start-up of DataEase. In this tutorial, you create a simple database form consisting of a list of company sales representatives, and you enter several records. You also ask a few questions of the data and print the list of sales representatives sorted first by identification number and then by name.

Before you can begin, you must install DataEase. Refer to Appendix A for the steps necessary to ready the program for use on your system. When you have installed DataEase, you are ready to begin the tutorial.

Starting DataEase

DataEase is designed to work best from a hard disk. To start DataEase, do the following:

1. Start your system and access the root directory on the hard disk containing DataEase. From the DOS prompt (probably C›), make a directory to hold your DataEase files. For example, to create a

directory with the name DEDATA, at the DOS prompt type the following:

MD \DEDATA

Press Enter. DOS creates the new directory but returns to the same prompt. If you see the message Unable to create directory, you probably already have used the directory name. Choose a different name and try the *MD* command again.

2. After you create a directory for your database files, switch to the directory on your hard disk containing the DataEase program files. From the DOS prompt, type *CD \DEASE*.

Press Enter. This command assumes that you have followed the instructions in Appendix A to install the program and that the program's system files are in the directory *C:\DEASE*.

3. To start DataEase and to tell the program where to store database files during your DataEase session, type *DEASE C:\DEDATA*. Press Enter. As DataEase loads, you see the DataEase Sign On screen, similar to figure QS1.1.

Fig. QS1.1.

The DataEase Sign On screen.

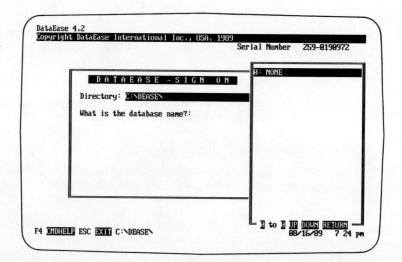

The screen states that the directory is C:\DEDATA\. DataEase stores any files you create during the current session in this directory on the hard disk. DataEase then asks you for a database name. The next section describes how to create the database to which you add data and how to respond to this prompt.

Creating the Order Tracking Database

When you work in DataEase, you must specify a *database* in which you want to work. Each database consists of one or more *forms* containing the data added to the database. In this tutorial, you create a database named *Order Tracking* and a form named *Sales Representative*. Quick Start 2 and the examples used throughout this book develop this database further into a simple order tracking system for a small manufacturer of widgets.

1. In a window on the right side of the initial Sign On screen, DataEase displays a list of available databases. In the example shown in figure QS1.1, no database has been created, and the only option displayed is 0: NONE. Press Enter to accept this option.

2. To specify a new database named Order Tracking, at the prompt, What is the database name?:, type *Order Tracking*. Because this database does not exist yet, DataEase asks whether you want to create the database. Answer this prompt by typing *y* and pressing Enter. DataEase informs you that the New database will use the filename letter O. DataEase uses this letter in the names of DOS files created during your DataEase session to identify them as parts of the Order Tracking database.

3. DataEase then asks for your name. The program considers the individual who initially names the database to be the *database administrator*. As the database administrator, you have the opportunity to assign a name and password that will be required to access the database. Later, you also can assign separate user names and passwords for other individuals. If you leave the database name and password blank, anyone can obtain access to your data. For this tutorial, type *Quick Start* as the database name. Press Enter. You can use upper- or lowercase letters. DataEase then prompts you for a password. Type *Que* as the password and press Enter. The password does not display as you type. Again, you can use upper- or lowercase letters. After you enter the password, DataEase displays the DataEase Main menu shown in figure QS1.2.

Defining a Form

You need to enter information about the sales representatives of your fictional company. DataEase makes entering such information into a database similar to typing the same data in a fill-in-the-blank form using a typewriter. Before you can begin entering information on your computer,

Fig. QS1.2.

*The DataEase Main
menu.*

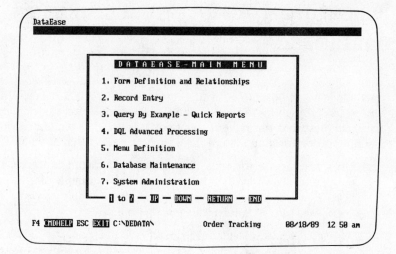

however, you must describe to DataEase what this form should look like
and the general nature of the data. Will the data consist of alphanumeric
characters (text), numbers, currency, or dates? How long will the longest
name be? How many characters are in the largest address? This process is
called *form definition*.

1. To define the form for entering the sales representatives' data, select
   1. Form Definition and Relationships from the Main menu.

   DataEase displays the Form Definition menu. At the bottom of the
   screen, the directory C:\DEDATA\ and the database name Order
   Tracking are displayed, as shown in figure QS1.3.

Fig. QS1.3.

*The Form Definition
menu.*

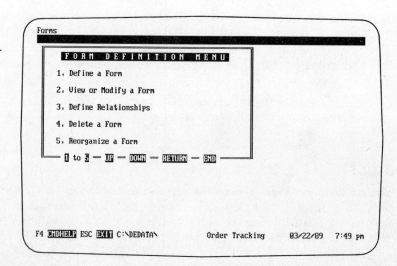

2. From the Form Definition menu, choose **1. Define a Form**. DataEase prompts you to enter the form name. Type *Sales Representative* and press Enter. DataEase displays the Form Definition screen, a mostly blank screen with two lines of text at the top and one line at the bottom. The top line identifies the form as the Sales Representative form. The second line includes instructions for defining fields and field names. In a DataEase form, a *field* is equivalent to a blank on a fill-in-the-blank form. The bottom line, the *function key line*, shows a list of keys and corresponding functions.

3. This Sales Representative form is used for entering sales representative data: identification number, name, address, phone number, hire date, salary, and number of dependents. To begin defining the form, press the down-arrow key five times and the Tab key twice to move the blinking cursor away from the top left corner of the screen. Notice that a position indicator, located on the top line of the screen, keeps track of the cursor's row and column. Your cursor should now be at position R6C13 (row 6 and column 13). Starting at R6C13, type *Sales Rep ID:*.

Press the space bar to move the cursor one space to the right; then press F10 (FIELD). DataEase displays the Field Definition screen shown in figure QS1.4, with Sales Rep ID already entered as the field name. DataEase took this name from the text you entered.

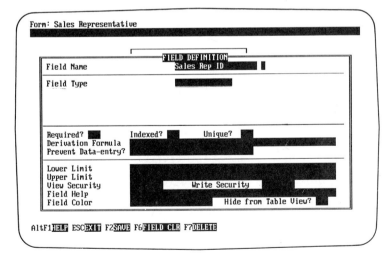

Fig. QS1.4.

The Field Definition screen.

4. Press Enter to move down to the field labeled Field Type. When you move to this field, six of the available field types are listed as a menu in the second line of the screen. This line is the *prompt line*. The field you are defining, Sales Rep ID, will contain an identification number for each sales representative.

5. This company uses Social Security numbers for identification. DataEase has a special field type for that purpose. Choose the *numeric string* field type by selecting 2: Numeric String.

   DataEase displays Numeric String in the field and moves the cursor down a line to the prompt, Is it a formatted string?. A menu listing four special numeric string formatting options replaces the field type menu in the prompt line.

6. To select field formatting for Social Security numbers choose 2: soc.sec.no.

   DataEase fills in the field with the formatting type, moves the cursor down to the Required field, and displays a menu with the choices 1: no 2: yes in the prompt line.

7. Leave the remaining fields blank and save the definition of the Sales Rep ID field by pressing F2 (SAVE), one of the function-key commands listed in the function key line. DataEase returns to the Form Definition screen and displays a highlighted bar to the right of Sales Rep ID:. This bar is 11 characters long and represents the Sales Rep ID field.

8. Define a field for the sales representative's first name. Use the cursor-movement keys to move the cursor to position R8C13. Type *First Name:* and press the space bar. Define a field at this position (R8C25) by pressing F10 (FIELD) to display the Field Definition screen. Press Enter at the field name First Name and choose 1: Text from the menu of field types in the prompt line.

9. After you select the text field type, DataEase moves the cursor to the next field and prompts you to specify a maximum length for the field. For this First Name field, type *15* to indicate that employees' first names are no longer than 15 characters. Press Enter, and DataEase moves the cursor to the Required field. Press F2 (SAVE) to save the field definition. DataEase returns to the Form Definition screen, adding a highlighted bar to the right of First Name:. This bar is 15 spaces long, the same size as the defined maximum field length.

10. Using a similar procedure, define the following fields:

Screen Prompt	Cursor Position of Prompt	Field Name	Field Type	Maximum Length
Last Name:	R8C43	Last Name	Text	20
Region:	R10C13	Region	Text	8
Date Hired:	R10C43	Date Hired	Date	
Dependents:	R12C13	Dependents	Number/ Integer	2
Salary:	R14C13	Salary	Dollar	6

To correct typing mistakes, erase the error with the Backspace key and retype the appropriate entry. You also can use the arrow keys to move the cursor around the form. When you are finished, your screen should look like figure QS1.5.

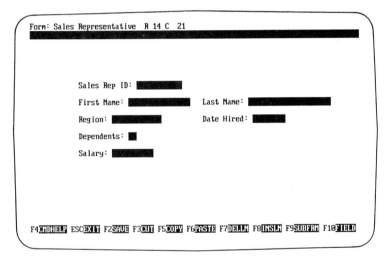

Fig. QS1.5.

The Sales Representative form.

11. When you complete the definition, tell DataEase you are finished by pressing F2 (SAVE). DataEase returns you to the Form Definition menu.

12. To return to the DataEase Main menu press Esc. You are ready to enter data into the form.

Entering Employee Data

Now that you have built a form to hold data about your sales representatives, you can enter the data. If you have ever typed information onto a fill-in-the-blank form, you already know how to complete the next series of steps:

1. From the Main menu, choose **2. Record Entry**. DataEase displays the DataEase Records menu (see fig. QS1.6).

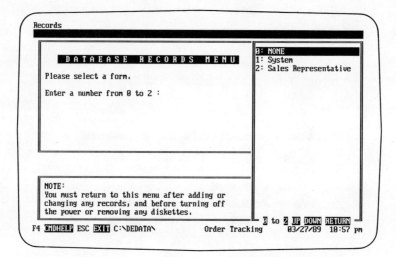

Fig. QS1.6.

The DataEase Records menu.

2. The right side of the Records menu screen includes a list of available forms. The option 0: NONE is highlighted by a menu selection bar. The third menu choice is 2: Sales Representative. The cursor is blinking in the middle of the screen at a prompt that instructs you to Please select a form. Enter a number from 0 to 2:. Type 2 or press the down-arrow key twice to move the highlighted bar to the Sales Representative option. Press Enter to select this form.

DataEase displays the Sales Representative form with the cursor in the Sales Rep ID field. Notice that the Sales Rep ID field already contains hyphens in the correct position for a social security number (see fig. QS1.7). The Date Hired field contains slashes, and the Salary field contains a decimal point. A message in the second line from the top of the screen says No record on screen.

```
 Sales Representative
 No record on screen

                    ┌─────────────────────────┐
                    │  Sales Representative Data  │
                    └─────────────────────────┘

        Sales Rep ID: ▌  - -

        First Name: ▌            Last Name: ▌

        Region:  ▌               Date Hired: ▌ / / ▌

        Dependents: ▌

        Salary:  ▌        ▌


  F4 CMDHELP  ESC EXIT  F2 SAVE  Sh-F1 TABLE  F3 VIEW  F7 DEL  F8 MODIFY  F9 BBE  F10 MULTI
```

Fig. QS1.7.

The Sales Representative form with the fields defined.

3. Type the first sales representative's identification number, *921-65-1234*. Do not type the hyphens. When the field is filled, the cursor moves to the First Name field. Notice that a message in the second line from the top of the screen says New Record on Screen. Type the following data into the remaining fields on the form. When data does not completely fill a field, press Enter or Tab to move to the next field. Do not type the comma in the Salary field. DataEase automatically adds the comma.

Field	Entry
First Name	Gertrude
Last Name	English
Region	Northern
Date Hired	01/04/71
Dependents	2
Salary	36,750

4. When you finish entering this data, press F2 (SAVE). DataEase displays a message in the top line of the screen indicating that the record has been written to disk. The second line of the screen now says Record 1 on screen. Clear this record by pressing F5 (FORM CLEAR), and the second line of the screen again says No record on screen.

5. Type the following data into the form by using the same procedure. Remember to press F2 (SAVE) and then F5 (FORM CLEAR) after you enter each record.

Sales Rep ID	First Name	Last Name	Region	Date Hired	Dep	Salary
541-67-5555	Emily	Bronson	Southern	06/10/75	0	23,875.00
230-76-2376	Tim	Jones	Eastern	11/23/69	3	41,400.00
111-33-8491	Harry	Albertson	Western	06/07/78	2	32,250.00
329-76-2219	Sharon	Kellogs	Northern	03/04/81	1	21,870.00

6. Toggle on Table View by pressing Shift-F1 (TABLE). Your screen should look like figure QS1.8. Press End to display a screen full of rows for entering data.

Fig. QS1.8.

The sales representative data in Table View.

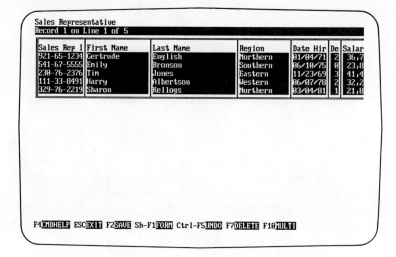

Notice that you do not have enough room on-screen to display the entire Salary field. Type the data for Samantha Green listed below. After you type the entry in the Dependents field (shortened to De on-screen) and press Enter, DataEase displays the Salary field in a screen by itself. Type Samantha's salary and press Enter. DataEase moves the cursor to the beginning of the next blank row for you to enter another record. Enter the last two records (listed below) using this table. Use the arrow keys to move around the table to correct errors, if necessary.

Sales Rep ID	First Name	Last Name	Region	Date Hired	Dep	Salary
448-09-6721	Samantha	Green	Southern	08/15/79	4	49,339.00
129-08-4562	Joseph	Jones	Western	10/02/65	1	75,900.00
987-31-9873	George	Quick	Eastern	05/21/83	3	53,000.00

7. When finished, press F2 (SAVE) to save the new records. DataEase
   displays the message Saved All Changes at the top of the screen.
   Press F5 (FORM CLEAR) to remove the extra blank rows. Your
   screen appears similar to figure QS1.9. Press Esc to return to the
   Records menu. Press Esc again to return to the Main menu.

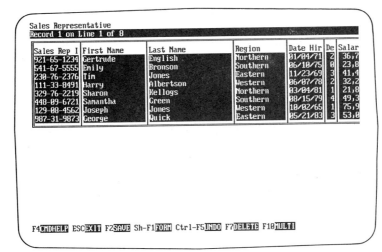

Fig. QS1.9.

*Data displayed in
Table View after
entering new records.*

Asking Questions of the Data

Imagine that you had entered data for 800 or even 8,000 sales
representatives, rather than just 8, and you want to find the record of one
representative to make a correction. With DataEase you easily can search
for the record of any sales representative, regardless of how many records
are in the database, by typing the Social Security number or name into the
form. The next several steps in this tutorial demonstrate how to use the
fill-in-the-blank method to ask the following simple questions of your data:

❏ What is the name of the sales representative whose Sales Rep ID is
   111-33-8491?

❏ How many dependents does Joseph Jones have?

❏ What is the salary of Emily Brunson, or is her last name Brinson?

To answer these three questions, complete the following steps:

1. Access the record-entry screen by selecting **2. Record Entry**. To
   select the Sales Representative form, choose 2: Sales Representative
   and press Enter. DataEase displays the form with all fields empty.

2. To answer the first question, DataEase needs to search the records for the one with a Sales Rep ID field containing the value 111-33-8491. To specify this criterion, press Alt-F5 (UNCHECKED) and type *111-33-8491* in the Sales Rep ID field. To search the Sales Representative records for a match, press F3 (VIEW). DataEase displays Harry Albertson's record.

3. The second question asks for the number of Joseph Jones' dependents. Clear the fields and prepare to enter search criteria by pressing Alt-F5 (UNCHECKED). Press Tab or Enter once to go to the First Name field. Type *Joseph* in the First Name field, press Enter, and type *Jones* in the Last Name field. Press F3 (VIEW) to search for a matching record. DataEase displays Joseph's record and shows that he has 1 dependent.

4. The last question requests the salary of Emily Brunson, but you are not sure whether Brunson is the correct spelling. You can use DataEase's special *Soundex* search feature to find the correct record even if you do not have the exact spelling. Clear the current record and prepare the form to accept search criteria by pressing Alt-F5 (UNCHECKED). Press Tab or Enter twice to skip the Sales Rep ID and First Name fields. In the Last Name field, type the Soundex character (tilde), followed by your best guess at the spelling, *Brunson*. Press F3 (VIEW) to start the search. The correct spelling is Bronson. DataEase finds and displays Emily Bronson's record and shows that her salary is 23,875.

5. Press Esc to return to the Records menu. Press Esc again to return to the Main menu.

Reporting Your Data

You usually do not enter records into a database form in any particular order. DataEase can retrieve any information from the form through the search process, regardless of the order of the records. When you display data on-screen or send data to the printer, however, you often want to see the information in order alphabetically, by date, by Sales Rep ID, and so on. In this portion of the tutorial, you can try out the DataEase reporting features that enable you to display or print data in sorted order. In this lesson, you display, in order by Sales Rep ID, the First Name, Last Name, and Salary fields for all records in the Sales Representative form. Then, you total the salaries of the sales representatives at the bottom of the report and print this information. Finally, you print the same data in alphabetical order by last name.

1. From the Main menu, select **3. Quick Reports**. DataEase displays the QBE-Quick Reports menu with the highlighted menu selection bar resting on the **1. Run Report** option (see fig. QS1.10).

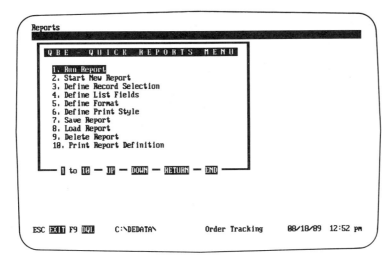

Fig. QS1.10.

The QBE-Quick Reports menu.

2. To start a new report, select **2. Start New Report**. DataEase displays a message at the top of the screen, New report Started, and moves the highlighted bar down to the **3. Define Record Selection** option.

3. Because your report is to include all records in the Sales Representative form, you can skip the third option on the Quick Reports menu. To specify which fields should be included in the report, select **4. Define List Fields**.

   DataEase displays a menu of forms on the right side of the screen. A prompt at the bottom of the screen instructs you to Select the Primary File for the Report.

4. Select 2: Sales Representative and press Enter. DataEase displays the Sales Representative form. A message in the top line of the screen says Select Fields. Another message in the next line says Press Space to mark field. Specify order reverse group count sum mean max or min.

5. To mark the first field you want included in the report, press the space bar at the Sales Rep ID field. DataEase places a 1 in the field, indicating that this field is the first to be in the report, and moves the cursor one space to the right.

6. Because you want the report sorted in order by this field, type *order* and press Enter. DataEase moves the cursor to the First Name field.

7. Mark the First Name and Last Name fields by pressing the space bar and Enter (do not type *order* in these fields). DataEase places the field sequence numbers, 2 and 3, in these fields. Skip the Department, Date Hired, and Dependents fields by pressing the Enter, Tab, or down-arrow key until the cursor is in the Salary field.

8. When the cursor is in the Salary field, press the space bar. DataEase places the field sequence number 4 in the field and moves the cursor one space to the right. To sum the salaries of all the sales representatives, type *sum* in the Salary field. Your screen should look like figure QS1.11.

Fig. QS1.11.

Selecting fields for the report.

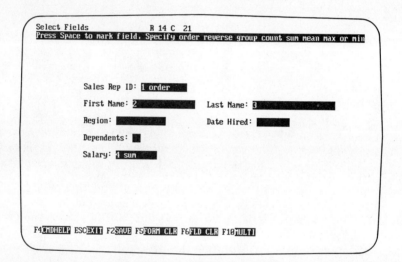

```
Select Fields              R 14 C  21
Press Space to mark field. Specify order reverse group count sum mean max or min




        Sales Rep ID: 1 order

        First Name: 2                 Last Name: 3

        Region:                       Date Hired:

        Dependents:

        Salary: 4 sum




    F4 CMDHELP  ESC EXIT  F2 SAVE  F5 FORM CLR  F6 FLD CLR  F10 MULTI
```

9. Save the field selections to memory (RAM) by pressing F2 (SAVE). DataEase returns to the Quick Reports menu. The highlighted menu selection bar now is resting on the **5. Define Format** option.

10. To display the report on-screen, select **1. Run Report**. DataEase displays a message at the top of the screen that says Press Return or 0 to proceed. Two options on this menu begin with the number 1: **1. Run Report** and **10. Print Report Definition**. Press Enter to select the Run Report option. (Pressing 0 prints the Report Definition.) The report displays on-screen. Your report should look like figure QS1.12. Notice that the report is in order by the sales representatives' identification numbers. Press any key to return to the Quick Reports menu.

```
                                    Running report
 END OF REPORT, SPACE: Return to Menu    PgUp: Scroll

 ================================================================
    Sales Rep      First          Last          Salary
       ID          Name           Name
 ----------------------------------------------------------------
    111-33-8491  Harry        Albertson          32,250.00
    129-88-4562  Joseph       Jones              75,900.00
    230-76-2376  Tim          Jones              41,400.00
    329-76-2219  Sharon       Kellogs            21,870.00
    448-89-6721  Samantha     Green              49,339.00
    541-67-5555  Emily        Bronson            23,875.00
    921-65-1234  Gertrude     English            36,750.00
    987-31-9873  George       Quick              53,000.00
 ----------------------------------------------------------------
    sum                                         334,384.00
 ================================================================



 F4 CMDHELP ESC EXIT C:\DEDATA\        ORDER TRACKING    07/17/89  11:11 pm
```

Fig. QS1.12.

The Quick Report.

11. Now that the report looks good on-screen, you can send the report to the printer. From the Quick Reports menu, select **6. Define Print Style**. DataEase displays the Print Style Specification screen (see fig. QS1.13).

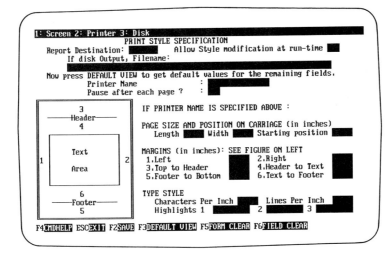

Fig. QS1.13.

The Print Style Specification screen.

12. The first field on the Print Style Specification screen is Report Destination. When the cursor is resting in this field, DataEase displays a list of three options in the top line of the screen. To indicate that the report should go to the printer, select 2: `Printer`. Accept the default values for the remaining questions by pressing F3 (DEFAULT VIEW). (See Appendix B for instructions on configuring DataEase for your printer.) To save the settings, press F2 (SAVE). DataEase returns to the Quick Reports menu, and the **7. Save Report** option is highlighted.

13. Make sure that your printer is set up properly (paper, ribbon, plugged in, connected to computer) and run the report again. Select **1. Run Report** and press Enter. DataEase prints the report as displayed on-screen and displays the Quick Reports menu with the **1. Run Report** option highlighted.

14. You can save this report definition to disk in case you want to run the report again later. Select **7. Save Report**. DataEase displays a window at the bottom of the screen. The program places the cursor in a field to the right of a prompt that instructs you to `Please enter the report procedure name`. Type the name *Sales Rep ID Order* and press Enter. DataEase saves the report procedure definition to a file on disk and displays the Quick Reports menu with the **2. Start New Report** option highlighted.

15. Modify the report so that the records are printed in alphabetical order by the representatives' last names. From the Quick Reports menu, select **4. Modify List Fields**. DataEase displays the Sales Representative form again.

16. Change the order of the fields to print in the following order: Last Name, First Name, Sales Rep ID, Salary. Clear all fields with F5 (FORM CLR). Move to each field in the order that the fields should appear in the report and press the space bar. DataEase places a field sequence number in each field. Type *order* to the right of the 1 in the Last Name field. Type *sum* to the right of 4 in the Salary field. When you finish, press F2 (SAVE) to save these selections. DataEase returns to the Quick Reports menu with the **5. Define Format** option highlighted.

17. To print the modified version of the report, make sure that your printer is ready. (If the page with the previous report is still in the printer, push the form feed button so that the new version of the report prints on a separate page.) Select **1. Run Report** and press Enter. DataEase prints the report, Last Name first and in alphabetical order by Last Name. DataEase then returns to the Quick Reports menu with **1. Run Report** highlighted.

18. You can save this modified version of the report under a different name. From the Quick Reports menu, select **7. Save Report**. DataEase displays a window at the bottom of the screen and asks Do you want to save modified report procedure under another name(y/n)? Answer by typing *y*, and DataEase displays another field for the new report procedure's name. Type the name *Last Name Order* and press Enter. DataEase saves the report and returns to the Quick Reports menu with the **2. Start New Report** option highlighted. Press Esc to return to the Main menu.

Quitting from DataEase

To quit DataEase, press Esc. DataEase displays a small window on top of the Main menu containing the question Exiting DataEase—Are you sure?. Answer by typing *y*, and DataEase returns you to DOS.

Summary

Quick Start 1 guided you through starting up DataEase, creating a simple database, entering several records, and asking a few questions of the data. You also printed a report sorted in two different ways. This simple exercise gave you a glimpse of the subjects covered in the first part of this book. Now that you have an idea of where you are headed, turn to Chapter 1 and learn the details of how to navigate DataEase.

1

Navigating DataEase

This chapter gets you started with DataEase by helping you find your way around in the program. This chapter explains the DataEase screen, menus, on-line help, and how to use the keyboard. You start by looking at how to sign on to DataEase and create a database. Then, you examine how DataEase looks on-screen and how the program requests and responds to your actions. Start in this chapter if you are new to DataEase, even if you are an experienced PC user. Seasoned DataEase users may want to at least skim this chapter for features new in DataEase 4.0.

This chapter assumes that you have started DataEase and that the DataEase Sign On screen is displayed. Refer to Appendix A for instructions on installing and running DataEase.

Signing On to DataEase

When you first start DataEase, the program displays the DataEase Sign On screen (see fig. 1.1). This screen shows the program name and version number on the top line of the screen, a copyright notice on the second line, and the serial number of your copy of DataEase on the third line. Within a window (a box on-screen), DataEase displays the DOS path of the current data directory (refer to Appendix A for information on starting DataEase from the desired data directory) and the prompt What is the database name?:.

At the Sign On screen, you select a database with which to work or indicate that you want to create a database. After you have been working with one DataEase database and want to change to another database, you have to exit DataEase and begin again.

Fig. 1.1.

*The DataEase Sign
On screen.*

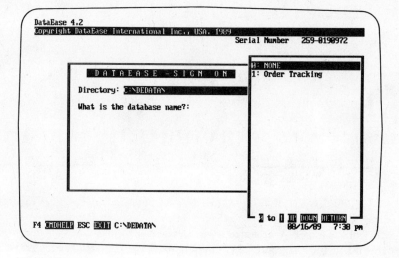

On the right side of the Sign On screen, DataEase displays a menu of
databases available in the current data directory. The first time you start
DataEase, the only database choice is 0: NONE. Even after you create a
database, the 0: NONE choice is listed first. After you create a database (for
example, the Order Tracking database from the first Quick Start lesson),
DataEase includes the new database in the list.

Creating a Database

To create a database, select 0: NONE by pressing Enter. At the prompt that
asks for the database name, type the name of the database you want to
create and press Enter. Follow the database naming rules listed in table 1.1.

Table 1.1
Database, User Name, and Password Naming Rules

Object Type	Rules
Database	2 to 19 keyboard characters (spaces are allowed)
User name	0 to 15 characters (including spaces and any displayable characters)
Password	0 to 8 characters (including spaces and any displayable characters)

After you enter the database name, DataEase displays the following message:

```
Database does not exist in specified directory
Create a new database (y/n) ?:
```

Type *y* and press Enter. DataEase displays the following message:

```
New database will use filename letter d
```

The variable, *d*, is a letter assigned by DataEase.

Understanding the Database Letter

DataEase assigns a letter to each database in the data directory. This letter is the *database letter*. DataEase uses the database letter in naming files containing data associated with the database. If you begin the database name with a letter, DataEase uses this letter as the database letter. If this letter has been used (because another database begins with the same letter), DataEase assigns the first unused letter in the alphabet.

Tip: Even though a DataEase database name can begin with any character, you should try to begin each database name in a directory with a different letter. In this way, you control how DataEase assigns the database letter. You also should avoid beginning a database name with a number, because doing so can affect the operation of the Sign On screen window menu (see the "Using Window Menus" section, later in this chapter).

Table 1.2 shows how DataEase names files. Forms, procedures, and the other files listed in table 1.2 are covered later in this book.

For example, if you create a form named *Sales Representative* (as in the first Quick Start) in the Order Tracking database, DataEase creates a DOS file in your current data directory with the filename *SALEOAAA.DBA*. The letters *SALE* are the first four letters of *Sale*s Representative; the letter *O* is the database letter for the Order Tracking database, and DataEase assigns the letters *AAA*. The filename extension that DataEase assigns to form definitions is DBA. When you add records to the form, DataEase places the data in a file named *SALEOAAA.DBM*. Only the filename extension is different.

If this process seems complicated and confusing, do not be concerned. You can give forms and procedures names, such as *Sales Representative* and *Quarterly Report*, that are descriptive and easy to identify and remember.

Table 1.2
DataEase Data Files

File type	DOS file name*
Form definition	*formdaaa*.DBA
Form records	*formdaaa*.DBM
Form index	*formdaaa*.I*nn*
Form error	*formdaaa*.E*nn*
Procedure definition	*procdaaa*.DBR
Data-entry form	*procdaaa*.DBF
Forms directory	RDRR*daaa*.DBM
Procedure directory	REPO*daaa*.DBM
Users	USER*daaa*.DBM
Configuration	CONF*daaa*.DBM
Printers	PRIN*daaa*.DBM
Screen style	SCRE*daaa*.DBM
Relationships	RELA*daaa*.DBM
Menus	MENU*daaa*.DBM

*File name conventions: the letters *form* represent the first four letters of the form name; the letters *proc* represent the first four letters of the procedure name; *d* represents the database letter; the letters *aaa* represent three letters assigned by DataEase; the letters *nn* represent a hexadecimal (base 16) number assigned by DataEase.

DataEase largely relieves you of the tedium of keeping up with DOS file names. For most purposes you need to be only generally aware that DataEase is creating files on your disk and that DataEase names these files in a systematic way.

Specifying a System Administrator Name and Password

After you specify the name of the new database, DataEase asks for your name. DataEase is not asking for your legal name, but for a *user name* you want to use for security purposes. The name you enter at this prompt is the *system administrator* name (also called the *database administrator* name) for the database (see table 1.1 for naming rules). The first Quick Start used *Quick Start* as the database administrator name. Refer to the "Defining Users" section of Chapter 9 for a discussion of how to add more user names for a database. You can leave the user name field blank. If you do provide a system administrator name, you have to enter the name each time you want to access the database, but you have better security.

After you provide a system administrator name or press Enter at the blank field without providing a name, DataEase prompts you for a password. This optional password is associated with the system administrator name. Table 1.1 lists password naming rules. Do not use a password that you cannot remember. Refer to Appendix A for information on how to specify the database name, your user name, and your password in the DataEase start-up command.

Tip: The primary purpose of DataEase user names and passwords is data security. When you are the only user of a database, you may not be concerned with limiting or preventing access by others. Leave the user name blank so that you do not have to type the name each time you want to use the database. If you assign a system administrator name when you first create the database, DataEase enables you to change the name later, but you cannot remove the name. Refer to Chapter 9 for a complete discussion of assigning, changing, and removing user names, passwords, and security levels.

Caution: When you share a database with other users, on a stand-alone computer or on a network, you probably should assign a system administrator name and password from the start. If you decide not to assign a system administrator name and password, anyone else who has access to DataEase on your computer (or on a shared network directory) can lock you out of the database by adding a user name and password. Someone else also can change, look at, and destroy information.

After you enter your name and password, DataEase displays the Main menu (see fig. 1.2).

Selecting an Existing Database

When you want to use an existing database, you can select a database from the list on the right side of the Sign On screen. Move the highlighted menu selection bar down to the database name and press Enter or type the database name at the prompt. You can move the menu bar in two ways: press the down-arrow key until the menu bar is on the name of the database you want to work with or type the number listed to the left of the database name. Press Enter to complete the selection.

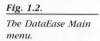

Fig. 1.2.

The DataEase Main menu.

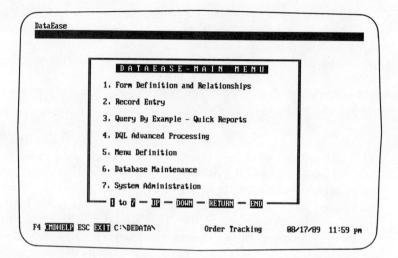

DataEase asks for your name, as the program does when you are creating a database. Type a valid user name and press Enter. If no system administrator or user name has been defined for the database, you can press Enter at the blank field.

After you enter a valid user name, you are asked for a password. Type the password associated with the user name (or system administrator name) that you just used. When no passwords have been defined, you can press Enter at the blank field. If you fail to enter a valid user name and password in three attempts, DataEase gives up and returns you to DOS.

After you enter your user name and password, DataEase displays the Main menu.

Using the DataEase Main Menu

The DataEase Main menu, shown in figure 1.2, provides a thumb-nail overview of the features of the program.

The first option, **1. Form Definition and Relationships**, accesses the part of the program that enables you to build DataEase *record-entry forms* and *form relationships* that are the basic building blocks of a DataEase database. Chapter 2, "Creating DataEase Record-Entry Forms," Chapter 3, "Modifying and Enhancing Record-Entry Forms," and Chapter 6, "Using Related DataEase Forms," describe how to create and use DataEase forms and relationships.

The second option on the DataEase Main menu, **2. Record Entry**, invokes the DataEase module that enables you to enter, view, and edit data in the forms created through the first option. Chapter 4, "Using DataEase To Enter, Edit, and View Data," covers the fundamentals of this part of DataEase. Chapter 6 follows up on this topic by covering entering, editing, and viewing data using DataEase *multiforms*.

The **3. Query By Example—Quick Reports** option provides a non-procedural method (without programming) of designing and printing reports from the data in your database. Chapter 5, "Using DataEase Quick Reports," describes how to use this part of DataEase to generate reports using data from one form at a time. Chapter 6 expands on this discussion, describing how to use Quick Reports to generate reports from multiple forms.

The **4. DQL Advanced Processing** option is the door to creating DataEase Query Language (DQL) procedures (programs). This part of DataEase is related to the Quick Reports section because Quick Reports can be saved as DQL procedures. Chapter 7, "Building Simple Procedures with DQL," Chapter 8, "Customizing DataEase Reports," and Chapter 11, "Building Full-Powered Procedures with DQL," discuss in detail how to use the many features and capabilities of DQL.

The fifth option, **5. Menu Definition**, accesses DataEase's impressive menu-generation facility. This part of DataEase enables you to design and build a custom menu system for your database. This option is explained in Chapter 10, "Creating Custom DataEase Menus."

The last two options on the Main men, **6. Database Maintenance** and **7. System Administration**, are described in Chapter 9, "Maintaining Your Database." These two options access capabilities to perform such maintenance operations as making a back-up copy of your database; defining user names, passwords, and security levels; exchanging data with other file formats, and controlling multiuser access.

Familiarizing Yourself with the DataEase Screen

The basic building block of a DataEase database is the DataEase form. The details of creating a DataEase form are covered in Chapters 2 and 3. The Field Definition screen, used to define a field in a DataEase form, is a good example of a typical DataEase screen. Figure 1.3 shows the Field Definition screen you see if you are adding a field named *Phone* to the Sales Representative form defined in the preceding Quick Start.

Title area　　Mode/cursor position area　　Message area

Fig. 1.3.

The Field Definition screen—a typical DataEase screen.

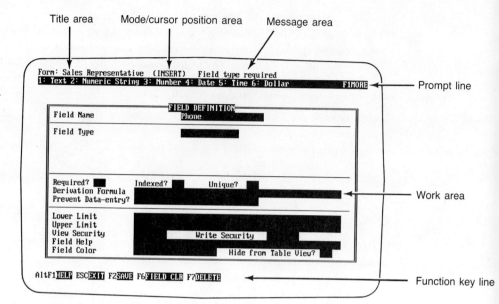

```
Form: Sales Representative  (INSERT)   Field type required
1: Text 2: Numeric String 3: Number 4: Date 5: Time 6: Dollar         F1MORE
```
Prompt line

```
                        ╔FIELD DEFINITION╗
Field Name                    Phone

Field Type




Required? ▮         Indexed? ▮      Unique?
Derivation Formula
Prevent Data-entry?

Lower Limit
Upper Limit
View Security           Write Security
Field Help
Field Color              Hide from Table View?
```
Work area

```
AltF1HELP ESCEXIT F2SAVE F6FIELD CLR F7DELETE
```
Function key line

Title Area

The left portion of the top line of the DataEase screen is called the *title area*. DataEase uses this portion of the screen to display the name of the current DataEase operation. Figure 1.3 shows that you are working on Form definition and that the name of the form is Sales Representative.

Mode/Cursor Position Area

The middle portion of the top line, the *mode/cursor position area*, shows the cursor position on-screen when you are editing a form or procedure. R1C1 means that the cursor is in row 1 and column 1 of the screen. This area of the screen also is used to show when DataEase is in *Insert mode*. By default, characters typed on-screen replace any characters already on-screen in the same position. You must switch to *Insert mode*, by pressing the Insert key, when you want to insert a character or characters without replacing existing characters. The first time you press Insert, DataEase turns on Insert mode and displays (INSERT) in the mode/cursor position area of the top line of the screen, as in figure 1.3. The next time you press Insert, DataEase turns off Insert mode and displays the cursor position in the mode/cursor position area.

Message Area

The right third of the top line is the *message area*. In this portion of the screen, DataEase displays messages about the progress of various operations and error messages. Figure 1.3 shows an error message in the message area.

Prompt Line

DataEase uses the second line of the screen, the *prompt line*, to display questions to the user and to list options. Options listed in the prompt line are called *line menus*. Line menus are discussed in the "Using Line Menus" section of this chapter.

Function Key Line

DataEase displays two kinds of information in the bottom line of the screen: a list of available function-key commands and status information. This line is called the *function key line* or *status line*. For convenience, this book uses *function key line*.

As explained in the "Using DataEase Function-Key Commands" section of this chapter, DataEase enables you to perform many operations by using function keys. The most commonly used function-key commands for an operation are listed in the function key line. To the right of each function key (or key combination) is an abbreviated name for the operation performed by the function key. The bottom line of figure 1.3 shows five function-key commands (the Esc key is considered a function key for this purpose): Alt-F1 (HELP), Esc (EXIT), F2 (SAVE), F6 (FIELD CLR), and F7 (DELETE).

When DataEase uses the full screen for a menu, the function key line displays the following function-key choices: F4 (CMDHELP) and ESC (EXIT). To the right of these two options, DataEase also displays several pieces of *status* information: the data directory, the database name, and the system date and time.

Work Area

The remaining 21 lines of the screen, below the prompt line and above the function key line, are where the majority of your work is done. This portion of the screen, therefore, is called the *work area*. Figure 1.3 shows the Field Definition form in the work area.

Using the DataEase Keyboard

DataEase works with any PC, AT, PS/2 keyboard, or equivalent. You should become familiar with your keyboard (see fig. 1.4). This book uses the labels found on the IBM Enhanced Keyboard to describe the keys you should press.

Fig. 1.4.

The IBM PC keyboard (top); the IBM Personal Computer AT keyboard (center), and the IBM Enhanced Keyboard (bottom).

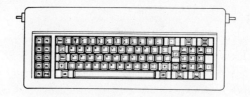

Using DataEase Function-Key Commands

As with many other popular programs, DataEase uses function keys F1 through F10. In most cases, a function-key command also can be executed through the DataEase pull-down menus (see "Using Pull-Down Menus" in this chapter); however, because using menus requires more keystrokes, this book suggests that you use the function-key method whenever possible.

To help you learn how and when to use DataEase commands, discussions in this book list the function key or key combination followed by the name of the function (in parentheses) as the name appears on the function key line. For example, when an instruction in the book says press Alt-F1 (HELP), you should press the Alt key and the F1 function key in combination. Do not type *HELP*.

Tip: If you have difficulty executing a key-combination command (with any program, not just DataEase), you may be trying to press both keys at the same instant. Try the following method instead: press the initial key of the key combination (Alt, Ctrl, or Shift) and hold down the key; using the other hand, press the second key; then release both keys. This method works every time.

Because you can have as many as 40 different functions assigned to these keys and key combinations at the same time, DataEase cannot possibly list all the functions in the function key line. DataEase, therefore, provides *pull-down* menus as an alternative to the function keys and to help you perform operations whose function keys are not listed in the function key line. Refer to the "Using Pull-Down Menus" section of this chapter for more on this topic.

Using DataEase Keystroke Commands

A few DataEase commands can be performed by combining the Alt key with a letter. For example, Alt-U turns on underlining, and Alt-E turns underlining off. These commands are called *keystroke commands*. Most DataEase commands, however, are executed by pressing a function key, pressing a function-key combination, or using menus.

Using the Cursor-Movement and Editing Keys

As you work with DataEase, you often need to move the cursor around the screen to enter and edit data. The keys you use are the *cursor-movement* keys and *editing* keys. The cursor-movement keys are the →, ↑, ←, ↓, Home, PgUp, PgDn, End, Tab, and Enter keys. The keys that assist you at editing data in DataEase are the Backspace, Tab, Insert, and Delete keys. The specific effect of cursor-movement keys and editing keys differs somewhat depending on whether you are creating or editing a form on-screen or are entering and editing data into a form.

Using these keys in form design is covered in Chapter 2, "Creating DataEase Record-Entry Forms," and Chapter 3, "Modifying and Enhancing Record-Entry Forms." Use of cursor-movement keys and editing keys during Record Entry is described in Chapter 4, "Using DataEase To Enter, Edit, and View Data."

Using DataEase Menus

DataEase uses four types of menus to make learning and using the program as easy as possible: *window*, *full-screen*, *line*, and *pull-down* menus. By selecting options from a menu, you always know exactly what your choices are, and you cannot make a syntax error.

Using Window Menus

Window menus are already familiar to you. The list of databases displayed on the Sign On screen is a window menu (see fig. 1.1). A window menu displays a numbered vertical list of options on the right third of the screen, surrounded by a border of double lines. When DataEase first displays this type of menu, a highlighted menu selection bar rests on the first (top) option. To select a window-menu option, you move this menu selection bar to the desired choice and press Enter. You can move the bar to the appropriate selection in three ways: type the option number, type the first letter, or use the cursor-movement keys.

DataEase numbers window menu options. You can move the menu selection bar by typing the number of the option you want to use. After you type the first digit of a two-digit number, DataEase moves the selection bar to the option with that number and displays the message Enter another Digit, or press Return. If you press Enter (Return), DataEase selects the highlighted option. When you type the next digit, DataEase moves the bar to the correct option.

You also can move the menu selection bar by typing the first letter of the menu selection name. When more than one option begins with the same letter, DataEase moves the bar to the first one (from top to bottom) in the list. If this option is not the one you want, use the down-arrow key to move the selection bar.

DataEase also enables you to use several cursor-movement keys to move the selection bar. Each press of the down-arrow key moves the bar down one option in the list. The up-arrow key moves the bar up one option at a time. The End key moves the bar to the last option, and the Home key moves the bar to the first option. When you have more than 19 options listed in the window menu, PgDn moves to item number 20. If you have more than 39 options, pressing PgDn again moves you to item 40, and so on. PgUp works in reverse of PgDn.

Regardless of the method you use to move the highlighted menu selection bar, when the bar rests on the option you want to use, Press Enter.

You also can use a fourth way to choose a window-menu option. DataEase presents a window menu when asking you to enter information into a field on-screen, such as when you are asked to fill in the database name on the Sign On screen. The menu is the easiest way to enter the answer, but you can type your answer. For a touch typist, typing may be easier than looking up at the screen to find the menu option.

Using Full-Screen Menus

The eight major menus in DataEase take up most of the middle of your screen and, therefore, are referred to as *full-screen* menus. The DataEase Main menu fits into this category (see fig. 1.2). Six of the other seven full-screen menus are accessed through one of the menu options found on the DataEase Main menu. The last menu, the Utilities menu, is accessed from the Administration full-screen menu. Table 1.3 lists each of these menus and the menus that they are called from. The inside front cover of each of the four manuals distributed with DataEase includes a menu tree showing how these full-screen menus are connected. DataEase's Menu Definition facility, described in Chapter 8, enables you to design your own custom full-screen menus called *user menus*.

Table 1.3
Full-Screen Menus

Menu	*Called from*
DataEase Main	Sign On screen
Form Definition	Main menu
Records	Main menu
QBE-Quick Reports	Main menu
DQL	Main menu
Maintenance	Main menu
Administration	Main menu
Utilities	Administration menu

You have only two ways to select an option on a full-screen menu. When the menu initially displays, no option is highlighted, but you can use the cursor-movement key method, described in the preceding section, to make a menu selection. The easiest method, however, is to type the menu option's number. You do not have to press Enter when you use this approach. For example, to access the Form Definitions menu (discussed in Chapters 2 and 3) from the Main menu, type *1*. DataEase immediately displays the Form Definition menu.

Using Line Menus

The third type of menu, the *line menu*, is strung out horizontally in the second line from the top of the screen (the prompt line). This menu has no highlighted menu selection bar. When using a line menu with options that do not all fit on-screen, DataEase places the option F1MORE at the right most end of the prompt line. Pressing F1 converts the line menu into a window menu, so that DataEase can display more options (refer to the "Using Window Menus" section for instructions on choosing options from a window menu). For example, the line menu in figure 1.3 shows the first six available field types. To see all the field types displayed as a window menu press F1. You do not, however, have to display a choice before you can select that option; you can select the option by typing the option number.

You also can select an option on a line menu by typing the first letter of the menu selection. When more than one option begins with the same letter, type the second letter. If multiple options begin with the same two letters, you may have to type a third, and so on. After you type enough letters to identify the option you want, DataEase fills in the rest for you.

The easiest way to select a numeric string field type from the line menu shown in figure 1.3 is to type *2*. DataEase places the words *Numeric String* into the Field Type field. You also can type *nume*, and DataEase fills in the rest. (Typing the first three letters is not enough because another option, 3: Number, also starts with *num*).

Using Pull-Down Menus

The fourth type of DataEase menu is the *pull-down* menu. Pull-down menus are available whenever the F4 (CMD HELP) function-key command appears in the function key line. You access pull-down menus by pressing F4 (CMD HELP). Figure 1.5 shows the first pull-down menu that displays when you press F4 (CMD HELP) while working on the Form Definition screen.

The options available on pull-down menus usually duplicate the effect of function-key commands and keystroke commands. For example, the first option listed on the pull-down menu in figure 1.5 is Exit & Save F2. Selecting this option from the pull-down menu has exactly the same effect as pressing F2 (SAVE). The primary purpose of pull-down menus, therefore, is to provide optional assistance with DataEase commands. Some commands appear on the pull-down menus that do not appear in the function key line. For example, Alt-F1 (HELP) is not listed in the function key line in figure 1.5 but is shown as More Help Alt-F1 in the pull-down menu. If you do not see the command you are looking for in the function key line, you can display a pull-down menu that shows all the options.

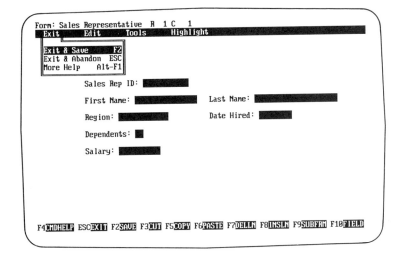

Fig. 1.5.

The Exit pull-down menu.

You have only one method for selecting options from pull-down menus. When you see the command you want, use the up- and down-arrow, Home, and End keys to move the highlighted menu selection bar to the desired option and press Enter. If you do not see the option you need on the first pull-down menu, use the right- and left-arrow keys to move between menus. For example, pressing the right-arrow key three times or the left-arrow key once from the Exit menu shown in figure 1.5 displays the Highlight menu shown in figure 1.6. When the correct menu is displayed, you can use the cursor-movement keys to move the selection bar to the desired option and press Enter, or you can use the function-key or keystroke command listed in the menu. Press Esc if you decide not to select an option. DataEase removes the pull-down menu from the screen.

Occasionally, the pull-down menu provides the only way to accomplish a desired operation. Because the three Highlight menu options that begin with CPI and the three options that begin with LPI do not have corresponding function-key commands or keystroke commands, these options must be selected through the pull-down menu.

Getting Help from DataEase

Even though DataEase is an easy program to learn and use, you may not always know what to do next. Whenever you are looking for a brief explanation or a memory jogger, use the *context-sensitive* DataEase help system. To access the DataEase on-line help system from any screen, press Alt-F1 (HELP). DataEase displays a screen of information specific to the task at hand, including a cross-reference to the DataEase documentation.

Fig. 1.6.

The Highlight pull-down menu.

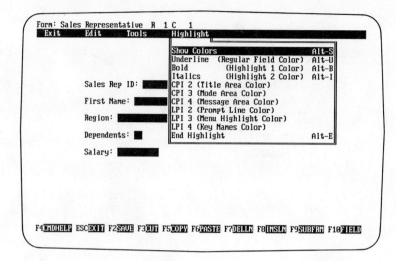

Suppose that you are working in the Field Definition screen shown in figure 1.3 and are not sure what characters are allowed for each field type. Press Alt-F1, and DataEase displays help information (see fig. 1.7). This screen tells you which characters are permitted for each type of field and the maximum field length. The screen also contains a cross-reference to the DataEase documentation, Pages 2:2-37 — 2:2-53. This reference means that pages 2-37 to 2-53 in Volume 2 of the DataEase documentation discuss how to define the field type for a DataEase record-entry form. A list of function-key commands at the bottom of the help window indicates that you can obtain more help by pressing F1 (MORE). If you press F1 (MORE), DataEase displays another screen of more general help, still relating to form definition.

Chapter 2 explains how you also can add two levels of your own custom help messages to DataEase record-entry forms.

You may want to display help messages automatically. While a Help screen is displayed, press Ctrl-F1 (Auto Help). The first time you press this toggle, Auto Help is activated. As you move from field to field in the Field Definition screen, DataEase displays the appropriate Help screens. While a Help screen is displayed, you can turn the Auto Help feature off by pressing Ctrl-F1 again.

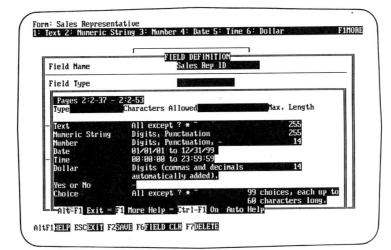

Fig. 1.7.

Context-sensitive help for defining a field type.

Chapter Summary

This chapter guided you around the DataEase program. The Sign On screen, the various parts of a typical DataEase screen, how the keyboard is used, four types of menus, and on-line help were explained. You now are ready to move on to more substantial information. Turn to Chapter 2 to learn how to create DataEase record-entry forms.

Creating DataEase
Record-Entry Forms

This chapter helps you develop a good understanding of DataEase forms—an understanding on which subsequent chapters build. New DataEase users should find this chapter especially helpful. The first section briefly explains what a *relational database* is. Several important DataEase concepts also are introduced, such as *form*, *record*, and *field*.

This chapter also covers the more practical topic of how to create the essential elements of a DataEase record-entry form. You learn how to design and enter prompts on the form, define fields, and create indexes.

When you feel comfortable with the basics of form definition presented in this chapter, turn to Chapter 3 to learn how to modify form definitions and add enhancements (derivation formulas, special form properties, security features, borders, custom color, and help messages).

Understanding Database Terminology

Because of their great speed and storage capacity, computers always have been good candidates for storing large amounts of information. Today, you can store thousands of pages of information on your desktop. This hardware capacity has created a need for software systems that can retrieve massive amounts of information quickly and easily. Relational database programs are designed for this purpose.

Understanding Databases

You probably have built and used databases all your life, even if you did not call them databases. Any time you collect information in an organized fashion that can be accessed randomly, you are creating a database. Following is a list of typical databases:

Telephone books
Card catalogs
Recipe cards
Rolodex files
Mailing lists

With computers, you can store data electronically, instead of on cards, in file cabinets, or in books. From this electronic storage, you can retrieve data almost instantaneously by using well-designed database programs.

Understanding Relational Databases

A relational database consists of a collection of related tables made up of rows (*records*) of data arranged in named columns (*fields*). Two tables are related when they contain columns with matching data. DataEase refers to each table in the database as a *form*. You can view the data one record at a time in a fill-in-the-blank style form or in a tabular fashion with multiple rows on-screen at one time. A relational database management system, such as DataEase, enables you to use data from any number of related tables at once.

This definition is an oversimplified description of the relational model, originally suggested in 1970 by Dr. Edgar F. Codd—then an IBM scientist. Although DataEase may not meet all of the criteria established by Dr. Codd to qualify as 100 percent relational, DataEase meets one of the most important goals of relational database technology: DataEase does an excellent job of handling many of the complexities of the underlying database structure automatically. You are free, therefore, to concentrate on the information you want to see, rather than how to access the information.

DataEase Forms

All data in DataEase is stored in forms made up of fields and records. A DataEase database is made up of a collection of forms related by matching fields.

The form is to DataEase what the worksheet is to 1-2-3. Although you have the option of entering and editing data in a tabular format (*Table View*), entering, editing, or viewing data in a DataEase database usually is performed one record at a time in a fill-in-the-blank style form.

Defining a form is like drawing a blueprint before constructing a building. You must define all the fields in a representative record before you can add any real data to the form. DataEase enables you to define as many as 255 fields per record. As you define each field, you must specify the field name (up to 20 characters) and the type of data that you intend to enter into the field (text, numbers, and dates, for example).

Designing a Database

As you design your database you should keep each form small, resisting the temptation to put everything into one form. Relational database technology gives you the ability to access data easily in multiple forms at the same time. Therefore, you rarely should create a database made up of only one DataEase form. Create multiple forms and use common fields to tie forms together. Keep four guidelines in mind as you decide which fields to include in each form:

1. Collect all the information necessary for the reports that must be generated.

2. Do not collect any information that will never be needed for a report.

3. Divide the data into logical and manageable categories.

4. Never enter the same information more than once.

The first two rules can be followed through thoughtful analysis of the real-life data that you now collect and the reports you currently generate or plan to generate. Careful attention to detail at this early stage of database design saves you countless hours in redesigning.

The fourth guideline is possible only if the third guideline is followed properly. For example, assume that your company sells widgets. Each widget order has fields for at least a customer, address, sales representative, model number, model name, price, and quantity. If you place all this information in one form, you quickly discover a number of built-in disadvantages.

First, you have no way of recording information about a sales representative until he or she makes a sale. Every time a sales representative makes a sale, you also have to enter all the data again. Similarly, customer information and product information have to be entered repeatedly.

A more efficient design divides the data into multiple forms: Widget Order, Retail Customer, Sales Representative, Order Detail, and Product, for example. You then can enter data into each form independently. You can add a new sales representative's name to the Sales Representative form, whether or not he or she has made a sale. You also can add a customer's name whether or not that customer has placed an order. In the Widget Order form, you can use a sales representative identification number to reference the appropriate sales representative data found in the Sales Representative form. You also can use a customer identification number to reference customer data in the Retail Customer form. In DataEase, this type of reference field is called a *match* field.

Figure 2.1 shows an example of a Widget Order form; figure 2.2 shows a Retail Customer form, and figure 2.3 depicts a Sales Representative form.

Chapter 6, "Using Related DataEase Forms," expands on this example and depicts the Order Detail and Product forms. That chapter discusses how match fields are used to define relationships between forms and explains how DataEase enables you to use the new multiform capability to put multiple related forms on the same screen (see fig. 2.4).

Fig. 2.1.

The Widget Order form.

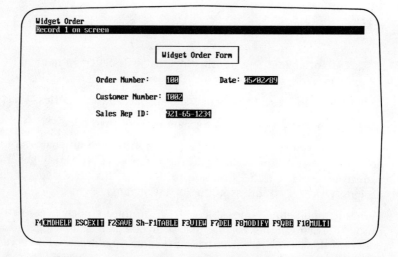

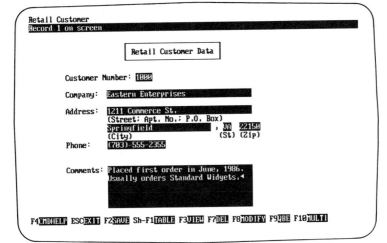

Retail Customer
Record 1 on screen

```
                    ┌─────────────────────┐
                    │ Retail Customer Data │
                    └─────────────────────┘

        Customer Number: 1000

        Company:  Eastern Enterprises

        Address:  1211 Commerce St.
                  (Street; Apt. No.; P.O. Box)
                  Springfield          , VA  22150
                  (City)                 (St) (Zip)
        Phone:    (703)-555-2355


        Comments: Placed first order in June, 1986.
                  Usually orders Standard Widgets.◄
```

F4 CMDHELP ESC EXIT F2 SAVE Sh-F1 TABLE F3 VIEW F7 DEL F8 MODIFY F9 QBE F10 MULTI

Fig. 2.2.

The Retail Customer form.

Sales Representative
Record 3 on screen

```
                    ┌───────────────────────────┐
                    │ Sales Representative Data  │
                    └───────────────────────────┘

        Sales Rep ID: 230-76-2376

        First Name: Tim          Last Name: Jones

        Region:     Eastern      Date Hired: 11/23/69

        Dependents: 3

        Salary:     41,400.00
```

F4 CMDHELP ESC EXIT F2 SAVE Sh-F1 TABLE F3 VIEW F7 DEL F8 MODIFY F9 QBE F10 MULTI

Fig. 2.3.

The Sales Representative form.

Fig. 2.4.

A multiform version of the Widget Order form.

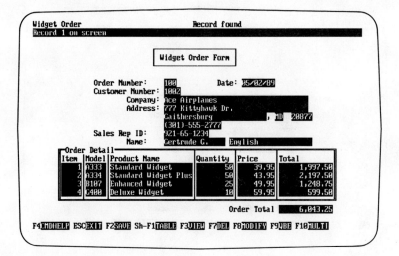

```
Widget Order                        Record found
Record 1 on screen

                        ┌─────────────────────┐
                        │  Widget Order Form  │
                        └─────────────────────┘

            Order Number:   100       Date: 05/02/89
         Customer Number:   1002
                 Company:   Ace Airplanes
                 Address:   777 Kittyhawk Dr.
                            Gaithersburg           , MD  20877
                            (301)-555-2777
             Sales Rep ID:  921-65-1234
                    Name:   Gertrude G.   English
    ┌─Order Detail─┐
    │Item│Model│Product Name        │Quantity│Price │Total    │
    │   1│A333 │Standard Widget     │      50│ 39.95│ 1,997.50│
    │   2│A334 │Standard Widget Plus│      50│ 43.95│ 2,197.50│
    │   3│B107 │Enhanced Widget     │      25│ 49.95│ 1,248.75│
    │   4│C400 │Deluxe Widget       │      10│ 59.95│   599.50│
    └──────────────────────────────────────────────┘
                                    Order Total   6,043.25

    F4:CMDHELP ESC:EXIT F2:SAVE Sh-F1:TABLE F3:VIEW F7:DEL F8:MODIFY F9:QBE F10:MULTI
```

> **Tip:** Design your database on paper first. Write the form names on a sheet of paper and list the field names below the form names. This "bird's-eye view" of your database will be invaluable as you actually begin to define the forms and later build multiforms (forms that combine fields from multiple related forms onto one screen) and reports. Keep this paper plan next to your keyboard as you work, and keep a copy in your files for later reference. A preplanned worksheet for the three forms shown in figures 2.1, 2.2, and 2.3 looks like the following:

Widget Order	Retail Customer	Sales Representative
Order Number	Customer Number	Sales Rep ID
Customer Number	Company	First Name
Sales Rep ID	Address	Last Name
Date	City	Region
	State	Date Hired
	Zip	Dependents
	Phone	Married
	Comments	Salary

This design process sometimes is called *normalization*. A normalized form is as small as possible, is easy to understand and change, contains no duplicate records, and contains little (if any) information already entered in another form. Forms in the database always are related to one or more other forms in the database by sharing a field with the same name and type—a *match field*.

Defining a DataEase Record-Entry Form

After you have designed your database on paper, the first step toward implementation is to define each form. From the DataEase Main menu select **1. Form Definition and Relationships**. DataEase displays the Form Definition menu shown in figure 2.5.

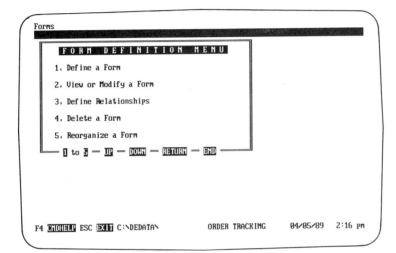

Forms

```
┌─────────────────────────────────────┐
│    FORM  DEFINITION  MENU            │
│                                      │
│  1. Define a Form                    │
│                                      │
│  2. View or Modify a Form            │
│                                      │
│  3. Define Relationships             │
│                                      │
│  4. Delete a Form                    │
│                                      │
│  5. Reorganize a Form                │
│  ── 1 to 5 ── UP ── DOWN ── RETURN ── END ── │
└─────────────────────────────────────┘
```

F4 CMDHELP ESC EXIT C:\DEDATA\   ORDER TRACKING   04/05/89   2:16 pm

Fig. 2.5.

The Form Definition menu.

From this menu choose **1. Define a Form**. DataEase asks you to enter the name of the form to be defined. At this prompt, type the name that you want to use for the form and press Enter. Form names can contain from 1 to 20 displayable ASCII characters, including spaces, but excluding brackets ([ ]), braces ({ }), and punctuation. Do not use DataEase Query Language terms, the word "data" or the word "form" in a form name. When you use a text name, the letters can be in upper- or lowercase. In menus, DataEase lists the form name exactly as you typed the name originally. If you type *widGeT oRDEr* as the name of the form, for example, DataEase lists widGeT oRDEr in all menus. When you need to use the form name in an operation, however, you can type *WIDGET ORDER*, *widget order*, or a combination of lower- and uppercase letters.

As you type the form name, you can use the Backspace key or the left-arrow key to erase the character to the left of the cursor and to move one space to the left. To clear the name completely and start over, press F6 (FIELD CLR). After you make corrections, press Enter or F2 (SAVE) to save the form name and continue with the form definition.

Tip: As you use DataEase, the program often displays form names in window and line menus. In Chapter 1, you learn to select an option from either of these menus by typing the first letter of the option. This feature does not work when the name starts with a numeric digit. You may want to choose form names, therefore, so that each form in a database begins with a different letter.

DataEase displays the Form Definition screen. The work area of this screen is completely blank. The form name is displayed at the top in the title area. A cursor blinks at position R1C1 (row 1, column 1), as indicated in the mode/cursor position area. DataEase also displays the message Type text and field names anywhere on form, press F10FIELD to define fields in the prompt line. In the function key line, DataEase shows you a list of commonly used function-key commands.

In DataEase, you use the Form Definition screen for two purposes. You define fields to receive data, providing name, type, size, and so on, for each field in the form. At the same time, you also create a fill-in-the-blank screen or template that surrounds the fields for use when you enter data. In many database programs, these two tasks are accomplished separately; DataEase simplifies the process by combining both functions.

Using the Form Definition Screen

The blank Form Definition screen is similar to a blank sheet of paper, 80 characters wide and 16 pages (screens) long. You create your fill-in-the-blank form on this electronic paper by typing text on-screen. The Form Definition screen has several simple editing capabilities similar to word processing programs.

Moving the Cursor

As you create the form, you move the cursor (blinking underscore) around on-screen. DataEase displays the cursor's current position in the mode/cursor position area on the screen's top line. The cursor always starts at R1C1 on a new Form Definition screen (row 1 and column 1). You can create a form that uses up to 80 columns and 16 pages, with each page containing 22 rows. You can use the arrow keys to move one position (column or row) in any direction. Table 2.1 lists the other cursor-movement keys available in the Form Definition screen. Table 2.2 lists the function-key commands available. Each of these function-key commands is discussed in this chapter, except F9 (SUBFRM), which is discussed in Chapter 6.

Table 2.1
Form Definition Cursor-Movement Keys

Key	Moves cursor to:
↑	Preceding line
↓	Next line
←	One position (space) to the left
Backspace	One position to the left
→	One position to the right
Home	Position R1C1
End	Column 1 in last line containing any text or field
Tab	Six positions to the right
Shift-Tab	Six positions to the left
Ctrl-→	Column 80, same row
Ctrl-←	Column 1, same row
Enter	Column 1, next row
PgDn	Down 21 rows, same column
PgUp	Up 21 rows, same column

Table 2.2
Form Definition Function-Key Commands

Function Key (KEY NAME)	Function
Esc (EXIT)	Returns to Form Definition menu without saving changes
Alt-F1 (HELP)	Provides help on current operation
F2 (SAVE)	Returns to Form Definition menu after saving all changes
F3 (CUT)	Cuts a block of text and/or fields
F4 (CMDHELP)	Displays pull-down menus
F5 (COPY)	Copies a block of text and/or fields
F6 (PASTE)	Pastes a cut or copied block of text and/or fields

Table 2.2—*continued*

Function Key (KEY NAME)	Function
F7 (DELLN)	Deletes a complete line (blank, text, and/or fields)
F8 (INSLN)	Inserts a new line at the cursor
F9 (SUBFRM)	Defines a subform to create a multiform
Shift-F9 (PRINT)	Prints form definition
F10 (FIELD)	Defines a field
Shift-F10 (FORM PROPERTIES)	Defines form properties
Alt-F10 (BORDERS)	Draws borders using the ASCII character set

As you edit the form and move the cursor past the bottom edge of the work area, DataEase scrolls the "electronic paper" up by one row. For example, if your cursor is in row 22 at the bottom of the work area and you move the cursor to row 23, DataEase scrolls row 1 out of the work area, off the screen. Anything you may have typed in row 1 is still there, but you cannot see it at the moment.

Tip: When you use the form for entering data, DataEase does not scroll the screen in this manner. Each 22 rows is treated as a separate page. When you move from the last field on one page to the first field on the next page, DataEase replaces the entire page on-screen with the page containing the current field.

Typing Text

Typing text on the Form Definition screen is straightforward. All the letters, numbers, and special characters on your keyboard are displayed as usual. You can type text on-screen as if you were using a typewriter or word processor. Unlike most word processors, however, DataEase does not have automatic word wrap. If you type a word over the right edge of the screen, DataEase does not wrap the entire word to the next line; instead, the program splits the word, wrapping to the next line only the character that you typed past column 80. You may want to press Enter, therefore, to move the cursor to the next line if you are about to type a word that does not fit.

Figure 2.6 shows text you might use as labels or prompts in a fill-in-the-blank form for data about your company's retail customers. This text has no effect on the actual data that you enter into the form. Text on the form primarily is used for labels and prompts to assist individuals who do data entry. You also must define record-entry fields to create the blanks that complete your fill-in-the-blank style form.

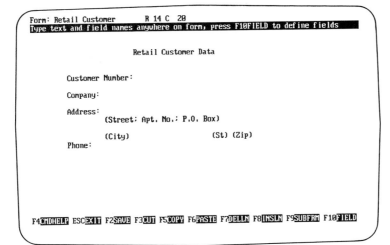

Fig. 2.6.

Typing text on the Form Definition screen.

Editing and Inserting Text

You have many ways to edit text on the Form Definition screen. The simplest way is to move the cursor to the incorrect text and type over that text. DataEase starts the editing session in the Replace mode, so that text typed on-screen replaces existing text at the same position. As you are typing text and make an error, you can press the Backspace or left-arrow key and then correct the mistake.

You may want to insert text between characters that you already have typed on the form. To insert text, press the Insert key. DataEase displays the message (INSERT) in the mode/cursor position. Move the cursor to the position where you want the new text to begin. Type the text, and DataEase inserts it at the cursor, pushing existing text to the right. Any text pushed past the right edge of the screen wraps to a new blank row inserted by DataEase.

Inserting a Blank Line

DataEase provides a function-key command for inserting a blank line. Place the cursor where the new line should go and press F8 (INSLN). DataEase inserts a blank line at the cursor position and pushes the line that was at the cursor down one line.

Deleting Fields and Text

DataEase also enables you to delete text from the form. You can delete one character at a time with the Delete key. Each time you press Delete, DataEase deletes the character or space at the cursor and pulls to the left any text that was to the right of the cursor.

For deleting larger amounts of text, DataEase provides two function-key commands: F3 (CUT) and F7 (DELLN). The former command deletes a contiguous block of text; the latter deletes exactly one line (row) of text. Both of these commands delete fields as well as text.

To delete the fields and text in a line, place the cursor in the line you want to remove and press F7 (DELLN).

To remove a contiguous block of fields and/or text, move the cursor to the first character, space, or field that you want to remove. This position is the *start* of the block. Press F3 (CUT) and move the cursor to the space or character to the right of the last character, space, or field to be deleted. This position is the *end* of the block and must be below or on the same line and to the right of the original position. The *block* consists of all the fields, text, and spaces between the two positions, reading from left to right and from top to bottom. The block includes the start position but not the end position. Press F3 (CUT) again to remove the block of text from the form. If you decide that you want to cancel the operation, press Esc before pressing F3 (CUT) the second time.

When you cut fields or text from the form using F3, DataEase places the removed block in an internal *buffer*. The block remains in this buffer until you press Esc, use F3 (CUT) again, use F5 (COPY) (discussed in the "Copying a Block" section of this chapter), or quit from DataEase. The next section describes how to use the fields or text in this buffer.

Moving a Block

You can move a block of fields or text around the form in DataEase. Use F3 (CUT) to place the block in the buffer. Then, place the cursor at the position where the block should begin and press F6 (PASTE). DataEase places a copy of the block at the new position. The block itself, however, remains in the buffer. You can use F6 (PASTE) to place multiple copies of the same block of fields or text on the form. DataEase adds a digit to field names in the duplicated block so that no two have the same name (for example, Address, Address2, Address3, and so on).

The F6 (PASTE) command also provides a way to *undo* a block deletion. If you accidentally delete a block by using the F3 (CUT) method, use F6 (PASTE) to place the block back at the original position. Remember that you have to use F6 (PASTE) while the deleted block is still in the buffer. (For example, before you press Esc, use F3 (CUT) again, or use F5 to copy.)

Copying a Block

Occasionally, you may want to copy a block of fields or text, without cutting the block from the original location. Move the cursor to the start of the block to be copied and press F5 (COPY). DataEase displays a line menu in the prompt line. Choose 1: Block from this menu. Move the cursor to the end of the block and press F5 (COPY) again. DataEase places the block in the buffer. Move the cursor to where you want the copy to begin and press F6 (PASTE). DataEase inserts the copy at the new position.

DataEase adds a digit to field names in the duplicated block so that no two fields have the same name. As is true for CUT and PASTE, after you use COPY and PASTE, the buffer still contains the block. You can PASTE the block again, if you want. DataEase flushes the buffer when you press Esc, use F3 (CUT), use F5 (COPY) again, or use F2 (SAVE).

Note: The other two options on the COPY line menu, 2: Form, and 3: Dictionary Field, are discussed in Chapter 3.

Defining Record-Entry Fields

The primary purpose of DataEase form design is the definition of record-entry fields. Record-entry fields are the blanks of the fill-in-the-blank form you are designing.

To begin defining a field, move the cursor to where you want the blank to appear and press F10 (FIELD). DataEase displays the Field Definition screen (see fig. 2.7). This screen is a fill-in-the-blank form. Use the cursor-movement keys listed in table 2.3 to move around on-screen. Several function-key commands are available from this screen; they are listed in table 2.4. Pull-down menus are not available.

Table 2.3
Field Definition Screen
Cursor-Movement Keys

Key	Moves cursor to:
↑	Preceding line
↓	Next line
←	One position (space) to the left, except from the left end of a field where the cursor moves to the preceding field
Backspace	One position to the left, erasing any character currently in that space
→	One position to the right, except from the right end of a field where the cursor moves to the next field
Home	First field
End	Last field
Tab	Next field
Shift-Tab	Preceding field
Enter	Next field
Page Up	First field

Table 2.4
Field Definition Function-Key Commands

Function Key (KEY NAME)	Function
Esc (EXIT)	Returns to Form Definition screen without saving changes
F1	Displays full-screen editor for typing *derivation formula* (available only when cursor is in derivation formula blank)
Alt-F1 (HELP)	Provides help on current operation
F2 (SAVE)	Returns to Form Definition screen after saving field definition
F5 (FORM CLR)	Clears all values from Field Definition form

Table 2.4—*continued*

Function Key (KEY NAME)	Function
F6 (FIELD CLR)	Clears value from current field in Field Definition form
F7 (DELETE)	Deletes field from form being defined

Assigning the Field Name

The first blank you must fill in on the Field Definition screen is the Field Name blank. Field names can contain from 1 to 20 letters, numbers, and spaces. As with form names, DataEase considers upper- and lowercase letters the same but displays the form name in menus just as you type the name.

Tip: You always should start field names with a letter so that you easily can select them from line and window menus. Also, do not use a DataEase *keyword* as a field name. A DataEase keyword is a word that has a special meaning in Quick Reports and DQL (DataEase Query Language) procedures. A complete list of keywords is included in Chapter 11.

DataEase often completes this field-naming step automatically. DataEase takes the first 20 printable characters and spaces from the text on-screen, starting with the first letter on the left end of the line, or at a previously defined field to the left of the field you are defining. DataEase drops leading and trailing spaces and keeps only one space between words. The program also drops any colon or question mark that you include at the end of the field prompt. For example, if you move the cursor to the right of the text Company: shown in figure 2.6 and press F10 (FIELD), DataEase displays the Field Definition screen shown in figure 2.7, with the field name Company already filled in.

To edit the field name, erase mistakes with the Backspace key and type the correction. You also can make corrections by moving the cursor with the ← or → keys and typing over existing text. To insert text, turn on Insert mode with the Insert key, move the cursor to the position where the new text should begin, and type the text. You also can press F6 (FIELD CLR) to erase the entire name and start over.

When the field name is typed as you want it, press Enter, ↓, or Tab to move to the next blank on the Field Definition screen. In addition to a field name, you always must specify field type and length. Other field characteristics are optional.

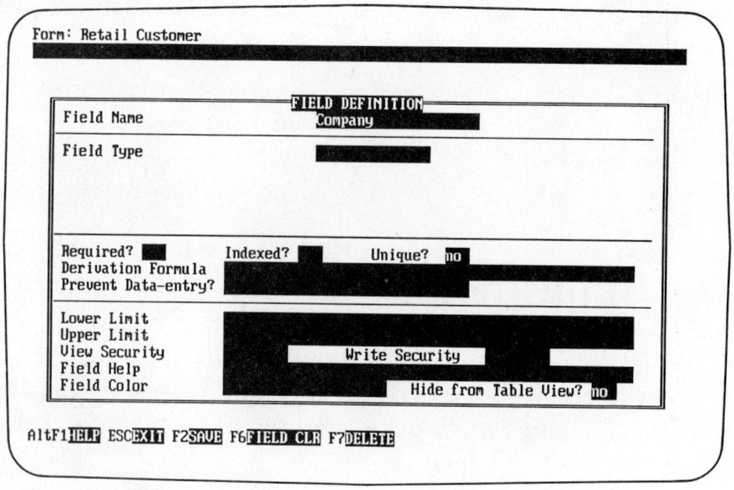

Fig. 2.7.

The Field Definition screen.

Assigning Field Type and Length

The purpose of the Field Type blank on the Field Definition screen is to inform DataEase what kind of data you intend to enter into this field. DataEase assists you in preventing entry mistakes for certain kinds of data and permits you to do calculations with other types of data. Choosing the field type, therefore, is an important part of defining each field. In addition to defining the field type, you also must decide the maximum length of the data value for each field. For some field types, DataEase prompts you to enter a maximum length. For other field types, DataEase uses a set default length. Table 2.5 lists the field types available in DataEase and their maximum lengths. The sections that follow describe when and how to select each field type and how to assign the field length.

Table 2.5
Field Types

Field Type	Properties
Text	Maximum 255 characters; any character except *, ?, and ~
Long:Text	Maximum 4,000 characters; any character except *, ?, and ~
Numeric String	Not normally used for calculation
Unformatted	Maximum 255 characters
Social Security Number	Format: *000-00-0000* where each *0* can be any positive integer

Table 2.5—*continued*

Field Type	Properties
Phone Number	Format: *(000)-000-0000* where each *0* can be any positive integer
Other format	Format is user-specified, up to 40 characters (for example, *00000-0000* for a ZIP Code).
Number	Accurate to 14 digits
Integer	Commas are inserted automatically.
Fixed point	Set number of digits to the right of decimal; commas inserted
Floating point	Variable number of digits to the right of the decimal; no commas inserted
Date	01/01/00 to 12/31/99; date calculations possible (North American format—see Appendix B)
Time	00:00:00 to 23:59:59; time calculations possible (time of day, not elapsed time)
Dollar	2 digits to the right of the decimal; automatic commas (see Appendix B)
Yes or No	*Yes* and *No* are the only possible values for this field type.
Choice	Custom list of up to 99 choices—up to 60 characters each; set of choices can be given a name for use in other fields

When the cursor moves into the Field Type field on the Field Definition screen, DataEase displays a line menu with the following options: 1: Text, 2: Numeric String, 3: Number, 4: Date, 5: Time, 6: Dollar, and F1MORE. DataEase displays the complete list of eight available field types if you press F1 (MORE). The two additional types that do not appear on the line menu are 7: Yes or No and 8: Choice. Choose the field type from the line menu, from the window menu, or by typing the field type in the space provided. Then, press Enter, the ↓ key, or Tab to move to the next question.

The field type you choose determines the next prompt you see. For several field types, you must specify a maximum field length, and for other field types, you must specify a specific format. The following sections describe when to select each field type, the various prompts that you see, and how to respond. After discussing field types, this chapter discusses two optional field definition characteristics—how to make a field required and how to index a field.

After you define all the desired field characteristics, press F2 (SAVE) to save the field definition to RAM. DataEase displays a highlighted bar with a length equal to the field's length. As you are working on the Form Definition screen, you can obtain a brief summary of a field's definition by moving the cursor into this highlighted field and pressing the space bar. In the prompt line, DataEase displays FIELD: followed by the field name, type, and length. DataEase also lists any of the following characteristics assigned to the field: required, indexed, unique, range, derived, and prevent data-entry.

Creating Text Fields

A *text* field can hold any data up to a maximum length of 255 characters. You normally use this type of field for text without a particular format. This field type, however, accepts any type of data including numbers, dates, and punctuation.

To specify the text field type, at the Field Type prompt on the Field Definition screen, choose 1: Text. Specify field length at the next prompt by typing a number from 1 to 255. For example, the Company, Address, City, and State fields in the Retail Customer form are text fields. You might give these fields lengths of 35, 35, 25, and 2, respectively.

You always should specify field length for text fields, unless you want the default value of one character. All other field characteristics are optional. After defining length, you can continue defining the optional field characteristics, or you can press F2 (SAVE) to indicate that you have finished defining the field. After you save the field definition, DataEase displays the field on the form as a highlighted bar. Figure 2.8 shows the Company, Address, City, and State fields in the Retail Customer form.

Creating Long:Text Fields

DataEase also provides a method for creating a group of single-line text fields that can hold as many as 4,000 characters. This type of field, a *long:text* field, provides capabilities similar to the capabilities of a word processor during Record Entry, including word-wrap. These capabilities are not available in regular text fields. Long:text fields most often are used for

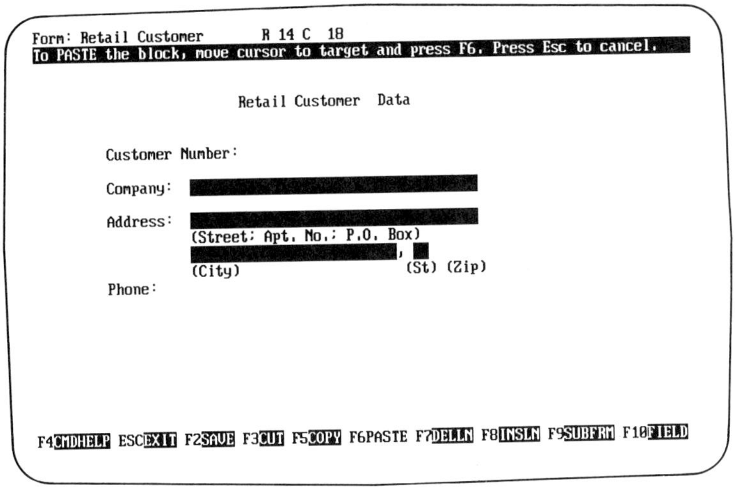

```
Form: Retail Customer        R 14 C  18
To PASTE the block, move cursor to target and press F6. Press Esc to cancel.



                     Retail Customer  Data


         Customer Number:

         Company: ████████████████████████████

         Address: ████████████████████████████
                  (Street: Apt. No.: P.O. Box)
                  ████████████████████, ██
                  (City)                (St) (Zip)
         Phone:




     F4 CMDHELP  ESC EXIT  F2 SAVE  F3 CUT  F5 COPY  F6 PASTE  F7 DELLN  F8 INSLN  F9 SUBFRM  F10 FIELD
```

Fig. 2.8.

The Retail Customer form with Company and Address fields.

recording narrative style information likely to go beyond one line in length. For example, you may want a Comments field in the Retail Customer form where you can place any special notes or information about the customer.

To create a long:text field, you first define its top line as an individual text field. To distinguish a long:text field from a normal text field, you name the field in a special way. Give the top line field of each long:text field a name beginning with the word *long* immediately followed by a colon and at least one letter. The name *Long:Comments*, for example, is a valid field name for the top line of a long:text field.

The length you assign to the top line of the long:text field determines the overall width of the entire field. The field *Long:Comments*, which is on the top line of the long:text field in figure 2.9, has a maximum length of 35, so that the entire long:text field (indicated by the reverse video block in fig. 2.9) is 35 characters wide.

After you define the top line, use the F5 (COPY) procedure, described in a previous section of this chapter, to make copies of this line. You must observe the following two rules as you place portions of a long:text field on the form:

❏ No other fields may be defined on the same line as any part of the long:text field.

❏ No other fields may be defined between portions of the long:text field.

The total number of characters that can be entered in all the parts of a long:text field cannot exceed 4,000.

The long:text field shown in figure 2.9 (to the right of the prompt Comments:) consists of five fields—a top line field—Long:Comments— and four copies—Long:Comments2, Long:Comments3, Long:Comments4, and Long:Comments5. These five fields appear as one block on-screen.

Fig. 2.9.

Adding a long:text field to the Retail Customer form.

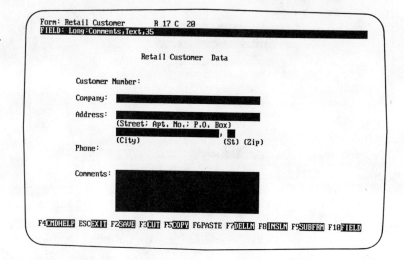

Chapter 4 describes how to enter and edit data in long:text fields.

Creating Numeric String Fields

Numeric string fields are a hybrid field type, somewhere between text and *number* fields. This type of field is intended to hold numbers that do not denote quantity but are used more like text, often for identification. Typical examples are Social Security numbers, phone numbers, and ZIP codes.

Like a text field, a numeric string field can hold up to 255 characters. During Record Entry, however, numeric string fields accept only numeric digits.

Numeric string fields are distinguished from number fields in several ways. First, numeric string fields can be 255 characters, but number fields can be no more than 14 digits in length. Numeric string fields also can contain formatting characters. You can define a format for a numeric string field that contains any printable character such as hyphens, parentheses, slashes, and letters. DataEase inserts commas and decimal points in number fields, but no other formatting characters are permitted. These formatting characters are inserted in the field by DataEase during Record Entry (not during Form Definition). Numeric string fields also retain leading zeros. If,

during Record Entry, you type *0012* into a number field, DataEase stores
the number as 12, dropping the leading zeros. If you type the same
number in a numeric string field, however, DataEase retains the zeros,
storing the value as 0012.

To create a numeric string field, at the Field Type prompt on the Field
Definition screen, select 2: Numeric String. DataEase displays another
prompt, Is it a formatted string? DataEase also displays a line menu with
the choices: 1: no format, 2: soc.sec.no., 3: phone no., and 4: other
format.

When the data contains no special formatting characters, punctuation, or
spaces, select 1: no format. Specify the maximum length of the field at the
next prompt. All other characteristics are optional. The Customer Number
field and the Zip field in the Retail Customer form have no formatting
characters. The Customer Number field has a length of 4, and the Zip field
has a length of 5 (see fig. 2.10).

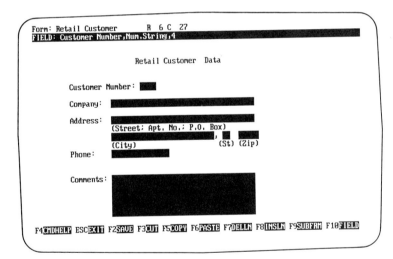

Fig. 2.10.

*Defining record-
entry fields for the
Retail Customer
form.*

For fields that will contain a Social Security number, choose 2:
soc.sec.no. During Record Entry, DataEase accepts data in the format
000-00-0000, and places the hyphens for you. You do not specify a field
length; DataEase sets the field at a length of 11 characters. The Sales Rep
ID field in the Sales Representative form is a numeric string/soc.sec.no.
field.

If the field is going to hold telephone numbers, select 3: phone no. from
the line menu. DataEase assumes that you will enter (during Record Entry)
phone numbers with the format (000)-000-0000 in a field 14 characters

long (digits and formatting characters, together). The Phone field in the Retail Customer form is an example of this type of field (see fig. 2.10).

When your data is a formatted string of numbers, but does not fit into the built-in social security or phone number molds, select 4: other format. At the prompt Define Numeric string format, type a typical data value. For example, you may want to use nine-digit ZIP codes with a hyphen between the first five digits and the last four digits. At the prompt, you can type *12345-1000* or just *00000-0000*. The actual digits you type do not matter; they represent where you will enter digits during Record Entry. All non-numeric characters you type in this format, however, are entered in the field during Record Entry. Therefore, you only type the nine digits, and DataEase inserts the hyphen for you.

Tip: During Record Entry, if you leave any portion of a numeric string blank, DataEase fills the empty spaces (or *pads* them) with zeros on the left side. Existing digits are pushed to the right, if necessary. Appendix B explains how to change this default setting on the System Configuration form so that DataEase does not pad empty spaces.

Creating Number Fields

You normally create *number* fields to contain numeric data that denotes a quantity; you may want to perform calculations with these numbers. For example, you always use a number field to record how many widgets are ordered by a particular customer. The number of dependents of an employee also is a numeric field.

To define a number field, choose 3: Number at the Field Type prompt on the Field Definition screen. DataEase displays a prompt, Number Type, and a line menu listing three types of number fields: 1: Integer, 2: Fixed point, and 3: Floating point.

Select 1: Integer when the data for this field will always consist of whole numbers (no decimals). DataEase then prompts for the maximum number of digits in this field. If a value in this field might be a negative number, leave room for a negative sign when you plan maximum field length. After you specify field length, you can continue to define the optional characteristics, or you can press F2 (SAVE). When you save the field, DataEase returns to the Form Definition screen and displays a highlighted bar to indicate the position of the field. Figure 2.11 shows the Sales Representative form. The Dependents field in this form is an integer field with a length of 2.

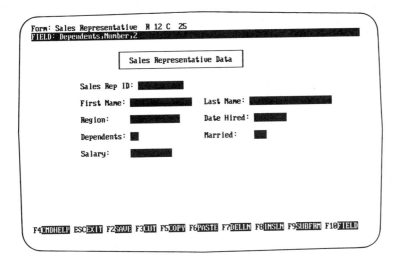

Fig. 2.11.

*Defining record-
entry fields for the
Sales Representative
form.*

During Record Entry, DataEase inserts commas as necessary. You do not,
however, have to allow space for commas when you specify field length on
the Field Definition form. DataEase adjusts the field highlight to
accommodate commas. For example, if you specify 5 as the maximum
number of digits in your data, DataEase allows 6 spaces in the field
highlight. Keep this process in mind when you are designing your form so
that you leave enough room on-screen between text prompts.

When the data for the number field includes decimal values, you have two
choices at the Number Type prompt on the Field Definition screen: 2: Fixed
point or 3: Floating point.

Select 2: Fixed point when the data values to the right of the decimal
point always contain the same number of digits. The most common
example is currency. Whenever a currency value includes cents, you
always should show two digits to the right of the decimal. After you select
2: Fixed Point at the Number Type prompt, DataEase asks you for the
maximum number of digits to the left of the decimal. Remember to
include one digit for a minus sign, if appropriate, but do not add digits for
commas. Type a number and press Enter. After you specify the number of
digits to the left of the decimal, DataEase asks for the number of digits to
the right of the decimal. Type this number and press Enter.

You can continue to define the optional characteristics, or press F2 (SAVE)
to save the field definition. When you save the field definition, DataEase
displays a highlighted bar on-screen long enough to accommodate the
digits to the left of the decimal, including commas, the decimal point, and
the specified number of digits to the right of the decimal. For example, if
you specify six digits to the left of the decimal and two to the right of the
decimal, the highlighted bar is 10 spaces long. The Salary field in the Sales
Representative form is a fixed point field (see fig. 2.11).

To make defining a fixed point number field with two digits to the right of the decimal quicker and easier, DataEase provides the 6: Dollar field type. Instead of choosing 3: Number and then specifying the number type and field length, select 6: Dollar at the Field Type prompt. DataEase then prompts you for the number of digits to the left of the decimal. DataEase assumes that you mean a fixed point number field with two digits to the right of the decimal. You must supply only the number of digits to the left of the decimal point. DataEase actually saves the field definition as a fixed point number. The final result is the same whether you choose 6: Dollar as the field type or choose 3: Number and then specify 2: Fixed point with two decimal places. Using either method, you cannot use dollar signs ($) in the data, but you can add dollar signs in a report.

The third type of number field is called *floating point*. Use a floating point field when you are not sure how many decimal places the data will have. To define this type of field, choose 3: Floating point. At the next prompt, specify the maximum number of digits by typing a number and pressing Enter. Continue to define the optional characteristics or press F2 (SAVE) to save the field definition. DataEase adds one space to the field length for the decimal point. For example, if you indicate six as the maximum number of digits in a floating point field, DataEase creates a highlighted bar seven spaces long. DataEase does not, however, insert commas into floating point fields during Record Entry. Therefore, do not add any spaces to the highlighted bar for commas.

Creating Date Fields

Tracking dates often is important when collecting business-related information. DataEase provides a *date* field type that enables you to record dates, automatically place today's date in records, and perform date calculations.

To create a date field, choose 4: Date at the Field Type prompt. You can add any of the optional characteristics or press F2 (SAVE) to save the field definition. After you save the definition, DataEase returns to the Form Definition screen and displays a highlighted bar eight characters long. The Date Hired field in figure 2.11 is a date field.

During Record Entry, you must enter the date in the format *MM/DD/YY* where *MM* represents the month; *DD* represents the day of the month, and *YY* represents the last two digits of the year. Because DataEase inserts the slashes, you type only the six digits. Refer to Appendix B for a description of how to use the System Configuration form to change the date format to international (DD/MM/YY) or metric (YY/MM/DD).

Refer to the "Using Derivation Formulas" section of Chapter 3 for an explanation of how to create fields that place today's date in each record and that can perform date calculations.

Creating Time Fields

Time fields provide capabilities similar to those provided by date fields. You can use these capabilities to track the time of day particular events occurred and to insert the time of day. You also can create derivation formulas that calculate the time that has elapsed since a certain event.

To create a time field, select 5: Time at the Field Type prompt on the Field Definition screen. You can add any of the optional characteristics or press F2 (SAVE) to save the field definition. After you save the definition, DataEase returns to the Form Definition screen and displays a highlighted bar eight characters long.

During Record Entry, you must enter time in the format *HH:MM:SS* where *HH* represents the hour; *MM* represents minutes, and *SS* represents seconds. Because DataEase inserts the two colons, you type only the six digits.

Refer to the "Using Derivation Formulas" section in Chapter 3 for an explanation of how to create fields that insert the time of day in each record.

Creating Yes-or-No Fields

When you are recording information in a database, you may want to create fields that require a simple yes or no response. Many of the DataEase prompts that you answer while designing your database require that you answer yes or no.

To create this type of field, choose 7: Yes or No at the Field Type prompt on the Field Definition screen. Continue to select optional characteristics, or press F2 (SAVE) to save the field definition. After you save the definition, DataEase displays a highlighted bar three characters long on the form. The Married field in figure 2.11 is a Yes-or-No field.

During Record Entry, when the cursor is in a Yes-or-No field, DataEase displays a line menu with the choices 1: no and 2: yes.

Creating Choice Fields

DataEase provides a unique field type called *Choice* that enables you to create custom line menus that display all available values for a field. This type of field can greatly reduce data-entry errors and save time.

To create a Choice field, choose 8: Choice at the Field Name prompt on the Form Definition screen. DataEase displays the prompt Optional choice type name: and displays the message Press F1 to see list of choices in the prompt line. If you want to use the list of options with another field in the same form without typing them again, type a name at this prompt and press Enter. Otherwise, leave the field blank and press F1. In either case, DataEase overlays the Field Definition screen with a screen entitled Field Choices. Initially, DataEase displays 15 blank lines. Ninety-nine lines are available by scrolling the screen with the cursor-movement keys. (If you type the name of a previously defined choice list at the Optional choice type name prompt, that list displays instead of the 15 blank lines.)

Starting at line 1 of the Field Choice screen, type a valid field value on each line. Type the choices in the order you want them to appear in a line menu during Record Entry. You can use the F7 (DELLN) and the F8 (INSLN) keys to assist you in editing the choices. You also can delete characters with the Delete key, the Backspace key, or the space bar. As usual, the Insert key toggles Insert mode. After typing all valid choices, each on its own line, press F2 (SAVE). DataEase returns to the Field Definition screen.

DataEase returns you to the Field Definition screen after you enter all the choices on the Field Choices screen. The cursor still is at the Optional choice type name prompt. Do not type a name in this space. If you do, DataEase tries to find a list by that name and then erases all the entries you just made. Instead, press Enter, Tab, or the down-arrow key to go to the next characteristic, or press F2 (SAVE) to save the field definition. After you save the field definition, DataEase displays a highlighted bar on the form. The length of the record-entry field on-screen is equal to the longest choice you typed on the Field Choices screen.

For example, you might define the Region field in the Sales Representative form as a choice field. Assuming that your company has four regions—North, South, East, and West—you type each region name on a line in the Field Choices screen, as shown in figure 2.12. Because North and South are five characters long, DataEase gives the field a length of five characters (see fig. 2.11). During Record Entry, the four regions display as a line menu when the cursor is in the Region field.

Because you can define as many as 99 choices for Choice fields, DataEase always cannot display every available choice in a line menu. During Record Entry, DataEase displays as many choices as will fit in a menu. If any options do not fit, DataEase adds the choice F1MORE at the right end of the prompt line. You then can press F1 to display the available choices in a window menu.

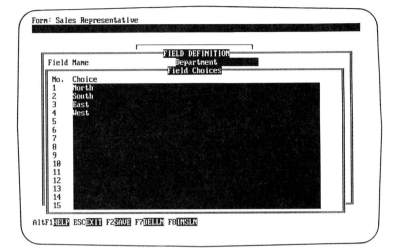

Fig. 2.12.

The Field Choices Screen.

Assigning the Required Field Characteristic

In every form, at least one field contains essential information. For example, in the Sales Representative field, the Employee Number identifies each employee, therefore, you do not want anyone to enter a Sales Representative record without entering the employee number. DataEase calls this type of field a *required* field.

To define a field as required, answer 2: Yes at the Required? prompt on the Field Definition form. During Record Entry, DataEase does not save a record until all required fields have valid entries.

Specifying a field as required is optional. If you save the field definition without first answering this prompt, DataEase assumes that the field is not required.

Tip: You should not make every field a required field. The first time you enter a particular record, you may not have an entry for every field. When you first start a record on a new customer in the Retail Customer form, for example, you may not have a customer's phone number. If you have defined the Phone field as required, you would have to enter a dummy phone number to save the record. If the field is not defined as required, however, you can leave the phone number blank, save the record, and enter the number later.

Assigning an Indexed Field

An index for a database form is similar to the index of a book. For example, if you want to look up discussions about numeric string fields in this book, you can turn to the index and look up *numeric string* alphabetically. The book index refers you to the appropriate pages. Like a book's index, a DataEase form index keeps track of the data in the field sorted in alphabetical or numerical (according to field type) order. The DataEase index is a separate file on the disk that is updated each time you add, delete, or modify a record in the field.

To assign an indexed field, respond 2: Yes to the Indexed prompt on the Field Definition screen. By default, DataEase will not index a field, unless you answer Yes. You can index as many as 254 fields in each form.

Always index fields that meet any of the following criteria:

❏ The field is a *match* field. For example, the Sales Rep ID Number and Customer Number fields in the Widget Order form (see fig. 2.1) are both used to make reference to records in other forms. The Sales Rep ID refers to a record in the Sales Representative form (see fig. 2.3), and the Customer Number refers to a record in the Retail Customer form (see fig. 2.2).

❏ The field is *unique*. Refer to the next section for a discussion of when you should define a field as unique. Each time you add or modify a record, DataEase checks the combined value of its unique fields for a duplication in the other records of the form. DataEase can perform this comparison much faster when each of the unique fields is indexed.

❏ The field will be used as the *primary* sort field in reports. (Refer to the "Grouping and Sorting Records" section of Chapter 5.) DataEase maintains the index in sorted order, so that the program can print a report in order by an indexed field without having to take the time to sort the form records again.

Initially, you should make a field indexed only if it meets one or more of the preceding three criteria. You always can add indexed fields later if you find that you often are searching or sorting on a field that you have not indexed. Assigning an indexed field unnecessarily actually can retard processing speed because DataEase has to rebuild each index file every time you add, delete, or modify a record in the form. Index files also reduce available disk space.

> **Tip:** As a rule-of-thumb, do not create more than eight indexed fields per form. This seems to be the point of diminishing returns. If you define more than eight indexed fields in a form, the increased processing overhead associated with maintaining the index files probably is greater than the gains from faster searching and sorting.

Based on the above criteria, for example, you should index the Customer Number field in the Retail Customer and Widget Order forms and the Sales Rep ID field in the Sales Representative and Widget Order forms. Because you probably want to search for records and sort reports based on the Last Name field in the Sales Representative form and the Company field in the Retail Customer form, you also should index those fields.

Assigning the Unique Field Characteristic

A cardinal rule of relational databases is that each record in every form should be unique—no duplicates. Make certain that no two records in the same form have exactly the same values in all fields. Following this rule results in the most efficient use of disk space and manpower for data entry.

DataEase can assist you in preventing duplicates if you specify one or more unique fields in the form definition. When you attempt to save a record during Record Entry, DataEase checks the unique fields in the current record against those in other records. The program determines whether a record with the same values in all unique fields—a duplicate—already exists. If a duplicate does exist, DataEase alerts you to that fact, through a screen message, and then asks if you want to replace the old record with the new. Refer to Chapter 4 for a more complete discussion of how DataEase handles duplicate records during Record Entry.

To specify that a field is unique, respond 2: Yes to the Unique? prompt on the Field Definition screen.

Always define at least one unique field per form. For example, the Sales Rep ID field in the Sales Representative form is a unique number; no two employees should have identical Social Security numbers (see fig. 2.11). Similarly, the Customer Number field in the Retail Customer form is unique. The Widget Order form also contains Sales Rep ID and Customer Number fields, but these fields should not be defined as unique, because a customer can make more than one order, and a sales representative can make more than one sale. Each value in the Order Number field, however, is used only once in the Widget Order form and should be defined as a unique field.

Sometimes a form does not contain a single field that uniquely identifies each record. In that case, you should designate a second unique field. DataEase combines the values from all of a form's unique fields to determine whether a new record duplicates an existing record.

For example, you might design a form named Order Detail to contain the information about each Widget order (see fig. 2.13). Because a customer might order several different models of widgets using the same order number, the Order Number field does not uniquely identify each record. By adding an Item Number field (the first model ordered is item 1; the second model ordered is item 2, and so on), you can combine the Order Number field and the Item Number field. You therefore assign the *unique* characteristic to each of these fields.

Fig. 2.13.

A form with two unique fields.

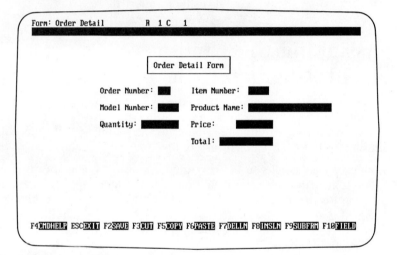

Saving the Field Definition

After you define the field name, type, and length, all other field characteristics are optional. You can save the field by pressing F2 (SAVE). If you do not define any optional characteristic before saving the field, DataEase enters a default value for each. All characteristics on the Field Definition screen that take a yes-or-no answer are given a setting of *no*. All other unanswered prompts remain blank (see fig. 2.14). You can modify the field definition and add one of the optional characteristics later. The "Modifying Form Definition" section of this chapter explains how to change existing characteristics and how to add new ones to DataEase fields.

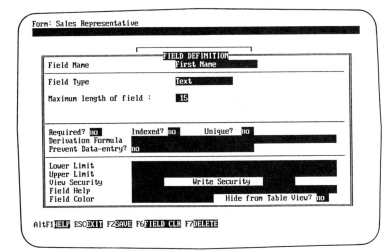

Fig. 2.14.

The default values of the optional field characteristics.

Saving the Form Definition

When you finish defining all fields and text on a form, you are ready to save the form definition to disk. To save the definition, press F2 (SAVE) from the Form Definition screen. DataEase saves the form definition to disk and returns to the Form Definition menu. Press Esc (EXIT) to return to the DataEase Main menu.

Table 2.6 shows the file-naming conventions used by DataEase when the program saves the form to disk. Assuming, for example, that the database letter for the Order Tracking database is *O*, DataEase saves the Retail Customer form definition to disk with the name *RETAOAAA.DBA*. The index file for the Customer Number field is saved with the name *RETAOAAA.I01*.

Table 2.6
DataEase Form Files

File type	*DOS file name**
Form definition	formdaaa.DBA
Form records	formdaaa.DBM
Form index	formdaaa.Inn
Form error	formdaaa.Enn

*File name conventions: the letters *form* represent the first four letters of the form name; the letters *proc* represent the first four letters of the procedure name; *d* represents the database letter; the letters *aaa* represent three letters assigned by DataEase, and the letters *nn* represent a hexadecimal (base 16) number assigned by DataEase.

Creating a Form on a Network

The procedure for defining a form in a shared database on a network is really no different than defining a form on a stand-alone system, with one exception. When you first specify a name for your form, DataEase checks the list of previously defined forms for a duplicate name (as usual) and also checks to see if another network user of the database already is defining a form by that name. If the form already exists or if another user is in the process of defining a form by the same name, DataEase displays the message Form formname already exists, where *formname* is the name you chose for the form. You have to use a different form name to continue.

Chapter Summary

This chapter has introduced you to many concepts fundamental to learning to use DataEase. The first portion of the chapter discussed the terms relational database, form, record, and field. The remainder of the chapter focused on how to create a simple DataEase record-entry form. You learned how to design and enter prompts on the form, define fields, and create indexes. Using the information in this chapter, you can create simple, no-frills DataEase forms. Refer to Chapter 3 to learn how to modify form definitions, how to reorganize forms, and how to add enhancements such as derivation formulas, special form properties, security features, borders, custom color, and help messages.

3

Modifying and Enhancing Record-Entry Forms

This chapter continues the discussion in Chapter 2. In that chapter, you learn how to create basic DataEase forms with text and fields. This chapter shows you how to modify DataEase forms, explains the effects that form modifications have on existing data, explains how to delete forms, and explains how to reorganize forms to recover disk space.

After you learn the mechanics of modifying a form, you become familiar with some of the modifications and enhancements you might want to make. This chapter explains how to add to field definition derivation formulas, security features, help messages, and color. You also learn how to change form properties like security level and encryption and how to add form enhancements such as borders and custom color.

The final portion of the chapter describes how you can save time when developing forms by copying text and fields from other forms and by using the DataEase Dictionary. You also learn how to print a copy of your form definition for easy reference and permanent documentation.

Modifying the Form Definition

Inevitably, you will need to make an adjustment or two to the definition of one or more forms in your database. Your database is never exactly the way you want it; you will always be able to think of improvements. This section describes the steps necessary to make changes to a form's definition.

Often, the most important aspect of any change you might make to the form is the effect the change has on the form's existing data. You can change the text on a form as much as you like without affecting existing data, but modifications to a field definition can have a dramatic effect on data already entered in that field. If you already have entered data into the form, be sure to read "Understanding the Effects of Field Modifications" in this chapter before making changes to a field definition.

To access the original form definition to make changes, select **1. Form Definition and Relationships** from the DataEase Main menu. After DataEase displays the Form Definition menu, select **2. View or Modify a Form**. DataEase displays a list of available forms. Select the form containing the definition you want to modify and press Enter. DataEase displays the Form Definition screen.

Caution: Each time you modify a form, DataEase makes a temporary copy to which changes are saved. When you press F2 (SAVE), DataEase attempts to copy the old records into the new definition. If you have insufficient room on your disk for old and new copies of the form files, DataEase abandons the changes you made to the form definition and saves the old version. Make sure that you have sufficient space on your data disk for two copies of the form's files before starting a form modification session.

Deleting a Field

Occasionally, you may want to remove a field from the form. To delete a field, place the cursor in the field's highlighted bar and press F10 (FIELD). DataEase displays the Field Definition screen. Press F7 (DELETE) and answer 2: Yes at the next prompt to confirm the deletion. DataEase deletes the field from the form and returns to the Form Definition screen. When you finish making changes, press F2 (SAVE). DataEase deletes the field's data from the database and returns to the Form Definition menu.

Caution: When you delete a field and then save the form definition with F2 (SAVE), all of the field's data is abandoned. If you accidentally delete a field and recognize the mistake *before* you press F2 (SAVE), pressing Esc (EXIT) returns you to the previous version of the form definition.

Redefining a Field

To make a change to a field's definition, move the cursor to the field's highlighted bar and press F10 (FIELD). DataEase displays the Field Definition screen you saw when you defined the field. Use the cursor-movement keys to move around the screen and make changes to the field characteristics. When you finish, press F2 to save the new field definition. You then can redefine other fields.

Understanding the Effects of Field Modifications

When you first define a DataEase form (before you add data), you do not have to worry about the effects of form modification. As soon as you add one record, however, you must be aware of the ramifications of redefining fields. The following sections describe the effects of changing field characteristics, as discussed in Chapter 2. Several other optional field characteristics also are discussed later in this chapter.

Changing Field Names

Changing only the name of a DataEase field has no effect on the field's data. You must modify other database objects that refer to the renamed field to reflect the new name. Refer to subsequent chapters in this book for information on creating and modifying reports, procedures, and multiforms that refer to DataEase record-entry forms.

Caution: If you change a field name and also change another characteristic during the same form modification session, DataEase assumes that you are defining a new field and discards all the existing data from the original field. If you need to change the field name and another characteristic, change the name first and save the form. Then, modify the form to change the characteristic. If you use this method, the original data is maintained.

Changing Field Types

You may want to change the field type of a field that already contains data. When you save the form definition, DataEase converts the data from the old field type to the new field type. During the conversion, DataEase strips any characters from the data that would not be valid if you were typing the data into the field. For example, a numeric string field accepts only numeric digits during Record Entry; during data conversion to a numeric string field, DataEase deletes all characters except numeric digits. The portion of your data that constitutes valid input into a field of the new field type is saved, but all other characters are stripped away. Table 3.1 summarizes the effect of the conversion process on data.

Table 3.1
Data Conversion Rules for Changing Field Type

New Field Type	Effect on Data
Text	None
Numeric string	Deletes all characters except numeric digits
Number	Deletes everything except digits, minus sign (−), and decimal point (.)
Date	Deletes everything except digits and slashes (/)
Time	Deletes everything except digits and colons (:)
Choice	Converts to choice number based on a match of source data to a choice value or a match of source data to a choice number. If neither match is found, the field is left blank.

Modifying a Choice Field

When you add data to a choice field, DataEase stores only the choice number for each record in the form's data (DBA) file. The actual choice values are stored in the form definition.

During form modification, if you make a change to the list of choices by adding a choice, editing a choice value, or rearranging choices, you must inform DataEase how to handle the choice numbers stored in existing records.

When you save the form after making such a change, DataEase displays the question Do Choice field changes require Choice Numbers in records to be updated?. If you do not want to rearrange choice values, respond 1: No to this question, even if you changed a choice value or added one or more choices to the end of the list.

For example, you can change the *North* choice to *Northeast* in the list of choices for the Region field in the Sales Representative form (see fig. 3.1), or you can add *Northeast* as a fifth option (see fig. 3.2). In either case, the choice numbers should not be updated.

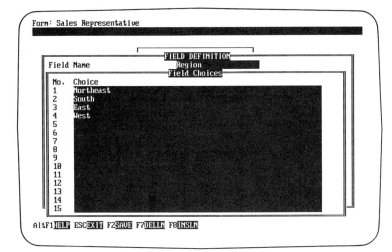

Fig. 3.1.

Changing choice North to Northeast.

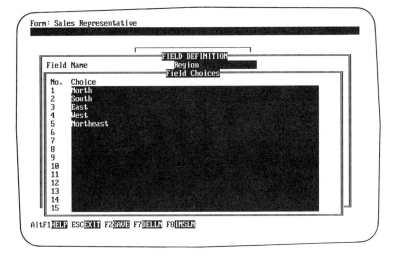

Fig. 3.2.

Adding a new choice, Northeast.

When you rearrange choices so that the choice numbers no longer correspond to their original values (see fig. 3.3), you must respond 2: Yes when DataEase asks whether choice numbers should be updated.

Never rearrange choices in the same modification session that you change or add choice values. Make necessary changes to existing choices, add any new values to the choice list, and save the form. Respond 1: No to the question of whether DataEase should update current choice numbers. In a subsequent modification session, you then can rearrange the choices (without making any further changes to the choice values or additions to

Fig. 3.3.

Rearranging choices. Northeast, South, East, and West have new choice numbers.

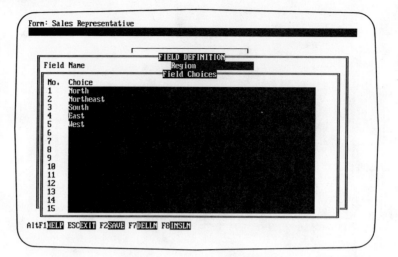

```
Form: Sales Representative

                          ┌─────FIELD DEFINITION─────┐
                          │        Region            │
   Field Name             └────Field Choices─────────┐
                                                      │
   No.  Choice                                        │
   1    North                                         │
   2    Northeast                                     │
   3    South                                         │
   4    East                                          │
   5    West                                          │
   6                                                  │
   7                                                  │
   8                                                  │
   9                                                  │
   10                                                 │
   11                                                 │
   12                                                 │
   13                                                 │
   14                                                 │
   15                                                 │

   AltF1 HELP  ESC EXIT  F2 SAVE  F7 DELLN  F8 INSLN
```

the choice list), save the form again, and answer 2: Yes to updating current choice numbers. You can add *Northeast* as the fifth choice for the Region field, as in figure 3.2, and save the form, answering 1: No to updating choice numbers. Then, in a subsequent form modification session, you can rearrange the choices so that *Northeast* appears second in the list of choices, as shown in figure 3.3. Save the form definition again, but answer 2: Yes so that DataEase updates the choice numbers to reflect the new order.

Caution: Tread carefully in this area. If you attempt to rearrange choices and modify choice values at the same time, you end up with corrupted data that you have to correct manually.

Changing Field Length

DataEase enables you to alter a field's length, even after you add data. Increasing field length is generally safe, but decreasing field length can result in some of your data being cut off (*truncated*). Table 3.2 summarizes how DataEase handles field length changes.

For example, if a Salary field in an existing record contains the value 125,250.00 and you shorten to 5 the number of digits to the left of the decimal, DataEase truncates the number from the left resulting in an incorrect value of 25,250.00.

Table 3.2
Effect of Field Length Changes

| Field Type | Effect | |
	Shorten	Lengthen
Text	Truncate from right	Add spaces to right
Numeric String	Truncate from right	Add zeros to left
Number		
Integer	Truncate from left	No effect
Fixed point (Dollar)		
Digits to left	Truncate from left	No effect
Digits to right	Truncate from right	No effect
Floating point	Truncate from right	No effect

Changing Required Status

Modifying a field's definition to change the Required characteristic from Yes to No or from No to Yes has no effect on existing data. If you change this characteristic from No to Yes, however, and then reorganize the form (discussed later in this chapter), DataEase checks to see if any records fail to have a value in this field. DataEase writes a list of records without an entry in the required field to an error file and displays the message Errors logged in File C:formdaaa.Enn. *C* represents the data drive; the letters *form* represent the first four letters of the form name; *d* represents the database letter; *aaa* represents three letters assigned automatically by DataEase, and *nn* represents a hexadecimal (base 16) number from 00 to 10 assigned by DataEase. Use the DOS TYPE command from the DOS prompt to read the file. You then can use Record Entry to add data to the fields that lack values in the required field.

Reassigning the Unique Characteristic and Indexed Fields

Changing the response to the Unique prompt on the Field Definition screen has no effect on current data values. If you change this field characteristic to unique, however, DataEase does not permit you to edit an existing record that duplicates another record (has a duplicate value in all unique fields). When you attempt to save the edited record, DataEase displays an error message explaining that a duplicate record exists. You can save the edited record only after you change the value in one of the unique fields so that it no longer duplicates another record. Refer to Chapter 4 for more information about entering and editing data with DataEase.

Adding or removing indexing from a field has no effect on current data.

Rearranging Fields and Text on the Form

All of the editing features available during initial form design are still available when you are modifying a form definition. For example, to rearrange fields and/or text on the form, use F3 (CUT) and F6 (PASTE). If you move fields or text around the form, existing data is not affected. If you delete a field with the F3 (CUT) command and do not PASTE the field somewhere else, however, all data in the field is abandoned. If you copy a field with F5 (COPY), a new field with the same field definition is created, but data is not copied to the new field.

Adding Fields

When you add a field to a form that already contains data, DataEase initializes the new field with a blank value in each existing record, unless you have defined a derivation formula. (Refer also to "Using Derivation Formulas" in this chapter.)

Saving a Modified Form

After you make all desired alterations to your form, save the new definition by pressing F2 (SAVE). DataEase displays the question Do you want to save modified form under another name? (y/n). Select 1: No to replace the original definition with the modified version.

Choose 2: Yes if you want to create a form with a different form name. Type a valid form name at the next prompt and press Enter. DataEase saves the definition to disk as a new form and then asks Do you also want to transfer the form data? (y/n). Respond 2: Yes, and DataEase copies the original data into the new form (resulting in two copies of the data) and returns to the Form Definition screen. If you answer 1: No, DataEase returns to the Form Definition screen without making a second copy of the data.

Tip: DataEase provides a utility for changing the database name (see Chapter 9) but does not provide a direct method of changing the name of a form. You effectively can accomplish the same result, however, using the form modification procedure. Follow the steps outlined in this chapter for displaying the form in the Form Definition screen. Move the cursor to one of the text prompts on the form and type any letter of the prompt again (on top of the existing letter, so that you actually make no changes). Save the form definition with F2 (SAVE). Because DataEase "thinks" you made a change to the form, the program asks whether you want to save the form definition under a new name. Respond 2: Yes and assign the new name to the form. When asked whether the data also should be copied, answer 2: Yes. DataEase copies the data to the form definition under the new name and returns to the Form Definition screen. You now have two identical copies of the form and its data, but with different names. View the new form to be certain that the copy is as good as the original and delete the original form using the procedure described in this chapter (viewing a form is discussed in Chapter 4).

DataEase saves the modified definition and returns to the Form Definition menu. When you delete a field, add a field, change a field type, or change a field length, DataEase also reorganizes the form. Refer to the next section for a description of form reorganization.

If you press Esc (EXIT) from the Form Definition screen, before you press F2 (SAVE), DataEase displays the prompt Do you want to abandon modified form data (y or n):. To discard all changes to the form and return to the old definition, select 2: Yes. Select 1: No if you want to continue modifying the form definition or use F2 (SAVE) to save the changes you already have made.

Network Considerations

The procedure for modifying a shared form on a network is the same as the procedure for a stand-alone system, except that only one user at a time can make changes to the definition. The "Using Multiuser Locking Options" section of Appendix B describes how to set the *form definition file lock*. With this lock set to *exclusive*, only one user at a time may access the definition. If the form definition file lock is set to *shared*, multiple users can view the definition provided that none of them make changes. When a user begins modifying the form definition, all other network users are locked out until the modified definition is saved.

Reorganizing a Form

As you use your DataEase database day after day, week after week, you may notice that processing seems to be getting slower. You also may notice that the database files on the disk are getting bigger and bigger. Even when you delete records, the disk files do not decrease in size because DataEase does not recover space used by deleted records. Instead, the program marks records for deletion (see Chapter 4).

If your database system seems to be getting slower over time, you may need to reorganize the forms in your database. Reorganizing a form has the following effects:

❏ Removes records marked for deletion during Record Entry or by a DQL procedure from the file, freeing otherwise unusable disk space

❏ Rebuilds the index file for each indexed field in the form, resulting in improved performance in searches and sorts

❏ Corrects *inconsistencies* in the form caused by power-outages or machine malfunctions that may have occurred during a record-entry operation. DataEase alerts you with an error message if such inconsistencies exist.

As explained in the preceding section, DataEase reorganizes the form when you delete a field, add a field, change a field type, or change a field length in the form definition. DataEase also provides a more direct method to reorganize a form. From the DataEase Main menu choose **1. Form Definition and Relationships** to display the Form Definition menu. Then, select **5. Reorganize a Form**. Choose the form you want to reorganize and press Enter.

Tip: DataEase makes a temporary second copy of the form and its data during the reorganization process. You need enough disk space on the data disk, therefore, for two copies of the form's files, or DataEase cannot complete the reorganization. Refer to Appendix B for instructions on how to establish a separate directory for temporary files.

When you are reorganizing a shared form on a network, DataEase prevents other network users from accessing the form. On the other hand, if someone else is using the shared form when you select the form for reorganization, DataEase informs you that the form is already in use and does not permit you to complete the procedure until the other user releases the form.

Deleting a Form

You may want to delete a form from the database. DataEase provides this option on the Form Definition menu.

To delete a form, from the DataEase Main menu select **1. Form Definition and Relationships**. DataEase displays the Form Definition menu. Next, select **4. Delete Form**. DataEase displays a window menu listing all the forms in the database. Select the one you want to delete and press Enter. If you have defined any *relationships* (discussed in Chapter 6), DataEase asks if you also want to delete them. Answer 2: Yes. DataEase then displays the prompt Are you sure you want to delete this form? (y/n). Respond 2: Yes to complete the deletion. DataEase confirms that the form is deleted by displaying the message Form deleted in the message area.

Caution: This operation erases from the disk the form definition, any records that you may have entered in the form, and all associated index files. DataEase provides no utility for recovering this data after it is deleted. File recovery programs, available from several software manufacturers, may or may not be able to recover deleted form files.

On a network, when you select the form to be deleted, DataEase locks all other users out. Conversely, if another user already is using the shared form when you attempt to select the form for deletion, DataEase indicates that the form is in use and does not permit you access.

Enhancing the Field Definition

Chapter 2 presents the basics of creating fields into which you can type data. This portion of Chapter 3 describes how you can add field characteristics that automatically will enter data based on values in other fields, values looked up from other forms, default values, system supplied date or time, and automatically sequenced values. This section also shows you how to add upper and lower limits on data that can be entered into a field, discusses security features, help messages, and color, and describes how to hide a field from Table View.

Using Derivation Formulas

A *derivation formula* is a special field characteristic through which you instruct DataEase to enter data automatically in the field. Based on a formula that you type on the Field Definition screen, DataEase derives the value of the field from the source(s) you specify. DataEase can derive a field value in five ways. The program can assign a constant *default* value to the field, *lookup* the value from another form, *calculate* the value using a formula, automatically increment the value in *sequence* based on the value of the same field in the preceding record, or provide the *current* value of one of eight system-determined parameters. Combining any of these derivation methods in the same derivation formula also is possible.

To create a derived field, position the cursor on the Form Definition screen where the field should be located and press F10 (FIELD). DataEase displays the Field Definition screen. Assign a field name, field type, and field length (if applicable). Normally, you do not make derived fields required, indexed, or unique. Move the cursor to the field to the right of the prompt Derivation Formula. Type the formula here according to the guidelines presented in the following sections. DataEase checks the formula's syntax when you press Enter, Tab, or the down-arrow key to move to the next field on-screen. If your formula does not evaluate to a value, DataEase displays the error message A value is required in the message area and positions the cursor beneath the offending part of the formula. You cannot move to another field on the Field Definition screen until you have corrected the error(s).

Notice that DataEase displays a message in the prompt line, Press F1 to use the Editor. While defining the derivation formula, you can access the full-screen DataEase Editor by pressing F1. The space provided for the formula on the Field Definition screen is only 50 characters long. If you type past the 50th character, DataEase invokes the Editor. The function-key commands listed in table 3.3 are available when editing the derivation formula in the full-screen Editor. Using this full-screen Editor, you can create formulas up to 4,000 characters in length.

You can return to the Field Definition screen from the Editor by pressing Esc or F2 (SAVE). In either case, you can see up to 50 characters of the derivation formula in the Field Definition screen Derivation Formula field. When you return to the Field Definition screen, DataEase checks the syntax of the formula and displays an error message if the formula does not evaluate to a value.

Table 3.3
Function-Key Commands for the Editor

Function Key (KEY NAME)	Function
Esc (EXIT)	Returns to Field Definition screen
Alt-F1 (HELP)	Provides help on current operation
F2 (SAVE)	Returns to Field Definition screen
F3 (CUT)	Cuts a block of text
F4 (CMDHELP)	Displays pull-down menus
F5 (COPY)	Copies a block of text
F6 (PASTE)	Pastes a cut or copied block of text
F7 (DELLN)	Deletes a complete line
F8 (INSLN)	Inserts a new line at the cursor
Alt-F10 (BORDERS)	Draws borders using the extended character set

Assigning a Default Value

The simplest type of derived field is a *default value*. To assign a default value to a field, type a *constant* value for the derivation formula.

A *constant* value (often referred to as a *constant*) is a valid DataEase value—text, numeric string, number, date, time, choice, or Yes-or-No—that you enter into the formula. For example, the number *356* when used in a derivation formula is referred to as a constant value. The value must be valid for the field type of the derived field. You may not include commas in number constants. Text constant values must be enclosed in double quotation marks. When typing numeric-string values, do not include formatting characters. You must include slashes in date constants, and include colons in time constants. For choice and Yes-or-No fields, enter the choice value rather than the choice number and do not enclose the value in quotation marks. Table 3.4 lists a few examples of constant values.

When you include only a constant as the derivation formula, DataEase enters that value in new records automatically. Suppose that most of your customers are from the state of Virginia. To speed Record Entry and reduce typing errors, you can assign *"VA"* as the default value for the State field in the Retail Customer form. During Record Entry (discussed fully in Chapter 4), you still can type another state code in the State field if you

Table 3.4
Example of Constant Values

Field Type	Valid Value	Invalid Value
Text	"Standard Widget"	Standard Widget
Numeric string	921651234	921-65-1234
Number, Dollar	125500.00	125,500.00
Date	01/31/89	013189
Time	09:45:30	094530
Yes-or-No	Yes	2
Choice	East	3

want to *override* the default (see the "Preventing Data-Entry" section of this chapter). If you just press Enter or Tab at a blank State field, however, DataEase inserts *VA* automatically.

Creating a Lookup Formula

One of your database design goals always should be to avoid entering the same information more than once. DataEase enables you to accomplish this goal by using the *lookup* operator in a derivation formula, creating a *lookup formula*. Data that is already entered in a DataEase form can be looked up and used in other forms, rather than you entering the data again.

For the lookup operation to be effective, you first must define a *relationship* between the form that contains the data and the form that contains the lookup formula. Chapter 6 discusses form relationships more fully, but an example is given here to provide the necessary foundation for the lookup operator. The two forms used in this example are the Product form and the Order Detail form, mentioned in Chapter 2.

Suppose that you have created a form named Product containing the fields shown in figure 3.4. (Price is the retail price charged customers. The Cost field contains the amount your company has to pay to produce the item.)

You have entered records for each of the widget models that your company sells. Now, you are designing the Order Detail form to record information about each order placed for widgets. This new form includes the following fields:

Order Detail

Order Number
Item Number
Model Number
Product Name
Quantity
Price
Total

The final form looks like figure 3.5.

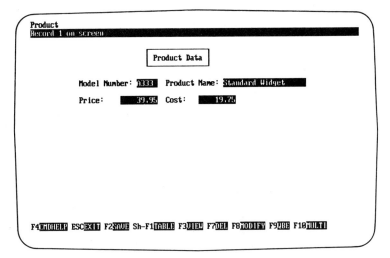

Fig. 3.4.

The Product form.

Fig. 3.5.

The Order Detail form.

The Widget Order form still is used to track orders. For each order, you have one record in Widget Order. By contrast, the Order Detail form should contain one record for each type of widget purchased. If a customer buys three types of widgets in one order, the Order Detail form contains three records for that order—one for each type of widget.

Notice that the Model Number, Product Name, and Price fields occur in the Product form and in the Order Detail form. The goal, in this example, is to use the lookup operator to derive at least some of the data in the Order Detail form from data already entered in the Product form.

First, you formally must define the relationship between Product and Order Detail. You must describe to DataEase which fields in Product and Order Detail to match up to search for data from Product. For example, you can provide the Model Number so that DataEase can search for the Product Name and Price. In this example, the Model Number field functions as the *match* field (often called the *link*) between the Product and Order Detail forms.

To define a relationship, select **1. Form Definition and Relationships** from the DataEase Main menu to display the Form Definition menu. Select **3. Define Relationships**, and DataEase displays the Relationship form, similar to figure 3.6, with the cursor at the Form 1: prompt.

Fig. 3.6.

The Relationship form.

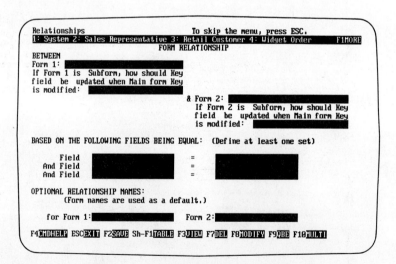

DataEase displays a list of the database forms as a line menu. Select the name of a form from this list. If you cannot see the name of the desired form in the line menu, press F1 (MORE) and then select the name from the window menu. In this example, you press F1 (MORE) and select 6: Order Detail. DataEase places the name of the form in the first field and then moves the cursor to the next prompt:

```
If Form 1 is Subform, how should Key
field  be  updated when Main form Key
is modified:
```

This prompt, new in DataEase 4.2, becomes significant when you use the two forms in a relationship in a Multiform. Chapter 6, "Using Related DataEase Forms," covers relationships and Multiforms in detail and explains when and how to respond to this prompt in the Relationships form. For now, press Tab to move the cursor to the & Form 2: prompt.

Next, choose the other form from the line menu. For this example, you press F1 (MORE) and choose 5: Product. DataEase enters the second form's name to the right of the & Form 2: prompt, and the cursor moves to the next prompt:

```
If Form 2 is Subform, how should Key
field  be  updated when Main form Key
is modified:
```

Press Tab to move the cursor to the first space to the right of the Field prompt, to the left of the first equal sign. This line of the Relationships form defines the *match* fields between the forms.

The line menu now lists the fields from the first form, Order Detail. Select the match field, 3: Model Number from the menu. DataEase types the field name, moves to the right of the equal sign, and lists the second form's fields as a line menu. Choose the second form's match field, 1: Model Number. DataEase types the field name to the right of the equal sign and moves the cursor to the next line (see fig. 3.7). Press F2 (SAVE) to save the relationship and Esc (EXIT) twice to return to the Form Definition menu.

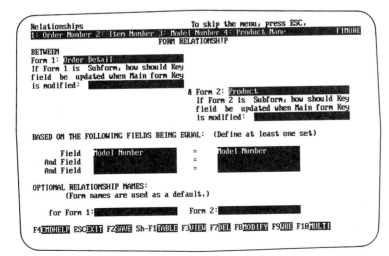

Fig. 3.7.

The Relationships form—Order Detail related to Product.

After the relationship between Product and Order Detail is defined, you can use the lookup operator in Order Detail to search for data from the Product form.

To use the lookup operator in a derivation formula, type the word *lookup*, the name of the relationship (the same as the name of the related form), and the name of the field to be looked up. When a form name or a field name contains a space or one of the *delimiter* characters $(- + */, ( ) = .)$ you also must enclose the entire name in quotation marks. For example, the definition of the Product Name field in the Order Detail form contains this lookup formula (typed in the Derivation Formula line of the Field Definition screen):

lookup PRODUCT "Product Name"

Figure 3.8 shows the formula as it appears in the Field Definition screen.

Note: The use of upper- and lowercase letters in this and other formulas is optional and intended only to make distinguishing the operator, form name, and field name easier when reading the formula.

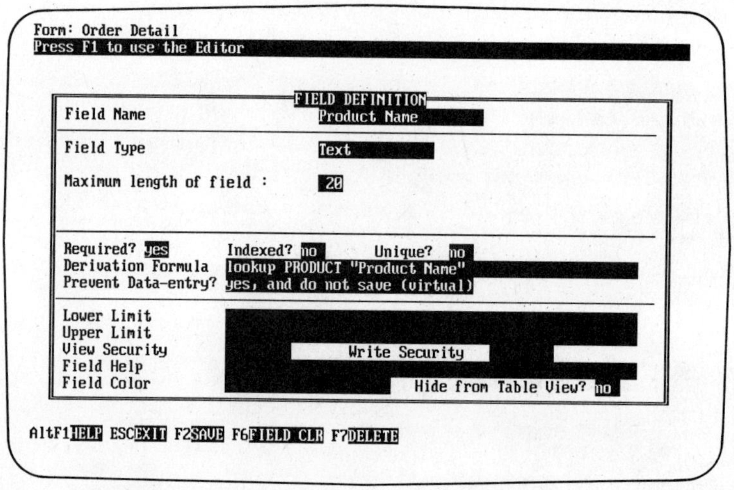

Fig. 3.8.

Using a lookup formula to derive the Product Name from the Product form.

```
Form: Order Detail
Press F1 to use the Editor

                        ┌─FIELD DEFINITION─┐
   Field Name            Product Name

   Field Type            Text

   Maximum length of field :    20


   Required? yes    Indexed? no     Unique? no
   Derivation Formula  lookup PRODUCT "Product Name"
   Prevent Data-entry? yes, and do not save (virtual)

   Lower Limit
   Upper Limit
   View Security              Write Security
   Field Help
   Field Color                    Hide from Table View? no

AltF1 HELP ESC EXIT F2 SAVE F6 FIELD CLR F7 DELETE
```

Similarly, to derive a value for the Price field in the Order Detail form, use this lookup formula:

lookup PRODUCT Price

You do not need double quotation marks in this formula, because the form name and the field name do not contain spaces or delimiter characters.

During Record Entry, DataEase uses the lookup formula to derive the correct value from the related database, using the value of the match field in each record. For example, when you enter *A333* in the Model Number field of the Order Detail form, DataEase uses that value to find the record in the Product form with the same value in its Model Number field. DataEase then retrieves the Product Name (in this case, Standard Widget) and Price (39.95) from the matching Product record and places these values in the corresponding Order Detail fields. You entered the data once in the Product form, but you can use it as many times as necessary in related forms, such as Order Detail.

Calculating a Field Value

DataEase offers an impressive array of formula-building tools including:

❏ *Arithmetic* symbols listed in table 3.5

❏ *DQL functions* including if, date, spell out, time, text, financial, scientific, trigonometric, and arithmetic functions. These functions are listed in Chapter 11.

❏ *DQL operators* including comparison, logical, statistical, conditional statistical, and relational statistical operators. These operators also are listed in Chapter 11.

Table 3.5
Arithmetic Symbols

Symbol	Meaning
*	Multiplication of number values
/	Division of number values
+	Addition of number values
−	Subtraction of number values

Using these tools with constant values and/or field values, you can create virtually any formula you need. Constant values are described in the "Assigning a Default Value" section earlier in this chapter. A *field* value in a formula takes on the value entered in a specified field. Because the value in a field may change from record to record, the final result of a DataEase formula that operates on one or more field value also may vary from record to record. To specify a field value in a formula, use the field name. When a field name contains any spaces or a delimiter character, enclose the name in quotation marks. For example, if you want to use the Date Hired field from the Sales Representative form, type *"Date Hired"* in the formula. Field values can be from the same record in the same form or from a matching record in a related form. You even can derive values from multiple records in a related form using DataEase's special relational statistical operators (discussed in Chapter 6).

For example, in the Order Detail form you want to show Quantity, Price, and Total where the value of the Total field is equal to the value of Quantity multiplied by the value of Price. You therefore define the Total field in the Order Detail form with this derivation formula:

Quantity * Price

During Record Entry, when you type the widget model number into the Model Number field, DataEase searches for the price and places it in the Price field (see the preceding "Creating a Lookup Formula" section). When you type the number of widgets ordered into the Quantity field, DataEase calculates the total price and places that value in the Total field.

Preventing Data Entry

The prompt Prevent Data-Entry appears immediately after the derivation formula line on the Field Definition screen. This characteristic is used exclusively in the definition of derived fields. With the cursor in this field on the Field Definition screen, DataEase displays three options in a line menu: 1: no, 2: yes, 3: yes, and do not save (virtual).

When the derivation formula is providing only a default value, the data entry person can override the default whenever necessary by typing a different value in the field. For fields with a default value, therefore, select 1: no at this prompt.

For all other types of derived fields, you almost always choose one of the other two options at the Prevent Data-Entry prompt. Most often, you want the derived value to be stored with the record, and you do not want the user to be able to change the value. In this case, you should respond 2: yes at the Prevent Data-Entry prompt. For example, the Price and Total fields in the Order Detail form should be stored as permanent values on the disk because you do not want anyone to be able to alter either amount after the order has been placed. You should answer 2: yes at the Prevent Data-Entry prompt in the Field Definition screen for both fields.

Occasionally, you may want the derived field to be recalculated each time you display a record, or you may not want to store the value to disk. In either case, you can select the third option, 3: yes, and do not save (virtual). Derived fields with this characteristic are called *virtual* fields. For example, you do not need to store the Product Name twice—in the Product form and the Order Detail form. To save disk space, select 3: yes, and do not save (virtual) at the Prevent Data-Entry prompt of the Product Name field definition screen in the Order Detail form. DataEase still searches for and displays the Product Name in the Order Detail form during Record Entry but does not store the value with the form's data on the disk. By contrast, you do not want to choose 3: yes, and do not save for the looked-up Price field. You may need to change the price of a particular model, and you do not want the new price to affect the records of previously consummated sales.

During Record Entry, the cursor does not rest on a field that has been defined to include this prevent data-entry characteristic.

Sequencing a Field Value

Identification numbers usually are assigned in sequence—for example, *18647, 18648, 18649,* or *702AA, 702AB, 702AC,* and so on. Keeping track of the last number used, however, could be a chore and is certainly a source for data-entry errors. DataEase provides a special operator, the *sequence from* operator, that automatically sequences a field. A field derived by this operator is referred to as a *sequence* field. Sequence fields can be text or numeric string fields.

To create a sequence field, type the sequence from operator in a derivation formula, followed by the starting value of the sequence. For example, to automatically increment the Order Number field in the Widget Order form, beginning at order number 100, use the following derivation formula:

    sequence from 100

You always should respond 2: yes to the Prevent Data-Entry prompt, so that no one will override the value in the sequence field. Even if you respond 1: no to this question, DataEase disregards any attempts during initial Record Entry to override a value, but you can edit the value after it is saved.

The starting value of a text sequence field can contain letters and/or numbers, but the starting value of a numeric string sequence field must contain only numbers. Sequencing is from right to left. Each digit sequences from *A* to *Z* (or *a* to *z*) or *0* to *9*.

Using System-Supplied Values

You may want to date-stamp or time-stamp a record when you create or modify the record. DataEase provides two ways to access your computer system date and time in a derivation formula.

When you want a derived field to store the date on which a record is created, use the following derivation formula:

    ??/??/??

Respond 2: yes to the Prevent Data-Entry prompt. When you first create the record during Record Entry, DataEase stores the system date in the derived field. Subsequent display of the record for the purpose of viewing or editing does not change the date in this derived field. The field always contains the original date of entry.

To create a derivation formula that stores the current system date when the record is modified, use either of the following derivation formulas:

current date

or

lookup current date

When the field is derived by one of these formulas, DataEase supplies the current system date each time you display a record. If you save a modified record with F8 (MODIFY), the date of the modification therefore is stored in the derived field (see Chapter 4). *Note:* You also must make sure that the Preserve old CURRENT DATE, etc. on modify? prompt on the Form Properties screen is answered 1: No. This option is the default answer. Refer to the "Using Form Properties" section later in this chapter.

Similarly, you can derive the system time with the formulas: *??:??:??*, *current time*, or *lookup current time*.

DataEase also supplies other useful information through the *current* keyword. Table 3.6 lists the system-supplied parameters accessible in derivation formulas.

Table 3.6
Derivation Formulas
Using the Current Keyword

Formula	System Parameter	Field Type
Current date	System date	Date
Current time	System time	Time
Current "user name"	Name used at sign on	Text
Current "user level"	User's security level	Number, Numeric string
Current computername	Workstation name (LAN)	Text

Deriving the Value

You create a derived field during form definition, but DataEase actually uses the derivation formula during Record Entry (see Chapter 4). DataEase calculates the formula and derives the value of the field when you move the cursor from the derived field to the next field during Record Entry. Fields with the *prevent data-entry* characteristic are derived as the cursor jumps over them to the next field (because the cursor never rests on this type of field). If you do not move the cursor past the field, DataEase derives its value when you press F2 (SAVE) to save the new record. Refer to the "Recalculating Derived Fields" section in Chapter 4 for instructions on how to rederive the field's value during Record Entry.

Modifying a Derivation Formula

Changing a derivation formula after you already have entered data does not change the value of the derived field in existing records, unless the field is a *virtual* field (see the "Preventing Data Entry" section earlier in this chapter). Reorganizing the form after changing the derivation formula also does not affect the value of the field in existing records, except when the field is blank. You can rederive fields, one record at a time during Record Entry; however, if you want to recalculate a derived field in all existing records, you must use a DQL procedure. Refer to Chapter 11 for more information on DQL procedures.

Setting Upper and Lower Limits—Establishing Validation Criteria

One method of reducing data-entry errors is to prohibit values outside given minimum or maximum limits. DataEase enables you to assign a *lower limit*, *upper limit*, or both to any text, numeric string, number, dollar, date, or time field.

To define a lower limit, type a derivation formula at the Lower Limit prompt. Typically, you type a constant as a lower limit. For example, you might want to place upper and lower limits on values entered into the Salary field in the Sales Representative form. To place a lower limit of $20,000.00 on the Salary field, you type *20000* at the Lower Limit prompt on the Field Definition screen. To establish an upper limit of $80,000.00, you type *80000* at the Upper Limit prompt on the Field Definition screen. If, during Record Entry, you try to enter a value below the lower limit, DataEase displays the error message Field value is too Low in the message area and specifies the lower limit value in the prompt line. Similarly, entering a value above the upper limit results in the message Field value is too High, and the upper limit value is specified in the prompt line.

Another effective way to reduce errors during Record Entry is to create a list of valid entries for a field and force the user to enter a value from the list. This type of list often is referred to as a *validation table*. A DataEase choice field contains a built-in validation table, but the upper/lower limit options provide a convenient alternative. To validate the value entered in a field against a list of values in another form, type the same lookup formula at the Upper Limit and Lower Limit prompts. For example, you may want DataEase to validate the Model Number field in the Order Detail form against the model numbers contained in the Product form. Enter the following formula at both `Limit` prompts in the Field Definition screen of the Order Detail form's Model Number field:

lookup PRODUCT "Model Number"

During Record Entry, DataEase checks the entered model number against all the model numbers in the Product form. If you enter a model number that does not exist in the validation table form, DataEase displays the error message `Field value is too High`. This message means that the value entered does not exist in the validation table. Refer to the "Using Dynamic Lookup" section in Chapter 6 for an explanation of how to display the validation table easily and how to select a valid entry from the list.

Changing the upper or lower limits characteristics has no effect on existing data; however, if you reorganize the form after changing the criteria, DataEase builds an error list file that specifies any records containing values outside the new limits.

Assigning Field-Level Security

DataEase enables you to assign any one of seven levels of security to each user you authorize to access your database: *High*, *Medium 1*, *Medium 2*, *Medium 3*, *Low 1*, *Low 2*, and *Low 3*. The procedure for assigning security levels is discussed in Chapter 9.

With DataEase, you can limit access to the records in a form and limit access to each field in the form. Access to form records is limited through the Form Properties screen, discussed in the "Using Form Properties" section of this chapter. Field access is controlled through the `View Security` and `Write Security` fields on the Field Definition screen.

To limit the ability to view the values in a field to users with a given security level or higher, select the appropriate security level from the line menu at the `View Security` prompt. Users that do not have the required view security level see a blank field. To limit the ability of users to modify a field, enter a security level at the `Write Security` prompt. The value is displayed, but the cursor does not move into the field, because the user cannot change values.

For example, you might want to limit those who may view the Sales Representative Salary field to individuals with a Medium 1 security level or higher, but permit only persons with a High security level to make changes to the field. Select 2: `Medium 1` at the `View Security` prompt on the Field Definition screen and select 1: `High` at the `Write Security` prompt.

Changing a security level characteristic has no effect on existing data.

Adding a Help Message to a Field

DataEase has many built-in messages including context-sensitive help messages. Because you are the most likely to know how and by whom your form is to be used, DataEase enables you to write help messages for use with your form. You can write form-level and field-level help messages. A help message that can be displayed from any field in the form during Record Entry can be added through the Form Properties screen, discussed in the "Using Form Properties" section of this chapter. When you want to add a help message specific to a single field, type the message in the field's Field Definition screen.

To add a field-level help message, access the Field Definition screen and move the cursor to the Field Help prompt. DataEase indicates in the prompt line that you should press F1 to access the Editor. As with the derivation formula line, 50 spaces appear on the Field Definition screen, but you have up to 4,000 total spaces for a help message by using the Editor. The function-key commands listed in table 3.3 are available for use in the Editor when creating the help message. Unlike the derivation line, the Editor is invoked automatically when you type the first character of the help message (see fig. 3.9).

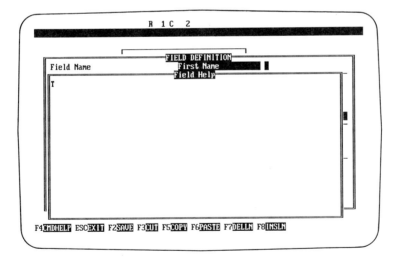

Fig. 3.9.

Using the Editor to create a field-level help message.

For example, you may want to explain to people adding records to the Sales Representative form that they also can type an employee's middle initial in the First Name field. Type the following message in the space next to the Field Help prompt:

Type first name and optional middle initial in this field.

Press F2 (SAVE) or ESC (EXIT) to return from the Editor to the Field Definition screen.

During Record Entry, you can display this help message any time the cursor is in the First Name field. Just press Alt-F1 (HELP). After users display the field-level help message, they still can display the normal DataEase help information, or any form-level help message that may be defined, by pressing F1 (MORE). Refer to Chapter 9 for an explanation of how to set the *help level* for specific users so that help messages are displayed without users pressing Alt-F1.

By default, the location of the help message window is near the bottom of the screen, just above the function key line (see fig. 3.10). You can change the size and position of a field-level help message window by typing a special numeric code at the beginning of the message in the Field Definition screen. The code follows the syntax

W, R, C, L

where *W*, *R*, *C*, and *L* represent integers. *W* is the window's width; *R* is the window's starting row on-screen; *C* is the starting column, and *L* is the total number of rows in the window. For example, to cause the First Name help message window to display in a window 50 characters wide (the minimum width), starting at position R5C7, and 3 rows long, you type the following message:

50,5,7,3 Type first name and optional middle initial in this field.

The message window now appears as shown in figure 3.11.

Fig. 3.10.

The default location of help messages.

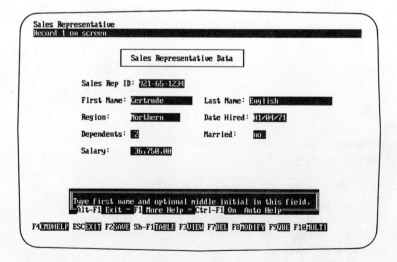

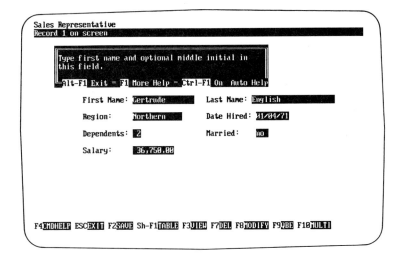

Fig. 3.11.

The help message with a different size and location.

DataEase also provides several special control characters that can be used to enhance and format help messages.

To maintain upward compatibility with earlier versions of DataEase, the vertical bar (|), sometimes called the *pipe* character, causes text that follows the pipe to start a new line. Using this character is an alternative to pressing Enter when typing the message in the Field Definition screen.

DataEase also enables you to emphasize portions of the message in three ways. On a color system, each emphasis setting represents a different foreground/background color combination, determined by the current screen style. Refer to Appendix B for instructions on customizing the screen style by using the Screen Style form. Normal help message characters display in the same foreground/background color combination as the highlighted menu selection bar in full-screen and window menus (referred to on the Screen Style form as *menu highlighting*). Characters enclosed in angle brackets (< >) display in the same color combination as the function key names on the function key line (*key names*). Characters enclosed in brackets ([ ]) display in the same color combination as normal text on the form (*all other*). Characters enclosed in braces ({ }) are displayed in the same color combination as normal record-entry fields on the form. These colors display only when you invoke the message during Record Entry, not on the Field Definition screen.

Changing a help message has no effect on existing data.

Highlighting the Field with Color

Previous versions of DataEase enabled you to highlight fields in three ways. DataEase now offers eleven foreground/background color combinations that can be applied to each field. These color combinations correspond to the eleven color combinations listed on the Screen Styles screen (see fig. 3.12). The Screen Styles screen is accessed through the Administration menu. Appendix B explains how to customize screen style colors and how to select a default screen style. See also "Highlighting the Form with Color," later in this chapter and "Defining a User's Screen Style" in Chapter 9.

Fig. 3.12.

The Screen Styles screen.

```
Screen Styles
Record 1 on screen
         SCREEN  STYLE  NAME : color

                    FOREGROUND    BACKGROUND    INTENSIFY?    BLINK ?

  Title Area        Brown         Black         yes           no

  Cursor/Mode Area  Cyan          Black         yes           no

  Message Area      Red           Black         yes           no

  Prompt Line       Black         Green         no            no

  Fields: Regular   Brown         Blue          yes           no
        Highlight 1 Light Gray    Red           yes           no
        Highlight 2 Brown         Black         yes           no
        Highlight 3 Black         Black         no            no
  Menu Highlighting Light Gray    Blue          yes           no

  Key Names         Light Gray    Red           yes           no

  All Other         Brown         Black         yes           no

 F4 CMDHELP  ESC EXIT  F2 SAVE  Sh-F1 TABLE  F3 VIEW  F7 DEL  F8 MODIFY  F9 QBE  F10 MULTI
```

You assign a specific color combination to a field through the Field Definition screen. Move the cursor to the Field Color prompt. DataEase displays a line menu in the prompt line that shows the names of four color combinations: 1: Regular, 2: Highlight 1, 3: Highlight 2, and 4: Highlight 3. Press F1 (MORE) to see the complete list, as shown in figure 3.13. Select an option from the line menu or the window menu. During Record Entry, DataEase displays the field in that color combination.

Changing a field color has no effect on existing data.

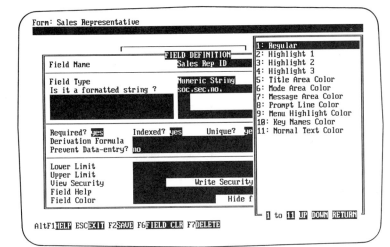

Fig. 3.13.

The Field Color window menu.

Hiding a Field from Table View

One of the most convenient new features of DataEase is the capability to switch the record-entry display from the traditional *Form View*, one record at a time, to *Table View*, multiple records in a tabular format. This feature is explored fully in Chapter 4.

A disadvantage of Table View, in contrast to Form View, is that usually all the fields of a form do not fit horizontally on-screen at once, forcing you to scroll the screen right and left to view all the data in any particular record. The last characteristic on the Field Definition screen enables you to suppress the display of a field during Table View, so that other fields that may be of more interest to you have more room. Suppressing fields reduces or even eliminates the need for left/right scrolling.

To prevent a field from displaying during Table View, move the cursor in the Field Definition screen to the Hide from Table View? prompt and select 2: yes. The default value is 1: no, so that all fields normally display in Table View.

Changing this characteristic has no effect on existing data.

Using Form Properties

Much of this chapter deals with altering the characteristics of individual fields on the form. DataEase also provides several characteristics that apply to the form as a whole. These characteristics are the *form properties*. To modify any of the properties of a form, from the Form Definition screen press Shift-F10 (FORM PROPERTIES). DataEase displays the first page of the two-page Form Properties screen, shown in figure 3.14.

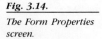

Fig. 3.14.

*The Form Properties
screen.*

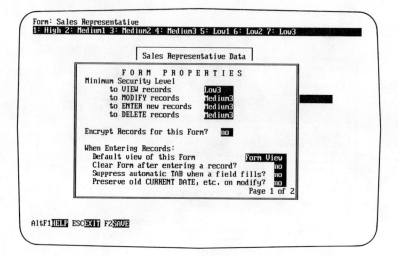

The following sections describe when and how to change any of the
properties listed on the Form Properties screen. Changing a form property
has no effect on existing records.

Assigning Form-Level Security

On the Users form, you can assign any one of seven levels of security to
each user authorized to access your database: *High*, *Medium 1*, *Medium 2*,
Medium 3, *Low 1*, *Low 2*, and *Low 3*. The procedure for assigning security
levels is covered in Chapter 9. Each user security level carries certain
default rights and restrictions to do such things as view, enter, modify, and
delete fields.

You can limit access to form records and each field in the form with
DataEase. You limit access to the field through the Field Definition screen,
discussed in the "Enhancing the Field Definition" section of this chapter.
You control records access with the four Minimum Security Level options
listed on the Form Properties screen. The minimum security level
requirements set on the Form Properties screen take precedence over the
default requirements and any field-level security requirements.

By default, users with the lowest security level can view any record in any
form in the database. To change the security level, access the first page of
the Forms Properties screen and at the to VIEW records prompt, select a
higher security level from the line menu. Any user with a security level
lower than the minimum is denied access to the form. If restricted users
try to view the form, DataEase displays the message You don't have access
to form name, where *form name* represents the actual form the user tries
to view.

Any user with a medium security level by default can enter, modify, and/or delete any record in any form of the database. To increase the security level required to perform one of these functions in a particular form, display the Form Properties screen and change the security level option entered in the corresponding Minimum Security Level field. Any user with a security level lower than the specified minimum who attempts an operation is shown the message Security Access denied.

Encrypting Records

If your data is particularly sensitive, you may want to take advantage of DataEase's data encryption capability. To *encrypt* (scramble) all data before storing it to disk, respond 2: yes to the Encrypt Records for this Form? prompt, on page 1 of the Form Properties screen. You must choose this form properties option before any record is entered for encryption to be effective on all records in the form.

Changing the Default View

Normally, during Record Entry, DataEase displays a form in Form View—one record at a time in a fill-in-the-blank style form. You then can display the form records in Table View by pressing Shift-F1 (TABLE VIEW). Figure 3.15 shows the Sales Representative form in Table View. Press Shift-F1 again to return to Form View.

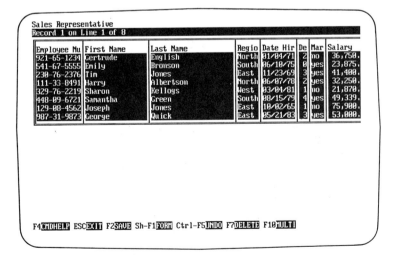

Fig. 3.15.

The Sales Representative form in Table View.

DataEase enables you to change this default setting for each form so that the form is displayed first in Table View. To make Table View the default view, access the first page of the Form Properties screen from the Form Definition screen. Then select 2: Table View at the Default view of this Form prompt. Save the form. The form displays in Table View each time you access it in Record Entry. Press Shift-F1 to display the form in Form View.

Clearing the Form during Record Entry

Each time you press F2 (SAVE) to save a record during Record Entry in Form View, DataEase (by default) does not clear the field values from the screen. This feature is convenient when the next record has some of the same field values as the one you just saved, but you are forced to press F5 (FORM CLR) if you want to enter the next record from scratch (see Chapter 4). DataEase (Versions 4.01 and higher) enables you to change this setting so that all fields are cleared when you press F2 (SAVE) during Record Entry in Form View.

To change the operation of F2 (SAVE) in Record Entry/Form View so that pressing F2 also clears the form, access the Form Properties screen from the Form Definition screen. Move the cursor to the Clear Form after entering a record? prompt and change the response to 2: yes. Save the form definition.

Suppressing Automatic Tab

As you enter data during Record Entry, when a field entry does not completely fill the field, you must press Tab or Enter to move the cursor to the next field. However, when a field entry fills the field's entry space, DataEase moves the cursor to the next field—a sort of *automatic tab*. For example, when entering data in the Sales Representative form, as soon as you fill the Sales Rep ID field, the cursor jumps to the First Name field. For touch typists who do not look at the screen as they type, however, this may not always be a desirable feature. If you are not looking at the screen, you do not notice that the cursor has jumped, and you may press Tab or Enter by habit. The cursor then moves to the wrong field, and the record's data is incorrect. You may suppress the automatic tab feature to eliminate this inconsistency.

To suppress automatic tab, display the Form Properties screen and move the cursor to the Suppress automatic TAB when a field fills? prompt. Change the selection to 2: yes. Save the form definition.

Preserving the Old System Supplied Values

As explained in the "Using System-Supplied Values" section earlier in this chapter, you may derive a field value from several system parameters: current date, time, user name, user level, and computername. When you enter or modify a record that contains a *current* derived field, DataEase stores the most current value. ***Note:*** This rule does not apply to the *??/??/??* or *??:??:??* derived formulas, but to those formulas that use the keyword *current*. For example, if you create a field named Date Modified with the derivation formula *current date*, DataEase stores a new date in the field when you create a record and each time you modify the record.

When you prefer to maintain the value of the original *current* date (the value that is current when you first enter each record), you must change one of the form properties. From the Form Definition screen, display the Form Properties screen by pressing Shift-F10 (FORM PROPERTIES). Move the cursor to the last prompt on the first page, Preserve old CURRENT DATE, etc. on modify? and change the selection to 2: yes. Save the form definition.

Adding a Help Message to a Form

DataEase provides built-in help messages but also enables you to create your own custom help messages. The "Adding a Help Message to a Field" section earlier in this chapter explains how to add a message to a *field*. You add a custom help message to a *form* through the Form Properties screen.

To add a form-level help message, display the Form Properties screen and press PgDn to display the second page (see fig. 3.16). The second page of the Form Properties screen is intended solely for the form's help message. This screen is not the DataEase Editor and none of the Editor function-key commands work. Type the help message, exactly as you want it displayed. You can use F6 (FIELD CLR) to clear a line at a time, but do not use F8 (MODIFY) because this key clears all the values in the Form Properties screen (an inexplicable quirk). The special emphasis codes (carets, brackets, and braces), described in the "Adding Help Message to a Field" section, also are available for use in form-level help messages. After you have typed the message, press F2 (SAVE) to save the message and return to the Form Definition screen. Save the form definition.

Fig. 3.16.

Page 2 of the Form Properties screen.

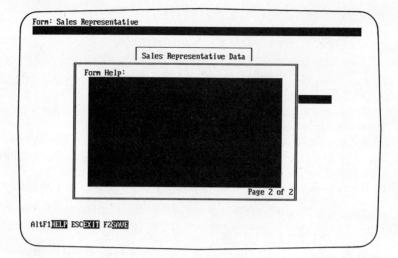

To display the custom help message during Record Entry, press Alt-F1 (see fig. 3.17). If the cursor is in a field that also has its own help message, the field-specific help message is displayed first. You then can see the form's help message by pressing F1 (MORE). To see any DataEase supplied help message, press F1 (MORE) while the field's help message is displayed.

Fig. 3.17.

A sample form-level help message.

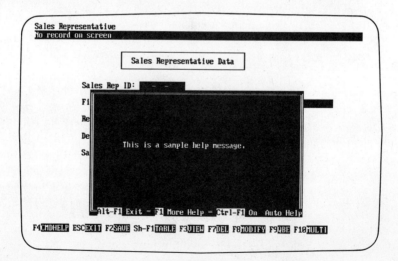

Enhancing a Form's Appearance

When you are satisfied that you have all the more substantive features of your form properly defined, you may want to turn your attention to how the form "looks" on-screen. With DataEase you can draw borders around portions of the form and modify screen color.

Adding Borders

To draw a border around part of the form, display the Form Definition screen and move the cursor where you want to place one corner of the desired border. Press Alt-F10 (BORDERS) to display a window menu that shows the border line choices and the extended character set (see fig. 3.18). For a border made up of double lines, select 1: Double Border from the menu. When you want a single-line border, choose 2: Single Border. DataEase then displays the message Move cursor to the opposite corner and press Alt-F10. Press Esc to Cancel. Move the cursor to the position of the corner diagonally opposite from the corner where you started, and press Alt-F10. DataEase draws the border. You can erase a border following a similar procedure, by choosing 3: Erase Border from the window menu. Figure 3.19 shows the Sales Representative form with a border around the words Sales Representative Data.

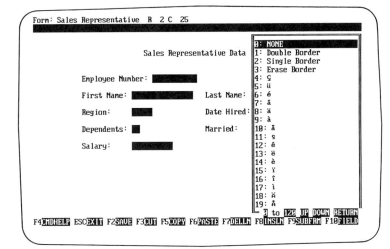

Fig. 3.18.

The Borders and Extended Character Set window menu.

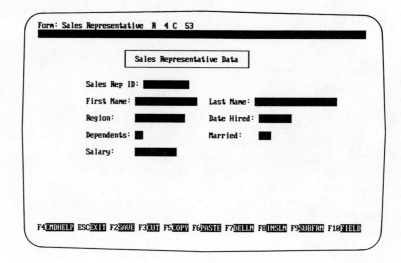

Fig. 3.19.

*The Sales
Representative form
showing a border
around the words*
Sales
Representative
Data.

Adding Color to the Screen

In addition to customizing the color of each field on a form, you can apply any of nine available color combinations to any part of the form. When you apply a new color to the form, you define a starting point and a stopping point. The new color combination is applied from the starting point to the stopping point, left to right, top to bottom. Application of color to the form screen works best when done one line at a time. To create blocks of color, you must create strips of the same color on successive lines in the form, all of the same length.

You can apply a color combination to a portion of the form screen in several ways. The easiest method (the most consistent, not the fewest keystrokes) is through the Highlight pull-down menu. First, move the cursor to the position where the new color should start. Press F4 (CMDHELP) to display the pull-down menus. Use the → or ← key to move to the Highlight menu (see fig. 3.20). Use the down-arrow key to move the highlighted bar to one of the nine color combinations (shown in parentheses in fig. 3.20): Regular Field, Highlight 1, Highlight 2, Title Area, Mode Area, Message Area, Prompt Line, Menu Highlight, or Key Names. These color combination names refer to those combinations used in the Screen Style screen. The other labels for these highlighting options (not in parentheses) refer to their effects printed in DataEase reports. Highlight the desired color combination name and press Enter. Then, move the cursor to the end of the area to which the new color should be applied and press Alt-E.

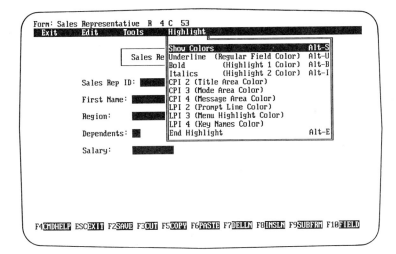

Fig. 3.20.

The Highlight pull-down menu.

As you apply the color attributes, DataEase types special codes on-screen at the beginning and end points. If you prefer, you can bypass using the Highlight menu and type the code yourself. The begin and end codes for the available color combinations are listed in table 3.7.

Table 3.7
Color Combination Codes

Color Combination Name	Begin Code	End Code
Regular Field	@u	@nu
Highlight 1	@b	@nb
Highlight 2	@i	@ni
Title Area	@c2	@c1
Mode Area	@c3	@c1
Message Area	@c4	@c1
Prompt Area	@p2	@p1
Menu Highlight	@p3	@p1
Key Names	@p4	@p1

Another way to apply three of the color combinations is with keystroke commands. Table 3.8 lists these commands.

Table 3.8
Color Combination Keystroke Commands

Keystroke Combination	Function
Alt-U	Begin Regular Field color
Alt-B	Begin Highlight 1 color
Alt-I	Begin Highlight 2 color
Alt-E	End new color combination
Alt-S	Show current colors

The new color combinations apply when the form is displayed during Record Entry, but you can preview their effects while still on the Form Definition screen. Press Alt-S, and DataEase displays the form and its fields in the same color combinations that will be used in Record Entry.

Copying Field Definitions from Other Sources

Try to avoid repetition of work whenever possible—even when defining a DataEase record-entry form. DataEase enables you to copy text and field definitions easily from any other form in the database and provides a ready-built list of commonly used field definitions in the Dictionary form.

Copying Text and Field Definitions from Another Form

A primary reason for copying a field definition, rather than redefining a field from scratch, is to ensure that fields used as *match* fields are defined in a similar manner. For example, you want to be sure that the Model Number field in the Order Detail form is defined in the same manner as the Model Number field in the Product form, because that field is used as a match field or link between the two forms. To make field definitions identical, copy the Model Number field definition from the form definition of Product to the form definition of Order Detail.

DataEase does not, however, enable you to copy fields and/or text selectively from another form. Instead, you must make a copy of the entire form and then delete the fields and text that you do not need.

To copy an existing form into the new Form Definition screen, place the cursor at the position where you want the copy to be placed and press F5 (COPY). Choose 2: Form from the line menu. DataEase displays a window menu containing a list of the forms in the database. Select the form you want to copy. DataEase inserts a copy of this form in the Form Definition screen at the cursor, complete with all text and fields.

After copying the old form into the new one, you need to delete the unneeded fields and text. Use the F3 (CUT) feature, described in Chapter 2 to discard the portions of the form that you cannot use. You then can use F3 (CUT) and F6 (PASTE) to position the portions of the old form that you are going to keep.

Using the Dictionary Form

DataEase (Versions 4.01 and higher) supplies an off-the-shelf list of 30 commonly used field definitions in the *Dictionary* form. Each time you create a database, DataEase installs a copy of this form in the database. The available fields are listed in table 3.9.

To copy a definition from the Dictionary form into a form you are defining, type the field name as text on the Form Definition screen. With the cursor to the right of this text, press F5 (COPY). Then, select 3: Dictionary Field from the line menu. DataEase displays a window menu listing the 30 available field names. Select the name of the field you need from the menu. DataEase returns to the Form Definition screen and displays the new field starting at the cursor. DataEase assigns the field's name based on the text that you typed on-screen prior to copying the field definition. If DataEase finds no text to the left of the field, the program uses the name of the field from the Dictionary form.

Table 3.9
Dictionary Form Fields

Field Name	Abbreviated Field Definition
Soc.Sec.No.	Numeric String, 11, Required, Indexed, Unique
I.D. Number	Numeric String, 5, Indexed, Derived, No entry
Salutation	Choice, 6, Derived
First Name	Text, 15, Derived
Middle Initial	Text, 2, Derived
Last Name	Text, 25, Indexed, Derived

Table 3.9—*continued*

Field Name	Abbreviated Field Definition
Company	Text, 40, Derived
Title	Text, 30, Derived
Salary	Number, 10, Range
Address1	Text, 30, Derived
Address2	Text, 30, Derived
City	Text, 25, Derived
State	Choice, 2
Zip	Numeric String, 5, Indexed
Telephone	Numeric String, 14
Extension	Text, 5
Birthdate	Date, 8
Marital Status	Choice, 9
Age	Number, 2, Derived
Quantity	Number, 6
Price	Number, 9
Price X Quantity	Number, 13, Derived, No entry
Description	Text, 40, Required, Indexed, Derived
Yes/No	Choice, 3, Derived
Today's Date	Date, 8, Derived, No entry
Spell Date	Text, 20, Derived
Time of Day	Time, 8, Derived
long:Comments1	Text, 50
long:Comments2	Text, 50
long:Comments3	Text, 50

You also can add field definitions to the Dictionary form, just as you add fields to any DataEase form. The field definitions you add, however, can be copied only from within the current database. The Dictionary form in a new database always starts with the default list of 30 field definitions.

Printing the Form Definition

Print the form definition after you are satisfied that your form design is perfect. This hard copy of the definition of each form in the database will be a great time-saver months later when you realize that you need to add a few features. This hard copy also will be helpful to those who must completely redesign their databases to meet the needs of their growing companies. Indeed, the printouts provided by DataEase should be only a small part of the documentation you should be compiling as you design and implement your database system.

To print a DataEase form definition, make sure that your printer is turned on, connected, has paper, ribbon, and so forth. From the Form Definition screen, press Shift-F9 (PRINT). DataEase sends the definition to the printer. This definition includes a picture of the form layout and a list of field definitions. The field definition list shows the status of the following characteristics: field name, field type, field length, required, indexed, unique, derived, range (upper/lower limit), prevent entry, and hide from Table View. The list also shows the size and offset (in bytes) of each field and the size of each record. Finally, the printed form definitions show the total amount of memory (RAM) required by the form.

Chapter Summary

This chapter continued the discussion in Chapter 2. In that chapter, you learned how to create basic DataEase forms with text and fields. This chapter showed you how to modify DataEase forms and explained the effect that form modification has on existing data. You also learned how to delete forms and how to reorganize forms to recover disk space and increase processing speed. A large portion of this chapter described some of the modifications and enhancements you may want to make to a field definition including: field derivation formulas, security features, help messages, and color. This chapter also demonstrated how to change form properties and how to add such form enhancements as borders and custom color. This chapter described how you can save time when developing forms by copying text and fields from other forms and by using the DataEase Dictionary. You also learned how to print a copy of your form definition—an important part of your permanent database documentation.

This chapter prepared you for the topic that comes next. The purpose for all the field types, derivation formulas, help messages, and so on, is to facilitate accurate and efficient record entry. Turn to Chapter 4 to learn the ins and outs of "Using DataEase To Enter, Edit, and View Data."

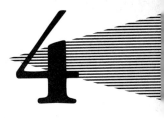

Using DataEase To Enter,
Edit, and View Data

Data entry and retrieval are the primary missions of any database management system. This chapter shows you several methods of entering, editing, and viewing data using DataEase forms—building on the foundation laid by Chapters 1, 2, and 3. Chapter 1 introduces you to DataEase, its screen, menus, and commands. Chapters 2 and 3 describe how to create a database and define DataEase forms. Now that you are familiar with the DataEase way of doing things and can define quite sophisticated record-entry forms, this chapter shows you how to use what you have learned.

Using DataEase Record Entry

The principal way to enter data into DataEase forms is through Record Entry. This section of the chapter describes how to access a form to enter data and explains which cursor-movement keys, function-key commands, and pull-down menus are available in Record Entry.

Accessing the Record-Entry Form

To add data to a DataEase form, start from the DataEase Main menu and select **2. Record Entry**. DataEase displays the DataEase Records menu, similar to figure 4.1. This window menu contains the names of all the forms defined in the database, listed in the order that you created them. Select the form on which you want to enter data.

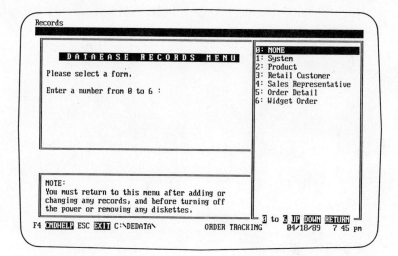

```
 Records
┌─────────────────────────────────────────────────────────────────┐
│                                            ┌──────────────────┐   │
│  ┌──────────────────────────────────┐      │0: NONE           │   │
│  │ D A T A E A S E   R E C O R D S   M E N U │1: System      │   │
│  │ Please select a form.            │      │2: Product        │   │
│  │                                  │      │3: Retail Customer│   │
│  │ Enter a number from 0 to 6 :     │      │4: Sales Representative│
│  │                                  │      │5: Order Detail   │   │
│  │                                  │      │6: Widget Order   │   │
│  │                                  │      │                  │   │
│  │                                  │      │                  │   │
│  │                                  │      │                  │   │
│  ├──────────────────────────────────┤      │                  │   │
│  │ NOTE:                            │      │                  │   │
│  │ You must return to this menu after adding or│             │   │
│  │ changing any records, and before turning off│             │   │
│  │ the power or removing any diskettes.        │             │   │
│  └──────────────────────────────────┘      └──────────────────┘   │
│                                          0 to 6 UP DOWN RETURN     │
│  F4 CMDHELP ESC EXIT C:\DEDATA\        ORDER TRACKING   04/18/89  7 45 pm │
└─────────────────────────────────────────────────────────────────┘
```

> **Tip:** On the DataEase Records menu is the name of a form that you
> did not define: the System form. The System form is actually a group
> of forms provided by DataEase. These forms hold information about
> users, DataEase configuration, printers, screen styles, relationships,
> and menus. You may access each of these forms through the Records
> menu or through the Administration menu (see Chapter 9 and
> Appendix B).

After you select the form name, DataEase displays the record-entry form,
just as you defined it, with the cursor resting in the first field. In the title
area, at the top left of the screen, DataEase displays the form name. The
message No record on screen is displayed in the prompt line. Figure 4.2
shows the Sales Representative form in a Record Entry session before any
records have been entered. You enter one record at a time on this screen.
When DataEase displays data in the fill-in-the blank form defined during
Form Definition, you are in *Form View*.

Entering Data in a Record-Entry Form—Form View

After the form is on-screen in Form View, entering data is easy. Type the
information into each field, just as you would fill in blanks on a fill-in-the-
blank form. As you type, DataEase fills in text, date, numeric string, floating
point, time, and choice fields from left to right. Integer fields, however, are

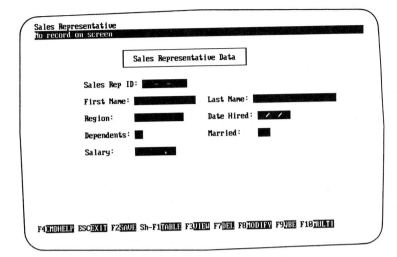

Fig. 4.2.

The Sales Representative form in Form View.

filled in from right to left. In a fixed point field, DataEase fills in the field from the decimal point to the left, until you type the decimal point, at which point numbers fill the field from the decimal point to the right.

If you make a typing mistake as you are entering the data, press the Backspace key. DataEase erases the last character that you typed. You then can type the correct character in its place.

When the value you type in a field does not fill all of the available space, use a cursor-movement key to move to the next field—usually Enter or Tab. When the value fills a field, the cursor jumps to the next field, unless the field is an integer field. (See the "Suppressing Automatic Tab" section of Chapter 3.)

After you enter a value in a field and move to another field, DataEase displays the message New Record on Screen in the prompt line.

Because the cursor rests in the first field on-screen when you start, you usually type the data in that field before moving to the next field. You normally move through the form from left to right, top to bottom, typing data in the fields as you go, but you do not have to follow this order. Table 4.1 lists the cursor-movement keys available during Record Entry. You can use these keys to move around the form and enter the data in any order that you choose.

Table 4.1
Form View Cursor-Movement Keys

Key	Moves cursor to
↑	Field above
↓	Field below
←	One space to the left; from left end of field, moves to preceding field
→	One space to the right; from right end of field, moves to next field
Backspace	One space to the left, erasing preceding character
Ctrl·←	Start of long:text line
Ctrl·→	End of long:text line
Home	First (top left) field of first page
End	Last (bottom right) field of last page
Tab	Next field
Shift-Tab	Preceding field
*Enter	Next field
PgDn	First field of next page (multipage forms only)
PgUp	First field of preceding page on multipage forms; first field of current page on single-page forms

* The DataEase documentation refers to the Enter key as the Return key, because earlier versions of DataEase referred to F2 as the Enter key.

When entering data in a text field, you may type letters, numbers, or any displayable character; DataEase limits what you can enter in other types of fields. Table 4.2 describes acceptable entries in each DataEase field type.

Because long:text fields are a series of text fields, they accept any displayable character. Long:text fields have a special feature known as *word wrap*. As you type a word that extends beyond the right end of a line in a long:text field, DataEase moves the entire word to the next line. Word wrapping keeps all the letters that make up a word on one line together.

DataEase performs additional checks on values entered in date and time fields:

❏ You must enter dates in the format *mm/dd/yy*, where *mm* stands for the month number in two digits; *dd* represents the two-digit day of the month, and *yy* is the last two digits of the year (assuming that

Table 4.2
Acceptable Entries during Record Entry

Field type	Acceptable characters
Text, Long:text	Any character except *, ?, and ~
Numeric String	Numbers only
Number	
Integer	Numbers, minus sign (−)
Fixed point	Numbers, minus sign (−), decimal (.)
Floating point	Numbers, minus sign (−), decimal (.)
Date	Numbers only
Time	Numbers only
$	Numbers, minus sign (−), decimal (.)
Yes or No	Yes, no, 1, or 2
Choice	Any choice value in the list of choices; any choice number in the list of choices

you do not change the default data format—see Appendix B). If you enter a value that is not a possible date, such as 31/12/89, DataEase beeps and displays the message Invalid Date in the message area (the correct entry for December 31, 1989 is 12/31/89).

❏ You must enter time in the format *hh:mm:ss*, where *hh* is hours (24-hour clock—00:00:00 is midnight); *mm* is minutes, and *ss* is seconds. If you enter an invalid time (45:14:00, for example), DataEase beeps and displays the message Invalid Time. (The correct entry for 2:45 p.m. is 14:45:00.)

In addition to the field type, DataEase uses the other characteristics that you assigned during form definition (discussed in Chapter 3) to check the validity of your data:

❏ *Field length* limits the number of characters you can type in a field.

❏ *Upper limits* and *lower limits* prevent you from entering any value outside the specified *range*.

❏ *Prevent data entry* prevents you from entering anything in a field. The cursor skips over a field with this characteristic.

❏ *Unique field* prevents you from adding a record in this field if the combination of all unique fields in the record duplicate the combination of fields in another record in the form data.

For you to enter data, your security level must meet or exceed the minimum level set by the *view security* and *write security* characteristics, and the security level must be set on the Form Properties screen.

Suspending Calculation of Derived Fields

Each time the cursor passes through a derived field or a field on which a derived field depends for its value, DataEase recalculates the derivation formula. If a form has only a few derived fields, this recalculation is not a problem, but sometimes you may enter data into a form with many derived fields. If the calculations required to derive these fields cause noticeable delays as you move from field to field, you may want to suspend the calculations until you finish entering data in the record.

To temporarily suspend the calculation of derived fields, press Alt-F9 (SUSPEND CALC). This key is a *toggle*, which means that until you execute the same command again or until the session ends, calculation of derived fields is suspended. (Nothing appears on-screen, however, to indicate that calculations are suspended.) After you have entered all the values in the record, press Alt-F9 (SUSPEND CALC) again to toggle calculations on. DataEase then derives all underived fields in the record, based on the values you have entered. DataEase also derives underived fields when you press F2 (SAVE).

You may want to force recalculation of a derivation formula to see the result of a derivation while calculation has been suspended. Each time you want DataEase to recalculate all the derived fields in the current record, press Ctrl-F9 (RECALCULATE).

Entering Data in Table View

DataEase also enables you to enter data in a tabular format referred to as *Table View.* In Table View, each row is a separate record, and each field is a column. Multiple records are displayed on-screen.

To access Table View, display the form in Form View, as described in the "Accessing the Record-Entry Form" section earlier in this chapter. Then, press Shift-F1 (TABLE). If no records have been entered in the form, DataEase displays a screen full of blank lines similar to those in figure 4.3. Each of these lines or rows represents a separate record, and each column represents a field. Each line in a long:text field is displayed as a separate column.

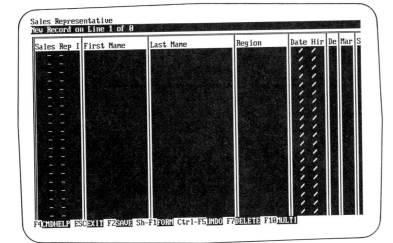

Fig. 4.3.

The Sales Representative form in Table View with no records entered.

The column width in Table View is determined by the field length. When field length is shorter that the field name, the field name in the column heading is truncated (cut off) at the right end. The seventh column in figure 4.3 is the Married field, for example. Married has a field width of only 3, but the entire length of the field name is 7 characters. The last four characters in the field name (*ried*), therefore, are truncated in the Table View column heading.

After you enter records in the form, access Table View to display the existing records in a tabular format, as shown in figure 4.4, with no blank lines.

To add new records to existing records in Table View, press the End key. The program scrolls all but two records off the screen and fills the work area with blank lines (see fig. 4.5). You still can view and edit existing records, but you also can enter new records into the blank lines.

Entering data into your form in Table View is similar to entering data in Form View. As you type the information into each field, data appears as described in the preceding section, "Entering Data in a Record-Entry Form—Form View." Data is filled in differently in long:text fields, however, because the word wrap feature does not work in Table View.

Fig. 4.4.

*The Sales
Representative form
in Table View with
eight records
entered—Edit/View
mode.*

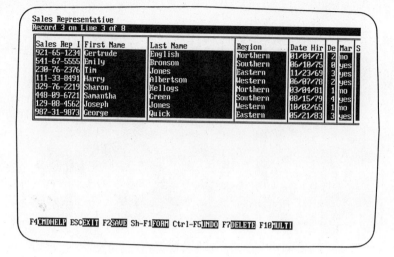

Fig. 4.5.

*The Sales
Representative form
in Table View in
Add mode.*

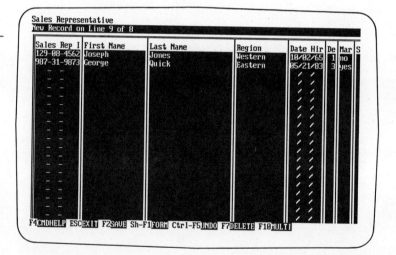

Tip: You may enter text into a long:text field during Table View and later notice in Form View that one or more words in the data are split onto multiple lines. To get DataEase to place the words together, display the record in Form View and move the cursor to the first character in the long:text field. Press insert to turn on the Insert mode and press the space bar, pushing the entire entry to the right until DataEase properly wraps the words together. Use the Backspace key to delete extra spaces.

When you first display a form in Table View, the cursor rests in the field on the left end of the first blank row on-screen. You usually type the data in that field before moving to the next one, therefore, and move through the table from left to right, top to bottom, typing data in the fields as you go. Table 4.3 lists the cursor-movement keys available during Record Entry in Table View. You can use these keys to move around the table and enter the data in any order that you choose.

Table 4.3
Table View Cursor-Movement Keys

Key	Moves cursor to
↑	Same column (field), preceding row (record)
↓	Same column in succeeding row
←	One space to the left; from left end of column, moves to preceding column
→	One position to the right; from right end of column, moves to next column
Backspace	One space to the left, erasing preceding character
Ctrl-←	First (left-most) column, same row
Ctrl-→	Last (right-most) column, same row
Home	Same column in first row of table
End	Same column in first blank row
Tab	Next column in same row; from last column, moves to first column in next row
Shift-Tab	Preceding column in same row; from first column, moves to last column in preceding row
*Enter	Next column in same row; from last column, moves to first column in next row
PgDn	Same column in first row of next screen
PgUp	Same column, top row, when cursor is not already at the top of the screen; from top row, moves to top row of preceding screen

*The DataEase documentation refers to the Enter key as the Return key, because earlier versions of DataEase referred to F2 as the Enter key.

Because you can have as many as 4,000 characters in a single record, you often do not have enough horizontal space in Table View to display all the fields on-screen at one time. DataEase still displays each record as a separate row, but displays only 80 characters at a time. The last column displayed on the right may not fit on-screen. As you move the cursor into the partially displayed field, DataEase makes this the left-most field, and displays a new set of columns on-screen.

Editing Data in a Record-Entry Form

You may need to correct a field value after you move the cursor to another field. Whether you are working in Form View or Table View, you can change the value in a field in one of four ways:

❑ Clear the current value and begin again.

❑ Type over the current value.

❑ Insert characters in the current value.

❑ Delete characters in the current value.

Move the cursor to the field with the cursor-movement keys and begin editing the data.

To clear the current value from the field, regardless of the field type, move the cursor to the field and press F6 (FIELD CLR). DataEase erases the current value and leaves the cursor in the field. This command clears one line of a long:text field. When the field is clear, you can type in the correct value.

When the field you are editing is a text, numeric string, date, time, choice, or yes-or-no field, DataEase places the cursor at the left end of the field. DataEase is in Replace or Overstrike mode by default; when you type a character, DataEase replaces any character currently displayed at the cursor and moves the cursor to the right. You can type the new value over the old entry, or when the new value contains fewer characters than the old value, press the space bar to erase the extra characters.

If you need to insert only a few characters in any of these field types (non-number fields), do not type the complete entry again. Instead, press the Insert key to turn on the Insert mode. DataEase displays the message (INSERT) in the cursor position/mode area of the top line of the screen. Move the cursor to the position in the field where the first character should be inserted and start typing the correction. As you type, DataEase pushes to the right any character at the cursor. Press Insert again to return to Overstrike mode. You can insert an entire blank line in a long:text field by pressing Shift-F8 (INSLN).

To delete characters in non-number fields, use the Delete key. Each time you press Delete, DataEase erases the character at the cursor and pulls to the left any text that is to the right of the cursor. To delete a line in a long:text field, press Shift-F7 (DELLN).

Editing a number field (integer, fixed point, dollar, or floating-point) is different than editing the other field types. When you move the cursor into a number field that already contains a value, DataEase places the cursor at the left-most digit. For integer and fixed point fields, this position may not be the left end of the field, but if you press the ← key, the cursor moves to the preceding field.

As with the other field types, when you use the Overstrike mode while editing a number field, digits at the cursor are replaced, and the cursor moves one space to the right. You cannot, however, add any digits to the left end of the number while in Overstrike mode, and you cannot type a decimal point unless the decimal is typed over a previous decimal.

When the Insert mode is on in a number field and the cursor is on the left side of the decimal point (in fixed and floating point fields), DataEase inserts numbers to the left of the cursor, pushing existing numbers to the left. You can use the Insert mode, therefore, to add digits to the left end of the number. When the cursor is on the right side of the decimal point, numbers are inserted at the cursor, and existing numbers are pushed to the right.

When the cursor is on the left side of the decimal in a number field and you press the Delete key, DataEase deletes the digit at the cursor, pulling any remaining digits that were to the left of the cursor one space to the right. If the cursor is on the right of the decimal when you delete a digit, all remaining digits are pulled from right to left.

Saving a New Record

After you enter data into a Form View record, you must save the record to add it to the form's data in memory (RAM). After every 10 records or if there is no keyboard activity for 30 seconds, DataEase adds the data to disk.

To save a record to RAM from Form View, press F2 (SAVE). DataEase displays the message New Record Written in the message area and the message Record *n* on screen—where *n* is the record number of the new record. Press F5 (FORM CLR) to clear all fields in the form. DataEase again displays the message No record on the screen, and you are ready to enter data in the next record.

Tip: DataEase normally does not clear the data from the form on-screen when you save a record. Instead, you must press F5 (FORM CLR). This design decision is intended to make data entry easier; the decision is based, however, on the sometimes incorrect assumption that the values you enter into most fields will change little, if any, from record to record. If you find that you most often clear the data from the preceding record before entering a new record, refer to the "Clearing the Form during Record Entry" section in Chapter 3. That section describes how to access the Form Properties screen and how to clear the form by pressing F2 (SAVE).

You can save a record in Table View in several ways. You can use the Save operation in Table View to save all unsaved records, not just the record that contains the cursor. DataEase displays the message Saved All Changes in the message area at the top of the screen. To save records in Table View, use one of the following methods:

❑ Press F2 (SAVE), as in Form View.

❑ Press F8 (MODIFY).

❑ When you begin to enter records in Table View, DataEase displays two existing records as the top two rows on-screen (see fig 4.5). If you scroll any other existing records onto the screen using the cursor-movement keys, DataEase saves any new records to RAM.

❑ DataEase can display up to 20 records on-screen at one time in Table View. When you finish entering the twentieth record on-screen and press Enter or Tab at the last field, DataEase scrolls all the records off the screen and displays a screen of blank lines, similar to those in figure 4.3. DataEase also saves any new records.

❑ Switch back to Form View. DataEase automatically saves to RAM any unsaved records.

After records are saved to RAM, press Esc (EXIT) to return to the Records menu and to write the records to disk.

Using Function-Key Commands and Pull-Down Command Menus

As in form definition, during Record Entry, most tasks can be accomplished with a function-key command. Several commands already have been described in this chapter. The remainder of the chapter describes how to use all but four of these commands (the remaining four are covered in

Chapter 6). For your convenience, all 29 available Form View function-key commands are listed in table 4.4. The 19 function-key commands available in Table View are listed in table 4.5.

Table 4.4
Form View Function-Key Commands

Function Key (KEY NAME)	Function
Esc (EXIT)	Returns to the Records menu (does not save the current record)
F1 (MORE)	Displays a window menu
*Shift-F1 (TABLE)	Displays, using Table View, records that match the criteria specified on the Form View screen; displays all records in Table View when no criteria is specified
Alt-F1 (HELP)	Provides help on current operation
F2 (SAVE)	Saves record on-screen as a new record
Shift-F2 (SAVE DEFAULT)	Saves record on-screen as the default record
F3 (VIEW)	Views the first record that matches the criteria specified on-screen; views next consecutive record when no criteria is specified
Shift-F3 (VIEW PREVIOUS)	Views previous consecutive record
Alt-F3 (CONTINUE SEARCH)	Views the next record that matches the criteria specified on-screen
Ctrl-F3 (VIEW RECORD #)	Views a particular record, specified by record number
*F4 (CMDHELP)	Displays pull-down command menus
F5 (FORM CLR)	Clears values from all fields on-screen

Table 4.4—*continued*

Function Key (KEY NAME)	Function
Shift-F5 (DEFAULT FORM)	Fills in values from all default record fields into the record on-screen; when no default record has been defined (or after switching to Table View and back to Form View), fills in values from last record saved
Alt-F5 (UNCHECKED)	Invokes unchecked mode to allow entry of search criteria
*Ctrl-F5 (UNDO)	Undoes unsaved changes to record on-screen
F6 (FIELD CLR)	Clears values from current field on-screen
Shift-F6 (DEFAULT FIELD)	Fills in values from corresponding default record field into the current field
F7 (DEL)	Deletes the displayed record
Shift-F7 (DELETE DEFAULT)	Deletes Default Form, unless cursor is in a long:text field
Shift-F7 (DELLN)	Deletes a line from a long:text field
F8 (MODIFY)	Saves the modified record on-screen, replacing the existing record
Shift-F8 (INSLN)	Inserts a blank line in a long:text field
F9 (QBE)	Accesses QBE—Quick Reports menu
Shift-F9 (PRINT)	Prints record on-screen
ALT-F9 (SUSPEND CALC)	Suspends calculation
*Ctrl-F9 (RECALCULATE)	Recalculates
F10 (MULTI)	Accesses a related form—multiview

Table 4.4—*continued*

Function Key (KEY NAME)	Function
*Alt-F10 (MULTIFORM)	*Ad-hoc* Multiform
*Ctrl-F10 (LOOKUP)	Displays related form in a window and in Table View to lookup and retrieve data—dynamic lookup

*New command in DataEase 4.0

Table 4.5
Table View Function-Key Commands

Function Key (KEY NAME)	Function
Esc (EXIT)	Returns to Records menu (does not save the current record)
End (ADD)	Accesses Add mode—displays blank lines to the bottom of the table for entering additional records
F1 (MORE)	Displays a window menu
Shift-F1 (FORM)	Switches to Form View from Table View, saving all changes, additions, and/or deletions made to records displayed in Table View
Alt-F1 (HELP)	Provides help on current operation
F2 (SAVE)	Saves all changes, additions, and/or deletions made to records displayed in Table View
F4 (CMDHELP)	Displays pull-down command menus
F5 (FORM CLR)	Clears all unsaved changes and/or additions from all fields and records in the table on-screen and returns to Edit/View mode (if in Add mode)
Shift-F5 (DEFAULT FORM)	Saves fill-in values from last record
Ctrl-F5 (UNDO)	Undoes unsaved changes to current record on-screen

Table 4.5—*continued*

Function Key (KEY NAME)	Function
F6 (FIELD CLEAR)	Clears values from current field on-screen
Shift-F6 (DEFAULT FIELD)	Fills in value from corresponding Default Record field into the current field
F7 (DELETE)	Marks current record for deletion—(deleted by pressing F2 (SAVE), F8 (MODIFY), scrolling more records in view, or returning to Form View
F8 (MODIFY)	Saves all changes, additions, and/or deletions made to records displayed in Table View (same as F2 (SAVE)
Shift-F9 (PRINT)	Prints all records in form in tabular format
ALT-F9 (SUSPEND CALC)	Suspends calculation
Ctrl-F9 (RECALCULATE)	Recalculates
F10 (MULTI)	Accesses a related form—multiview
Ctrl-F10 (LOOKUP)	Displays related form in a window in Table View to lookup and retrieve data—dynamic lookup

It may take a while for you to commit all of the function-key commands to memory. Meanwhile, you can use the pull-down command menus, new with Version 4.0. If you do not see the command you are looking for in the function key line, you can display a series of pull-down menus to see all the options.

Press F4 (CMDHELP) to access the pull-down command menus from any field, in Form View or Table View. DataEase displays the Exit menu at the top left of the screen and a list of the available pull-down menus in the prompt line. Figure 4.6 shows the Exit pull-down menu and the list of nine Form View Command menus: Exit, Edit, Tools, Search, Table, Multi Form, Report, Default, and Multi-User. The comparable Table View Exit menu is shown in figure 4.7. The list of pull-down menus available in Table View is only slightly different than that in Form View. The Form menu replaces the Table menu, and the Search menu and the Report menu are not available.

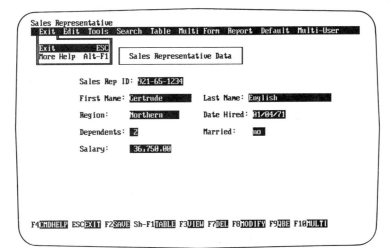

Fig. 4.6.

The Exit menu in Form View.

Fig. 4.7.

The Exit menu in Table View.

Use the ↑, ↓, Home, and End keys to move the highlighted menu selection bar to the desired pull-down menu option and press Enter. To move to another menu, use the → or ← key. For example, pressing the → key once from the Exit menu shown in figure 4.6 displays the Edit menu shown in figure 4.8. After a menu is displayed, you can use the cursor keys to move the selection bar to the desired option and press Enter. You still can use the function-key or keystroke command listed in the menu, if you prefer. To leave the pull-down menus without selecting an operation, press Esc (EXIT).

Fig. 4.8.

The Edit pull-down menu.

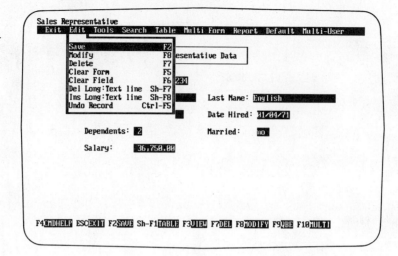

Although the primary purpose of pull-down menus is to provide optional assistance with DataEase commands, sometimes the pull-down menu provides the only way to accomplish a desired operation. Because the five Multi-User menu options, shown in figure 4.9, do not have corresponding function-key commands or keystroke commands, they must be selected through the pull-down menu.

Fig. 4.9.

The Multi-User pull-down menu.

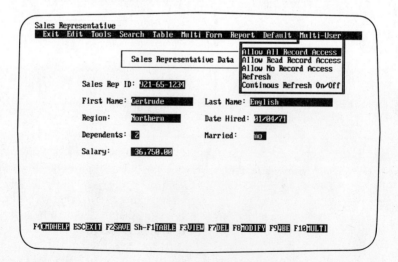

Because using menus always requires more keystrokes than the equivalent function-key command, you should use the function-key method when available. The remainder of this chapter explains when and how to use the many record-entry commands.

Quitting from Record Entry

To quit from Record Entry, with no pull-down menu displayed, press Esc (EXIT). DataEase displays the message Exiting in the prompt line and returns to the DataEase Records menu (see fig. 4.1). You can choose another form to work with or press Esc (EXIT) again to return to the DataEase Main menu.

Caution: You always should use the Esc (EXIT) command to return to the Records menu before you turn off your computer or remove the data disk. DataEase does not save to disk all the data you entered until you return to the Records menu. By using Esc (EXIT), you can ensure that all records are saved to disk. If you do not exit properly from Record Entry, you most likely will lose at least some of the data you entered.

Summoning Help

Context-sensitive help is available as you enter data, just as during other DataEase operations. As Chapter 1 explains, you can press Alt-F1 (HELP) at any time to make the help system available, even if DataEase is displaying a pull-down command menu. Indeed, the second option listed in the Exit pull-down menu is More Help, which invokes the context-sensitive help system. This option is listed on the menu because Exit is the first menu you see after pressing F4 (CMDHELP). If you cannot remember which function-key command summons context-sensitive help, press F4 (CMDHELP) to see the Exit menu.

When you invoke context-sensitive help while displaying a pull-down command menu, DataEase provides a short description of the highlighted selection (see fig. 4.10). DataEase displays a short description of each option as you move the highlighted menu selection bar around the pull-down menu system (see fig. 4.11). To receive continuous help, choose More Help from the Exit menu or press Alt-F1 (HELP), from the pull-down menus. After you select an option from a menu, execute a function-key command, or press Esc, the pull-down menus and corresponding help messages are no longer displayed.

Fig. 4.10.

The More Help *option on the Exit menu, in Form View, with context-sensitive help.*

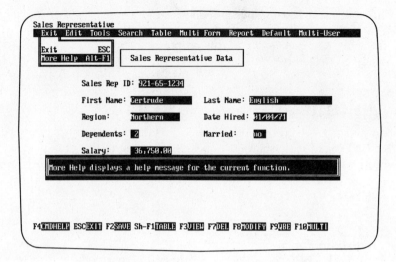

Fig. 4.11.

The Del Long:Text line *option on the Edit menu, in Form View, with context-sensitive help.*

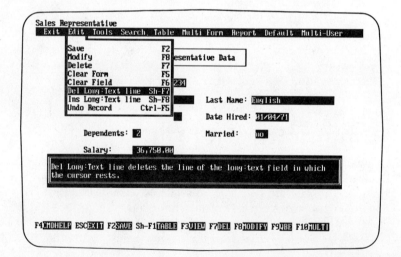

Tip: If you want the help to be displayed automatically, change the help level on your User Information form to **2. Automatically** (refer to Chapter 10) and restart DataEase. The next time you press F4 (CMDHELP), the context-sensitive help messages are displayed; you no longer need to press Alt-F1 (HELP).

Viewing Existing Records

You must be able to view your data after you enter it into a form. When you enter customer data, for example, you want to be able to call that information up easily on-screen for reference. DataEase provides several methods for finding a particular record or group of records and displaying them on-screen, one at a time (Form View) or as a group (Table View). These methods also are used to find and display records that you need to modify.

To view existing data in a DataEase form, select **2. Record Entry** from the Main menu. DataEase displays the Records menu. Select the form containing the data you want to view. DataEase displays the blank record-entry form in Form View with the cursor resting in the first field. In the title area, at the top left of the screen, DataEase displays the form name. The message No record on screen appears in the prompt line.

Viewing Existing Records in Record Order

DataEase stores records in the order that they are saved. The first record you add to a form is record number 1; the second record you add is record number 2, and so on.

Viewing Records in Form View

You easily can view each of the existing records in the same order that you entered them after you have the blank record-entry form on-screen in Form View.

To view the first record in the form data, press F3 (VIEW) from the blank record-entry form. DataEase displays the message Record found in the message area at the top of the screen, and the message Record 1 on screen in the prompt line. The program fills in the fields on-screen with values from the first record in the form data. Figure 4.12 shows record number 1 of the Sales Representative form.

You can view the next record in sequence by pressing F3 (VIEW) again. DataEase displays the message Record found in the message area, and Record 2 on screen appears in the prompt line.

Each time you press F3 (VIEW), DataEase displays the next record in the order that it was added to the form data. When you reach the last record and press F3 (VIEW) again, DataEase beeps, clears all fields, and displays the message No more records in the message area and the message No record on screen in the prompt line. Press F3 (VIEW) once more, and DataEase starts at record number 1 again.

Fig. 4.12.

*The first record in
the Sales
Representative form.*

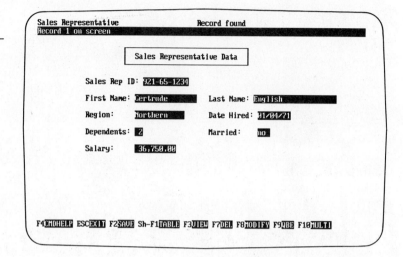

DataEase also enables you to move in reverse record order through the form data. Press Shift-F3 (VIEW PREVIOUS) to see the previous record, in the reverse order that the records were added to the form data. Press Shift-F3 (VIEW PREVIOUS) at a blank form for DataEase to display the last record saved.

Viewing Records in Table View

When you switch to Table View from a blank form, DataEase also displays records in the order they were saved. With the cursor in the first line of the table, DataEase displays in the prompt line the message Record 1 on Line 1 of *n*, where *n* is the total number of records in the form data. You can use the cursor-movement keys listed in table 4.3 to move around the table. As you move the cursor to other rows in the table, the record number in the message changes. The second row is record number 2; the third is record number 3, and so on. DataEase can display as many as 20 records in Table View on the same screen. If you move the cursor past the 20th row, DataEase displays a new page including the next group of up to 20 records. Each time you move the cursor past the top or bottom edge of the screen, DataEase *pages* up or down through the form data, 20 records at a time.

Viewing Records in Index Order

Chapter 2 discusses why and how to create an indexed field. As you add records to a form with an indexed field, DataEase keeps a special list of the records in order by the values in the indexed field (alphabetical order for text fields, numeric order for number fields, chronological order for date fields). This list is the index file. One use for this index file is to display records in indexed order.

To view form records in order by the values in an indexed field, display a blank record in Form View, press Alt-F5 (UNCHECKED), and type an asterisk (*) in the indexed field. Then, press F3 (VIEW). DataEase displays the first record in index order. To see the next record in order by the value in the indexed field, press Alt-F3 (CONTINUE SEARCH).

You also can view the records in Table View in indexed order. Display a blank record in Form View, press Alt-F5 (UNCHECKED), type an asterisk (*) in the indexed field, and press Shift-F1 (TABLE). DataEase displays all records in the form in indexed order in Table View.

For example, the Product form contains a list of all the types of Widgets your company sells. If you press Shift-F1 (TABLE) at a blank form, DataEase displays the product list in the order the records were saved (see fig. 4.13). To display the products in alphabetical order by product name, press Alt-F5 (UNCHECKED), type an asterisk in the Product Name field, and press Shift-F1. Because Product Name is an indexed field, DataEase displays the product list in alphabetical order by that field, as shown in figure 4.14.

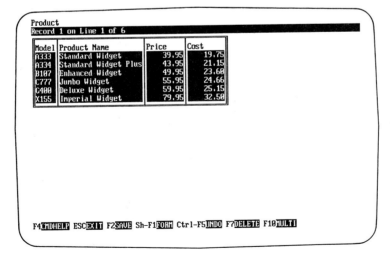

Fig. 4.13.

The Product form in record number order.

Fig. 4.14.

The Product form in alphabetical order by the indexed field product name.

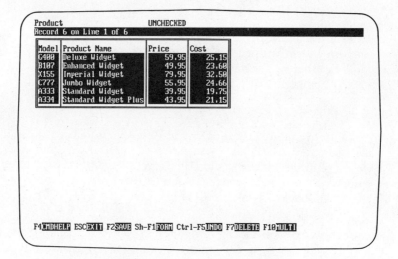

```
Product                      UNCHECKED
Record 6 on Line 1 of 6

Model Product Name       Price  Cost
C400  Deluxe Widget       59.95  25.15
B187  Enhanced Widget     49.95  23.60
X155  Imperial Widget     79.95  32.50
C777  Jumbo Widget        55.95  24.66
A333  Standard Widget     39.95  19.75
A334  Standard Widget Plus 43.95 21.15



F4 CMDHELP ESC EXIT F2 SAVE Sh-F1 FORM Ctrl-F5 UNDO F7 DELETE F10 MULTI
```

Searching for Individual Records

Scrolling through the data one record at a time is fine when the form contains a small number of records, but becomes tedious and unworkable when searching through thousands of records. Fortunately, DataEase provides search capabilities that enable you to locate quickly a specific record for viewing.

To search for a record that meets a given criteria, always start in Form View. Then, press Alt-F5 (UNCHECKED) to clear all fields and turn off field derivations. DataEase displays the word UNCHECKED in the mode/cursor position area at the top of the screen, indicating that the form is in Unchecked mode. Unchecked means that as you enter values in the form, DataEase does not perform the normal validity checks on the following: date fields, time fields, required fields, lower limits, upper limits, unique fields, and fields assigned the prevent data-entry characteristic. DataEase also does not perform field derivations while in Unchecked mode. The restrictions listed in table 4.2, however, still apply. You can search for records, but you cannot save a record while the form is UNCHECKED.

When you are in Unchecked mode, type a value in at least one field. This value is referred to as a *search criterion*. You can enter values in any number of fields in the form. Because the form is in Unchecked mode, you can even type a value in derived fields and fields to which you assigned the prevent data-entry characteristic. All the values you type in the form make up the search criteria. You want DataEase to find the first record that matches values in each of the fields in which you enter a value. If you leave a field blank, DataEase does not have to match that field. (The record you are looking for can have any value in that field.) When you finish entering the search criteria, press F3 (VIEW). DataEase displays the first record that matches the search criteria.

Tip: DataEase is not sensitive to the case of the characters used to specify search criteria. If you type a search criterion in lowercase and the actual data value contains the same characters but in uppercase, DataEase still considers it a match.

To see the next record that matches the criteria, press Alt-F3 (CONTINUE SEARCH). DataEase displays the next record that matches if one exists in the form data. When DataEase can find no more records that match the criteria, press Alt-F3 (CONTINUE SEARCH) to clear the form. The message No more records appears, and No record on screen is displayed in the prompt line. If you press F3 (VIEW), DataEase displays the next sequential record in the file, whether or not it matches the criteria.

To view the record of customer number 1005, for example, press Alt-F5 (UNCHECKED) and type *1005* in the Customer Number field, as shown in figure 4.15. Press F3 (VIEW), and DataEase displays the record for Signal Plumbing (see fig. 4.16).

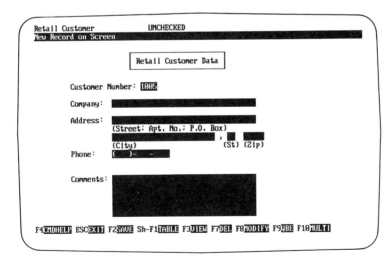

Fig. 4.15.

The Retail Customer form in Unchecked mode—specifying the search criteria.

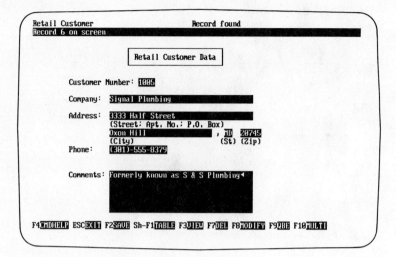

Fig. 4.16.

The matching Retail Customer record.

> **Tip:** The most efficient way to search for a specific record is to build a search criteria that specifies a value for each field assigned the unique field characteristic. When you press F3 (VIEW), you never have more than one matching record. To search for the record of a particular customer in the Retail Customer form, for example, enter the Customer Number as the search criteria. Customer Number is the only unique field in the Retail Customer form, and you can never retrieve more than one customer when you specify that number. When searching for a particular record in the Order Detail form, however, you must specify both Order Number and Item Number. Both have the unique field characteristic; specifying just the Order Number is not enough to find a unique record.

Searching for Multiple Records

You may want to view a group of records that meet the same criteria. For example, you might want to see a list of all sales representatives in the Northern region. Using the procedure described in the preceding section, you can see only one record at a time and must press Alt-F3 to see each matching record.

To display a group of matching records on-screen, use Table View. While still in Form View, press Alt-F5 (UNCHECKED) and build the criteria, as explained in the preceding section. Then, instead of pressing F3 (VIEW), press Shift-F1 (TABLE). DataEase displays all the matching records in Table View. Press Shift-F1 (FORM) to return to Form View.

To display a list of all sales representatives from the Eastern region, for example, you should display the Sales Representative form in Record Entry and press Alt-F5 (UNCHECKED). Then, enter *Eastern* in the Region field and press Shift-F1 (TABLE). DataEase displays the list of Eastern region sales representatives (see fig. 4.17).

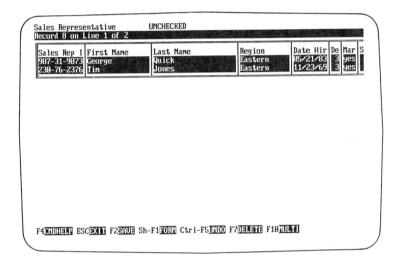

Fig. 4.17.

The sales representatives from the Eastern region.

Using Wildcards in Search Criteria

Ideally, when you want to view a particular record or a group of records, you know precisely what criteria to enter. In many situations, however, you may not be sure of the proper spelling of the value that you want DataEase to match. DataEase provides two *wildcard* characters to help you solve this problem. When specifying a search criteria, you can use the asterisk (*) to represent any number of characters. The question mark (?) can be used to represent one character. These wildcard characters are valid in all field types except number fields (integer, fixed point, dollar, and floating point) and choice fields.

If you want to view the record of a customer that called you last week, for example, but you can remember only that her company name includes the word *Airplane*, clear the form and invoke Unchecked mode with Alt-F5 (UNCHECKED). Then, type *Airplane* in the Company field and press F3 (VIEW). DataEase displays the record of the company Ace Airplanes.

When you know exact position of certain characters in the criterion, use the question mark (?) wildcard character. You may want to find the record of a sales representative, for example, but you can recall only that his Sales Rep ID has a 3 as the third and fourth digits. Press Alt-F5 (UNCHECKED) and enter the search criterion *???-33-????*. Then, press F3 (VIEW). DataEase searches the data in the Sales Representative form and displays the record of the employee with the Sales Rep ID 111-33-8491.

Wildcard characters also provide a way to group records. You can create search criteria that multiple records match by using wildcards. You can, for example, display the records of all Sales Representatives hired in the 1970's. Press Alt-F5 (UNCHECKED) and enter the search criteria *??/??/7?* in the Date Hired field. Press Shift-F1 (TABLE), and DataEase displays all the records with hire dates that have a year value beginning with the number 7.

Performing a Soundex Search

One of the more interesting capabilities of DataEase Version 4.0 is the *soundex* or "sounds like" search. Instead of searching for an exact match, the program searches for a value that contains the same consonant pattern, regardless of the vowels. To specify a soundex or "sounds like" search, type the tilde (˜) followed by your best guess at the word's spelling.

You can search for the record of a sales representative, for example, even if you are unsure of the spelling of the name. Assume that you know the last name is Brinson, Brunson, or Bronson—you guess Brinson. You also know that the first name begins with an E. To locate this record, display the blank Sales Representative form and press Alt-F5 (UNCHECKED) to invoke Unchecked mode. Then, type *E** in the First Name field and *˜Brinson* in the Last Name field (see fig. 4.18). Press F3 (VIEW) to complete the search. DataEase displays the record of Emily Bronson.

If you want to use wildcards and the soundex search in the same field, the wildcard characters (* or ?) must precede the tilde (˜).

Searching for the Record Number

Sometimes searching for a record by its record number is convenient. If you have deleted a record, but have not reorganized the form, this search method provides a convenient method of viewing and restoring the deleted record.

To search for a record by record number, press Ctrl-F3 (VIEW RECORD #) from any record in Form View. DataEase displays the prompt Enter the Record number to view ? in the prompt line. The cursor blinks in the

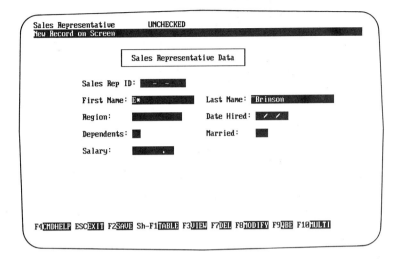

Fig. 4.18.

Specifying a search criteria—using the * wildcard and the soundex (˜) search characters.

prompt line, to the right of the question mark. Type the record number at the cursor and press Enter. DataEase displays the target record and the message Record found in the message area and indicates the record number in the prompt line.

When you delete a record (see "Deleting a Record" in this chapter), DataEase does not remove the record immediately from the records file on disk. The deleted record remains in the file until you reorganize the form. DataEase does not reassign the record numbers of a deleted record until the record is removed during reorganization. Until then, you can access the deleted record using this search-by-record-number operation. Press Ctrl-F3 (VIEW RECORD #), specify the number of the deleted record, and press Enter. DataEase beeps, displays the record, and indicates This is a deleted record in the message area. The program also displays the record number in the prompt line. You can *undelete* this record by pressing F8 (MODIFY). The record is added back to the list of active records. After you reorganize a form, all deleted records are gone.

Modifying and Deleting Records

You often need to correct, update, and even remove many of the records already entered into a database. In DataEase, you modify and delete records in a Record Entry session. The paragraphs that follow describe how to modify records, delete records, abandon modification, and recover deleted records.

Modifying a Record

Three basic steps are required to modify an existing record, and you already know how to perform the first two:

1. View the target record in Record Entry.

2. Make the desired changes to the field values.

3. Update the record in memory.

Viewing the record for the purpose of modifying it is no different than viewing the record just for reference. Refer to the previous "Viewing Existing Records" section in this chapter to refresh your memory of how to view a record that you may want to edit.

When you have the record on-screen that needs to be corrected or updated, use the techniques discussed in the "Editing Data in a Record-Entry Form" section, earlier in this chapter, to make the modifications. The methods used to edit a new record and to edit a previously saved record are similar, but you should understand clearly how they differ:

❏ In Form View, when you make a change to a field value in an existing record and move the cursor to another field, DataEase displays the message, Record n Revised on screen in the prompt line, where n is the record number of the target record (see fig. 4.19). This message is the only on-screen clue that you are modifying an existing record. For a new record, the message would be New Record on Screen, and this message would not change, regardless of how many changes you make to the values in the form fields. Be careful not to modify an existing record when you really intend to add a new record.

❏ In Table View, when you make a change to a field value and move the cursor to another column, DataEase displays the message Record n on Line l of r Modified, where n is the record number; l is the line or row number in the table, and r is the number of rows in the table (see fig. 4.20). DataEase also changes the color of the modified row. When you are editing a new record (not yet saved), the message in the prompt line is New Record on Line l of r, where l is the line number in the table, and r is the number of lines in the table that are saved to RAM. Because DataEase does not change the color of a new record that you are editing, you easily can tell the difference between adding a new record and modifying an existing record.

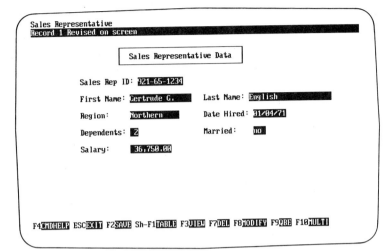

```
Sales Representative
Record 1 Revised on screen


                    ┌─────────────────────────────┐
                    │    Sales Representative Data │
                    └─────────────────────────────┘

        Sales Rep ID: 921-65-1234

        First Name: Gertrude G.      Last Name: English

        Region:     Northern         Date Hired: 01/04/71

        Dependents: 2                Married:    no

        Salary:     36,750.00




    F4 CMDHELP  ESC EXIT  F2 SAVE  Sh-F1 TABLE  F3 VIEW  F7 DEL  F8 MODIFY  F9 QBE  F10 MULTI
```

Fig. 4.19.

Modifying a record in Form View.

```
Sales Representative
Record 4 on Line 4 of 8 Modified

┌───────────┬────────────┬────────────┬─────────┬─────────┬──┬────┬─┐
│Sales Rep I│First Name  │Last Name   │Region   │Date Hir │De│Mar │S│
│921-65-1234│Gertrude G. │English     │Northern │01/04/71 │2 │no  │ │
│541-67-5555│Emily       │Bronson     │Southern │06/10/75 │0 │yes │ │
│230-76-2376│Tim         │Jones       │Eastern  │11/23/69 │3 │yes │ │
│111-33-8491│Harry T.    │Albertson   │Western  │06/07/78 │2 │yes │ │
│329-76-2219│Sharon      │Kellogs     │Northern │03/04/81 │1 │no  │ │
│448-09-6721│Samantha    │Green       │Southern │08/15/79 │4 │yes │ │
│129-08-4562│Joseph      │Jones       │Western  │10/02/65 │1 │no  │ │
│987-31-9873│George      │Quick       │Eastern  │05/21/83 │3 │yes │ │
└───────────┴────────────┴────────────┴─────────┴─────────┴──┴────┴─┘




    F4 CMDHELP  ESC EXIT  F2 SAVE  Sh-F1 FORM  Ctrl-F5 UNDO  F7 DELETE  F10 MULTI
```

Fig. 4.20.

Modifying a record in Table View.

The last step in modifying an existing record is to save the changes to
memory:

❏ In Form View, to save the modifications—replace the existing record
with the modified version—press F8 (MODIFY). DataEase saves the
new version of the record to memory in place of the old version and
displays the message Record *n* updated, where *n* is the record
number. Do not press F2 (SAVE), because a new record is added to
the form data, putting two versions of the same record in your
database.

❏ In Table View, you do not have to be so careful. After you modify a record, you can press F8 (MODIFY) or F2 (SAVE). Each function-key command has the same effect, saving the changed record to RAM, as a replacement for the old version. If you scroll records on or off the screen, or if you return to Form View (by pressing Shift-F1), DataEase saves the modified record in place of the original.

Tip: To prevent the possibility of creating a duplicate record by pressing F2 (SAVE) in Form View when you should have pressed F8 (MODIFY), always assign the unique field characteristic to at least one field in the form. When you change a field value in an existing record and press F2, DataEase beeps and displays the message Record already exists as *n*, where *n* is the record number. DataEase also displays the prompt, Do you want to modify that record (y/n)? Type *y*, and DataEase modifies the existing record. The result is the same as pressing F8 in the beginning. If you type *n* at the prompt, DataEase aborts the save but continues to display the revised record on-screen.

Note: If you change the value of a field and press F2 (SAVE), a new record is created, leaving the old record intact. To avoid this result, you also should assign the prevent data-entry characteristic to the unique field when possible (when the unique field is an automatically sequenced derived field, for example).

Deleting a Record

The steps to delete a record are almost the same as those used to modify a record. To delete a record in Form View or Table View, display the record on-screen (refer to "Viewing Existing Records," earlier in this chapter) and indicate whether the record should be deleted in one of the following ways:

❏ In Form View, press F7 (DEL). DataEase displays a window containing the question Are you sure you want to delete the record? Select 2: Yes, Delete Record. DataEase displays the message Record deleted in the message area. The program also displays the message Deleted Record *n* on Screen in the prompt line, where *n* is the record number. DataEase does not remove the record from the screen. Do not press F8 (MODIFY) or F2 (SAVE) or you undo the deletion (see the "Recovering Deleted Records," later in this chapter). After you clear the screen, you no longer can access this record with F3 (VIEW).

❏ In Table View, place the cursor in the row to be deleted and press F7 (DELETE). DataEase displays the message Record Marked Deleted in the message area. The program displays the message Record *n* on Line *l* of *r* Deleted in the prompt line, where *n* is the record number; *l* is the line or row number in the table, and *r* is the number of rows in the table. DataEase also changes the color of the deleted row, but does not remove the row from the screen. To complete the deletion, you must save the change in one of the ways described in the preceding section.

Abandoning Modifications

Whether in Form View or Table View, you can abandon a change that you have made, but you must do so before saving the modification to RAM—before pressing F8 (MODIFY). Use one of the following methods:

❏ Press Ctrl-F5 (UNDO). DataEase displays the message Discarded Record Changes. In Form View and Table View, all fields in the current record are returned to their original values, as previously saved.

❏ Press Esc (EXIT). In Form View, DataEase asks if you want to abandon the record on-screen. Answer 2: yes, and DataEase abandons any modifications you made to the record and returns to the Records menu. In Table View, DataEase asks if you want to abandon the changes on-screen. Answer 2: yes. (Any unsaved changes in other records also are abandoned.)

❏ Press F5 (FORM CLR). In Form View and Table View, DataEase asks Do you want to discard the entered data? Answer 2: yes. Only the changes you made are discarded—not the original record. In Form View, DataEase clears all values from the screen and displays the message No record on screen in the prompt line. In Table View, all unsaved changes are discarded, even those made in other unsaved records. All fields are returned to their original values.

The first method, Ctrl-F5 (UNDO), is usually the best choice when you want to discard the changes in the record you are viewing.

After you have saved a change with F8 (MODIFY), the change cannot be discarded. You must type the old values in the fields if you want to reverse the modification.

Recovering Deleted Records

When you delete records from a DataEase form, the data is not removed immediately from the records file. DataEase maintains all deleted records and does not reassign record numbers until you reorganize the form (see "Reorganizing a Form" in Chapter 3). When you reorganize a form, all deleted records are removed from the records file, and the remaining records are renumbered. Think of records that are deleted but still maintained in the records file as *inactive* records. Until you reorganize the form, you can reactivate an inactive record. In DataEase, this reactivation is called *recovering* deleted records.

To recover a deleted record still in the records file, you must know the record number. Press Ctrl-F3 (VIEW RECORD #), type the record number at the prompt Enter the Record number to view?, and press Enter. DataEase displays the record but beeps and indicates This is a deleted record in the message area. The program also displays the message Deleted Record *n* on Screen in the prompt line, where *n* is the record number. To recover the record with the same record number, press F8 (MODIFY). DataEase reactivates the record with the same field values. If you press F2 (SAVE), DataEase adds the record as a new record to the end of the form data, with a new record number. (A *Sequence from* derived field also is given a different value when the record is saved as a new record.)

When you delete a record in Table View but have not yet saved the change, you can abandon the deletion by pressing Ctrl-F5 (UNDO). After you save the changes in Table View, however, you must return to Form View and use the Ctrl-F3 (VIEW RECORD #) method to recover the deleted record.

Creating and Using a Default Record

Computers always excel at repetitive tasks. Using DataEase, you can get your PC to enter values automatically that tend to be repeated throughout several records in a form, for example. If you frequently enter certain values in some or all of the fields in a DataEase form, you should create a *default record* that contains these default values. You then can enter all these values in a subsequent record with one keystroke.

To create a default record, display a blank form in Form View. Then press Alt-F5 (UNCHECKED) to deactivate normal validity checking and to prevent field derivations. Fill in the field values that you expect to repeat often. Finally, press Shift-F2 (SAVE DEFAULT). DataEase displays the message Default record written in the message area.

As explained in Chapter 3, you can create a default value for a field during form definition by using a derivation formula. The method described here, however, enables you to establish default values on-the-fly. This method is so simple that you may want to create a default record for a Record Entry session when you know that a large number of records will have the same entries in several fields.

After you have created a default record, you can enter all the default values at once into a new record by pressing Shift-F5 (DEFAULT FORM). DataEase fills in the fields of the record on-screen with the values that you entered in the default form. You should execute this command before entering values in any fields in a new record.

To use only one field from the default record, move the cursor to the target field and press Shift-F6 (DEFAULT FIELD). DataEase fills in the field with the default value from the default record, without affecting other fields.

To delete the default record, press Shift-F7 (DELETE DEFAULT). This function-key combination is the same as Shift-F7 (DELLN), which deletes a line from a long:text field, therefore, the command is effective only when the cursor is not in a long:text field.

Perhaps the most convenient aspect of the default record feature is that you do not have to create a default record to use a default record. DataEase uses the last record saved as an ad-hoc default record if you have not created a default record or have not deleted the default record.

Printing a Record in Record Entry

Any time you are working in Record Entry, you can print a copy of one record in Form View or the entire table in Table View. When in Form View, press Shift-F9 (PRINT) to print the record-entry form and the field values from the current record. From Table View, Shift-F9 (PRINT) prints all records in the form in tabular format. This feature provides a quick-and-easy method of producing a hard copy of a record or table. Do not confuse these copies with DataEase reports (discussed in Chapters 5 and 8).

Entering, Editing, and Viewing Records on a LAN

Using DataEase Record Entry on a Local Area Network (LAN) is not very different from using Record Entry on a stand-alone PC. If you are working with a database in your private data directory, there is no difference at all.

If you are using DataEase on a LAN, you probably are working with a shared database in a shared data directory. You therefore need to develop an understanding of how DataEase handles the inevitable competition for data resources that occurs when multiple network users attempt to access the same data at the same time.

Understanding the Default Minimum Locks

When you use DataEase Record Entry to enter, edit, or view a shared form on a network, DataEase places certain restrictions on simultaneous access by multiple network users. These restrictions are *locking rules*, and the minimum locks placed automatically by DataEase are *default minimum* locks. You can add more restrictive locks using several mechanisms, but you cannot remove these minimum locks.

When you update a shared database by adding records, modifying existing records, or deleting records, DataEase places a lock on the record or records with which you are working that prevents other users from reading or changing the record. The user updating the record has *exclusive* access. This lock applies only to records that you are currently updating. The lock does not prevent other users from accessing other records in the same form.

If you are in the middle of updating the address of a customer in the Retail Customer form, for example, DataEase does not permit another user to display the same customer's record until you finish making the modification. Instead, the program displays a conflict message indicating that the resource (record) is in use. If the record that you just changed was already on another user's screen when you changed it, that user's copy is no longer correct. The user may modify his version of the record and try to save that version. DataEase displays the message Record modified since it was read and prevents the user from saving his changes. He first must find out what changes you made. He can use the *refresh* option explained in the next section.

If you are only viewing a shared record—making no changes, additions, or deletions—DataEase prevents other users from making changes to the record you are viewing while your computer reads the data from the disk; otherwise the program gives all users complete access to the data.

One of the configuration options, discussed in Appendix B, enables you to place a more restrictive lock on multiuser access to records in Record Entry. Instead of allowing multiple users to modify records at the same time, you can specify *shared* access. Multiple users can view the same record at once, but while you are viewing a record, another user cannot update that record. Similarly, if another user already is viewing a record, you are not permitted to modify it. When access is shared, you avoid the situation where two or more users are modifying the same record.

The most restrictive access type, *exclusive* access, prevents more than one user from even viewing the same record at the same time. Normally restricting access to records to this extent is not necessary to protect the integrity of the data. In most cases, shared access or even the default minimum lock is sufficient protection.

Using the Multi-User Pull-Down Menu

While you are using Record Entry, you can override the current record-locking rule with the options on the Multi-User pull-down menu. To grant maximum access to the records in the form, display the Multi-User pull-down menu and select Allow All Record Access (Allow All File Access in Table View). This option enables multiple users to view and update the same record; remember, however, that when changes are being made, only one user's changes can be saved.

To grant shared access, choose Allow Read Record Access from the Multi-User menu (Allow Read File Access in Table View). For exclusive access, select Allow No Record Access (Allow No File Access in Table View).

During a Record Entry session when all users can view and modify records at the same time, you need a method of keeping your data current. To cause DataEase to read and display the most up-to-date information from the disk, select Refresh from the Multi-User menu. This command overwrites any unsaved entries or changes you make to the record displayed on-screen. In Table View, DataEase refreshes all records displayed in the table. To update your screen every few seconds with changes other users are making, select Continuous Refresh On/Off. This option is toggled off by default.

Chapter Summary

This chapter showed you how to use DataEase Record Entry. Everything discussed in this chapter is accomplished through the **2. Record Entry** choice on the DataEase Main menu. You learned how to enter new records, and how to view, modify, and delete existing records in Form View and Table View. Now that you know how to define a form and add data, you are ready to move on to building reports. Chapter 5 describes how to create reports using the DataEase Quick Reports facility.

Using DataEase
Quick Reports

Just as you would never start out on a long trip without some idea of your final destination, you should never design or build a database until you have a clear vision of how the final output will look. All the data entry, editing, and viewing you can muster is worth little if the output it produces doesn't please or inform your audience. Often it's easiest to look at the overall design of the end product first and work backward to determine what data you need to collect to produce the desired results. This chapter introduces you to the fundamentals of using DataEase Quick Reports.

The DataEase reporting features provide all the capability you would expect from a full-featured database program, and then some. This chapter introduces you to the basics of the Quick Reports, which provide a relatively easy method of generating a wide variety of reports without the need for programming. An underlying DataEase philosophy is that a computer program should do as much of the work for you as possible. The DataEase Quick Reports feature lives up to this philosophy.

In this chapter, you learn about tools that you can put to use immediately, and the chapter lays a foundation for understanding and using the powerful DataEase Query Language (DQL), introduced in Chapter 11.

To present DataEase report design fundamentals clearly, this chapter works with only one database table at a time, but keep in mind that DataEase is meant to be used as a relational database, using information from many forms to build the output you are looking for. Some of DataEase's most exciting features involve creation of reports from multiple related forms, including multiforms. Study this chapter to learn the basic terminology and develop a sound design approach. Then turn to Chapter 6 for a discussion of how to use related DataEase forms in Quick Reports.

An Overview of the DataEase Report Design

So far in this book, you have learned how to design database forms, enter and edit data, and retrieve particular records from these forms for viewing. With the DataEase Quick Reports feature, you can produce and control the output of data from your database to a printer, your screen, or a disk file.

Understanding DataEase Quick Reports

Anytime that you display or print some or all the information you have collected with DataEase, you are producing a *report*. In the broadest sense, then, viewing a record in Record Entry is creating a simple report. In DataEase, you use the Quick Reports facility or the DQL Advanced Processing facility to produce reports from your data that cannot be generated by printing records in Form View or Table View.

The DataEase Quick Reports module enables you to create reports in nine different formats without programming. Figure 5.1 shows the easiest report format to create with DataEase—the columnar Quick Report. This report is essentially a version of your form data arranged in columns, and is similar to the Record Entry Table View. In addition to columnar format, you can generate reports in eight other formats: File Per Line, Record Entry, Template, GrafTalk Chart, Custom, Export, Mailing Labels, and CrossView.

Fig. 5.1.

A columnar Quick Report.

```
                                         Running report
         END OF REPORT, SPACE: Return to Menu   PgUp Home LEFT RIGHT Arrows: Scroll

         =====================================================================================
         Sales Rep      First            Last           Region        Date      Depe Mar
           ID           Name             Name                         Hired     nden ied
                                                                                 ts
         -------------------------------------------------------------------------------------
         921-65-1234 Gertrude G,   English         Northern      01/04/71    2 no
         541-67-5555 Emily         Bronson         Southern      06/10/75    0 yes
         230-76-2376 Tim           Jones           Eastern       11/23/69    3 yes
         111-33-8491 Harry T,      Albertson       Western       06/07/78    2 yes
         329-76-2219 Sharon        Kellogs         Northern      03/04/81    1 no
         448-89-6721 Samantha      Green           Southern      08/15/79    4 yes
         129-88-4562 Joseph        Jones           Western       10/02/65    1 no
         987-31-9873 George        Quick           Eastern       05/21/83    3 yes
         =====================================================================================



         F4 CMDHELP ESC EXIT C:\DEDATA\         Order Tracking    07/23/89  11 87 pm
```

DataEase enables you to print the report on paper, preview the report on-screen, and create a text file that can be imported into a word processing program for inclusion in a longer document.

DataEase also enables you to create Quick Reports that draw data from several related forms at once and from the new (in DataEase 4.0) multiforms. Creation of multiple form and multiform reports is covered in Chapter 6.

In DataEase, each report design is saved as a *report definition*, and each report definition is associated with a particular DataEase form called its *Primary* form. The distinction between the report's Primary form and other related forms is significant when you generate reports from more than one form (discussed in Chapter 6, "Using Related DataEase Forms"). For now, the Primary form you select for a report is simply the one whose data you want to print.

Design Considerations

As you begin to design a DataEase Quick Report, and try to decide which report format is best, you should consider the following questions:

❏ Can you visualize the way the report will look? Building the report is easier if you sketch it on paper first. Better yet, if you are duplicating an existing form, work from it. Perhaps fill in some data so that you get a better idea of what the final product will look like.

❏ Will your new report replace an existing report or form? When practical, design your report definition to look as much like the current form or report as possible. This consideration has little to do with computer software but a lot to do with human nature and resistance to change.

❏ Will data be arranged in rows and columns, or in some other fashion? A telephone list of your department's employees, for example, should probably be a columnar table with each employee's name and phone number on a single row. But a report to print mailing labels to the same employees would have to arrange the data about each employee vertically in several rows.

❏ Should the information be arranged in a particular order? Normally you don't just "dump" data on the page from your database. Instead, you organize it so that it is easy to use and understand. Even a simple list of telephone numbers usually is arranged in alphabetical order by each person's last name.

❏ Will records be grouped? A phone book for your entire company also might be grouped by department or division for convenience.

❏ Will summary computations be necessary? When your data includes numeric information you often will want to perform summary computations, such as subtotals, that require that the data be appropriately grouped in the report.

❏ Is all the necessary information in one form, or will some have to be drawn from other forms in the database? To be able to create a report from multiple forms, the primary form must be related or linked to each of the other forms. Use of data in reports from multiple forms is discussed in Chapter 6.

You also should keep in mind the basic report-building capacities of DataEase, which are summarized in table 5.1.

Table 5.1
DataEase Report Format Capacities

Feature	Capacity
Fields	255
Relationships	100
Grouping	No limit—any number of levels
Width of page	4,000 characters
Length of page	352 lines (16 screens by 22 lines)
Reports	2,000 per database

If you cannot decide which report format is best even after answering the questions listed in this section, try the columnar format; this format is most likely to present your data satisfactorily with a minimum of effort on your part.

Accessing the QBE—Quick Reports Menu

Before you can design and print a report, you must have already defined and added data to a DataEase form. Then, you can access all the Quick Report features through the QBE—Quick Reports menu. Start at the DataEase Main menu and select **3. Query By Example—Quick Reports**. DataEase displays the QBE—Quick Reports menu, shown in figure 5.2.

As in earlier versions of the program, DataEase 4.0 enables you to access Quick Reports from within the Record Entry facility. While in a record-entry screen, press F9 (QBE) to display the QBE—Quick Reports menu (see fig. 5.2). Use this method of starting the Quick Reports module when you are entering or editing data and want to see the results in a report

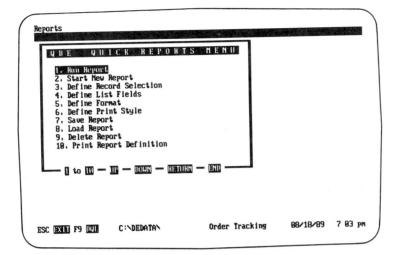

Reports

```
┌─ Q B E   Q U I C K   R E P O R T S   M E N U ─┐
│ 1. Run Report                                  │
│ 2. Start New Report                            │
│ 3. Define Record Selection                     │
│ 4. Define List Fields                          │
│ 5. Define Format                               │
│ 6. Define Print Style                          │
│ 7. Save Report                                 │
│ 8. Load Report                                 │
│ 9. Delete Report                               │
│ 10. Print Report Definition                    │
└────────────────────────────────────────────────┘

  1 to 10 — UP — DOWN — RETURN — END

ESC EXIT F9 MENU    C:\DEDATA\      Order Tracking    08/18/89   7 03 pm
```

Fig. 5.2.

The QBE—Quick Reports menu.

immediately. When you're finished and have returned to the QBE—Quick Reports menu, return to Record Entry by pressing Esc (EXIT). DataEase returns you to the record-entry screen at which you invoked Quick Reports.

Defining a Quick Report

DataEase divides the process of defining a new Quick Report into 10 distinct steps or phases, each of which is an option on the QBE—Quick Reports menu. The purpose of each step is summarized in the following list:

1. Begin defining a new report by selecting **2. Start New Report** from the QBE—Quick Reports menu. Selecting this option is mandatory whenever another report definition is already in RAM and you want to start fresh.

2. Select **3. Define Record Selection** when you want to limit the report to only a portion of the records in the form data. DataEase uses all the form's records if you don't select this option.

3. To indicate that only selected fields be included in the report, choose **4. Define List Fields**. By default, all fields are included.

4. Select one of nine predefined report formats through the menu choice **5. Define Format**. The default format is Columnar, which prints each record as a separate row and each field as a separate column, with the field names as column headings. This format is similar in appearance to Table View in Record Entry.

5. Choose between sending the report to the screen, to the printer, or to a disk file with the **6. Define Print Style** option on the QBE—Quick Reports menu. By default, reports go to the screen.

6. You can save a report definition so that you can use it again later. Select the **7. Save Report** option on the QBE—Quick Reports menu.

7. To make modifications to a previously saved Quick Report, load it into RAM with the **8. Load Report** selection.

8. When you no longer need a particular report definition, you can delete it with the **9. Delete Report** command.

9. Make a hard copy of the report definition by choosing **10. Print Report Definition**.

10. Generate the report output (to screen, printer, or file) by choosing **1. Run Report**.

At a minimum, to define and print a new report, you first must select **2. Start New Report**, and then select at least one of the following options:

3. Define Record Selection
4. Define List Fields
5. Define Format
6. Define Print Style

Only then can you run the report with the **1. Run Report** option. DataEase assumes the default settings for any steps that you skip.

When you want to use the report definition during a subsequent Quick Reports session, you have to save it with the **7. Save Report** option. Later, you can run the saved report with the **1. Run Report** selection or retrieve the definition from the disk for modifications with **8. Load Report**.

Starting a New Quick Report

When you begin defining a new Quick Report, you need to clear any previous definition from RAM. This step is necessary only when you are defining a second or subsequent report definition without returning to the DataEase Main menu. If you just displayed the QBE—Quick Reports menu and have not yet selected any option from that menu, there is no definition in RAM to clear away.

To clear any existing report definition from RAM, select **2. Start New Report** from the QBE—Quick Reports menu. Before DataEase abandons the existing report settings, it displays the prompt Are you sure? in a pop-up window. (When no definition has been loaded and no selections have been made from the QBE—Quick Reports menu, DataEase doesn't ask this question.) Respond by selecting 2: yes. DataEase displays New report Started in the message area at the top of the screen and moves the menu selection bar down to the third option on the QBE—Quick Reports menu, as shown in figure 5.3.

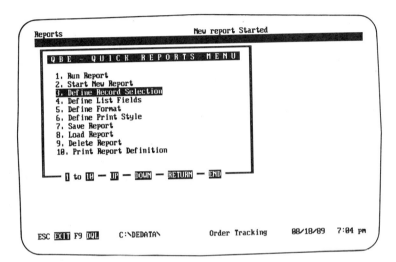

Defining Record Selection

Sometimes you want to include all the form data records in the report. When that is the case, you can skip the record selection phase of form definition. By default, DataEase includes all form records in the report.

Often, however, you will want to include only a select group of records in the report. To explicitly define the record selection, choose **3. Define Record Selection** from the QBE—Quick Reports menu.

The report definition phase is often the first menu selection you make after starting a new report definition. DataEase displays a list of all available forms in the database in a window menu. Select the name of the form (the Primary form) for which you are designing the report. DataEase displays the Record Selection screen, which is a blank record from the Primary form that looks like a record-entry screen. The Record Selection screen displays the instruction Select Records in the Title area at the top left of the screen. It also displays the message Specify the Field Selection Criteria in the prompt line. For example, the Record Selection screen for the Retail Customer form is shown in figure 5.4.

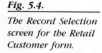

Fig. 5.4.

The Record Selection screen for the Retail Customer form.

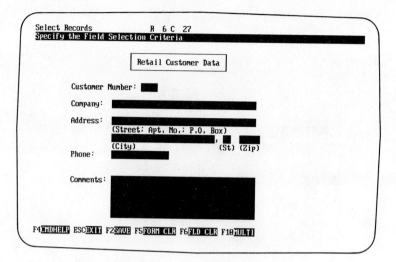

Specifying Selection Criteria

The Record Selection screen operates in much the same manner as the record-entry form in Unchecked mode. You use selection criteria to specify which records are to be included in the report, just as you do to specify which records you want to view while in Record Entry (refer to Chapter 4 for more details on how to use selection criteria in Record Entry). When you run the report, DataEase includes only records that match the values you type in each field in the Record Selection screen.

While you are typing the selection criteria, you can use the cursor-movement keys listed in table 5.2 and the function-key commands listed in table 5.3. Press F2 (SAVE) or Esc (EXIT) when you finish typing the search criteria to save your entries and return to the QBE—Quick Reports menu.

Table 5.2
Cursor-Movement Keys

Key	Cursor Movement
↑	Field above
↓	Field below
←	One space to the left; from left end of field, moves to previous field
Backspace	One space to the left, erasing previous character
→	One position to the right (does not move to next field)
Ctrl-←	Start of field

Table 5.2—*continued*

Key	Cursor Movement
Home	First (top left) field of first page
End	Last (bottom right) field of last page
Tab	Next field
Shift-Tab	Previous field
*Enter	Next field
PgDn	First field of next page (multipage forms only)
PgUp	First field of current page; when cursor is already in first field of current page, moves to first field of previous page on multipage forms

* The DataEase documentation refers to the Enter key as the Return key. This is because earlier versions of DataEase referred to F2 as the Enter key.

Table 5.3
Function-Key Commands

Function Key (Name)	Function
Esc (EXIT)	Saves entries and return to QBE—Quick Reports menu (same as F2)
F1 (MORE)	Displays a window menu
Alt-F1 (HELP)	Provides help on current operation
F2 (SAVE)	Saves entries and returns to QBE—Quick Reports menu (same as Esc)
*F4 (CMDHELP)	Displays pull-down Command menus
F5 (FORM CLR)	Clears values from all fields on-screen
F6 (FIELD CLR)	Clears value from current field on-screen
F10 (MULTI)	Multiview—accesses a related form.

*New command in DataEase 4.0

Suppose that you want to print a mailing list of all your customers in Virginia. You choose **3. Define Record Selection** from the QBE—Quick Reports menu and then choose Retail Customer from the window menu. Move the cursor to the State field and type *VA*, as shown in figure 5.5. This selection criteria limits the records that will be included in the report to those with the value VA in the State field. Press F2 (SAVE) or Esc (EXIT) to return to the QBE—Quick Reports menu. DataEase saves the selection criteria to RAM (not to disk) and displays the QBE—Quick Reports menu.

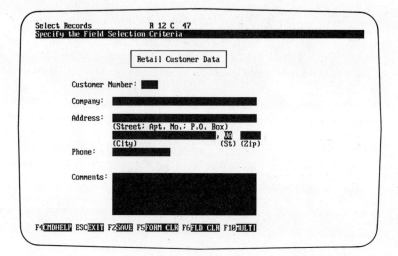

Fig. 5.5.

Selecting all the customers in Virginia (VA).

Tip: Notice that when you return to the QBE—Quick Reports menu, option 3 on the menu has now become **3. Modify Record Selection**. The word Define in the menu option name has become Modify because you specified the record selection criteria. When you start a new report, the choice changes back to **3. Define Record Selection**.

There are several differences between entering selection criteria in the Record Selection screen and entering selection criteria in Record Entry. You must enter formatting characters for date fields (slashes), time fields (colons), and decimal points in number fields but don't enter commas in number fields and don't enter formatting characters in numeric string fields. For example, you can type *111338491*, but not *111-33-8491*, to indicate a criterion in a social security number numeric string field. Match values can be constants, field names including fields from related forms, DataEase functions, and statistical summaries from related forms.

Typing values in the Record Selection screen is a little different than typing in a record-entry form. Formatting characters that normally appear in date, time, and numeric string fields when you use the form in Record Entry don't appear in the form during Quick Reports record selection. Similarly, the decimal point does not appear in number fields in the Record Selection screen. Each field is completely empty.

As you type a criterion in a Record Selection field, you may run out of room within the defined field length. If this happens, DataEase automatically expands the entry space on-screen as you type. After you finish typing the criterion and press Enter or Tab to move to the next field, the space contracts to the original field length and appears to truncate the criterion. The entire criterion entry reappears when you press Shift-Tab to move back into the field.

When you finish entering a criterion in a field and move to the next field, DataEase seldom displays an error message. But, when you save the Record Selection screen, any syntax errors cause DataEase to beep, move the cursor to the top left field in the form, and display the message value is required in the message area at the top of the screen. This message is your only clue that you made a mistake somewhere in specifying the selection criteria. DataEase will not save the selection criteria until the syntax is corrected.

Selecting Ranges with Record Selection Operators

The record selection operators, listed in table 5.4, are available to select a range of records for inclusion in the report. Table 5.4 also lists several examples of how you might use these operators. If you don't specify an operator, DataEase assumes the = operator (equal to). You must explicitly indicate the = operator only when the criterion contains a DataEase function (see Chapter 11) or statistical operator. Text values must be enclosed in double quotation marks when used with a record selection operator, but choice fields must not be enclosed in quotation marks.

Table 5.4
DataEase Record Selection Operators

Operator	Meaning	Examples
=	Equal to	=day(current date)
>	Greater than	>25000 >"G" >12/31/81
<	Less than	<39.95 <13:15:00

Table 5.4—*continued*

Operator	Meaning	Examples
>=	Greater than or equal to	>=18.7
<=	Less than or equal to	<=07/04/57
between *n* and *m*	Between and including *n* and *m*	between 3 to 5
and	Joins two criteria; both must be true to match	>3 and <5
or	Joins two criteria; match if either is true	<3 or >5
not	Reverses meaning of following operator	not=North

Tip: DataEase enables you to convert a Quick Report into a DQL procedure (this feature is described in Chapter 7). If your Quick Report record selection criterion includes the *and* or the *or* operator, be aware that DataEase will generate a DQL query statement with incorrect syntax. To correct the problem, you must edit the DQL procedure manually. For example, if you include the selection criteria

>12/31/87 and <01/01/89

in the Date Hired field, DataEase generates the DQL statement:

with Date Hired >12/31/87 and <01/01/89

The correct syntax for this command is:

with Date Hired >12/31/87 and Date Hired <01/01/89

The meaning of this and other DQL commands is covered in Chapters 7 and 11.

Using the Define List Fields Option

In any single report, you seldom include every field from a form. If you want to produce a mailing list from the Retail Customer form, for example, you don't need to include the Customer Number, Phone, or Comments fields. The company's name and address are enough.

The **4. Define List Fields** selection on the QBE—Quick Reports menu provides a method for you to indicate which fields you want in the report. In addition, it enables you to sort records in ascending (A to Z, 0 to 9) or descending (Z to A, 9 to 0) order and to group the records in the report according to the occurrence of like values in a specified field. You also can use this menu option to calculate certain summary statistics computed from multiple records.

Selecting Fields

DataEase makes selecting fields for the report very simple. First, choose **4. Define List Fields** from the QBE—Quick Reports menu. DataEase displays the Field Selection screen. (If you skipped the Record Selection step, you also must specify the name of the Primary form before DataEase displays the Field Selection screen.) This screen, like the Record Selection screen, is a version of the record-entry form; no formatting characters or decimal points are displayed in the fields. DataEase displays the title `Select Fields` in the title area, and the following message:

```
Press Space to mark field. Specify order reverse group count sum
mean max or min
```

Figure 5.6 shows the Field Selection screen for the Retail Customer form.

With the Field Selection screen for the Primary form displayed, move the cursor (using the cursor-movement keys listed in table 5.2) to the field that you want to display first in the report and press the space bar. DataEase places the number 1 in the field. This number is called the *list* number and indicates the order in which DataEase will display the fields in the report. Move the cursor to the next field you want DataEase to include in the report and press the space bar again. DataEase places a 2 in the field. Continue this procedure until you have numbered all the desired fields. DataEase numbers the fields in the order that you select them with the space bar. Figure 5.7 shows the Field Selection screen for Retail Customer after selecting the five fields to be included in the mailing list report: Company, Address, City, State, and ZIP.

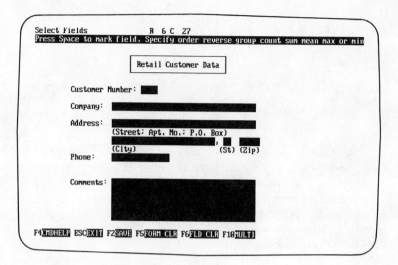

Fig. 5.6.

The Field Selection screen for the Retail Customer form.

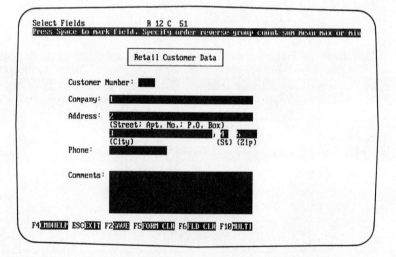

Fig. 5.7.

Selecting fields for the Retail Customer mailing list.

As an alternative to allowing DataEase to assign the list numbers automatically, you can type them. After you begin using the manual method, however, you should stick with it. If you try to switch to the space bar method, DataEase may not assign the correct number in sequence.

If you make a mistake in specifying the list numbers, use either the Del key or the F6 (FLD CLR) to clear the field. Then, enter the correct number. DataEase does not automatically renumber any other fields. You must correct each mistake manually. If you want, you can clear the entire form with F5 (FORM CLR) and start over from the beginning using the space bar method.

When all the fields for the report have been numbered, press either Esc (EXIT) or F2 (SAVE) to return to the QBE—Quick Reports menu.

Grouping and Sorting Records

As you assign the field list numbers in the Field Selection screen, you also can indicate how DataEase should group the records in the report. For example, in a customer mailing list, you may want the records grouped by ZIP code.

Type the word *group* in the field to the right of the list number, and DataEase groups records according to the values in that particular field. To group Retail Customer records by ZIP code, you should type *group* to the right of the number 5 in the ZIP field. All customer records with the same ZIP code are placed together in the report. In addition to grouping records, the group keyword causes DataEase to sort the records in ascending order according to the value in the group field. In the customer mailing list example, the customer records are not only grouped by ZIP code but also sorted by ZIP code. The customer records with the lowest ZIP code number appear first in the report.

You can create multiple levels of grouping by placing the group keyword in several fields in the Field Selection screen. The group with the lowest list number is the *primary* sort field. For example, you might want customers sorted by state and then by ZIP code. You type the word *group* after the number 4 in the State field, as well as typing *group* after the number 5 in the ZIP field. In our example form, the State field is only two characters long. Therefore, when you type *group* in the field and move to another field, the group keyword is hidden, as shown in figure 5.8.

Figure 5.9 shows the report that results from the field selections and groupings in figure 5.8. Notice that DataEase groups the customers from Maryland (MD) first, and then the customers from Virginia (VA). There are two Virginia customers from ZIP code 22150. Because DataEase lists each field value only once, MD, VA, and 22150 are displayed once each in the report.

When you want every occurrence of a sorted field to be displayed in the report, use the order keyword instead of group. Typing *order* in a field in the Field Selection screen causes DataEase to sort the records in ascending order according to the values in that field, just as when you use the group keyword. The difference is that DataEase displays each value in the field.

Fig. 5.8.

*Grouping records
using the Field
Selection screen.*

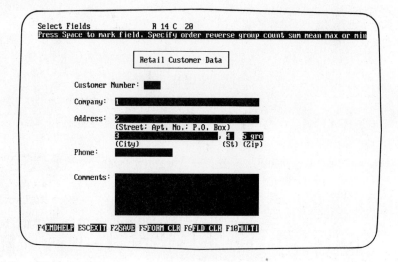

Fig. 5.8.

*Grouping records
using the Field
Selection screen.*

Fig. 5.9.

*A customer mailing
list grouped by ZIP
and State.*

Figure 5.10 shows the same report as figure 5.9 after using the order keyword in the State and ZIP fields instead of group. DataEase sorts the records based on any group fields before sorting on order fields.

Sometimes you want to sort records in descending order rather than ascending order. You may, for example, want to see a list of your sales representatives in descending order by salary. To sort records in a report in descending order use the keyword *reverse* in the Field Selection screen instead of group or order.

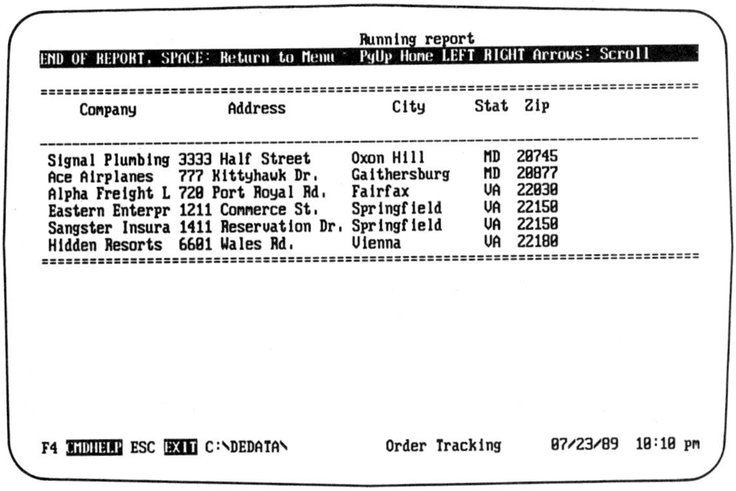

```
                              Running report
 END OF REPORT, SPACE: Return to Menu   PgUp Home LEFT RIGHT Arrows: Scroll

 ==============================================================================
    Company           Address          City      Stat  Zip
 ------------------------------------------------------------------------------
    Signal Plumbing 3333 Half Street    Oxon Hill      MD   20745
    Ace Airplanes   777 Kittyhawk Dr.   Gaithersburg   MD   20877
    Alpha Freight L 720 Port Royal Rd.  Fairfax        VA   22030
    Eastern Enterpr 1211 Commerce St.   Springfield    VA   22150
    Sangster Insura 1411 Reservation Dr.Springfield    VA   22150
    Hidden Resorts  6601 Wales Rd.      Vienna         VA   22180
 ==============================================================================




   F4 CMDHELP ESC EXIT C:\DEDATA\         Order Tracking    07/23/89  10:10 pm
```

Fig. 5.10.

A customer mailing list sorted by ZIP and State.

Calculating Statistics

In Quick Reports, DataEase enables you to calculate several statistics: count, sum, mean (average), maximum, minimum, variance, standard deviation, and standard error. DataEase calculates these statistics using the values in a specified field from all records included in the report. Whenever you also have grouped records using the keyword group, DataEase calculates the statistics for each grouping as well as for the entire report.

Table 5.5 lists the available statistic keywords and the statistics they generate. Note that only the keywords count, max, and min can be used with nonnumeric field types. All the other statistic keywords can be used with only number fields (integer, fixed point, floating point, and dollar).

Suppose that you want to see a list of your sales representatives' salaries, totaled within each region, with a grand total at the end of the report. You access the Field Selection screen for the Sales Representative form and add list numbers to the Last Name, Region, and Salary fields. (Because Region is a choice field, selections will be grouped in order by choice number rather than alphabetically.) Type *group* in the Region field and *sum* in the Salary field. To display the salaries in descending order within each region, you also can use the keyword *reverse* in the Salary field. The completed Field Selection screen is shown in figure 5.11. You can use this field selection to generate the report shown in figure 5.12.

Table 5.5
Field Selection Screen Statistic Keywords

Keyword	Statistic
*count	Number of records meeting record selection criteria
sum	Total of values in number field
mean	Average of values in number field
max	Highest value in field
min	Lowest value in field
variance	Statistical variance of values in number field
std.dev.	Standard deviation of values in number field
std.err.	Standard error of the standard deviation of values in number field

*New in DataEase 4.0.

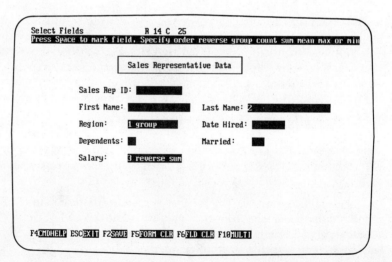

Fig. 5.11.

Using the sum keyword in the Field Selection screen to total sales representative salaries.

```
                           Running report
END OF REPORT, SPACE: Return to Menu   PgUp: Scroll
       Last Name                    Salary
-------------------------------------------------
Northern Region
         English                  36,750.00
         Kellogs                  21,870.00
      Subtotal                    58,620.00
Southern Region
         Green                    49,339.00
         Bronson                  23,875.00
      Subtotal                    73,214.00
Eastern Region
         Quick                    53,000.00
         Jones                    41,400.00
      Subtotal                    94,400.00
Western Region
         Jones                    75,900.00
         Albertson                32,250.00
      Subtotal                   100,150.00
-------------------------------------------------
Total                            334,384.00
=================================================

F4 CMDHELP ESC EXIT C:\DEDATA\        Order Tracking    07/23/89  10:27 pm
```

Fig. 5.12.

A report showing salaries grouped in descending order, subtotaled by Region, and totaled at the end of the report.

Specifying Report Format

After you have determined which fields and records you want to include in the Quick Report, you need to indicate how the fields of each record are to be arranged. Should there be one record per line or one field per line? Maybe the report should look like the record-entry form? If you are printing mailing labels, the fields should be formatted in that fashion. The **5. Define Format** option on the QBE—Quick Reports menu enables you to choose from a number of predefined and custom formats for your report, any of which can be tailored to fit your specific requirements.

To make the selection of a report format as easy as possible, DataEase permits you to skip the Define Format part. By default, DataEase assumes that you want the fields arranged in columns, with each record in a separate row.

For example, assume that you are creating a sales representative salary list and have completed the Field Selection screen as shown in figure 5.11 (fields are Last Name, Region, and Salary; Region contains the keyword group; Salary contains the keywords sum and reverse). If you skip the Define Format step, the report looks like the one in figure 5.13. Fields are arranged in columns, and each person is a separate row. The records are grouped and subtotaled by Region, with a grand total of the salaries at the end of the report. The subtotal for the Western region and the grand total do not show in the figure.

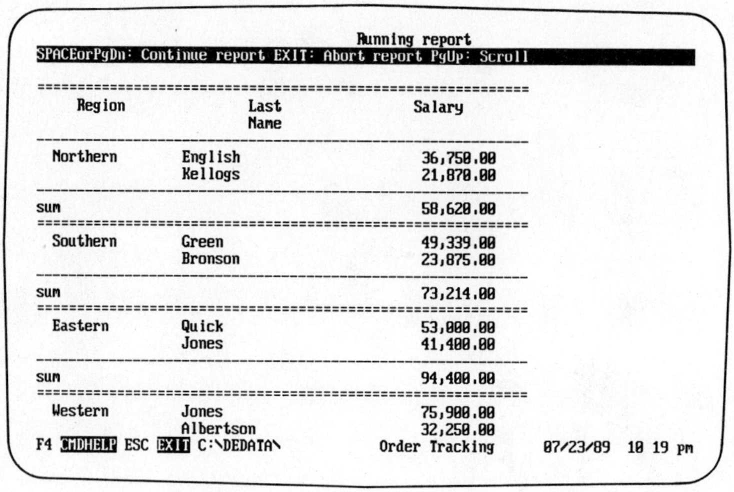

Fig. 5.13.

A sales representative salary list in columnar format, grouped by Region, with subtotals and a grand total.

```
                                    Running report
SPACEorPgDn: Continue report EXIT: Abort report PgUp: Scroll

===================================================================
         Region          Last            Salary
                         Name
       ----------------------------------------------------------
       Northern       English             36,750.00
                      Kellogs             21,870.00
       ----------------------------------------------------------
       sum                               58,620.00
       ===================================================================
        Southern      Green               49,339.00
                      Bronson             23,875.00
       ----------------------------------------------------------
       sum                               73,214.00
       ===================================================================
       Eastern        Quick               53,000.00
                      Jones               41,400.00
       ----------------------------------------------------------
       sum                               94,400.00
       ===================================================================
       Western        Jones               75,900.00
                      Albertson           32,250.00
F4 CMDHELP ESC EXIT C:\DEDATA\         Order Tracking     07/23/89  10 19 pm
```

Many times, the default columnar format is not appropriate for the report you need to create. For this reason, DataEase provides nine format types from which you can choose during Quick Reports, including two ways to create your own customized report format.

The predefined formats do save time when you design your report, but there are times when you will want to modify the position of fields or would like to change, add, or delete text. DataEase provides a number of options within Quick Reports that enable you to modify the predefined format of your report.

To access the format definition facility, choose **5. Define Format** from the QBE—Quick Reports menu. If you have not yet selected a primary form, choose the appropriate form from the window menu. DataEase displays the Format Selection screen, a mostly blank screen with a two-line prompt near the top of the work area (see fig. 5.14).

The first line of the prompt in the Format Selection screen specifies the minimum line length (report width) needed to display the defined fields in a columnar format. DataEase arrives at this number by combining the lengths of the fields specified in the Field Selection screen, and allowing additional spaces at the beginning of the line, end of the line, and between fields. Every field is given at least four spaces. When DataEase builds a columnar report, it also spreads the fields evenly across the report width, inserting from one to four spaces between fields and one or two spaces at the beginning and end of the line.

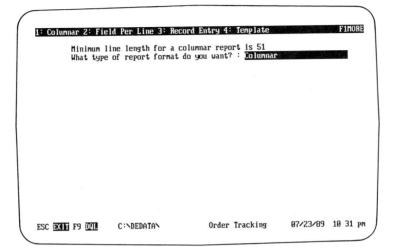

Fig. 5.14.

The Format Selection screen.

Assume, for example, that the field lengths for the Sales Representative fields you want included in the report are as follows:

Field	Length
Last Name	20
Region	12
Salary	13
	45

When DataEase calculates the minimum width for the report, it totals the field lengths—in this case 45. DataEase adds 1 space between each field—2 more spaces altogether—bringing the total number of spaces to 47. Finally, DataEase places 2 spaces at the beginning of the line and 2 at the end of the line, which makes the total line length 51 as shown in figure 5.14.

Below the prompt that displays the minimum line length, DataEase asks which type of report format you want and provides the default choice Columnar. DataEase also provides, in a line menu, all nine format options:

```
1: Columnar
2: Field Per Line
3: Record Entry
4: Template
5: GrafTalk Chart
6: Custom
7: Export
8: Mailing Labels
9: CrossView
```

These format choices are discussed in the sections that follow.

After you choose the type of report format, the procedure for completing this phase of Quick Reports design varies from format to format.

Understanding Report Format Elements

A DataEase report format can be as short as three lines or as long as 16 screens (22 lines each). Whether long or short, the elements of all DataEase reports can be divided into three categories: formatting commands, format text, and fields. Together, these elements describe the output of one record from the primary form. The report itself is made up of multiple records arranged in this format.

Format text and fields are analogous to text and fields in the record-entry form. You use format text to describe and enhance the report data just as you use text in a record-entry form to describe the field entries. Each field in the format represents the data from the corresponding field in the form data. Both format text and the report fields appear in the final output in precisely the positions defined in the report format. This design approach often is referred to as *WYSIWYG*, "What you see is what you get."

The Formatting Commands control what appears in the report between records. They control such features as the position of report headers, footers, group headers, and the trailers, including summary statistical operations. The eight basic formatting commands are

.header
.footer
.group header
.items
.group trailer
.end
.page
.call

Notice that each formatting command begins with a period or dot. For that reason, these commands are sometimes referred to as *dot commands*. Each formatting command must be on a line by itself and must begin in column 1. When you use one of the predefined formats (all but the custom format), DataEase inserts all the necessary formatting commands for you. To learn when and how to add and delete formatting commands yourself, see Chapter 8, "Customizing DataEase Reports."

Using the Columnar Format

The default Quick Reports format is the columnar format. This format is similar in appearance to the Table View in Record Entry, with field names across the top and records arranged in rows.

When you select 1: Columnar on the second line of the Format Selection screen (see fig. 5.14), DataEase adds a third line to the prompt. If you have assigned one or more group fields on the Field Selection screen, DataEase asks Do you want Group Headers and Trailers?

A *group header* is text or fields that appear in the report above the first record in each grouping. Group headers usually are used to label the grouping—to describe the information that follows. A *group trailer* appears just after the last record in every grouping. Group trailers most often contain totals or subtotals and other statistics calculated across the records in the grouping. Respond 2: yes to this prompt when you want DataEase automatically to insert the appropriate formatting commands to create a header and trailer for each of the groupings in your report. DataEase also automatically moves the group field to the group header and inserts statistical fields in the group trailer (see fig. 5.15).

Because columnar reports need a significant amount of horizontal space, DataEase compares the calculated minimum line length to the default report width of 80 spaces. When the fields that you have selected for your report require more than 80 spaces, DataEase asks What line length do you desire for the report? and suggests the default width of 80 spaces. Type the desired line length and press Enter. When you specify a line length that is shorter than the minimum line length, DataEase displays a fourth line in the Format Selection screen that asks report must be edited to fit into this line length! OK? Respond 2: yes, and DataEase displays the report format in the Format Definition screen. (If you answer 1: no, the screen returns to the first question, What type of report do you want?) Figure 5.15 shows a Format Definition screen.

If the line length required to accommodate the fields you have chosen is less than 80 spaces, DataEase inserts extra spaces between fields to position them evenly across the report width. The resulting format may be longer than the minimum line length displayed on the Format selection screen.

The minimum line length suggested by DataEase and the line length you type at the screen prompt are both just guidelines. The actual line length you should use for designing your report is determined primarily by your printer. DataEase enables you to define a format as wide as 4,000 spaces, but the line length (report width) is limited to the maximum number of characters your printer can print on one line. Most standard carriage dot-matrix printers can print 80 characters per line when set to print 10

Fig. 5.15.

The columnar report format on the Format Definition screen.

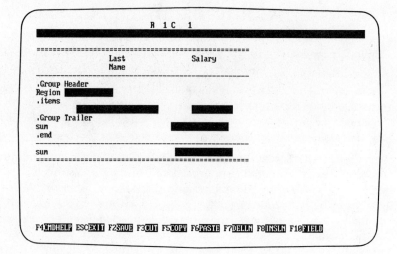

characters per inch (cpi). At 12 cpi, your printer can print 96 characters on a line. In compressed mode, or 17 characters per inch, you can squeeze up to 136 characters on one line. Wide carriage printers usually can handle 50 percent longer line lengths. However, if the report is sent to the screen, it may be up to 4,000 characters in width.

> **Tip:** As you calculate the line length for your report, make sure that you leave room for any left and right margin you want. Page size (paper size in inches) and margin widths are set using the **6. Define Print Style** option on the QBE—Quick Reports menu, but you have to take margin size into account when you figure line width.
>
> You may, for example, want to specify a one-inch margin on the left and right sides of the report on a page that is 8 1/2-inches wide. Subtracting 10 spaces per margin, or a total of 20 spaces, from the 85 spaces (10 cpi multiplied by 8 1/2-inches) leaves 65 spaces. The line length for your report should be no more than 65 characters.

Figure 5.15 shows the columnar report format in the Format Definition screen for the sales representative salary list, which includes group header and group trailer, as automatically defined by DataEase. Even though DataEase calculated the minimum required line length to be 44 spaces, with the group header and group trailer added, the minimum line is actually 52 spaces.

The predefined columnar format consists of a blank line at the top of the screen, followed by a double line (a line of equal signs), and then one or more lines displaying the field names selected in the Define List Fields step (or all the field names, if you skip that step). Below the field names is a line of hyphens. Everything in this format, up to this point, is *format text*. It will appear at the beginning of the report and at the top of every page in the report exactly as it appears on-screen.

Beneath the line of hyphens is the first formatting command. When you specify that you want group headers and trailers included in the report, the first command is the .group header command shown in figure 5.15. DataEase displays one .group header command in the columnar report format for each group field you specify on the Field Selection screen.

In the case where you don't specify a group field or choose not to include group headers and trailers, .items is the first command.

Whenever DataEase automatically creates a group header, it includes the group field's name as format text on the first line after the .group header command. The area between this command and the next formatting command is the group header. Any text or fields that you place in the group header appear in the report just above the first record in the grouping of records. DataEase places the group field and its field name in the group header (see fig. 5.15).

DataEase places the .items command after all group headers. There is always one (and only one) .items command in a report format. This command marks the beginning of the items area of the report. The items area extends from the .items command to the next formatting command. Any text or fields that you place in the items area appear in the report output once for each record in the primary form. In the predefined columnar format, DataEase places each field that you specified in the Field Selection screen into its own column in the items area. Each highlighted bar in figure 5.15 below the .items line represents a form field and is lined up beneath its field name.

The next formatting command is the .group trailer command. DataEase inserts one .group trailer command for each .group header command. The area that extends from the .group trailer command to the next formatting command is the group trailer for the group field.

Any text or field that you place in the group trailer appears in your report below the last record in the grouping. When you include a statistic keyword in a field, DataEase places the statistic name and a corresponding statistical function field in each group trailer. The statistic is calculated at every grouping level and at the end of the report. Figure 5.15 contains only one group trailer, for the Region field. The field that appears to the right of the text sum calculates a salary subtotal for each Region.

The last formatting command is the .end command. Any text or fields that you place after this command appear only once in the report, after all records have been processed. DataEase places statistical function fields after the .end command. For example, the field to the right of the word sum and after the end command in figure 5.15 produces a grand total of all the salaries, which appears in the report output at the end.

Figure 5.16 shows the report that results from the format shown in figure 5.15.

Fig. 5.16.

The sales representative salary list report resulting from the format shown in figure 5.15.

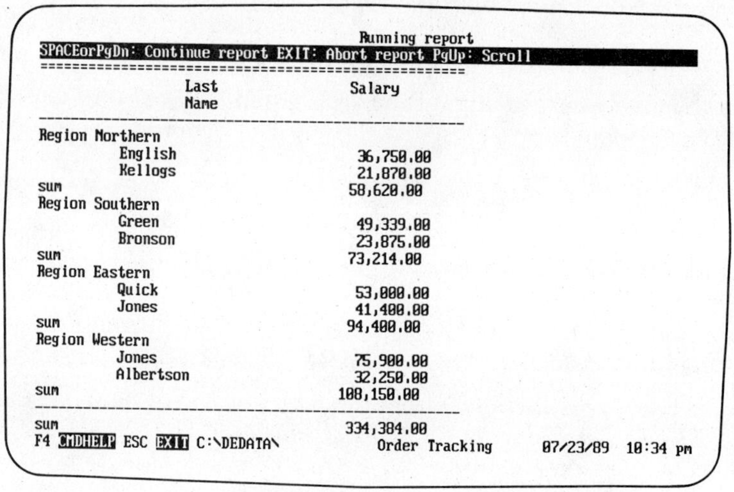

```
                                      Running report
SPACEorPgDn: Continue report EXIT: Abort report PgUp: Scroll
===========================================================
                        Last            Salary
                        Name
-----------------------------------------------------------
Region Northern
            English                   36,750.00
            Kellogs                   21,870.00
   sum                                58,620.00
Region Southern
            Green                     49,339.00
            Bronson                   23,875.00
   sum                                73,214.00
Region Eastern
            Quick                     53,000.00
            Jones                     41,400.00
   sum                                94,400.00
Region Western
            Jones                     75,900.00
            Albertson                 32,250.00
   sum                               108,150.00
-----------------------------------------------------------
   sum                               334,384.00
F4 CMDHELP ESC EXIT C:\DEDATA\         Order Tracking   07/23/89  10:34 pm
```

Editing a Report Format

Although the report shown in figure 5.16 contains all the necessary information, you still could improve its composition. DataEase enables you to edit the report format using the same full-screen editor features you are familiar with from the form definition process. Table 5.6 lists the available cursor-movement keys, and table 5.7 shows the function-key commands that you can use to edit the format.

In some respects, editing a report format is quite similar to editing the definition of a record-entry form. You can add, change, or delete format text using the cursor-movement keys, function-key commands, and by typing text on-screen. Neither adding or deleting text affects the data that appears in the report. You also can adjust the horizontal position of text or fields by using the Insert mode to "push" the field to the right and the Del key to "pull" it to the left. The same text and data is printed in the report, but in a different horizontal position.

Table 5.6
Report Format Definition Cursor-Movement Keys

Key	Cursor Movement
↑	Previous line
↓	Next line
←	One position (space) to the left
Backspace	One position to the left
→	One position to the right
Home	Move to position R1 C1
End	Column 1 in last line containing any text or field
Tab	Six positions to the right
Shift-Tab	Six positions to the left
Ctrl-→	Column 81, same row; column 121, 161, 201, and so on
Ctrl-←	Column 1, same row
Enter	Column 1, next row
PgDn	Bottom row of screen, same column
PgUp	Top row of screen, same column

Figure 5.17 shows the same report format as figure 5.15 after some editing to make the report easier to read. Several lines of text have been deleted, and a few have been added. The two occurrences of the word sum in figure 5.15 have been changed to Subtotal and Total, respectively, to describe more explicitly the statistical function sum field that each word labels. The field name Last Name is now all on one line, instead of on two lines, as it was in figure 5.15. The text "Region" has been moved to the right of the Region field in the group header. Several fields also are repositioned horizontally. The final version of the report is shown in figure 5.12.

When you finish editing a report format, press F2 (SAVE) or Esc (EXIT) to return to save the format and return to the QBE—Quick Reports menu.

Table 5.7
Report Format Definition Function-Key Commands

Function Key (Name)	Function
Esc (EXIT)	Returns to QBE—Quick Reports menu after saving all changes (same as F2)
Alt-F1 (HELP)	Provides help on current operation
F2 (SAVE)	Returns to QBE—Quick Reports menu after saving all changes (same as Esc)
F3 (CUT)	Cuts a block of text or fields
F4 (CMDHELP)	Displays pull-down menus
F5 (COPY)	Copies a block of text or fields
F6 (PASTE)	Pastes a cut or copied block of text or fields
F7 (DELLN)	Deletes complete line (blank, text, or fields)
F8 (INSLN)	Inserts a new line at the cursor
Shift-F9 (PRINT)	Prints the report definition
F10 (FIELD)	Defines a field
Alt-F10 (BORDERS)	Draws borders; ASCII character set

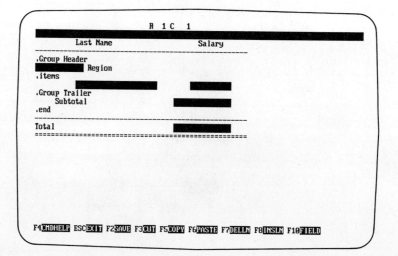

Fig. 5.17.

An edited version of the sales representative salary list columnar report format (see fig. 5.15).

Using Field-Per-Line Format

The most obvious weakness of the columnar format style is that the
horizontal orientation limits the number of fields you can display per
record. The field-per-line format solves this problem by orienting fields
vertically, one per line.

When you want to place each field on a separate line in the report, select
2: Field Per Line at the second line on the Format Selection screen.
DataEase displays a report format similar to figure 5.18. DataEase places a
field on each line. The field names are arranged in a column on the left
side of the screen. The corresponding fields are in a column on the right
side of the screen. Figure 5.18 shows all the fields from the Sales
Representative form in the field-per-line format. These fields would not all
fit horizontally on a normal size page (8 1/2-inches wide) but fit nicely in
a vertical orientation.

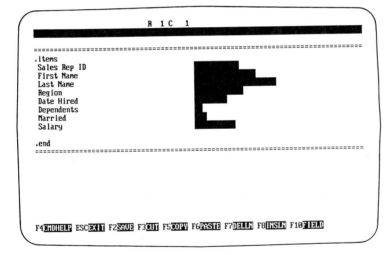

Fig. 5.18.

The field-per-line
format.

As shown in figure 5.18, DataEase labels statistical function fields in the
field-per-line report format a bit differently than in the columnar report
format. For example, in the field-per-line format, DataEase automatically
labels a sum field with the text sum of *f*, where *f* is the field name. By
contrast, in the columnar format, DataEase inserts the word sum as the
label for a sum field (see fig. 5.15). DataEase does not automatically add
group headers and trailers to the field-per-line format. Figure 5.19 shows
the report that results from the field-per-line format shown in figure 5.18.

You can edit this format as described in the "Editing a Format" section.
When the format is as you want it, press F2 (SAVE) or Esc (EXIT) to save
the format to RAM and return to the QBE—Quick Reports menu.

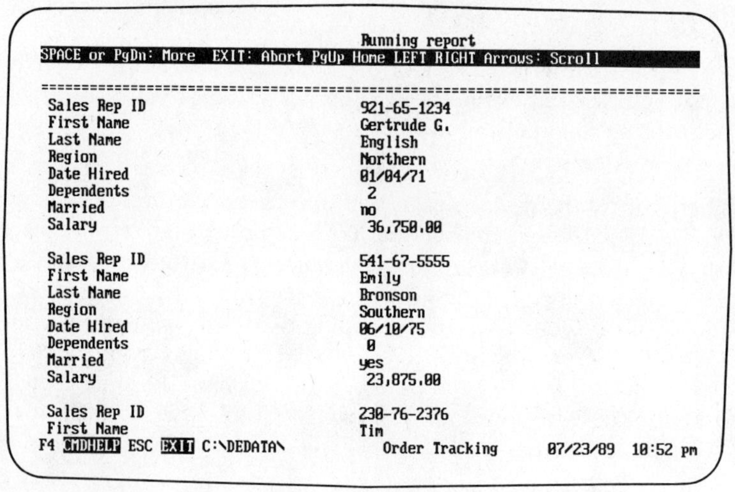

Fig. 5.19.

The Sales Representative form data in a field-per-line format report.

```
                               Running report
 SPACE or PgDn: More  EXIT: Abort PgUp Home LEFT RIGHT Arrows: Scroll

 ================================================================
 Sales Rep ID              921-65-1234
 First Name                Gertrude G.
 Last Name                 English
 Region                    Northern
 Date Hired                01/04/71
 Dependents                2
 Married                   no
 Salary                     36,750.00

 Sales Rep ID              541-67-5555
 First Name                Emily
 Last Name                 Bronson
 Region                    Southern
 Date Hired                06/10/75
 Dependents                0
 Married                   yes
 Salary                     23,875.00

 Sales Rep ID              230-76-2376
 First Name                Tim
 F4 CMDHELP ESC EXIT C:\DEDATA\      Order Tracking     07/23/89  10:52 pm
```

Using Record-Entry Format

The record-entry report format is a copy of the fields and text from the record-entry form. To choose this format, select 3: Record Entry from the line menu on the Format Selection screen (see fig. 5.14). DataEase displays a screen similar to figure 5.20—the record-entry report format for the Sales Representative form.

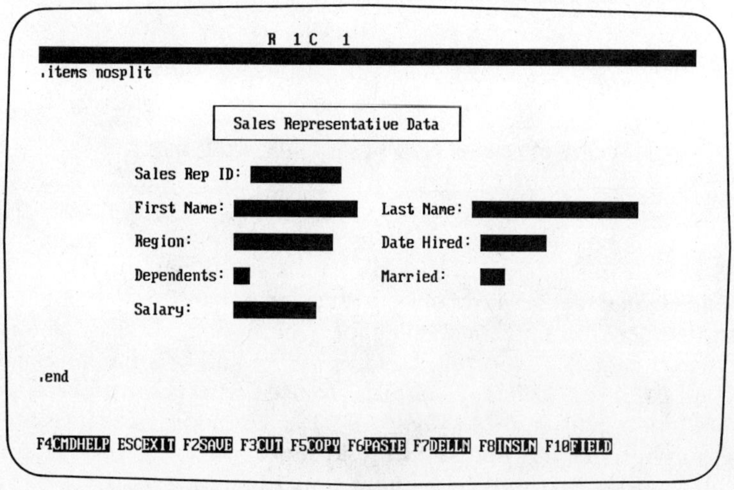

Fig. 5.20.

The record-entry report format for the Sales Representative form.

```
                          R 1 C 1

 .items nosplit

                    ┌──────────────────────────┐
                    │  Sales Representative Data │
                    └──────────────────────────┘

        Sales Rep ID: ████████

        First Name: ████████████    Last Name: ██████████████

        Region: ████████            Date Hired: ████████

        Dependents: █               Married: ████

        Salary: ██████████

 .end

 F4CMDHELP ESCEXIT F2SAVE F3CUT F5COPY F6PASTE F7DELLN F8INSLN F10FIELD
```

DataEase always uses all fields in the record-entry format, regardless what selections you make on the Field Selection screen. DataEase does not automatically insert group headers and trailers or display statistical function fields in the predefined record-entry format. You, therefore, can skip the Field Selection screen when you are using the record-entry format unless you want the records sorted in a particular order.

Notice that DataEase uses the .items nosplit formatting command at the beginning of the record-entry format instead of the .items command that is used in the other format types. This formatting command, a variation of the .items command, prevents data from one record from being split between two pages. When the data from one record will not fit on the current page, DataEase doesn't print any of the record's data on that page. Instead, the program starts on a new page. When one record is too large to fit on one page, however, DataEase has no choice but to split the record.

You can edit this format as described in the "Editing a Format" section. When the format is as you want it, press F2 (SAVE) or Esc (EXIT) to save the format to RAM and return to the QBE—Quick Reports menu.

Using the Template Format

The template report format is not really a single format type, but provides a means to select a report format of your own design, referred to as a *template*. You design the template using the Form Definition facility, described in Chapters 2 and 3 of this book. The specifics of designing a report template are discussed in Chapter 8.

Tip: Normally, you define all your report templates in a separate database. You never use them to enter data, and by placing them in another database, you cannot confuse a template with a normal record-entry form.

To use a previously defined report template, select 4: Template on the second line of the Format Selection screen. DataEase then prompts you for the name of the template file. Specify the DOS file name of the file that contains the template form definition (.DBA extension) and press Enter. DataEase copies all text from the template form to the Format definition screen and copies each field definition with a matching field name in the primary form.

Because template files can be stored on other directories and other disks, you can create a limitless number of report templates to use over and over.

You can edit this format as described in the "Editing a Format" section. When the format is as you want it, press F2 (SAVE) or Esc (EXIT) to save the format to RAM and return to the QBE—Quick Reports menu.

Using the GrafTalk Chart Format

One of the software packages in the DataEase family of products is the presentation graphics program DataEase GrafTalk. If you are a GrafTalk licensee, you can pass data directly to GrafTalk and display a graph or chart based on that data without leaving DataEase. This can be done through the GrafTalk chart format of Quick Reports.

Using the Custom Format

Although the several predefined formats help you generate informative reports with a minimum of effort, sometimes the only way to design a report exactly as you want is to design it yourself. The custom format enables you to do this.

To design a custom format, choose 6: Custom from the second line of the Format Selection screen. DataEase displays a blank Format Definition screen in which you can design the report format. All the formatting commands are available, as well as the fields from the primary form. You can, of course, type whatever format text you want to appear in the report.

Refer to Chapter 8, "Customizing DataEase Reports," for a complete discussion of creating a custom format, including a description of when and how to use each available formatting command and how to add, subtract, and modify report fields.

Using the Export Format

The export format is not one format, but nine. Each creates a copy of selected form data in a format that can be read by another program. Using the export format option, you can create a data file in a format readable by one of the following programs:

1-2-3
Symphony
GrafTalk
MultiMate
WordPerfect
WordStar

CrossView
Any program that can read variable-length ASCII files
Any program that can use fixed-length ASCII files
Any program that uses Data Interchange Format (DIF) files

To use the export format feature, select 7: Export on the second line of the Format Selection screen. DataEase displays the prompt What is the export format? You choose the desired format from a line menu.

Exporting to Lotus 1-2-3 or Symphony

Choose 1: Lotus 1-2-3 at the third line of the Format Selection screen when you want to use the data in Lotus 1-2-3 or Symphony. DataEase next asks whether you want to include field names in the format. Respond 2: yes, and DataEase creates a format with the following single line:

.export Lotus 1-2-3 With Field Names

If you answer 1: no to the prompt, DataEase creates the single line format:

.export Lotus 1-2-3

DataEase does not display fields or text on the Format Definition screen, and you should not add any. The single command line is intended solely to create a Lotus worksheet disk file that can be used by Lotus 1-2-3 Release 1A, Lotus 1-2-3 Release 2, or Lotus Symphony. The worksheet will contain a row for each record in the form data that meets the selection criteria you specified in the Record Selection screen. Don't edit this format, just press F2 (SAVE) or Esc (EXIT) to save the format and return to the QBE— Quick Reports menu.

Don't attempt to run the report until you have changed the print style to 3: Disk (see "Defining Print Style" later in this chapter). When providing a file name on the Print Style Specification screen, use the file name extension that matches the target program (see the list in table 5.8). Because DataEase exports only data, no formulas, your file will be compatible with all three Lotus programs. Sorting, grouping, and statistical operators don't have any effect on data exported to a file in the Lotus format.

Table 5.8
Export Format File Name Extensions

Target Program	Extension
Lotus 1-2-3 Release 1A	.WKS
Lotus 1-2-3 Release 2	.WK1
Lotus Symphony	.WRK
MultiMate	.DOC

Exporting to GrafTalk

Choose 2: GrafTalk at the third line of the Format Selection screen when you want to use the data in DataEase GrafTalk. You use this option to create a file that you can use later with GrafTalk. You should use the GrafTalk Chart format rather than export format when you want to load and run the GrafTalk program from within DataEase.

Exporting to MultiMate

To create a data file that can be merged with MultiMate word processing files, for example, select 3: MultiMate as the export format. DataEase displays a format similar to the one shown in figure 5.21. DataEase places each field name on a separate line of the format, followed by the corresponding field on the next line. Special box drawing characters mark the beginning and end of each field and the end of the record. Don't edit this format; just press F2 (SAVE) or Esc (EXIT) to save the format and return to the QBE—Quick Reports menu.

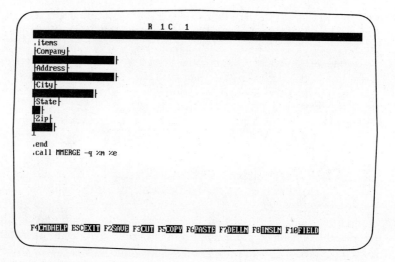

Fig. 5.21.

An export format to create a file that can be merged with MultiMate word processing files.

Before running the report, you must choose 3: Disk as the Report Destination on the Print Style Specification screen and assign a file name with the extension .DOC (see "Defining Print Style," later in this chapter).

When you run the report, the formatting command *.call MMERGE -q %m %e* runs a DataEase conversion program that creates the output file in a format usable by MultiMate.

Exporting to WordPerfect

To create a data file that can be merged with WordPerfect word processing files, select 4: WordPerfect as the export format. DataEase displays a format similar to the one shown in figure 5.22. DataEase places all fields on a single line of the format, with the code @[120A] at the end of each field and the code @[050A] at the end of the record, followed by a backslash (\ ). Don't edit this format. Press F2 (SAVE) or Esc (EXIT) to save the format and return to the QBE—Quick Reports menu.

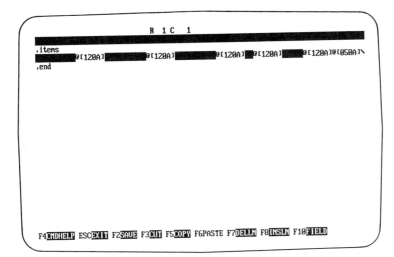

Fig. 5.22.

An export format to create a file that can be merged with WordPerfect word processing files.

Before running the report, you must choose 3: Disk as the Report Destination on the Print Style Specification screen and assign a file name (see "Defining Print Style" later in this chapter). When you run the report, DataEase generates WordPerfect secondary merge file. The code @[120A] produces the WordPerfect Merge Code (^R) for end of field, and the code @[050A] produces the WordPerfect Merge Code (^E) for end of record. The backslash suppresses the carriage return that DataEase would otherwise add automatically.

Exporting to WordStar Mail-Merge Format

To create a data file that can be merged with WordStar word processing files, select 5: Mail-merge as the export format. DataEase asks whether you want to include field names. Respond 1: no to produce a file without field names. When you respond 2: yes, DataEase displays a format similar to figure 5.23. DataEase places all field names, separated by commas, on a single line above the .items formatting command. Each field name is enclosed in double quotation marks. The fields, separated by commas, appear all on one line between the .items and .end commands. Text fields are enclosed in double quotation marks, but number fields and numeric string fields are not. You can edit the field names, but don't remove the quotation marks. Press F2 (SAVE) or Esc (EXIT) to save the format and return to the QBE—Quick Reports menu.

Fig. 5.23.

An export format to create a file that can be merged with WordStar word processing files.

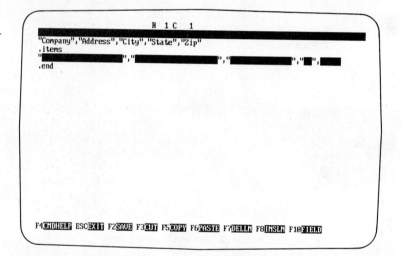

Before running the report, you must choose 3: Disk as the Report Destination and assign a file name (see "Defining Print Style" later in this chapter). When you run the report, DataEase generates a file that can be merged with WordStar documents.

Exporting to ASCII Format

Nearly every popular word processing, spreadsheet, and database program can import at least one of the formats already discussed in this chapter. If yours will not, it probably will import an ASCII (American Standard Code for Information Interchange) file. But, even ASCII files come in two types:

variable length, and fixed length. The word "length" refers to the length of the data fields. Consult your program's documentation to determine which type of ASCII format it can import.

To create a data file in a variable-length ASCII format, choose 6: Variable Length as the export format. DataEase prompts you with the message FIELD SEPARATOR character (If new line, press RETURN):. This means that you should type a character that will be used in the file to separate fields, and then to press Enter. Your program's documentation may call this field separator a "delimiter." The most commonly used field separator is the comma. Do not use a character that appears in the data as a field separator. If you want each field to be placed on a separate line without a field separator, press Enter without typing any character.

DataEase next asks whether you want to include field names in the format. Respond 2: yes and DataEase creates a format similar to that shown in figure 5.24, with the field names typed above the .items command. This line will become the first row in the output file. If you don't want field names, respond 1: no to the prompt. You can edit the field names, but don't remove the field separator characters.

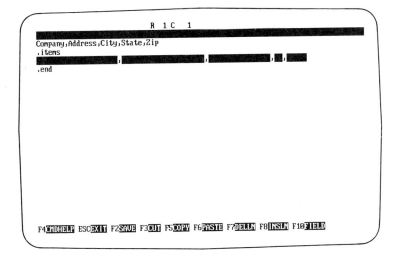

Fig. 5.24.

A variable length ASCII format with commas as field separators.

By default, DataEase uses the carriage return to separate records. If your program uses a different record separator character, type this character at the end of the field line, followed by a back slash (\ ). If, for example, your program uses the percent character (%) to separate records, type %\ at the right end of the format line that contains the fields, just after the last field. The percent character is added to the end of every record, and the backslash suppresses the carriage return that DataEase would otherwise add.

Press F2 (SAVE) or Esc (EXIT) to save the format and return to the
QBE—Quick Reports menu.

To create a data file in a fixed-length ASCII format, choose 7: Fixed Length
as the export format. DataEase displays a format similar to that in figure
5.25. The long highlighted bar appears to be one field, but is all the fields
(selected in the Field Selection screen) side by side. The backslash at the
end of the fields line suppresses the carriage return that DataEase
otherwise inserts automatically. The format is fixed length because every
record is exactly the same length. Records are separated by neither a
separator character nor a carriage return. Data is stored in the output file
as a continuous stream. At some point, you will have to provide the
individual field lengths and the total record length to the target program
that is going to use this file.

Fig. 5.25.

*A fixed-length ASCII
format.*

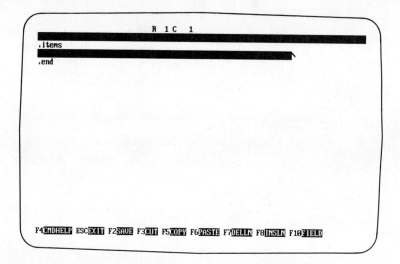

Don't attempt to edit this format. Press F2 (SAVE) or Esc (EXIT) to save
the format and return to the QBE—Quick Reports menu. Before running
the report, you must choose 3: Disk as the Report Destination on the Print
Style Specification screen and assign a file name (see "Defining Print Style"
later in this chapter). When you run the report, DataEase generates an
ASCII file in the format you have chosen.

Exporting to DIF Format

DIF stands for Data Interchange Format. This format originally was
developed for use with the pioneer spreadsheet program VisiCalc, but it
can be used by many other spreadsheet, word processing, and database
programs.

To export DataEase data into a DIF file, select 8: DIF as the export format. DataEase asks whether you want to include field names. Respond 1: no to produce a file without field names. When you respond 2: yes, DataEase displays a format similar to figure 5.26.

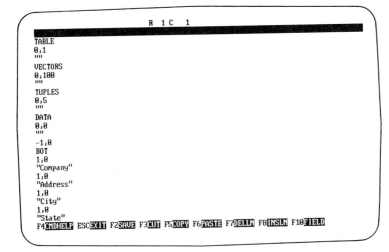

Fig. 5.26.

A DIF format.

Don't edit this format. Press F2 (SAVE) or Esc (EXIT) to save the format and return to the QBE—Quick Reports menu. Before running the report, you must choose 3: Disk as the report destination and assign a file name on the Print Style Specification screen (see "Defining Print Style" later in this chapter). When you run the report, DataEase generates the DIF file with the file name you have assigned.

Using the Mailing Labels Format

One of the most common needs in any business is an easy method of generating mailing labels. After you have the names and addresses in the computer, it should be a simple matter to spit them out onto labels, but with most programs that is not usually the case. Fortunately, one of DataEase's report format options does an excellent job of producing mailing labels with minimal effort on your part.

To produce a mailing labels report format, select 8: Mailing Labels at the second line of the Format Selection screen. DataEase displays another prompt asking, How many labels across? Look at the labels you want to use and respond appropriately to this question (the default is 2) and press Enter.

Next, DataEase asks for the number of columns in the label, which means the width of a label in spaces. To determine the proper number, use a ruler to measure from the left edge of the left most label to the left edge of the label to its right. Then, multiply this width by the horizontal spacing of your printer. For example, most sheets of 2-up mailing labels (each row has two labels) contain labels that are 4 inches wide. If your printer prints at 10 characters per inch (often called pica spacing), you multiply 10 by 4. The number of spaces per label is therefore 40. Enter the correct number in the space provided (the default is 40) and press Enter. DataEase displays a format similar to figure 5.27.

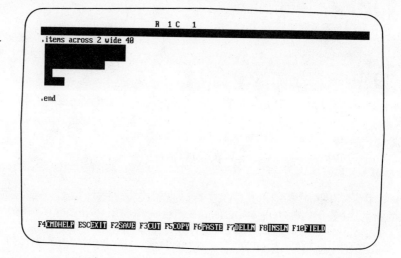

Fig. 5.27.

A mailing labels report format.

The first line in the format is the formatting command

.items across *n* wide *m*

where *n* is the number of labels in each row, and *m* is the width of a single label. This command, a variation of the .items command, causes DataEase to print *n* records across the page. Each record takes up *m* spaces in width.

DataEase places each field on a separate line, and the number of fields determines the number of lines that will be printed on each label. DataEase automatically adds one extra blank line. For example, you might include the Company, Address, City, State, and ZIP fields when creating mailing labels from the Retail Customer data. Because you have indicated five fields, DataEase creates a format with six lines (five plus one blank line) in the detail area (between the .items command and the .end command), as shown in figure 5.27.

Tip: You also should measure your labels vertically. Use the ruler to measure the distance in inches from the top of one label to the top of the next label. Multiply this number by 6, because normal spacing is 6 lines per inch. Make sure that there are exactly this many lines in the detail area. You may have to edit the format. For instance, to print on 1-inch labels, the format shown in figure 5.27 contains the correct number of lines (6) between the .items command and the .end command. But, to print 1 1/2-inch labels, you would need to insert three more lines, with the F8 (INSLN) command. In defining the Print style, you must specify a page length of 0 to print on continuous form labels.

You can edit the format to move several fields on the same line using the F3 (CUT) and F6 (PASTE) commands. Be careful not to move any fields above the .items command or below the .end command. If you type any text on the format, in the detail area, the text is printed on every label.

Press F2 (SAVE) or Esc (EXIT) to save the format and return to the QBE—Quick Reports menu. When you run the report, DataEase prints an address on each label.

Using the CrossView Format

DataEase CrossView is a powerful, multidimensional data analysis program also available from DataEase International. If you are a licensee of both programs, you easily can pass data from DataEase to CrossView as if they were the same program.

To create a CrossView-compatible file and then start CrossView from within DataEase, select 9: CrossView from the menu at the second line of the Format Selection screen. When DataEase produces a format, press F2 (SAVE) or Esc (EXIT) to return to the QBE—Quick Reports menu.

Before running the report, select **6. Define Print Style**, change the report destination to 3: Disk, and specify a file name. Finally, select **1. Run Report** from the QBE—Quick Reports menu. DataEase swaps itself to disk and loads CrossView. Refer to the CrossView documentation for further instructions on using a DataEase file with CrossView. When you finish using CrossView, DataEase reloads itself into RAM so that you can continue to work.

Defining Print Style

DataEase reports don't always have to be printed. Indeed, you may find that you display reports on-screen more often than you print them, at least until you work the kinks out. By default, if you don't specify otherwise, DataEase sends the report to the screen. Whenever you want the report displayed on-screen, rather than printed, skip the print style step.

To select a different output device—printer or disk—and to change such settings as printer name, page size, and margin, select **6. Define Print Style** from the QBE—Quick Reports menu. DataEase displays the Print Style Specification screen, shown in figure 5.28. As you work on this screen, the function-key commands listed in table 5.9 are effective.

Fig. 5.28.

The Print Style Specification screen.

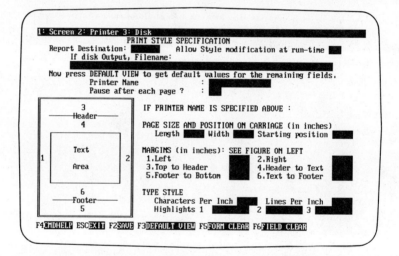

```
1: Screen 2: Printer 3: Disk
                    PRINT STYLE SPECIFICATION
    Report Destination: ▓▓▓▓▓    Allow Style modification at run-time ▓
           If disk Output, Filename: ▓▓▓▓▓▓▓▓▓▓▓▓▓▓▓▓▓▓▓▓▓▓

   Now press DEFAULT VIEW to get default values for the remaining fields.
            Printer Name            :
            Pause after each page ? : ▓▓▓▓▓▓▓▓

   ┌────────────────┐   IF PRINTER NAME IS SPECIFIED ABOVE :
   │       3        │
   │ ──Header──     │   PAGE SIZE AND POSITION ON CARRIAGE (in inches)
   │       4        │      Length ▓▓▓▓  Width ▓▓▓▓  Starting position ▓▓▓▓
   │                │
   │                │   MARGINS (in inches): SEE FIGURE ON LEFT
 1 │    Text        │ 2    1.Left          ▓▓▓▓   2.Right          ▓▓▓▓
   │    Area        │      3.Top to Header ▓▓▓▓   4.Header to Text ▓▓▓▓
   │                │      5.Footer to Bottom ▓▓  6.Text to Footer ▓▓▓▓
   │       6        │
   │ ──Footer──     │   TYPE STYLE
   │       5        │      Characters Per Inch ▓▓▓   Lines Per Inch ▓▓▓
   └────────────────┘      Highlights 1 ▓▓▓     2 ▓▓▓       3 ▓▓▓

   F4 CMDHELP  ESC EXIT  F2 SAVE  F3 DEFAULT VIEW  F5 FORM CLEAR  F6 FIELD CLEAR
```

Table 5.9
Quick Reports Print Style Specification Screen
Function-Key Commands

Function Key (Name)	Function
Esc (EXIT)	Saves entries and returns to QBE—Quick Reports menu (same as F2)
Alt-F1 (HELP)	Provides help on current operation
F2 (SAVE)	Saves entries and returns to QBE—Quick Reports menu (same as Esc)

Table 5.9—*continued*

Function Key (Name)	Function
F3 (DEFAULT VIEW)	Retrieves settings from the System Configuration form
*F4 (CMDHELP)	Displays pull-down Command menu
F5 (FORM CLEAR)	Clears values from all fields on-screen
Shift-F5 (DEFAULT FORM)	Fills in values from the last Print Style Specification saved
*Ctrl-F5 (UNDO)	Undos unsaved changes to record on-screen
F6 (FIELD CLEAR)	Clears value from current field on-screen
Shift-F6 (DEFAULT FIELD)	Fills in value from corresponding field in the last Print Style Specification saved

*New command in DataEase 4.0

Assigning the Report Destination

When DataEase first displays the Print Style Specification screen, the cursor rests in the field to the right of the prompt Report Destination. DataEase displays a line menu with the following options: 1: Screen, 2: Printer, and 3: Disk.

To specify that the report should be printed, select 2: Printer. Then, press F3 (DEFAULT VIEW). DataEase fills in the printer name, responds no to Pause after each page?, and specifies the page length and width. This information is taken from the System Configuration form. Refer to Appendix B for instructions on how to set and modify options on the System Configuration form.

You may want to be able to print the report from a disk file, because your printer is not currently available or because you want to send a disk to someone else. For a disk file output, select 3: Disk in the Report Destination field. You also must specify a file name in the blank line beneath the prompt If disk Output, Filename:. If you don't specify a disk and directory, DataEase places the file in the default data directory (see Appendix A).

DataEase creates a file containing ASCII characters. Later, you can print this file using the DOS COPY command. For example, if you create a disk file named LABELS.TXT, you can print this file from the DOS prompt:

COPY LABELS.TXT PRN

For this procedure to work properly, the printer definition selected on the Printer Name line of the Print Style Specification screen must match the printer connected to the computer when you use the COPY command.

> **Tip:** If you intend to use the disk file as input for another program, a word processing program for example, leave the Printer Name line blank. DataEase then creates an ASCII file without the special codes used to control printers.

To allow some flexibility later, you may want to respond 2: yes to the prompt Allow Style modification at run-time. This will give you an opportunity to switch the report to a different print style immediately before running the report.

Changing the Page Size

When you finally are ready to print the report, you need to make sure that the page size and position are properly set. The default page size is 8 1/2-by-11-inches. If these settings are not correct for your report, use the cursor-movement keys to move the cursor to the Length or Width prompts. Make the appropriate change or changes, specifying paper size in inches.

Setting the Margins and Type Style

To help ensure that your report looks as good as possible, DataEase enables you to adjust the margin settings so that the report is positioned just where you want it on the page. Six different margins can be set and modified. These six margins are numbered on the Print Specification screen. A diagram identifies the location of each margin by number. You can adjust each of these margins by typing a length, in inches, in the space to the right of the respective prompt.

By default, DataEase prints reports at 10 characters per inch horizontally and 6 lines per inch vertically. You can modify both of these settings on the Print Style Specification screen. You probably will seldom, if ever, change the Lines Per Inch vertical spacing setting but may frequently adjust the horizontal spacing setting. Elite spacing (12 characters per inch) is frequently used to squeeze a few more words on each line. For a change in either vertical or horizontal spacing to be effective, your printer must support the new setting. Most printers can print several different size characters and at various vertical spacing settings. Check your printer manual for the supported selections.

You also can add up to three special printing features, such as boldface or underline, to your report using the last three options on the Print Style Specifications screen. These options are labeled Highlight1, 2, and 3. With your cursor on one of these options, DataEase displays the following line menu choices: 1: Bold, 2: Underline, 3: Italicise, 4: Special 1, 5: Special 2, ...12: Special 9. (Appendix B explains how to define the highlights named Special 1 through Special 9.)

Select the special effect that you want applied to the entire report. By indicating a different effect in each of the three Highlight spaces, you can apply as many as three effects to the entire report. Also see Chapter 8 for a discussion of how to add printer control commands to the report format. Printer control commands override the printer effect applied through the three Highlight options on the Print Style Specification screen.

Saving the Print Style Specification

After you have made all the entries or changes you want to the Print Style Specification screen, press F2 (SAVE) or Esc (EXIT) to save the new settings to RAM and return to the QBE—Quick Reports menu.

Running the Report

You now know how to define a report, but you still haven't learned how to run it.

To run a report that is already loaded in RAM (such as one you just defined), select 1: Run Report from the QBE—Quick Reports menu. DataEase sends the selected fields and records to the output device specified in the Print Style Specification, using the specified report format.

When a report is sent to the screen, DataEase automatically pauses after each page. Although the report is paused, you can use the cursor-movement keys to move around the report. Press the space bar to continue the report.

You also can print a report that has been saved to disk without first loading it in memory. Clear any report from memory with **2. Start New Report**. Then, from the QBE—Quick Reports menu, choose **1. Run Report**. DataEase lists all available Quick Report definitions and DQL Procedures. Select the report you want to run and press Enter. DataEase runs the report and then returns to the QBE—Quick Reports menu.

Saving a Quick Report Definition

Even though creating DataEase Quick Reports is relatively quick and easy, you don't want to have to start from scratch each time. As you may have already discovered, DataEase enables you to save a Quick Report definition to disk for use at a later time.

When you complete the essential Quick Reports steps, you should save the definition. From the Quick Reports menu, Press **7. Save Report**. DataEase displays the prompt Please enter the report procedure name: Type a report name up to 20 characters long and press Enter. If this is the first time you have saved the report, DataEase saves to the specified disk file all the report settings and selections currently in RAM and displays the message New report created in the message area at the top of the screen. The program also adds the new report name to the prompt line, to the right of Current report:.

When you already have saved the Quick Report definition and try to save it again, DataEase asks Do you want to save modified report procedure under another name(y/n):. To replace the old version with the modified settings, answer this prompt 1: no. When you want to create a report file, leaving the original unchanged, respond 2: yes. DataEase then asks for a new name. Type a report name up to 20 characters long and press Enter. DataEase saves the new version of the report with the new name.

Of course, the purpose of saving a report definition to disk is to use it again at a later time. To load a previously saved Quick Report definition, choose 8: Load Report from the QBE—Quick Reports menu. DataEase displays the available Quick Reports and DQL Procedures in a window menu on the right side of the screen. Move the highlighted selection bar to the report you want to use and press Enter. DataEase loads the report settings to RAM and displays the message Report r Read where r is the name of the Quick Report definition you selected. DataEase also shows the name of the report definition in the prompt line. You now can use the definition to print a report, or can use it as a starting point to create a different report. Refer to Chapter 8 for a full discussion of how to enhance and customize DataEase reports.

Deleting a Quick Report Definition

Occasionally, you may need to clear old report definitions from the data disk to make more room or just to clear away obsolete files. To delete a Quick Report definition, select **9. Delete Report** from the QBE—Quick Reports menu. Choose the name of the report to be deleted from the window menu that lists all available Quick Report definitions and DQL Procedures and press Enter. DataEase asks you to confirm the deletion. Answer 2: yes. DataEase deletes the report definition, and displays the message report deleted in the message area.

Printing a Report Definition

DataEase provides two ways to print a hard copy of the Quick Report definition. From the Quick Reports menu select **10. Print Report Definition** or from the Format Definition screen press Shift-F9 (PRINT). Both methods print a listing that includes the record selection, field selection, report format, and field descriptions, as well as the memory required by the report definition when in use. You should print a copy of every report definition and file it away with the printouts that you have made of the record-entry form definitions. Both printed definitions will come in handy later when you make significant changes to your system. Without the hard copies to jog your memory, you might have to begin designing the system from scratch.

Chapter Summary

This chapter has shown you how to start a Quick Report, define record selection, select fields, specify a Quick Report format, define print style, group and sort records, calculate report statistics, save a Quick Report definition, load a previously saved Quick Report definition, delete a Quick Report definition, print a Quick Report, and print the Quick Report definition. This chapter presented a number of tools that you can put to use immediately and laid a foundation for understanding and using the powerful DataEase Query Language (DQL) introduced in Chapter 11.

Now that you have been introduced to the fundamentals of defining, entering, viewing, editing, and reporting individual DataEase forms, you are ready to explore the use of related forms. Turn to Chapter 6 to learn how to define and use DataEase relationships, and DataEase Multiforms.

Part II

Intermediate DataEase

Includes

Quick Start 2:
Tapping the Power of DataEase

Using Related DataEase Forms

Building Simple Procedures with DQL

Customizing DataEase Reports

Maintaining Your Database

Creating Custom DataEase Menus

Quick Start 2

Tapping the Power of DataEase

This is the second of two Quick Start lessons presented in this book. Each lesson precedes a major division of the book, previewing the topics to be covered, and taking you step-by-step through examples of techniques and concepts that are discussed in chapters that follow.

Quick Start II is designed with the assumption that you have finished Part I of this book or are generally familiar with the information covered there. Now that you have discovered how easy it is to work with the fundamental features of DataEase, you are ready to move on to the more powerful capabilities of the program.

This lesson gives you a taste of the topics presented in Part II of the book, from creation and use of Multiforms to menu generation. The various portions of the lesson must be completed in sequence, but the tutorial should be completed at your own pace.

First, you will build several forms and enter a number of records. The lesson is based on these forms, along with the Sales Representative form designed in Quick Start I.

The focus of Quick Start II is on design and use of DataEase Multiforms. You will design and build a DataEase Multiform—a new feature in DataEase 4.0—and then use the Multiform to enter and view records. You also will generate a Quick Report that uses data from the Multiform. Finally, you

209

will use the DataEase custom menu generator to design a custom menu, making it easy to use the Multiform and report that you create.

You will have a good idea of some of the most important capabilities of DataEase after completing this lesson.

Building the Database

Before you can begin this lesson, you need to have a few forms with which to work. If you have not already done so, build the Sales Representative form described in Quick Start I.

Modify the definition of Sales Representative to change the Region field to a *choice* field. Use the choices:

1. Northern
2. Southern
3. Eastern
4. Western

When you save the new form definition, respond 2: yes to the prompt Do Choice field changes require Choice Numbers in records to be updated? DataEase replaces the text that you entered earlier in each Region field with the appropriate choice number.

Use the procedures that you learned in Part I of the book to create the following forms and relationships. These are the same forms that have been used to create the book's screen examples.

Build the Retail Customer form according to the following definitions, so that its appearance is similar to figure QS2.1:

Field name	Cursor position of field name	Field definition
Customer Number	R6 C27	Num.String,4,Required, Indexed,Unique
Company	R8 C20	Text,35
Address	R10 C20	Text,35
City	R12 C20	Text,25
State	R12 C48	Text,2
Zip	R12 C53	Num.String,5
Phone	R14 C20	Num.String,phone no.
Long:Comments	R17 C20	Text,35

Field name	Cursor position of field name	Field definition
Long:Comments2	R18 C20	Text,35
Long:Comments3	R19 C20	Text,35
Long:Comments4	R20 C20	Text,35
Long:Comments5	R21 C20	Text,35

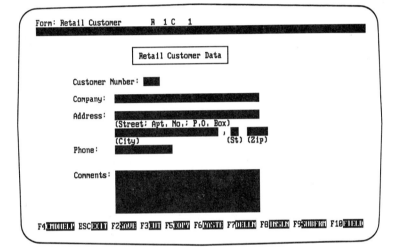

Fig. QS2.1.

The Retail Customer form.

Build the Widget Order form according to the following definitions, so that its appearance is similar to figure QS2.2:

Field	Cursor position of field name	Field definition
Order Number	R6 C33	Num.String,3,Required,Indexed, Unique,Derived,Formula: *sequence from 100*
Date	R6 C52	Date,8
Customer Number	R8 C33	Num.String,4,Required
Sales Rep ID	R10 C33	Num.String,11,Required

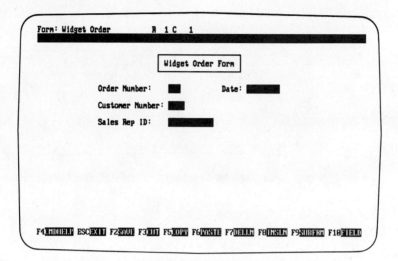

Fig. QS2.2.

The Widget Order form.

Build the Product form according to the following definition, so that its appearance is similar to figure QS2.3:

Field	Cursor position of field name	Field definition
Model Number	R6 C27	Text,5,Required,Indexed,Unique
Product Name	R6 C48	Text,20,Required
Price	R8 C23	Fixed point,5.2
Cost	R8 C42	Fixed point,5.2

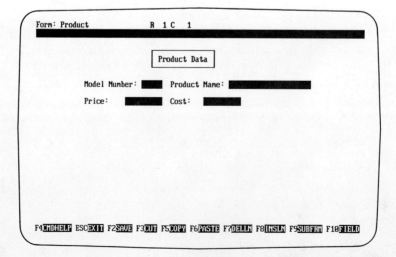

Fig. QS2.3.

The Product form.

Build the Order Detail form according to the following definition, so that its appearance is similar to figure QS2.4:

Field	Cursor position of field name	Field definition
Order Number	R7 C32	Num.String,3,Required,Indexed, Unique,Hide from Table View
Item Number	R7 C54	Integer,4,Required,Unique
Model Number	R9 C32	Text,5,Required,Indexed,Range Lower limit: *lookup PRODUCT "Model Number"* Upper limit: *lookup PRODUCT "Model Number"*
Product Name	R9 C54	Text,20,Required,Derived,Virtual Formula: *lookup PRODUCT "Product Name"*
Quantity	R11 C28	Integer,7
Price	R11 C51	Fixed point,5.2,Derived,No entry Formula: *lookup PRODUCT Price*
Total	R13 C47	Fixed point,8.2,Derived,No entry Formula: *Price * Quantity*

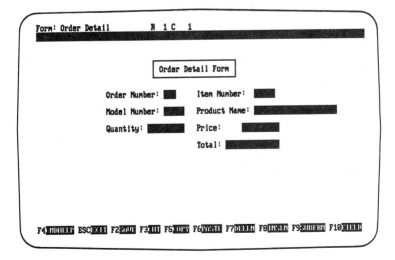

Fig. QS2.4.
The Order Detail form.

Define a relationship between Widget Order and Sales Representative, based on Sales Rep ID = Sales Rep ID, as shown in figure QS2.5. Define a relationship between Widget Order and Retail Customer, based on Customer Number = Customer Number.

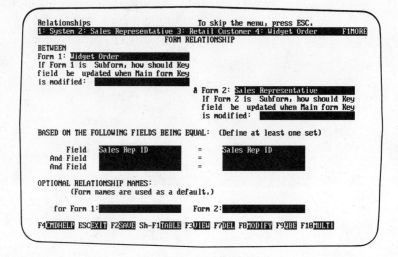

Fig. QS2.5.

The Widget Order-Sales Representative relationship.

Define a relationship between the Widget Order form and Order Detail form based on Order Number = Order Number, as shown in figure QS2.6.

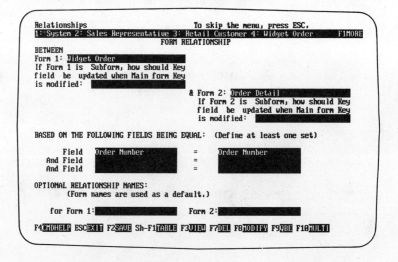

Fig. QS2.6.

The Widget Order-Order Detail relationship.

Define a relationship between the Order Detail form and the Product form based on Model Number = Model Number.

Use Form View or Table View to enter the following data (you can't use Table View for the Order Detail form because the Order Number field is hidden):

Retail Customer

Customer number	Customer data	Customer number	Customer data
1000	Eastern Enterprises 1211 Commerce St. Springfield, VA 22150 (703)-555-2355 Placed first order in June, 1986. Usually orders Standard widgets. Contact Joe Silver.	1001	Alpha Freight Lines 720 Port Royal Fairfax, VA 22030 (703)-555-1119 Usually orders Deluxe widgets. Ask for Bridget.
1002	Ace Airplanes 777 Kittyhawk Dr. Gaithersburg, MD 20877 (301) 555-2777 Call Sam the last Tuesday in each month.	1003	Hidden Resorts 6601 Wales Rd. Vienna, VA 22180 (703) 555-9662 Likes Imperial Widget. Contact Ms. French.
1004	Sangster Insurance 1411 Reservation Dr. Springfield, VA 22152 (703) 555-9995 Contact S. Saurus.	1005	Signal Plumbing 3333 Half Street Oxen Hill, MD 20745 (301) 555-8379 Formerly known as S & S Plumbing.

Product

Model #	Product name	Price	Cost
A333	Standard Widget	39.95	19.75
A334	Standard Widget Plus	43.95	21.15
B107	Enhanced Widget	49.95	23.60
C777	Jumbo Widget	55.95	24.66
G400	Deluxe Widget	59.95	25.15
X155	Imperial Widget	79.95	32.50

Widget Order

Order #	Date	Cust ID #	Sales Rep ID
100	05/02/89	1002	921-65-1234
101	05/08/89	1003	329-76-2219
102	05/09/89	1000	987-31-9873
103	05/12/89	1005	111-33-8491
104	05/15/89	1005	129-08-4562
105	05/16/89	1003	329-76-2219
106	05/23/89	1001	541-67-5555

Order Detail

Order #	Item #	Model #	Quantity
100	1	A333	50
100	2	A334	50
100	3	B107	25
100	4	G400	10
101	1	A333	15
101	2	X155	10
102	1	G400	35
102	2	A333	10
103	1	G400	22
103	2	X155	5
104	1	B107	45
105	1	G400	30
106	1	A334	22
106	2	B107	15

Creating and Using a Multiform

This database can be used to keep track of orders placed for any of the several types of widgets produced by your company. However, data entry is not as easy as it could be. As it now stands, you must enter the order number, date, customer number, and employee number in the Widget Order form. Then, you must switch to the Order Detail form to enter the item number, model number, and quantity for each type of widget ordered. DataEase looks up the product name and price and multiplies price by quantity to arrive at an amount that you should charge for each type of widget. This method gets the job done but is a bit tedious. You must type the order number several times for each order. In addition, there is no per-order total on-screen to tell you how much to charge each customer for all the types of widgets that a particular customer ordered. A DataEase *Multiform* enables you to easily eliminate these deficiencies.

Creating a Multiform

To create a DataEase Multiform, you first must decide which will be the *main* form and which will be the *subform*. This decision is based on the nature of the *relationship* between the forms. The relationship between Widget Order and Order Detail can be described as a one-to-many relationship. Each single record in Widget Order can correspond to several records in Order Detail. In other words, many records in Order Detail can have the same Order Number, because a single customer might buy more than one type of widget. When you are building a Multiform for a one-to-many relationship, make the *one-side* form the main form. Widget Order is on the *one-side*, so it is the main form. Order Detail is on the *many-side*, and is therefore the subform.

1. To create a Multiform, you first display the definition of the main form. The main form in this case is Widget Order. From the DataEase Main menu, select **1. Form Definition and Relationships**. DataEase displays the Form Definition menu.

   Choose **2. View or Modify a Form**.

   DataEase displays a list of available forms in a window menu. Move the selection bar to Widget Order and press Enter. DataEase displays the Widget Order form in the Form Definition screen (see fig. QS2.2).

2. Move the cursor to position R12C1. To begin defining the subform, press F9 (SUBFORM). DataEase displays the Subform Definition screen as a window in the middle of the Form Definition screen (see fig. QS2.7). Notice that the prompt line contains a menu with three options: 1: Sales Representative, 2: Retail Customer, and 3: Order Detail.

3. At the Relationship Name prompt of the Subform Definition screen, select 3: Order Detail. This is the third relationship that you just defined. Type the number 4 at the Minimum prompt and press Enter or Tab. Also, type 4 at the Maximum prompt and press Enter or Tab. DataEase moves the cursor to the last field on the Subform Definition screen and displays a line menu with the options: 1: Automatic Table, 2: Automatic Form, and 3: Custom Form. Select 1: Automatic Table. Finally, press F2 (SAVE) to save the subform definition. DataEase displays the Order Detail form, beginning in row 12 of the Form Definition screen, as shown in figure QS2.8. The subform is in Table View. Notice that the Order Number field from Order Detail is not shown in the subform, because you assigned the *hide-from-Table-View* characteristic to that field in the form definition.

Fig. QS2.7.

The Subform Definition screen.

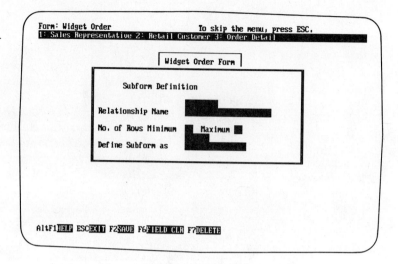

Fig. QS2.8.

The main form Widget Order with the embedded subform Order Detail.

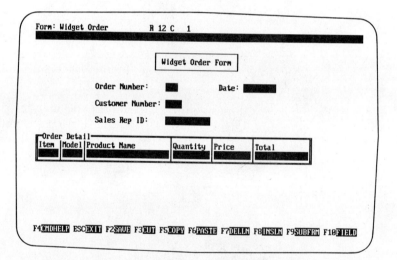

4. To center the first line of the subform, turn on Insert mode by pressing the Insert key and then press the space bar six times (ending at position R12C7). Press the down-arrow key once and the left-arrow key six times. While still in Insert mode, press the space bar six times again to center the second row of the subform. Repeat this process two more times until all four rows of the subform are centered. The subform should begin at column 7 and end at column 74.

Adding a Running Total

The Widget Order Multiform could be used as it appears at this point, without further modification; however, you still can improve it by adding a running total.

1. Use the arrow keys to move the cursor to position R17C48 and type *Order Total:*. Press the space bar once, moving to position R17C61.

2. To add a field that will calculate a running total, press F10 (FIELD). DataEase displays the Field Definition screen with the field name Order Total already filled in. Define the field as a Dollar field with 8 digits to the left of the decimal (fixed point, 8.2). Type the following formula in the Derivation Formula line:

   sum of "ORDER DETAIL" Total

   Select 3: yes, and do not save (virtual) at the Prevent Data-entry prompt. Save the field definition by pressing F2 (SAVE). The completed Multiform is shown in figure QS2.9.

```
Form: Widget Order          R  1 C  1

                    ┌─────────────────────┐
                    │  Widget Order Form   │
                    └─────────────────────┘

          Order Number: ██        Date: ███████

       Customer Number: ██

           Sales Rep ID: ████████

      ┌─Order Detail─────────────────────────────────────────┐
      │Item │Model│Product Name     │Quantity│Price │Total   │
      │     │     │                 │        │      │        │
      └─────┴─────┴─────────────────┴────────┴──────┴────────┘

                                   Order Total: █████████

F4 CMDHELP  ESC EXIT  F2 SAVE  F3 CUT  F5 COPY  F6 PASTE  F7 DELLN  F8 INSLN  F9 SUBFRM  F10 FIELD
```

Fig. QS2.9.

The completed Multiform.

3. To save the Multiform, press F2 (SAVE), and respond 1: no to the prompt Do you want to save modified form under another name? (y/n). DataEase returns to the Form Definition menu. Press Esc (EXIT) to display the DataEase Main menu.

Viewing and Entering Data with a Multiform

Now that you have designed a Multiform that looks organized, you must test it to be certain that it actually works properly. You will use the new Multiform to view the records you already have entered and to add a few more records. In addition to observing your Multiform in action, you also will discover how you can look up information on-the-fly from related forms not included in the Multiform.

1. To access the Widget Order Multiform in Record Entry, select **2. Record Entry** from the DataEase Main menu. Then, choose 5: Widget Order from the window menu and press Enter. DataEase displays the Multiform, Widget Order, with no record on-screen.

2. As you would with any DataEase form, press F3 (VIEW) to display the first record in your data. Because Widget Order is the main form, DataEase displays the first record in that form's data, which is order 100. The subform has expanded to a length of four rows and displays all four items from order 100. At the bottom of the Multiform, DataEase calculates the Order Total by adding the values in the Total column of the subform (see fig. QS2.10).

Fig. QS2.10.

Viewing a record with the Multiform.

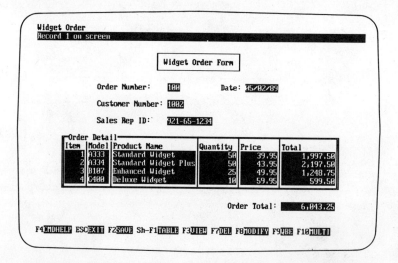

3. To view each of the other records, press F3 (VIEW) six more times, each time pausing long enough to make certain that the numbers really add up. Press F3 (VIEW) one more time to display a blank

form. DataEase beeps and displays the message No more records in the message area and the message No record on screen in the prompt line.

4. Now you can begin adding some new data using the Multiform. Starting in a blank form, with the cursor in the Order Number field, press Enter or Tab. Because Order Number is an automatic sequencing field, DataEase types the number *107* and moves the cursor to the Date field. Type the date *06/01/89* in the Date field and the cursor jumps to the Customer Number field.

5. You must enter the Customer Number for each transaction, but DataEase can give you some assistance, at least when the customer is already in the Retail Customer data. While the cursor is in the Customer Number field, press Ctrl-F10 (LOOKUP). DataEase displays a window menu on the right side of the screen listing the three relationships that you defined for Widget Order: 1: Sales Representative, 2: Retail Customer, and 3: Order Detail. Move the highlighted selection bar to 3: Retail Customer and press Enter. DataEase displays a window on the right side of the screen containing a list of the customers currently in the Retail Customer form data (see fig. QS2.11). This DataEase feature is called *dynamic lookup*. Use the down-arrow key to move down to Customer Number 1004, Sangster Insurance and press Enter. DataEase brings the Customer Number back to Widget Order and enters it into the Customer Number field. Press Enter or Tab to move to the Sales Rep ID field. Using a similar procedure, enter the Employee Number for Tim Jones (*230-76-2376*). Press Enter or Tab to move to the first field in the subform. DataEase displays the message New Sub Record on Line 1 of 0 in the prompt line.

6. This subform is in Table View. Each row represents a separate record in Order Detail. DataEase enters the order number *107* into the hidden Order Number field automatically. Type the number *1* in the Item field in the first row, and press Enter or Tab. Use the *dynamic lookup* feature, Ctrl-F10 (LOOKUP), to enter the model number for Standard Widget Plus (*A334*). Notice that DataEase fills in the Product Name and Price automatically. Press Enter or Tab to move to the Quantity field. Type the number *20* and press Enter or Tab. DataEase multiplies the Quantity by the Price and enters the result (*879.00*) into the Total column. The running total at the bottom of the form, the Order Total field, also reflects the total price of the first item in the order. Use a similar procedure to add two more items to order number *107*:

Item	Model	Product Name	Quantity
2	B107	Enhanced Widget	10
3	X155	Imperial Widget	5

Press F2 (SAVE) to save all the entries on the Multiform. DataEase
displays the message New Record Written in the message area,
informing you that the record is successfully saved to RAM. Press F5
(FORM CLEAR) to clear the form for the next order.

Fig. QS2.11.

*Performing a
dynamic lookup
from the Widget
Order Multiform to
the Retail Customer
form.*

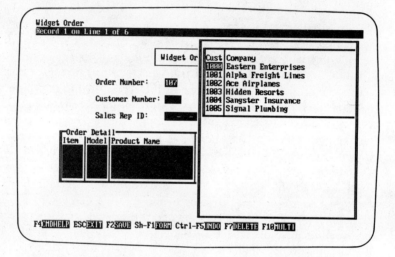

7. Use a similar procedure to enter the following orders:

    Order Number: 108
    Date: 06/05/89
    Customer Number: 1002
    Sales Rep ID: 921-65-1234

Item	Model	Product Name	Quantity
1	A333	Standard Widget	15
2	G400	Deluxe Widget	5

    Order Number: 109
    Date: 06/07/89
    Customer Number: 1001
    Sales Rep ID: 448-09-6721

Item	Model	Product Name	Quantity
1	G400	Deluxe Widget	25
2	B107	Enhanced Widget	30
3	A333	Standard Widget	50

Order Number: 110
Date: 06/15/89
Customer Number: 1000
Sales Rep ID: 987-31-9873

Item	Model	Product Name	Quantity
1	A333	Standard Widget	5
2	A334	Standard Widget Plus	5
3	B107	Enhanced Widget	5
4	C777	Jumbo Widget	5

Order Number: 111
Date: 06/21/89
Customer Number: 1004
Sales Rep ID: 230-76-2376

Item	Model	Product Name	Quantity
1	A334	Standard Widget Plus	15
2	B107	Enhanced Widget	10

Order Number: 112
Date: 06/26/89
Customer Number: 1001
Sales Rep ID: 448-09-6721

Item	Model	Product Name	Quantity
1	A333	Standard Widget	29

Order Number: 113
Date: 06/30/89
Customer Number: 1005
Sales Rep ID: 111-33-8491

Item	Model	Product Name	Quantity
1	B107	Enhanced Widget	17
2	G400	Deluxe Widget	8

After saving the last record, press Esc (EXIT) to return to the
DataEase Records menu. Press Esc (EXIT) and you are back at the
DataEase Main menu.

Generating Reports from a Multiform

Your Multiform works nicely for entering and viewing data. The next goal in the lesson is to use the Multiform data to create printed output. There are several ways to do this in DataEase. The simplest way is from Record Entry—in effect, printing the screen. This will give you a printed copy of the order form. You also can use the Quick Reports module to generate reports that use data from multiple records. You might want to generate a sales summary, for example. Finally, you can use the DQL to add features not available in Quick Reports. In this portion of the lesson, you will print a Widget Order record-entry screen, create a sales summary as a Quick Report, and then convert the Quick Report to a DQL procedure.

Printing the Record-Entry Screen

First, you will print a copy of the order form for order number 113 from Record Entry.

1. Start at the DataEase Main menu and select **2. Record Entry**. From the DataEase Records menu, choose the Widget Order form and press Enter. DataEase displays a blank order form.

2. To display order 113, press Alt-F5 (UNCHECKED), type *113* in the Order Number field, and then press F3 (VIEW). DataEase fills in the form with the values from order number 113.

3. Now you can print the order form. Make sure that your printer is on, connected to your computer, loaded with paper, and so on. Press Shift-F9 (PRINT). DataEase prints the order form, just as it appears on-screen, except that it does not print the blank rows in the subform.

Creating a Quick Report

Next, you will design a DataEase Quick Report that displays all the sales in the Widget Order data, grouped by sales representative, and sorted within each group by order number. You want to see the total sales for each sales representative and a grand total at the end of the report. You want also to see the order number, date, customer, and total for each order.

1. If you are still displaying the Widget Order record-entry screen, Press F9 (QBE) to display the QBE—Quick Reports menu. If you already returned to the DataEase Main menu, select **3. Query By Example—Quick Reports** to display the QBE—Quick Reports menu.

2. You want this sales report to include all the records in the data, so you can skip the *define record selection* step and go right to selecting fields. From the QBE—Quick Reports menu, choose **4. Define List Fields**. *Note:* If you returned to the DataEase Main menu before accessing Quick Reports, you also have to select the Multiform name, 5: Widget Order, from a window menu. DataEase displays the Field Selection screen—a copy of the Multiform.

3. Move the cursor to the Sales Rep ID field. You want this field to be included in the report. Press the space bar, and the number 1 appears, indicating that this is the first field selected for the report. To cause records to be grouped by the values in Sales Rep ID, type the word *group* to the right of the number 1.

4. Press Home to move to the Order Number field and press the space bar again. The number 2 will appear. To sort the records in each group by Order Number, type the word *order* in the Order Number field.

5. Press Enter or Tab to move the cursor to the Date field. Press the space bar, and the number 3 appears. Repeat this procedure for the Customer Number and Order Total fields. DataEase assigns them, respectively, the numbers 4 and 5.

6. You want a total of all the Order Totals, so type *sum* in the Order Total field, to the right of the list number 5. The completed Field Selection screen is shown in figure QS2.12.

Fig. QS2.12.

The Field Selection screen.

7. Press F2 (SAVE) or Esc (EXIT) to save the selections and return to the QBE—Quick Reports menu.

8. Next, you need to define the format of the report. Select **5. Define Format** from the QBE—Quick Reports menu. Choose 1: Columnar format type, and select 2: yes after the Do you want Group Headers and Trailers? prompt appears. DataEase displays the report format shown in figure QS2.13.

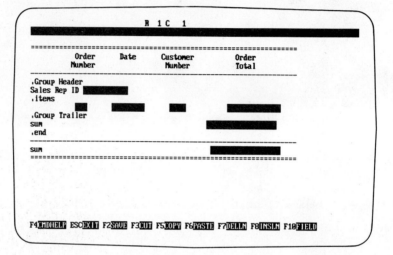

Fig. QS2.13.

The predefined columnar format, with group headers, group trailers, and sum fields.

9. Before you make any changes to the report format, you should test the report. Press F2 (SAVE) or Esc (EXIT) to return to the QBE—Quick Reports menu and select **1. Run Report**. The report looks similar to the report in figure QS2.14. Press the space bar to see the remainder of the report, including the grand total at the end. Press the space bar again to return to the QBE—Quick Reports menu.

Adding Fields from Related Forms

The report looks fairly good, but could stand a few improvements. It would be nice, for example, to see the names of the sales representatives and the customers in the report, rather than just identification numbers. You now will add the First Name field and the Last Name field to the report format, in place of the Sales Rep ID field. Similarly, you will add the Company field and remove the Customer Number field. You also will make

```
                              Running report
 SPACEorPgDn: Continue report EXIT: Abort report PgUp: Scroll

 ================================================================
        Order        Date     Customer        Order
        Number                Number          Total
 ----------------------------------------------------------------
 Sales Rep ID 111-33-8491
          103        05/12/89    1005           1,718.65
          113        06/30/89    1005           1,328.75
 SUM                                            3,047.40
 Sales Rep ID 129-08-4562
          104        05/15/89    1005           2,247.75
 SUM                                            2,247.75
 Sales Rep ID 230-76-2376
          107        06/01/89    1004           1,778.25
          111        06/21/89    1004           1,158.75
 SUM                                            2,937.00
 Sales Rep ID 329-76-2219
          101        05/08/89    1002           1,398.75
          105        05/16/89    1003           1,799.50
 SUM                                            3,197.25
 Sales Rep ID 448-09-6721
          109                    1001           4,994.75
 F4 CMDHELP  ESC EXIT  C:\DEDATA\        Order Tracking    08/10/89   1:13 pm
```

Fig. QS2.14.

The Quick Report using the predefined format.

a few adjustments to the appearance of the report, such as lining up the Order Total column, adding a line of hyphens above the group subtotal, inserting a blank line in the header, and adding a blank line in the trailer.

1. When you selected fields to include in this report, you did not include the sales representative's name or the customer's name. Indeed, these fields are not even in the Widget Order form. The sales representative's name consists of the First Name and the Last Name fields from the Sales Representative form. The customer's name is the Company field in the Retail Customer form. The easiest place to add these names to the report is on the Field Selection screen. From the QBE—Quick Reports menu, select **4. Modify List Fields** to display the Field Selection screen (see fig. QS2.12).

2. Press Tab or Enter until the cursor is in the Order Total field (this action helps DataEase "remember" how many fields already have been selected). Press F10 (MULTI) to see a window menu containing a list of available relationships, each of which you defined earlier in this lesson. Move the selection bar to 1: Sales Representative and press Enter. DataEase displays the Sales Representative form so that you can select the fields.

3. In the Sales Representative Field Selection screen, move the cursor to the First Name field and press the space bar. The number 6 appears, indicating that this is the sixth field selected for use in the current report. Press Tab or Enter to move the cursor to the Last Name field and press the space bar again. DataEase types the number 7 in the field. Press Esc (EXIT) to return to the Widget Order

screen. *Note:* Do not press F2 (SAVE), because it returns you to the QBE—Quick Reports menu. If you do press F2, by accident or by habit, just press 4 and modify List Fields again.

4. To select the Company field, press F10 (MULTI), and choose the relationship 2: Retail Customer. DataEase displays the Retail Customer screen. Press Tab or Enter to move the cursor to the Company field. Then, press the space bar. DataEase types the number 8. You have finished selecting fields, so press F2 (SAVE), returning to the QBE—Quick Reports menu.

5. Now that you have selected three additional fields, you must place them on the report format. From the QBE—Quick Reports menu, choose **5. Modify Format**. Respond 2: yes to the prompt Do you want to keep the existing report format?. DataEase redisplays the Format Definition screen containing the columnar report format (see fig. QS2.13).

6. First, move the cursor to R4C34, the letter N in the word Number. Because you are going to replace the Customer Number field with the Company field, this heading will not be accurate. Press the space bar six times to erase the word Number.

7. Next, move the cursor to position R7C10 and type a colon (:). The cursor is now at position R7C11, the first letter in the word ID. You are going to delete this word and the Sales Rep ID field to its right. Press F3 (CUT). Move the cursor past the end of the Sales Rep ID field to position R7C25 and press F3 (CUT) again. DataEase removes the word and the field and positions the cursor at position R7C11 again. Press the space bar once to move the cursor to R7C12.

8. Position the sales representative's first name here. Press F10 (FIELD) to display the Report Field Definition screen, as shown in figure QS2.15. DataEase displays a line menu containing the available fields, but not all choices are visible. Press F1 (MORE) to see the complete list and select 6: First Name. Text appears as the field type and 15 as the field length on the Report Field Definition screen. Move the cursor to the Supress Spaces field and change the response to 2: yes.

   This response suppresses any extra spaces between the First Name and Last Name fields. Press F2 (SAVE). DataEase saves the First Name field to the report format and returns to the Format Definition screen. The First Name field now appears to the right of the words Sales Rep:.

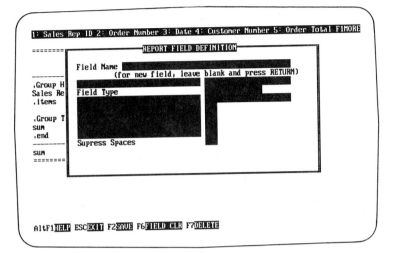

Fig. QS2.15.

The Report Field Definition screen.

9. Move the cursor to R7C28 and place the Last Name field by pressing F10 (FIELD) and selecting 7: Last Name from the line menu. DataEase displays the Report Field Definition screen. Press F2 (SAVE) to save the field definition and return to the Format Definition screen. Your screen should look like figure QS2.16.

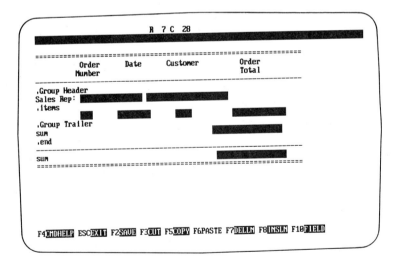

Fig. QS2.16.

Adding the sales representative's name.

10. Press Enter to place the cursor on the .items command, in row 8. Press F8 (INSLN) to insert a blank line. This Line will separate the header from the detail in the report output.

11. Move the cursor to R10C35, the Customer Number field. To delete this field, press F3 (CUT), move the cursor to R10C39, and press F3 (CUT) again. DataEase deletes the field and pulls the Order Total field to the left.

12. Use the left-arrow key to position the cursor at R10C30. To place the Company field here, press F10 (FIELD), and select 8: Company. DataEase displays the Report Field Definition screen, with the cursor in the field length space. Press F6 (FIELD CLEAR), to clear the current length. Type *18* as the new field length. Press F2 (SAVE) to save the definition and return to the Format Definition screen. Your Report Definition screen should appear similar to figure QS2.17.

Fig. QS2.17.

Adding the Company field.

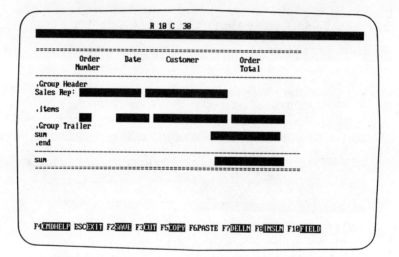

13. Move the cursor to position R12C1, to the letter s in the word sum. Type the word *Total*, replacing the word sum. Notice that the Order Total field on row 12, the group sum, is not properly aligned with the other fields in the column. Press the Insert key to toggle on Insert mode and press the space bar. This pushes the field over one space, lining it up vertically with the other two Order Total fields. Press F8 (INSLN) to insert a blank line at row 12. The Total line becomes row 13. Your screen should look like figure QS2.18.

14. Move the cursor to position R12C45. Type 17 hyphens (-) to create a line above the Order Total field that will contain the group total.

15. Position the cursor on the .end command (R14C1). Press F8 (INSLN) to insert another blank line.

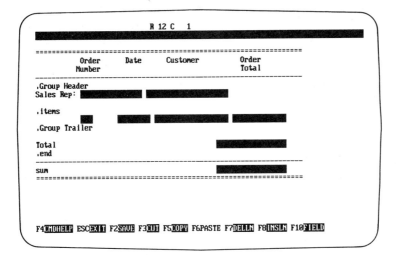

Fig. QS2.18.

Labeling the group sum.

16. Press the down-arrow key three times to position the cursor at R17C1. Type *Grand Total*, replacing the word sum. The completed report format is shown in figure QS2.19.

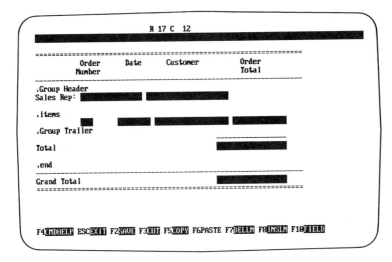

Fig. QS2.19.

The completed report format.

17. To save the form, press F2 (SAVE) or Esc (EXIT). DataEase saves the form and returns to the QBE—Quick Reports menu.

18. To run the report to screen again. Choose **1. Run Report** from the QBE—Quick Reports menu to see the report (see fig. QS2.20).

Fig. QS2.20.

The completed Quick
Report.

19. Now, change the output device to Printer. From the QBE—Quick
    Reports menu, select **6. Define Print Style** to display the Print Style
    Specification screen. Select 2: Printer as the Report Destination.
    Then, press F3 (DEFAULT VIEW) to retrieve the default printer
    settings from the System Configuration form. Save the new settings
    by pressing F2 (SAVE) or Esc (EXIT). Make sure that your printer is
    ready and run the report again. This time the report prints to your
    printer.

20. Save the report to disk. Select **7. Save Report** from the QBE—Quick
    Reports menu. Type *Widget Quick* as the report name and press
    Enter. DataEase saves the report, and again displays the QBE—Quick
    Reports menu. The prompt line includes the message Current
    report: Widget Quick. Press Esc (EXIT) to leave Quick Reports and
    return to the DataEase Main menu.

Creating a Menu

You have completed the design of your database, including a handy
Multiform, and a report. You are ready to tie everything together with a
menu system.

1. From the DataEase Main menu, select **5. Menu Definition**. DataEase
   displays the Menu Definition screen. Type the name *Widget Order* at
   the MENU NAME prompt and press Enter. Press Enter at the SECURITY
   LEVEL prompt to accept the default value, 7: Low3. The cursor moves
   to the MENU TITLE prompt.

2. Type the name *Widget Order* as the menu title and press Enter. The cursor moves to the CHOICE DESCRIPTION field (column) for menu choice number 1.

3. This first menu choice will be used to access the Widget Order Multiform in Record Entry. Type the choice description *Enter a Widget Order* and press Enter. DataEase moves the cursor to the FUNCTION TYPE field and displays a line menu that lists the available functions.

4. Select 3: record entry from the line menu. DataEase moves the cursor to the FUNCTION NAME field and displays a line menu containing a list of the available forms (and Multiform).

5. Choose Widget Order at the FUNCTION NAME field. DataEase moves the cursor to the CHOICE DESCRIPTION field for menu choice number 2.

6. Type *Print Company Sales Report* and press Enter. At the FUNCTION TYPE prompt, select 5: procedure. Then, at the FUNCTION NAME field, choose Widget Quick from the list of procedures/reports in the line menu (you may have to press F1 (MORE) to see it). DataEase moves the cursor to the third CHOICE DESCRIPTION field. The completed Menu Definition screen is shown in figure QS2.21.

Fig. QS2.21.

The Menu Definition screen.

7. To save the menu, press F2 (SAVE). Then, press Esc (EXIT) to return to the DataEase Main menu.

8. To see the menu in operation, you must define a new user for whom this menu is the *start-up menu*. From the DataEase Main menu, select **7. System Administration**. DataEase displays the Administration menu. Choose **1. Define Users** to display the User Information form.

9. Type a fictitious user name, *Menu Test*, and press Enter. Use the cursor-movement keys to move to the Start-up Menu: field, without filling in any other fields. Type *Widget Order* in the Start-up Menu: field. Press F2 (SAVE) to save the new user information. Press Esc (EXIT) twice to return to the DataEase Main menu.

10. To test the menu, exit from DataEase and then sign onto the Order Tracking database again as user *Menu Test* (no password). DataEase displays the menu you designed (see fig. QS2.22). Test each option and then press Esc (EXIT) to leave DataEase.

Fig. QS2.22.

The Widget Order menu.

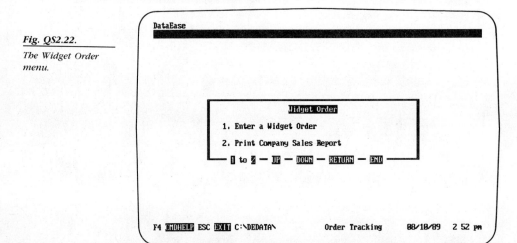

Summary

This lesson has given you a first-hand look at many of the features discussed in Part II of this book. You have designed and built a DataEase *Multiform* and have used the Multiform to enter and to view records. You also generated a Quick Report that uses data from the Multiform. Finally, you tied the entire lesson together with a custom DataEase menu. Turn now to Chapter 6 for a full discussion of using related DataEase forms and then explore the remainder of Part II in which you begin to master the real power of DataEase.

Using Related
DataEase Forms

Part II of this book, "Intermediate DataEase," builds upon the many fundamental concepts presented in Part I that now have become familiar to you. This first chapter of Part II explains more fully several important concepts that have been held in abeyance. But, now that you are fully armed with a good understanding of basic database/DataEase terminology, you are ready to learn how to tap the real power of DataEase.

DataEase is one of several popular database programs whose design is based on the *relational model*. As explained in Chapter 2, forms in a DataEase database can be *related* one to another. DataEase enables you to use data from any number of related DataEase forms at the same time, almost as easily as you can use data from one form. This chapter explains how to define a *relationship* between two DataEase forms and then explores the many benefits of doing so.

Read this chapter to learn how to create and use DataEase *Multiforms*, a feature that is new in DataEase 4.0. Multiforms enable you to work with data from several related forms on the screen at the same time in ways that would require complex programming in most other popular database programs. You learn how to design and build Multiforms and how to use them for entering, viewing, and editing data. You also are introduced to DataEase's other powerful multiple-form Record Entry features: *Multiview*, *Ad-Hoc Multiform*, and *Dynamic Lookup*. Finally, the last portion of the chapter integrates many of the concepts presented so far in the book by discussing how to use related forms and Multiforms to generate DataEase Quick Reports. When you are finished with this chapter, you will be ready to begin working with the DataEase Query Language discussed in Chapter 7.

235

Defining DataEase Relationships

To use many of DataEase's most powerful features, you must first explicitly define the relationships between forms in your database. Therefore, developing an understanding of how DataEase forms are related one to another is important.

Understanding Forms' Relationships

As suggested in Chapter 2, a simple rule of thumb is that two forms are "naturally" related when they each have at least one field with the same name, often called a *link* between the forms. In this sense, the Widget Order and Retail Customer forms are *linked* by the Customer Number field; Widget Order and Sales Representative are linked by the Sales Rep ID field; Widget Order and Order Detail are linked by the Order Number field and Order Detail and Product are linked by the Model Number field.

> Forms may be related by multiple link fields, but for the sake of clarity, this chapter discusses only related forms with a single link field.

When you use related DataEase forms, you are really interested in how particular records are related. More precisely, a specific record in a form is related to one or more records in another form when the value in its link field *matches* (is the same as) the value of the link field in the related form. Indeed, DataEase refers to the field that links related forms as the *match* field.

A record from Widget Order is *related* to a record from the Retail Customer form when the values in the respective Customer Number fields *match*. Figure 6.1 shows the Widget Order record for order number 100. The Customer Number field in that record contains the number 1002. Through the Ad-Hoc Multiform feature (discussed later in this chapter), you see that this number corresponds to the record for Ace Airplanes in the Retail Customer data, which contains the same value in the Customer Number field. The Widget Order for order number 100 therefore is related to the Ace Airplane record in the Retail Customer form.

DataEase enables you to work with many related forms at once but requires that you first explicitly define the match field(s) between each pair of forms. This procedure is called defining the relationship between the forms. In fact, DataEase enables you to define relationships between forms even when you haven't used exactly the same field name in each of the related forms. However, giving link fields the same name in both related forms is usually less confusing.

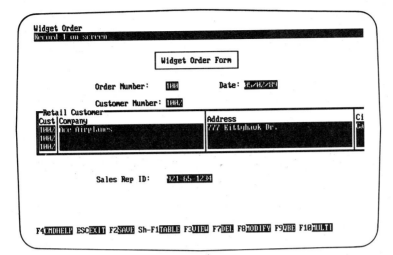

Fig. 6.1.

The Widget Order record for order number 100 and the related Retail Customer record for Ace Airplanes.

Because information can be related in many different ways in real life, defining a few terms to describe form relationships may be helpful. For instance, when the value of a form's match field can occur only once in the form data—such as each value in the Customer Number field in the Retail Customer form—the form is said to be on the *one-side* of the relationship. When the data in a match field is not necessarily unique—the Customer Number field in the Widget Order form, for example—it is called the *many-side* of the relationship. Therefore, a *one-to-many* relationship exists between Retail Customer and Widget Order. In other words, you enter data about a customer only once but then use it many times in processing orders.

The relationship between two forms is expressed from the point of view of one of the forms. This form is referred to as the *primary* form. The other form is called the *secondary* form. For example, if you consider Widget Order as the primary form, the relationship between Widget Order and Customer can be described as a *many-to-one* relationship. Four types of relationships are possible:

❏ *One-to-one.* A unique field in the primary form is linked to a unique field in the secondary form. One record in the primary form corresponds to one and only one record in the secondary form.

❏ *One-to-many.* A unique field in the primary form is linked to a non-unique field in the secondary form. One record in the primary form links to a group of records in the secondary form.

❏ *Many-to-one.* A non-unique field in the primary form is linked to a unique field in the secondary form. A group of records in the primary form corresponds to only one record in the secondary form.

❏ *Many-to-many*. A non-unique field in the primary form is linked to a non-unique field in the secondary form. A group of records in the primary form corresponds to a group of records in the secondary form.

Relational database systems in general and DataEase in particular can be used most effectively if you avoid designing many-to-many relationships into your database. DataEase provides several methods of displaying data from multiple forms on the same screen as long as their relationship is one-to-one, one-to-many, or many-to-one. However, the program cannot display all related records in a many-to-many relationship on-screen.

Recognizing Relationships

As you work with multiple forms, DataEase does not automatically recognize the relationship between forms. You have to explicitly define the relationships in each database in a system-supplied form called the Relationships form. Therefore, you must have a clear understanding of how the forms in your database should be related, and you must have properly structured the forms for the necessary links to do the job efficiently. The following guidelines will help you:

❏ A match field to which you have assigned the unique characteristic in the form definition is a one-side match field. A one-side match field should be indexed.

❏ A match field to which you do not assign the unique characteristic is a many-side match field. A many-side match field does not have to be indexed.

The forms used as examples in this book have the following relationships:

Forms	Relationship
Widget Order-to-Order Detail	One-to-many
Widget Order-to-Retail Customer	Many-to-one
Widget Order-to-Sales Representative	Many-to-one
Order Detail-to-Product	Many-to-one
Widget Order-to-Product	Many-to-many

In each case, the one-side match fields are indexed: the Order Number field in Widget Order, the Customer Number field in Retail Customer, the Sales Rep ID field in Sales Representative, and the Model Number field in Product. Through the respective index files, DataEase is able to retrieve the related records from each of these forms quickly and efficiently.

The most difficult relationship to understand is between Widget Order and Product. Each order a customer places for widgets can potentially include more than one product, and each product can be found in more than one order. This situation meets the definition of a many-to-many relationship. To avoid dealing with this relationship directly, the Order Detail table was created to buffer, or link, the two tables together.

At times you may want to see information from both Product and Widget Order—the many-to-many related forms—on-screen together. For instance, as you enter a new order for widgets into the database, you naturally want to see the model number, product name, and price of each of the widgets ordered on the same screen with the order number, date, customer number, and sales representative's number (Sales Rep ID).

However, the Product Name field and the Price field appear only in the Product form, and the Customer Number and Sales Rep ID fields appear in the Widget Order form. Fortunately, DataEase permits use of multiple levels of relationships when displaying data from several forms through the Multiforms and Multiview features. Widget Order is related to Order Detail, and Order Detail is related to Product. Through a series of matching fields, all the related information can be displayed together on-screen at the same time.

Using the Relationships Form

After you have designed and built your database, and you recognize the relationships between the various DataEase forms, you have to formalize these relationships on the system-supplied Relationships form. DataEase automatically builds a Relationships form for each database you create. Each relationship you define becomes a record in this form. You must define the relationship between DataEase forms before you can use the data from the forms together on the same screen or in the same report.

To define a relationship on the Relationships form, from the DataEase Main menu, select **1. Form Definition and Relationships** to display the Form Definition menu. Then select **3. Define Relationships**, and DataEase displays the Relationships form, similar to figure 6.2, with the cursor at the Form 1: prompt.

While the cursor is in the first field of the Relationships form, DataEase displays a list of the available forms in the database as a line menu. Select the name of one of the related forms from this list. For example, to define the relationship between Widget Order and Order Detail, you select 4: Widget Order. DataEase places the form's name in the first field and moves the cursor to the entry space to the right of the following prompt:

```
If Form 1 is Subform, how should Key
field  be  updated when Main form Key
is modified:
```

This field is new in DataEase 4.2 and is referred to in this book as a *referential integrity* field. The field becomes significant when you use the two forms in the relationship in a Multiform. The purpose and use of this prompt are discussed in "Editing Multiform Records—Ensuring Referential Integrity," later in this chapter. For now, press Tab to move the cursor to the & Form 2: prompt.

When the cursor is in the space to the right of the & Form 2: prompt, the line menu again displays the list of available forms.

Fig. 6.2.

The Relationships form.

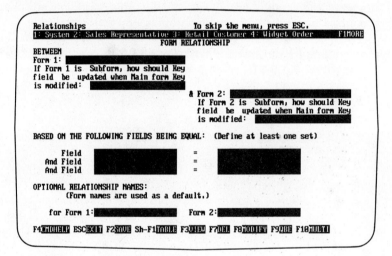

> **Tip:** You also can access the Relationships form through the DataEase Records menu. First, select **2. Record Entry** from the DataEase Main menu, and then select 1: System from the DataEase Records menu. DataEase displays a second list of forms, shown in figure 6.3. Choose 5: Relationships. DataEase then displays the Relationships form.

Now, choose the other related form from the line menu. If you cannot see the name of the form listed in the menu, press F1 (MORE) and then select the form from the window menu. For instance, you can choose 5: Order Detail. DataEase enters the second form's name and moves the cursor to the entry space to the right of the following prompt:

```
If Form 2 is Subform, how should Key
field  be  updated when Main form Key
is modified:
```

6.3.

DataEase
rds menu list of
m forms.

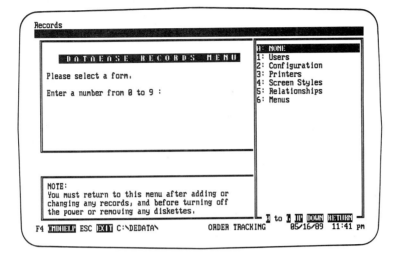

```
 Records
┌─────────────────────────────────────────────────────────────────────┐
│                                                                       │
│   ┌──────────────────────────────────────┐ ┌──────────────────────┐  │
│   │                                        │ │0: NONE               │  │
│   │    D A T A E A S E   R E C O R D S   M E N U │ │1: Users              │  │
│   │                                        │ │2: Configuration      │  │
│   │  Please select a form.                 │ │3: Printers           │  │
│   │                                        │ │4: Screen Styles      │  │
│   │  Enter a number from 0 to 9 :          │ │5: Relationships      │  │
│   │                                        │ │6: Menus              │  │
│   │                                        │ │                      │  │
│   │                                        │ │                      │  │
│   │                                        │ │                      │  │
│   │ ┌─────────────────────────────────────│ │                      │  │
│   │ │NOTE:                                 │ │                      │  │
│   │ │You must return to this menu after adding or │ │               │  │
│   │ │changing any records, and before turning off │ │               │  │
│   │ │the power or removing any diskettes. │ └─ 0 to 6  UP DOWN RETURN ─┘ │
│   └──────────────────────────────────────┘                          │
│   F4 MINIHELP  ESC EXIT  C:\DEDATA\         ORDER TRACKING   05/16/89  11:41 pm │
└─────────────────────────────────────────────────────────────────────┘
```

Refer to "Editing Multiform Records—Ensuring Referential Integrity," later
in this chapter, for a description of the purpose and use of this second
referential integrity field. For now, press Tab to move the cursor to the
first space to the right of the Field prompt, to the left of the first equal
sign. This line defines the match fields between the forms.

The line menu is now a list of the fields from the first form. You select the
match field from the line menu. DataEase types the field name, moves to
the right of the equal sign, and lists the second form's fields as a line
menu. You choose the second form's match field. DataEase types the field
name and moves the cursor to the next line. For example, if you are
defining a relationship between Widget Order and Order Detail, you select
the Order Number field as the match field on both sides of the equal sign.

DataEase permits you to use as many as three match fields in a relationship
definition. If you use all three fields, the records in the two forms are
related only when the three fields match.

You also can assign a special name to the relationship. By default, you refer
to the relationship by the names of the forms involved. For example, when
working with the Widget Order form in a Multiform or report definition,
you refer to the relationship with the Order Detail form as the Order
Detail relationship. Similarly, when working with the Order Detail form,
the same relationship is called the Widget Order relationship.

Alternatively, you can fill in the last line of the Relationships form with
optional relationship names that you then can use in place of the form
names. For example, you can type *Widget Transaction* as the optional
name for both form 1 and form 2, and then refer to the Widget Order-to-
Order Detail relationship as the Widget Transaction relationship.

Finally, to save the relationship, you press F2 (SAVE). Because this screen
is actually a system-supplied DataEase record-entry form, it works the same

as any other form during Record Entry. The screen contains one record for each relationship you define in the database. After saving the record currently displayed on the form, you have a choice of pressing F5 (FORM CLEAR) and entering another new relationship or pressing Esc (EXIT) twice to return to the Form Definition menu. If you do the latter, then you press Esc (EXIT) again to return to the DataEase Main menu.

Whenever you want to modify a relationship definition, use the techniques and procedures described in Chapter 4 for viewing and editing existing records.

Tip: The Relationships form sometimes can be conveniently displayed as a table. Press Shift-F1 (TABLE) and DataEase displays the currently defined relationships in Table View. You can scroll through, edit, and add to this table in the same manner as any DataEase form data in Table View.

Creating Multiforms

Arguably, the most significant new feature in DataEase is its Multiform capability. A Multiform is a record-entry form that enables you to enter and view records from multiple forms simultaneously on one screen. Designing this type of form with DataEase takes just a few keystrokes but would take pages of programming code to accomplish using more traditional database programs. DataEase is not the only program that boasts this cutting-edge technology, but the DataEase implementation is by far the easiest to understand and use.

Taking Preliminary Steps

You must take a number of steps to prepare for building a Multiform. You already know how to perform these steps; you just need to learn the proper sequence.

As always, the first step is to design your database and identify the relationships between the forms. Decide which form contains data that is most central to the database—usually the form that is related to the greatest number of other forms. For instance, the Widget Order form is the focal point of the Order Tracking database. You have to add a record to this form every time an order is placed. This form also is related to the Order Detail, Retail Customer, and Sales Representative forms. This central or *master* form becomes the *main* form in the Multiform definition. Always use the form on the one-side of a relationship as the main form.

Next, you must define each individual form using the procedures described in Chapters 2 and 3. As you define the form that you have identified as the main form, keep in mind that you will be adding fields from other forms, called *subforms*, later. Fields from two different forms cannot be placed on the same line in the Form Definition screen, so start planning where you may want to place subform fields. Figure 6.4 shows the Widget Order form. Notice that its fields take approximately half of the screen, leaving plenty of room for fields from subforms. You can add up to 32 subforms to one Multiform.

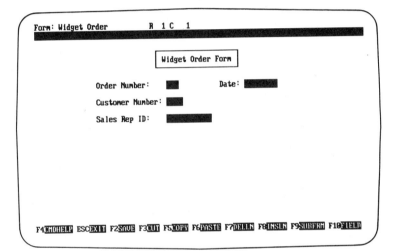

Fig. 6.4.

The Widget Order form.

The final preliminary step is to define the relationship between each subform and the main form. This step is necessary before you can add any of the subform's fields to the Multiform. For instance, if you want to add fields from the Order Detail form, the Retail Customer form, and the Sales Representative form to Widget Order, you must first define the relationships between Widget Order and each of the other forms.

Selecting the Relationship

To build a Multiform, first display the main form in the Form Definition screen. Then, move the cursor to the row on the form where you want a subform to be inserted. Press F9 (SUBFORM), and DataEase displays the Subform Definition screen, a window in the center of the work area, as shown in figure 6.5.

The cursor is in a field to the right of the prompt Relationship Name. DataEase displays a line menu containing a list of the available relationships. You may have to press F1 (MORE) to see a complete list.

Choose, from the line menu, the name of the relationship that links the main form to the desired subform. This is normally the name of the subform itself. If you assigned an optional name to a relationship, you can choose that name instead of the subform name.

Specifying the Number of Records

The second prompt on the Subform Definition screen asks for the `No. of Rows Minimum`. This number determines the lowest number of related records from the subform to be displayed in the Multiform. The number

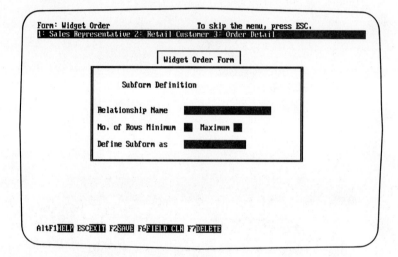

Fig. 6.5.

The Subform Definition screen.

you type here should be based on the type of relationship that exists between the main form and the subform. When the subform is a one-side field, you type the number *1* and press Enter. When the subform is a many-side form, you can type any whole number from *1* to *99*. Whenever you use this Multiform for entering, viewing, and editing records, DataEase always provides space for the specified minimum number of subform records. When the number of actual matching records is less than this minimum, the remaining space remains blank.

After specifying the minimum number of records, you also indicate the `Maximum` number. Again, for a one-side field, the maximum number of subform records is always *1*, but for a many-side field, the maximum can be up to *99*. When you specify a higher value for the `Maximum` field than you did for the `Minimum` field, DataEase always displays the minimum number of records and then adds records as necessary up to the specified maximum.

Selecting the View

At the last field on the Subform Definition screen, you choose whether you want the subform fields displayed in Table View, in Form View, or in a custom format that you design. When the cursor is in the field to the right of the prompt Define Subform as, the line menu contains three options: 1: Automatic Table, 2: Automatic Form, and 3: Custom Form. The effect of each of these options is explained in the sections that follow. After you select the subform view, press F2 (SAVE) to complete the subform definition.

Whenever DataEase places fields from a subform on the Form Definition screen, they appear as highlighted bars, just as main form fields do. In order to determine the identity of any subform field, you can move the cursor to the field and press the space bar. DataEase displays, in the prompt line, the name of the subform followed by a colon (:) and the field name. For example, the Company field from Retail Customer is displayed as Retail Customer: Company.

Selecting Table View

Select 1: Automatic Table at the Define Subform as prompt, on the Subform Definition screen, to display the related subform record or records in Table View. This view is ideal when the subform is on the many-side of a one-to-many relationship. DataEase displays a table with the number of rows determined by the values you specified as the Minimum and Maximum number of rows. Press F2 (SAVE), and DataEase inserts a row of the subform in Table View. The table consists of a single row containing all the fields from the subform (see the following tip), a row of field name headings, and a double line border (see fig. 6.7).

Tip: When you define a form that you plan to use as a subform, you should assign the *hide-from-table-view* characteristic to the match field that links this form to the main form. The match field is already on the Multiform as one of the fields in the main form. With this characteristic assigned, if you display the subform in Table View, DataEase knows not to display the match field again.

This trick provides the same benefit even if you never create a Multiform *per se* but occasionally use the ad-hoc Multiform feature also discussed in this chapter. You can use this technique to prevent any field from appearing in a subform Table View, not just to match fields.

The Widget Order form (see fig. 6.4), for instance, doesn't look much like an order form since the detail of the order—the widgets being ordered—is not shown. The Multiform feature, however, enables you to display the master Widget Order record and the detail records from Order Detail all on the same screen.

To do so, place the cursor wherever you want the new subform rows to start and press F9 (SUBFORM). Next, specify 3: Order Detail as the relationship. Assuming that most orders are for no more than 4 types of widgets, specify 4 as both the minimum and maximum number of rows. Finally, select 1: Automatic Table as the subform view. Press F2 (SAVE) and DataEase adds all the fields from the subform to the Form Definition screen, starting at column 1.

You often will want to use the Insert mode to push the four rows of the table (field row, heading row, and two border rows) to the right so that the table appears in the center of the screen. You now can use this form to enter, view, and edit records from both Widget Order and Order Detail.

On color systems, DataEase changes the foreground color and sometimes (depending on the capabilities of your display adapter) the background color of the subform area. Monochrome systems display the text in high intensity. This new color scheme (for example, black on cyan on a VGA screen) is temporary, visible only while on the Form Definition screen. Screen colors return to the usual screen style whenever you use the Multiform for adding, viewing, or editing data.

Selecting Form View

When you want to display the subform in Form View, choose 2: Automatic Form. This option works best when the subform is on the one-side of a relationship. Press F2 (SAVE), and DataEase places a copy of all fields from the subform in Form View on the Form Definition screen.

Tip: You should delete the subform match field from the Multiform. It always will contain the same value as the corresponding match field in the main form, making it unnecessary and possibly confusing. Use F3 (CUT).

For example, in order to see the customer's name, address, and phone number on the Widget Order screen, place the cursor at the position where you want to see the fields from Retail Customer, perhaps just below the Customer Number field, and press F9 (SUBFORM). DataEase displays the Subform Definition screen.

First, select 2: Retail Customer relationship. Then, because only one record from Retail Customer corresponds to a single Widget Order record (Retail Customer is on the one-side), specify 1 for both the minimum and maximum number of rows (records). Finally, select 2: Automatic Form at the Define Subform as prompt, and press F2 (SAVE) to return to the Form Definition screen.

DataEase inserts, at the cursor, the entire Retail Customer form, all the text, and every field from the form definition. You then can delete the blank lines and unnecessary text so that Multiform is still a single screen in length. You also can delete the Retail Customer: Customer Number field, because its value duplicates the main form's Customer Number field. Figure 6.7 shows the result. Note that the Long:Comments fields from Retail Customer have been removed not only to save space, but because they may contain notes you do not want displayed every time you enter, view, or edit an order.

On systems with color displays, DataEase uses a different foreground color for text in the subform area and perhaps (depending on the capabilities of your display adapter) a different background color. On a monochrome system, the subform text appears in a higher intensity. These color variations are intended only to make it easier for you to identify the subform area(s) on the Form Definition screen. During Record Entry, screen colors return to the screen style selected in the System Configuration form unless you specifically use one of the methods described in Chapter 3 for adding color to the subform area of the form.

Creating a Custom View

Choose 3: Custom Form at the Define Subform as prompt on the Subform Definition screen to indicate that you want to place subform fields onto the Form Definition screen manually. This option is especially suitable for placing a small number of subform fields into the Multiform. After selecting this option, press F2 (SAVE) to return to the Form Definition screen. DataEase displays the prompt line Move cursor to end of table and press F9. (This prompt means that you should move the cursor to the end of the subform area and press F9.

Use the down-arrow key to move down at least one row. Allow as many rows as you think you will need for the subform fields. Press F9 to indicate the end of the custom subform area. In order to make room for the subform, DataEase may have to insert one or more blank lines on a color screen; the subform area will appear highlighted in blue. Type any text that you would like included in the subform area of the form.

Finally, to place an actual subform field on the Multiform, position the cursor at the position where you want the field to appear and press F10 (FIELD). DataEase displays a window in the center of the screen that prompts, Select Existing Field as shown in figure 6.6, and the line menu lists all the available fields from the subform. Choose one of the fields and press F2 (SAVE). DataEase places the field on-screen, starting at the cursor position.

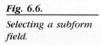

Fig. 6.6.

Selecting a subform field.

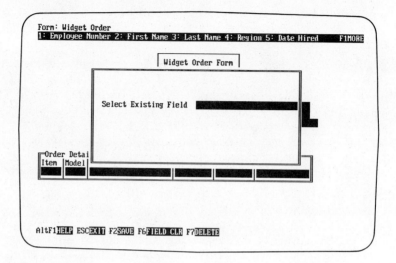

For example, the Widget Order form shown in figure 6.4 would be more informative if it displayed the sales representative's name (the First Name and Last Name fields from the Sales Representative form) as well as the sales representative's identification number (the Sales Rep ID field). To display this information, first position the cursor in the row where you want the two fields to be located, probably just below the Sales Rep ID field. Press F9 (SUBFORM). DataEase displays the Subform Definition screen.

Next, choose 1: Sales Representative from the line menu in order to specify the relationship. This relationship, between Widget Order and Sales Representative, is many-to-one, many orders to each customer. Therefore, you specify *1* as both the minimum and maximum number of rows.

In the last field of the Subform Definition screen, choose 3: Custom Form, and press F2 (SAVE) to return to the Form Definition screen. DataEase prompts you to move to the cursor to the end of the subform area (table) and press F9. Press the down-arrow key at least once and then press F9. DataEase inserts sufficient space to accommodate the subform area.

Next, type *Name:* in the subform area. Then, to place the First Name field with the cursor in the subform area to the right of the word Name:, press F10 (FIELD). DataEase prompts you to select a field from the list of subform fields listed in the line menu (see fig. 6.6). Choose 2: First Name and press F2 (SAVE). DataEase adds the First Name field to the form. You then can move the cursor to the right of this new subform field and add the Last Name field in a similar manner. Figure 6.7 includes these two fields from the Sales Representative form. Now, when you enter a sales representative's identification number in the Sales Rep ID field, his or her name is displayed in these subform fields.

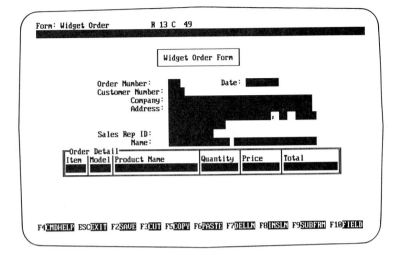

```
Form: Widget Order          R 13 C  49

                    ┌─────────────────┐
                    │ Widget Order Form │
                    └─────────────────┘
         Order Number:          Date:
         Customer Number:
              Company:
              Address:

         Sales Rep ID:
              Name:
     ┌Order Detail───────────────────────────────────────┐
     │Item │Model│Product Name      │Quantity│Price│Total │
     │     │     │                  │        │     │      │

  F4 CMDHELP  ESC EXIT  F2 SAVE  F3 CUT  F5 COPY  F6 PASTE  F7 DELLN  F8 INSLN  F9 SUBFRM  F10 FIELD
```

Fig. 6.7.

The Widget Order Multiform in the Form Definition screen with subform fields from Retail Customer, Sales Representative, and Order Detail.

As described in the preceding section, if you are using a color screen, DataEase uses a different foreground color for text in the subform area and perhaps (depending on the capabilities of your display adapter) a different background color. On a monochrome system, the subform text appears in a higher intensity. These color variations are intended only to make it easier for you to identify the subform area(s) on the Field Definition screen. During Record Entry, screen colors return to the screen style selected in the System Configuration form.

Modifying and Enhancing a Multiform

After you have added a subform to a form definition, creating a Multiform, you can still apply most of the modifications and enhancements described in Chapter 3. The main form portions of the Multiform can be modified as usual. In the subform areas, you can add and delete text and fields. You cannot, however, directly modify the definition of any subform field from within the Multiform's Form Definition screen. Instead, you must first display the definition of the subform and then make any desired modification. Any changes you make to the definition of the subform field are reflected in the Multiform the next time you use it.

On the other hand, if you add a field to the subform's definition, the field is not included in the Multiform. You have to add it manually if you want it to be displayed in the Multiform. The procedure for adding a subform field to the Multiform is described in the preceding section, "Creating a Custom View."

Printing a Multiform Definition

As when defining any form, you should always create a hard copy of the Multiform definition. To print a DataEase Multiform definition, first make sure that your printer is turned on and connected, and that it has paper, a ribbon, and all the other essentials. Then, from the Form Definition screen, press Shift-F9 (PRINT). DataEase prints the definition, including a picture of the form layout and a list of field definitions from the main form and all subforms.

The field definition list shows the status of the following characteristics: field name, field type, field length, required, indexed, unique, derived, range (upper/lower limit), prevent entry, and hide from Table View. The printed definition also shows the size and offset (in bytes) of each field, as well as the size of each record. Finally, it shows the total amount of memory (RAM) required by the form.

Creating Relational Statistical Derived Fields

Chapter 3 introduced you to the concept of derivation formulas and explained how to create derived fields. Among other topics, that chapter explained how to create a field whose value is derived from a matching record in another related form. The derivation formula for this type of field uses the *lookup* operator.

DataEase also enables you to construct a field whose value is derived from multiple matching records. The derivation formula for this type of field uses one of the *relational statistical operators*. A relational statistical operator not only *looks up* values from a related form but also performs a statistical operation on the data. The syntax for this type of operator is as follows:

operator RELATIONSHIP fieldname

RELATIONSHIP is the name of a relationship, and fieldname is the name of a field in the related form. The following five relational operators are available for use in a derivation formula:

❏ *count of*—counts the number of matching records in a related form.

❏ *highest of*—returns the highest value in the specified field from among the matching records in the related form.

❏ *lowest of*—selects the lowest value in the specified field from the matching related records.

❑ *sum of*—calculates the arithmetic sum of the field's values in the matching related records.

❑ *mean of*—produces the arithmetic mean (average) of the values in the specified field in the matching related records.

You can use relational operators in derivation formulas whether or not you also define a subform. Relational operators are, however, often used in conjunction with subforms, especially when the subform contains multiple matching records. They enable you to build a formula that performs calculations across multiple records in a related form.

The Widget Order Multiform shown in figure 6.7, for example, could use a field that displays the total price of all the widgets ordered. The Total field in the Order Detail subform shows the product of Quantity times Price for each type of widget ordered by the customer but does not show a grand total. The *sum of* relational operator is perfect for adding an Order Total field.

To create such a field, first position the cursor below the Order Detail subform and type a label for the field, *Order Total* for instance. Then, press F10 (FIELD). DataEase picks up the label as the field name. You then define the field as a fixed point field, using the following derivation formula:

    sum of "ORDER DETAIL" Total

This formula calculates the arithmetic sum (total) of the values in the Total field in the matching records from Order Detail. (The relationship name, Order Detail, is enclosed in double quotation marks because it contains a space.) The match field between Widget Order and Order Detail is the Order Number field. Thus, this formula calculates a sum of the Total field for all the records in Order Detail with the same order number. Figure 6.8 shows the completed Widget Order form that includes the Order Total field.

Figure 6.9 shows the same form in Record Entry, displaying data relating to Order Number 100. Notice that information is displayed from the Widget Order, Retail Customer, Sales Representative, and Order Detail forms. In addition, two of the fields from Order Detail—Product Name and Price—are actually *looked up* from the Product form. Literally pages of programming code would be required to duplicate the effect of this form if you used many of the best known database programs.

Fig. 6.8.

The completed Widget Order Multiform, including the relational statistical field Order Total.

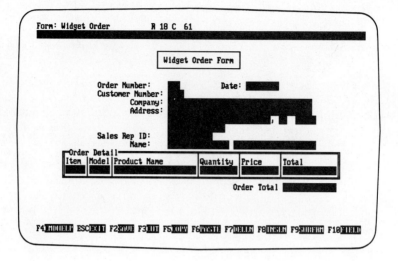

Fig. 6.9.

Using the Multiform to view information relating to order number 100.

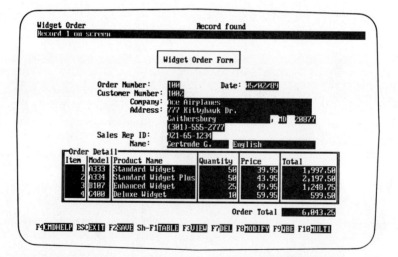

Tip: As with any derived field, you should never permit the user to enter a value in a relational statistical field. You should at least assign the prevent data-entry attribute. An often better choice, however, is to assign the virtual characteristic to this type of field; that is, select 3: yes, and do not save (virtual) at the Prevent Data-entry prompt on the Field Definition screen. DataEase then recalculates the value of the derived field each time it is used, thus always reflecting the current values in the related records.

Entering, Editing, Viewing, and Printing Data in a Multiform

The procedures for entering, editing, viewing, and printing records in a Multiform during Record Entry combine methods you have already learned. Chapter 4 described the procedure for using Record Entry with a single form as well as the differences between using Form View and using Table View. You draw on all of these techniques when you use a Multiform during Record Entry because a Multiform may have Form View and Table View areas on the same screen.

Accessing a Multiform in Record Entry

To access a DataEase Multiform for the purpose of entering, editing, viewing, or printing records, start from the DataEase Main menu and select **2. Record Entry**. DataEase displays the Records menu. Select the name of the Multiform from the window menu, and DataEase displays the Multiform with all fields blank and the cursor resting in the first field. In the title area, at the top left of the screen, DataEase displays the form name. The message No record on screen appears in the prompt line.

Entering New Records in a Multiform

You enter new records in a Multiform in much the same manner as with any other DataEase form, as described in Chapter 4. You can use the Form View cursor movement keys (listed in Chapter 4 in table 4.1) to move around the Multiform unless the cursor is in a tabular subform area (that is, a subform area displayed in Table View).

If the cursor is in a tabular subform area, use the Table View cursor-movement keys (see table 4.3 in Chapter 4). In a tabular subform area, when all the rows are filled, press End. DataEase scrolls several records off the screen to display more blank rows. As you move the cursor from field to field on the Multiform, DataEase displays status messages in the prompt line that inform you when the cursor is in a subform field.

You can use the arrow keys to move between main form fields and subform fields, just as you do in a standard record-entry form. DataEase 4.01, however, provides a quicker way to move around the multiform.

When the cursor is in a main form field, do the following:

❑ Press Ctrl-PgDn to move the cursor to the last saved record in the first subform below the cursor.

❏ Press Ctrl-PgUp to move the cursor to the last saved record in the first subform above the cursor.

When the cursor is in a subform field, do the following:

❏ Press Ctrl-PgDn to move the cursor to the first main form field below the cursor or to the last saved record in the first subform below the cursor, whichever comes first.

❏ Press Ctrl-PgUp to move the cursor to the first main form field above the cursor or to the last saved record in the first subform above the cursor, whichever comes first.

Press F2 (SAVE) to save the record. Even if the cursor happens to be in a subform field when you save the record, DataEase saves all values from every field on the form to their respective main form and subform data files. You can then press F5 (FORM CLEAR) to display a blank form for the next record.

Viewing Records in a Multiform

The procedure for viewing records in a Multiform is the same as the procedure for viewing records in a regular record-entry form, described in Chapter 4. Keep in mind, however, that only search criteria placed in a main form field are used to find a particular record; any criteria placed in a subform field is ignored.

Editing Multiform Records—Ensuring Referential Integrity

A Multiform is often more than just a convenient way to enter data into multiple forms, bringing together all the essential information in your database about a particular entity or event. It can depict in one screen (or series of screens) the relationships between all the forms in the database.

In the Order Tracking example, each record in the Widget Order Multiform contains all the essential information about a single order for widgets. It displays information from the Retail Customer, Sales Representative, Order Detail, and Product forms, and of course the Widget Order form. In other words, it shows information about the order from every form in the database.

DataEase Multiforms provide an incredibly easy way to pull related information together but not without potential pitfalls. Entering a new record using a DataEase Multiform is practically foolproof; DataEase stores the data in the appropriate files according to the links you explicitly establish.

However, the process of making changes to this data and the steps required to delete Multiform records are not quite as straightforward. The source of strength in a relational database—the capability of linking forms through match fields—can prove to be a serious weakness if the match fields are not properly maintained. The process of maintaining the correct relationship between particular records in a database is sometimes referred to as ensuring *referential integrity*.

To ensure that related records stay related, observe the following rules:

1. Each Multiform record must be unique.

2. When modifying a Multiform record,

   ❏ If the relationship between the main form and a subform is one-to-many or one-to-one, make sure that the match field of each subform record always has the same value as the match field in the main form record. Otherwise, the link is lost.

   ❏ If the relationship between the main form and a subform is many-to-one, you should *never* change the value of the subform match field. Changing it would destroy any link between the subform record and other main form records.

3. When deleting a Multiform record,

   ❏ If the relationship between the main form and a subform is one-to-many or one-to-one, remove all matching records in the subform before removing the related main form record.

   ❏ If the relationship between the main form and a subform is many-to-one, *never* delete a subform record when you delete the main record. A subform record on the one-side of a many-to-one relationship could be related to multiple main form records.

DataEase provides varying degrees of assistance in enforcing these rules, as explained in the following paragraphs. You can establish the following design policy that enables you to forget about rules 2b and 3b altogether:

Never use a many-to-one relationship in a Multiform. Use virtual lookup fields instead.

To follow this suggestion, for example, you need to modify the Widget Order Multiform designed earlier in this chapter. Both the Widget Order-to-Retail Customer relationship and the Widget Order-to-Sales Representative relationship are many-to-one relationships. You can replace the subform areas from Retail Customer and Sales Representative with virtual lookup fields from the same forms (lookup fields with the prevent data-entry, virtual characteristic, see Chapter 3).

The remainder of the chapter assumes that you will follow this advice and avoid using many-to-one relationships in Multiforms. In all figures and examples in the rest of the chapter, Customer subform fields and Sales Representative subform fields in the Widget Order multiform are replaced by lookup fields. The Widget Order Multiform looks the same on-screen. In that case, the three rules can be simplified a little:

1. Each Multiform record must be unique.

2. When modifying a Multiform record, make sure that the match field of each subform record always has the same value as the match field in the main form record. Otherwise, the link is lost.

3. When deleting a Multiform record, remove all matching records in the subform before removing the related main form record.

The paragraphs that follow discuss how to implement these rules to ensure referential integrity.

Ensuring Uniqueness

The best way to ensure that every Multiform record is unique—the first rule listed in the preceding section—is to define the main form and each subform so that each of their records must be unique. As explained in Chapter 2, DataEase prevents you from entering duplicate values in any field or combination of fields to which you have assigned the unique characteristic.

In the Order Tracking database example, the Order Number field in Widget Order is unique. DataEase therefore prevents you from adding a record to Widget Order with the same value in the Order Number field as an existing record. You cannot have two records in the Widget Order form data with order number *100*, for example.

In the Order Detail form, however, which is on the many-side of the one-to-many relationship between Widget Order and Order Detail, both Order Number and Item Number are assigned the unique characteristic. DataEase combines the two unique field characteristics to prevent you from adding a record that duplicates the values in both fields. You may very well have several records with order number 100, but you should only have one that is item 1 for order 100.

Changing a Match Field Value

The second rule ensures that you don't sever the link between main form record and subform record(s). Suppose that a customer places an order for three different kinds of widgets. To record this transaction, you have to add one record to the Widget Order form and three records to Order

Detail. Using the Widget Order Multiform (displayed in fig. 6.7), entering this order is quick and easy. When you enter a number in the main form Order Number field, DataEase enters the same number in the Order Number field of each record in the Order Detail subform (even though you have chosen to hide the Order Number field from the Table View of the subform).

If an hour later, however, you realize that you used the wrong order number, using the Multiform again to correct the mistake would be most convenient. When you display the record in the Multiform and change the value in the Order Number field in the Widget Order main form, you want DataEase to make a corresponding change to the Order Number field in each Order Detail record. DataEase 4.2 now updates subform records if you first make the proper entry in the Relationships form. Previous versions, including 4.0 and 4.01, do not update the subform records.

"Using the Relationships Form," earlier in this chapter, postponed the discussion of the two referential integrity fields (again see fig. 6.2 and the accompanying text). The entries you make in these two fields determine how DataEase handles updating match field values in Multiforms. You must make an entry in one of these two fields when you plan to use together in a Multiform two related forms—one form as the main form and the other as a subform.

First, you display the Relationships form record that defines how the two forms are related. For example, the Widget Order Multiform uses Widget Order as the main form and Order Detail as a subform. To display the Relationships form record for these two forms, select **1. Form Definition and Relationships** from the DataEase Main menu and then **3. Define Relationships** from the Form Definition menu. Press F3 (VIEW) until DataEase displays the record that shows the relationship between Widget Order and Order Detail (see fig. 6.10).

When the correct Relationships record is displayed, move the cursor to the referential integrity field for the form that will be used as the subform. In the Widget Order Multiform example, Order Detail is listed as Form 2 (again see fig. 6.10), so move the cursor to the field that follows the prompt:

```
If Form 2 is Subform, how should Key
field be updated when Main form Key
is modified:
```

The term *Key field* in this prompt means the match field. When the cursor is in a referential integrity field in a Relationships form record, DataEase displays three options in a line menu: 1: Cascade (Update), 2: Null (Blank), and 3: Restrict (Don't Update). Your choice from this menu determines whether DataEase will make corresponding changes to subform match field values each time you modify the value of a main form match field. The choice also determines whether DataEase will delete

Fig. 6.10.

The Relationships form record showing the relationship between Widget Order and Order Detail.

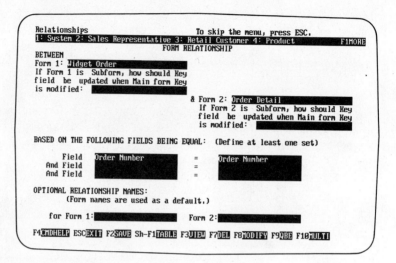

```
Relationships                          To skip the menu, press ESC.
1: System 2: Sales Representative 3: Retail Customer 4: Product        F1MORE
                            FORM RELATIONSHIP
BETWEEN
Form 1: Widget Order
If Form 1 is  Subform, how should Key
field be  updated when Main form Key
is modified:

                                    & Form 2: Order Detail
                                      If Form 2 is  Subform, how should Key
                                      field  be  updated when Main form Key
                                      is modified:

BASED ON THE FOLLOWING FIELDS BEING EQUAL:  (Define at least one set)

        Field  Order Number          =     Order Number
      And Field                       =
      And Field                       =

OPTIONAL RELATIONSHIP NAMES:
        (Form names are used as a default.)

      for Form 1:                    Form 2:

F4 CMDHELP ESCEXIT F2SAVE Sh-F1TABLE F3VIEW F7DEL F8MODIFY F9QBE F10MULTI
```

subform records when you delete a related main form record. The remaining paragraphs in this section discuss how the three referential integrity field options operate when you edit a Multiform. Refer to "Deleting Records in a Multiform," in this chapter, to learn how these three options operate when you delete a record using a Multiform.

Select 1: Cascade (Update) in a referential integrity field in order to cause DataEase to enforce referential integrity when you edit a Multiform. With this option activated, a change to the value of a main form match field "cascades" through the transactions subform match field values.

For example, suppose that the order number for the Widget Order Multiform record shown in figure 6.11 should be 200 instead of 100. To ensure that DataEase will update the Order Number values in Order Detail records when you make a change to an Order Number value in the Widget Order Multiform, display the Relationships form record that relates Widget Order to Order Detail (again see fig. 6.10). Select 1: Cascade (Update) in the referential integrity field for Order Detail. Press F8 (MODIFY) to save the modified Relationships form record.

Now return to Record Entry and edit the Multiform record. When you change the number in the Order Number field to 200, DataEase repeats the change throughout all the Order Detail records that are part of the same transaction, maintaining the referential integrity (link) between these related records.

The purpose of the other two options available in the referential integrity field is to break the link between related records. Choose 2: Null (Blank) to cause DataEase to insert a blank, or null, value into subform match fields when you modify the transaction's main form match field value. With this

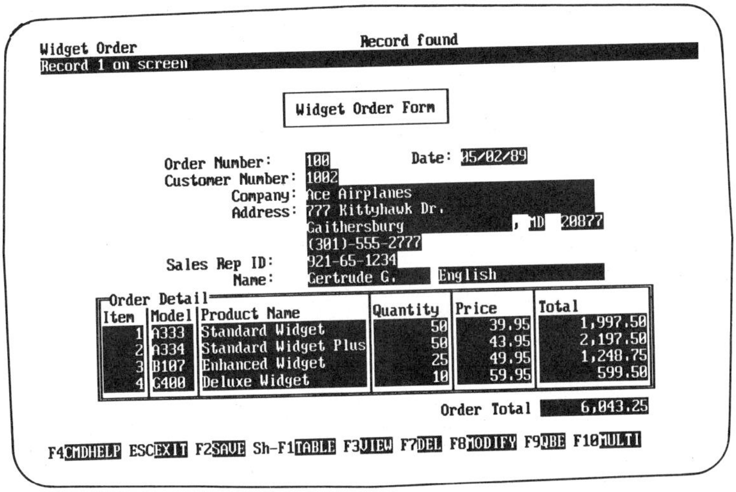

Fig. 6.11.

Order number 100 in the Widget Order Multiform.

option selected, any change to a main form match field value results in so-called "orphan" subform records—subform records that are no longer linked to a particular main form record.

Select 3: Restrict (Don't Update) when you want DataEase to make no change to subform match field values. This setting is the default and is the way previous versions of DataEase operate. With 3: Restrict (Don't Update) selected as the referential integrity field option, if you edit the Multiform record shown in figure 6.10 and change the Order Number from 100 to 200, DataEase does not change the corresponding Order Number values in the transaction's Order Detail records. The Order Number value in the Widget Order record is 200, but the value in each Order Detail record is still 100. The link between these records is broken.

> **Caution:** The referential integrity enforcing features described in this section are active only when you are modifying a Multiform in Record Entry, while in Form View. If you switch to Table View or use a DQL procedure to modify the value of the match field in the main form record, DataEase does not update the match field values in the related subform records.

Deleting Records in a Multiform

The third aspect of the referential integrity problem arises when you decide to delete a record. To avoid "orphan" subform records, you must never delete a main form record without deleting the matching subform record(s).

Suppose that a customer calls and cancels order 100 (again see fig. 6.11). You decide to remove the record of the order from the database. If you delete the record only from the Widget Order form, without deleting the related records from the Order Detail main form, you will leave in the Order Detail subform four records that have no match in Widget Order. DataEase helps you avoid this mistake; but the procedure varies depending on the referential integrity selection you made for the subform in the Relationships form.

In most cases, you should select 1: Cascade (Update) as the referential integrity setting for a form that is to be used as a subform in a Multiform. As explained in the preceding section, this setting assists you in enforcing referential integrity whenever you modify a match value in the main form. The 1: Cascade (Update) setting also makes deleting an entire transaction easy. To delete from a Multiform an entire record— main form record and all subform records—display the record in Record Entry and press F7 (DELETE). DataEase displays the message Are you sure, and what do you want to Delete? in a pop-up window. If the cursor is in a main form field, DataEase displays the following options in a line menu: 1: No, Do not Delete and 2: Yes, Delete Record. Select the first option to cancel the deletion. Choose the second option to delete the main form record and all subform records. When the cursor is in a subform field, DataEase displays the options 1: No, Do not Delete; 2: Yes, Delete Main and All Sub Records; and 3: Yes, Sub Record Only. Choose the first option to cancel the deletion. Select the second option to delete the main form record and all subform records. Select option 3 to delete only the subform record in which the cursor is resting.

Occasionally, you may select 2: Null (Blank) as the referential integrity setting for a subform. With this setting, follow the procedure described in the preceding paragraph to delete a Multiform record.

If you select 3: Restrict (Don't Update) as the referential integrity setting for a subform (or if you have not upgraded to DataEase 4.2), use the following procedure to delete a Multiform record. Display, in Record Entry, the Multiform record you want to delete and press F7 (DELETE). DataEase displays the message Are you sure, and what do you want to Delete? in a pop-up window. If the cursor is in a main form field, DataEase displays the following options in a line menu: 1: No, Do not Delete; 2: Yes, Main Record; and 3: Yes, Main and All Sub Records. When the cursor is in a subform field, DataEase displays a fourth option, 4: Yes, Sub Record Only. Select the third option to delete the main form record and all related subform records.

Caution: If you include a many-to-one relationship in a Multiform, choosing not to follow the advice given earlier in this chapter, you should never choose an option that deletes the main record and all subform records. If you do, you will delete the record in the one-side subform data even though the record may be linked to other main form records.

Recovering Deleted Multiform Records

As explained in Chapter 4, when you delete records from a DataEase form, DataEase does not immediately remove the data from the records file. DataEase enables you to recover any deleted record, including a Multiform main form record or subform record, as long as you have not reorganized that form (see "Reorganizing a Form" in Chapter 3). The procedure for recovering a deleted Multiform record varies depending on whether it is still displayed on-screen and whether you want to recover a main form record or a subform record.

To recover a deleted main form record still displayed on-screen, just press F8 (MODIFY). DataEase displays the message Record n updated where n is the main form record number. This command does not, however, recover deleted subform records. When the main form record is no longer displayed, you must use the Ctrl-F3 (VIEW RECORD #) method described in Chapter 4 to recover it.

To recover subform records deleted with the 3: Yes, Main and All Sub Records option, you must display the subform alone in Record Entry and recover each record one at a time using the Ctrl-F3 (VIEW RECORD #) procedure. Recovering a Multiform subform record deleted with the 4: Yes, Sub Record option is a little easier. If the subform is marked deleted but is still displayed on the screen, press Ctrl-F5 (UNDO). DataEase restores the record (unmarks it for deletion) and displays the message, Discarded Record Changes.

Printing Multiform Records

You learned in Chapter 4 that you can print a DataEase record directly from the record-entry screen. In fact, you can print multiple records from Table View in Record Entry. The same feature is available in a Multiform to print a copy of the current record, including any text that is part of the record-entry form. When all you want is a printout of one record, this method may often be the easiest and most convenient.

To print a single Multiform record, first display the target record in Record Entry using one of the methods described in Chapter 4 for viewing records. Make sure that your printer is ready, and press Shift-F9 (PRINT). DataEase prints a copy of the Multiform just as it appears on-screen with all text and data including all subform records associated with the on-screen main form record. DataEase does not print blank lines that may appear on-screen in a subform area. Even when the Multiform extends to several screens on your monitor, DataEase prints the entire record.

In the Order Tracking example, this Shift-F9 (PRINT) command proves to be the most natural way to print an invoice. Imagine that you have filled out an order form on-screen (the Widget Order Multiform) and that you want a hard copy for the customer. All you have to do is press Shift-F9 (PRINT), and you have an instant invoice.

This method of printing a record has obvious limitations. It can only print one record, and it doesn't give you any opportunity to modify the format in any way. Compare this quick-print capability to the Quick Reports facility discussed near the end of this chapter. Experiment with both reporting methods so that you learn how to benefit most from all of DataEase's features.

Using Other Multiple Form Record-Entry Capabilities

The DataEase Multiform feature is impressive, but it is by no means the only multiple form capability that DataEase has. Whenever you are working with related forms in Record Entry but have not previously defined a Multiform, DataEase provides the capability of quickly creating a temporary Multiform, referred to as an *ad-hoc Multiform*, by pressing a single keystroke combination.

Sometimes you don't need or want records from multiple forms on one screen, but you would like to be able to "jump" easily to a related record in another form for viewing or editing. DataEase provides this capability as well, referred to as the *multiview* feature.

Other times, you not only want to view or edit related records, but you want to browse through all records in a related form, locate a value in a record, and then copy it back to the original form. DataEase enables you to perform this feat by using its *dynamic lookup* feature. The paragraphs that follow explain how to use these multiple form features of DataEase.

Using Ad-Hoc Multiforms in Record Entry

In addition to providing the capability of defining Multiforms through the Form Definition screen, DataEase enables you to create temporary Multiforms during a Record Entry session—so called ad-hoc Multiforms. To create a Multiform from within Record Entry, position the cursor in the match field and press Alt-F10 (MULTIFORM). DataEase inserts the related form in Table View below the field that contains the cursor and displays at least three rows in Table View, even if only one matching record exists. When more than three matching records occur, DataEase expands the size of the table.

You might be interested, for example, in displaying a list of the sales made by a particular sales representative from within the Sales Representative form. You could, of course, take the time to design a Multiform, but you don't have to. You first display the sales representative's record in the Sales Representative record-entry form and place the cursor in the Sales Rep ID field, the match field between Sales Representative and Widget Order. Then, you press Alt-F10 (MULTIFORM). DataEase inserts Widget Order as a subform in Table View, as shown in figure 6.12, and lists in the subform the orders sold by the sales representative whose record you have displayed.

An Ad-Hoc Multiform always displays as an automatic table. The Automatic-Form and Custom-Form options of predefined Multiforms are not available here.

When the Ad-Hoc Multiform is displayed, you can use it in the same manner as a predefined tabular Multiform. However, keep in mind the referential integrity concerns discussed earlier in this chapter.

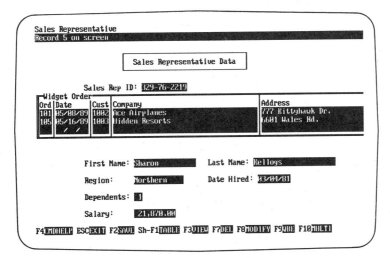

Fig. 6.12.

An Ad-Hoc Multiform showing the sales made by Sharon Kellogs.

You can use this feature many times during a Record Entry session, even from within a subform. The position of the cursor determines the relationship that DataEase displays and the location of the subform.

If you are using an Ad-Hoc Multiform, press Esc (EXIT) to remove the subform from the screen. When you have displayed multiple ad-hoc subforms, DataEase removes them one at a time, in the order they were added, each time you press Esc (EXIT).

Using Multiview to View and Edit Related Forms

In an ideal world, you could create one Multiform that would enable you to enter, view, and edit all records in all forms in your database. You have already seen, however, that some form relationships are not suitable for inclusion in a Multiform—many-to-one relationships, for instance. Even though Multiforms are in many ways convenient, you must still perform some tasks in the record-entry forms on which they are based.

The DataEase Multiview feature enables you to switch from one form to a related form in Record Entry at literally the touch of a single key. To switch from a displayed record-entry form to a related form, place the cursor in a match field or in a lookup field and simply press F10 (MULTI). DataEase displays the first related record in the related form. You then can use the form for viewing, editing, and even entering new data, as described in Chapter 4. When you are finished, and you have saved any changes or additions, press Esc (EXIT) to return to the original form.

Sometimes a form is related to more than one other form. For example, Widget Order is related to the Order Detail, Retail Customer, and Sales Representative forms. When you press F10 (MULTI), instead of switching immediately to another form, DataEase displays a window menu listing the available relationships so that you can choose the form you want to display (see fig. 6.13).

An earlier section in this chapter strongly suggested that you not include many-to-one relationships in a Multiform. Because of the Multiview feature, you can follow this advice without penalty. You can use virtual lookup fields to display data from a many-to-one subform and then use Multiview to display the actual related form (as opposed to a subform) if you ever need to view or edit the related form data.

The Widget Order Multiform, for example can display the Retail Customer fields Company, Address, City, State, Zip, and Phone as derived lookup fields with the prevent data-entry, virtual characteristic (see "Editing Multiform Records—Ensuring Referential Integrity" earlier in this chapter). Suppose that you are entering data about an order into the Multiform, however, and you discover that the customer's address has changed. You

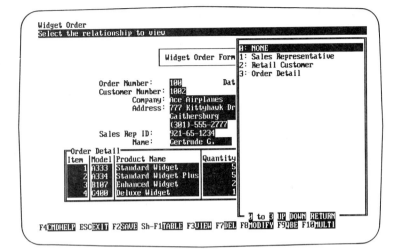

Fig. 6.13.

Displaying a list of related forms for use with Multiview.

cannot, of course, make any change to the *looked-up* Address field in the Widget Order Multiform, but you can use Multiview to switch to the Retail Customer form. You place the cursor in the Customer Number field in the Multiform and press F10 (MULTI). DataEase immediately displays the matching customer's record in the Retail Customer record-entry form. You then can edit the address, press F8 (MODIFY) to record the change, and press Esc (EXIT) to return to the Multiform.

Retrieving Data with Dynamic Lookup

One of the most useful new features of DataEase 4.0 is aptly called dynamic lookup. This feature takes the lookup field capability the next logical step.

Suppose that you are entering an order placed by the customer Hidden Resorts, but you can't remember their customer identification number. With most programs you would probably type up a little "cheat-sheet" listing all the customer numbers and tape it to the side of your monitor. DataEase, however, makes that method seem crude and passé.

To look up a value from a related form, place the cursor in the match field in the primary form and press Ctrl-F10 (LOOKUP). DataEase immediately displays a pop-up window in the right side of the screen containing the related form in Table View. Use the cursor-movement keys listed in table 6.1 to browse through the table to find the record you're looking for. When the cursor is in the target row, press Enter. DataEase removes the pop-up window and fills in any related fields in the primary form with the *looked-up* data. DataEase also displays the message Returned to *formname*, in which *formname* is the name of the primary form.

Table 6.1
Dynamic Lookup Cursor-Movement Keys

Key	Moves cursor to:
Tab	Next column (field) to right
Ctrl-Tab	Preceding column (field) to left
Ctrl-→	Last column (field) to right
Ctrl-←	First column (field) to left
↓	Next row in same column
↑	Preceding row in same column
Home	Same column, first row
End	Same column, last row

In this example, with the cursor in the Customer Number field in Widget Order, you press Ctrl-F10 (LOOKUP). Because Customer Number is the match field between Widget Order and Retail Customer, DataEase displays the Retail Customer records in Table View in a pop-up window (see fig. 6.14). You then move the cursor down to the target record, Hidden Resorts, and press Enter. DataEase removes the table from the screen, and fills in the Widget Order field Customer Number and the related lookup fields from Retail Customer with the values from the Hidden Resorts record, as shown in figure 6.15.

Fig. 6.14.

Using Dynamic Lookup to find a customer's identification number.

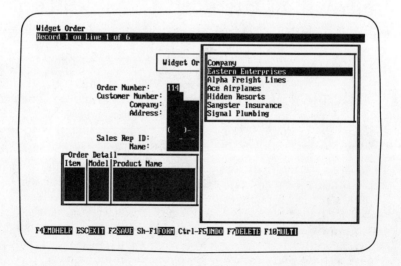

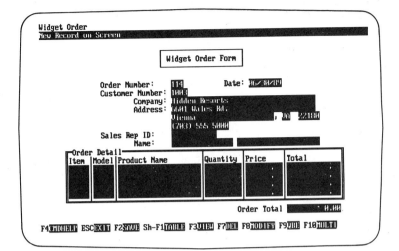

Widget Order Form

Order Number: 114   Date: 06/30/89
Customer Number: 1003
Company: Hidden Resorts
Address: 6601 Wales Rd.
Vienna   , VA 22180
(703) 555-5000

Sales Rep ID:
Name:

Order Detail
Item | Model | Product Name | Quantity | Price | Total

Order Total   0.00

F4 CMDHELP ESC EXIT F2 SAVE Sh-F1 TABLE F3 VIEW F7 DEL F8 MODIFY F9 QBE F10 MULTI

Fig. 6.15.

Data retrieved from the Retail Customer form using the Dynamic Lookup feature.

Building Quick Reports Using Related Forms and Multiforms

Chapter 5 covers DataEase Quick Reports extensively, but using Quick Reports to combine data from Multiforms and multiple related forms is explained in the following paragraphs. Just as DataEase provides several ways to access multiple forms in Record Entry, it gives you a choice of methods for generating a multiple form Quick Report. You can create a report from a Multiform (new in DataEase 4.0); you can use the multiview feature to select fields from related forms, or you can use a combination of these two approaches. A third method of creating multiple form reports uses DataEase *relational operators* and is discussed in Chapter 7.

Designing a Multiform Quick Report

If you know how to create a report from a single form, you know how to create a report from a Multiform. The steps are nearly identical:

❏ Access the QBE—Quick Reports menu in one of the three methods described in Chapter 5: from the DataEase Main menu, from Record Entry, or by loading a previously saved Quick Report definition from the DQL menu.

❏ Begin defining a new report by selecting **2. Start New Report** from the QBE—Quick Reports menu. Selection of this option is mandatory whenever another report definition is already in RAM and you want to start fresh.

❏ Select **3. Define Record Selection** when you want to limit the report to only a portion of the records in the Multiform data.

DataEase uses all Multiform records if you skip this option. You can specify record selection criteria in main form fields, subform fields, or both.

❑ Choose **4. Define List Field** to indicate which fields should be included. By default, only main form fields are included.

❑ Select one of nine predefined report formats through the menu choice **5. Define Format**. The default format is Columnar format.

❑ Choose between sending the report to the screen, to the printer, or to a disk file through the **6. Define Print Style** option on the QBE—Quick Reports menu. By default, reports go to the screen.

❑ You can save a report definition so that you can use it again later. Select the **7. Save Report** option on the QBE—Quick Reports menu.

❑ To make modifications to a previously saved Quick Report, load it into RAM with the **8. Load Report** selection.

❑ When you no longer need a particular report definition, you can delete it with the **9. Delete Report** choice on the menu.

❑ Make a hard (paper) copy of the report definition by choosing **10. Print Report Definition**.

❑ Generate the report output (to screen, printer, or file) by choosing **1. Run Report**.

Refer to chapter 5 for more specifics on completing each of these steps. Then, take a look at Chapter 8 for details on customizing DataEase reports.

Using Multiview to Generate Quick Reports from Related Forms

In addition to using Multiforms to design a report that draws data from multiple related forms, you can use the DataEase Multiview feature in the Record Selection screen and the Field Selection screen. In fact, you can use Multiview and Multiform together to include fields in the report that are not displayed in the Multiform.

Specifying Record Selection Criteria in Related Forms

Sometimes you may want to select records for inclusion in the report based on a field value in a related record. As usual, you select the **3. Define Record Selection** option from the QBE—Quick Reports menu and choose the primary form. Specify any desired selection criteria in the primary form Record Selection screen, as described in Chapter 5.

Then, to access the related form, press F10 (MULTI). DataEase displays a window menu containing a list of available relationships—forms that are related to the primary form. Select one of these relationships, and DataEase switches to the related form in the Record Selection screen. Now, you can specify any desired selection criteria in this form. After you have finished, press Esc (EXIT) to return to the primary form.

You can repeat this process for each related form if you need to. When you have specified all record selection criteria, press F2 (SAVE) to save your entries in the Record Selection screens and return to the QBE—Quick Reports menu.

When you run the report, DataEase applies the primary form selection criteria first, selecting records from the primary form. Then the program selects records from the related (secondary) forms that match both the records from the primary form and the specified secondary record selection criteria. Only records that pass both sets of selection criteria are listed in the report.

You may, for example, be interested in seeing a list of all sales representatives, grouped by sales region, who made a sale that totaled over $2,000. The Sales Representative form contains the names and regions of all the sales representatives but does not contain their order totals. Suppose that you decide to make Sales Representative the primary form. You select **3. Define Record Selection** from the QBE—Quick Reports menu and then choose Sales Representative. DataEase displays the Sales Representative form in the Record Selection screen. You need not enter any selection criteria in this screen because you want to include all sales representatives who have made a sale totaling more than $2,000. The selection criteria must be placed in the Order Total field, which is found in Widget Order.

To switch to the Widget Order Record Selection screen, you press F10 (MULTI) and choose Widget Order. DataEase then displays the Widget Order Multiform in the Record Selection screen. You move the cursor to the Order Total field and type *>2000*. Then, you press Esc (EXIT) to return to the primary form and press F2 (SAVE) to save the criteria and return to the QBE—Quick Reports menu. Figure 6.16 shows a report that includes records selected by this criteria (**Note:** This is not the default columnar report, but a slightly modified version.)

Defining List Fields Options in Related Forms

Just as record selection criteria may involve multiple forms, your reports may often include fields from several related forms. To select a field from a related form, first use the **4. Define List Fields** option on the QBE—Quick Reports menu to display the primary form in the Field Selection screen. Move from field to field in the primary form, pressing the space bar at each field to be included in the report. Recall from Chapter 5 that DataEase places a list number in each field indicating the order in

Fig. 6.16.

*A report showing
sales representatives
who have sales.*

```
                                    Running report
 END OF REPORT. SPACE: Return to Menu   PgUp Home LEFT RIGHT Arrows: Scroll
 ==========================================================================
 Sales Rep ID  First Name        Last Name         Region        Salary
 --------------------------------------------------------------------------
 921-65-1234   Gertrude G.       English           Northern       36,750.00
 448-89-6721   Samantha          Green             Southern       49,339.00
 129-88-4562   Joseph            Jones             Western        75,900.00
 987-31-9873   George            Quick             Eastern        53,000.00
 ==========================================================================




   F4 CMDHELP ESC EXIT C:\DEDATA\        Order Tracking    08/16/89   7 19 pm
```

which it will appear in the report. Alternatively, you can type the list
numbers yourself.

Then, to display the related form, press F10 (MULTI). DataEase displays a
window menu containing a list of all available relationships. Select the
appropriate relationship, and DataEase displays the related form. Use the
space bar method or type list numbers to select a field or fields from the
related form. You also can specify statistics for related fields, but not
sorting or grouping (see the discussion of these options in Chapter 5).

After you have selected all the desired related fields, press Esc (EXIT) to
return to the primary form. You can then continue to select fields in the
primary form or use F10 (MULTI) again to access another related form.

When you have selected all fields to be included in the report and
specified all other desired List Fields options, press F2 (SAVE). DataEase
saves the Field Selection screen entries and returns to the QBE—Quick
Reports menu.

All other aspects of Quick Reports design using multiple forms are as
described in Chapter 5 for individual forms.

Chapter Summary

This chapter has shown you how to design and build Multiforms and how
to use them for entering, viewing, and editing data. You also were
introduced to DataEase's other powerful multiple form features: ad-hoc
Multiform, Multiview, and Dynamic Lookup. Finally, the last portion of the
chapter discussed how to use related forms and Multiforms to generate
DataEase Quick Reports. However, many powerful DataEase capabilities
have yet to be covered. Turn now to Chapter 7 for an introduction to the
DataEase Query Language.

Building Simple Procedures with DQL

Every DataEase capability you have seen so far can be accomplished with absolutely no need for programming. You can build a database; enter, view, and edit data, and generate impressive reports without writing one line of programming code. Even the powerful Multiforms discussed in Chapter 6 can be created completely through menus and function-key commands. Indeed, this power-without-programming nature of DataEase is what attracts many users. This chapter, however, gives you a first glimpse at some of the programmable capabilities of DataEase available through DataEase Query Language (DQL) procedures.

This chapter introduces you first to DQL fundamental concepts and terminology, such as query and procedure. A clear understanding of these concepts will help you to learn how to use DQL quickly and easily. The remainder of the chapter discusses the portion of a DQL procedure that performs record and field selection—the query. It explains in detail how to start a procedure and define a simple query to retrieve information, sort records, group data, and use relational operators. This chapter also explains how to modify a query, save a query to RAM, save a procedure to disk, and print a hard copy of a procedure's definition. As you go through this chapter, keep in mind that building a DataEase query is only part of the story. Take a look also at Chapter 8 for specifics on how to create data-entry forms and custom procedure/report formats and at Chapter 9 for help in creating menus that can tie all your DQL procedures and Quick Reports together into one easy-to-use system.

When you are comfortable with simple procedures and custom reports, you will be ready to tackle the full power of DQL discussed in the last chapter of this book.

Accessing DQL

To create a procedure you first must access the DQL menu. DataEase provides three ways to access the DQL menu. The most obvious method is through the DataEase Main menu. You select **4. DQL Advanced Processing**, and DataEase displays the DQL menu shown in figure 7.1.

Fig. 7.1.

The DQL menu.

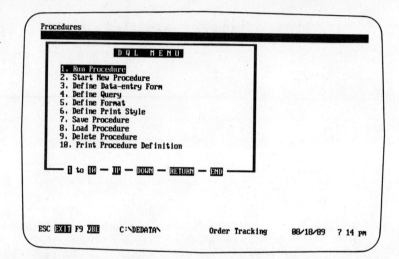

The second way to display the DQL menu is from the QBE—Quick Reports menu. Normally, you only use this method when you have been working with a Quick Report and want to convert it to a DQL procedure. From the QBE—Quick Reports menu, press F9 (DQL). DataEase displays a window on-screen with the question Convert current Quick report into a DQL Procedure? Respond 2: yes, and DataEase displays the Quick Report as a query. Then press F2 (SAVE). DataEase saves the query and displays the DQL menu.

Note: After you convert a Quick Report into a DQL procedure you cannot convert it back to a Quick Report because the DQL procedure overwrites the Quick Report on disk.

You also can access the DQL menu from the QBE—Quick Reports menu by loading a previously saved DQL procedure. From the QBE—Quick Reports menu, select **8. Load Report**. Then, select the name of a DQL procedure. DataEase loads the procedure in RAM and displays the DQL menu.

Overviewing DQL

The DataEase Query Language or DQL is an extension of much of what you have already learned about DataEase, particularly DataEase Quick Reports. The steps you take to create a DQL procedure are very similar to the steps you take to create a Quick Report, as you can see by comparing the DQL menu to the QBE—Quick Reports menu. This first portion of the chapter builds on the understanding of reports you have already gained from the preceding chapters in this book and helps you to focus quickly on the terms and concepts that are new.

If you replace the word "Report" in the QBE—Quick Reports menu with the word "Procedure," the QBE—Quick Reports and DQL menus look quite similar. A good place to start learning about DQL is to examine the similarities and differences in the two menus and to learn the meaning of the terms *procedure*, *data-entry form*, and *query*.

Defining a Procedure

You have already learned how to create reports using the DataEase Quick Reports feature (see Chapters 5 and 6). A DQL procedure can duplicate a Quick Report exactly, but it replaces the fill-in-the-blank procedure of Quick Reports with a command line approach. More importantly, DQL procedures give you control over DataEase reports not available in Quick Reports.

In addition to the capabilities available in Quick Reports, DQL enables you to create a series of menus that make your database easy for even the most computer-fearing person to use. A Quick Report can retrieve and print data from your database and calculate a few simple statistics, but you can use DQL to design a procedure to add, modify, or delete records and to perform any mathematical or statistical calculation that you can think of. In fact, you can design a series of DQL procedures that provide a complete menu-driven, custom-designed database that can process complex transactions, including entering new records, posting changes to existing records, and making ad-hoc or prescheduled multi-record updates to multiple forms in the database.

Actually, two types of DQL procedures exist: *processing* procedures and *control* procedures. Processing procedures work directly with data and enable you to retrieve, list, add, delete, modify, and sort data from your database. Control procedures are used to link processing procedures together. Unless specifically stated otherwise, all procedures discussed in this chapter are processing procedures.

In many ways, designing a DQL procedure is similar to designing a Quick Report. Much of what you have already learned from Chapters 5 and 6 applies to designing procedures. The following aspects of the Quick Report design process, described in Chapter 5, and the DQL procedure design process are nearly the same:

❏ *Starting the design*. When you begin designing a Quick Report or a procedure, you select the Start option from the respective menu so that DataEase clears any existing Quick Report or procedure from memory (RAM).

❏ *Defining output format*. The method of designing an output format is identical for Quick Reports and DQL procedures. Chapter 5 describes how to create reports in columnar, field-per-line, Record Entry, GrafTalk chart, mailing label, and a number of export formats. Chapter 8 describes in detail how to create custom and template output formats. All these formats can be used in Quick Reports and DQL procedures.

❏ *Defining print style*. Print styles, including the output device (screen, printer, or disk), page size, margin settings, and type style, are assigned on the Print Style specification screen, whether for a Quick Report or for a procedure.

❏ *Saving and loading the definition*. As you design a Quick Report or procedure, you are building its definition in RAM. As with a Quick Report, you can save a DQL procedure to disk so that you can load and use it later. The file that DataEase creates on disk to hold the definition has the same file name extension (.DBR) whether it is a Quick Report definition or a DQL procedure definition. For this reason, you also can load a DQL procedure from the QBE—Quick Reports menu and a Quick Report from the DQL menu.

❏ *Deleting a definition*. The method for deleting a Quick Report definition and a procedure definition is the same: you choose the Delete menu option. In fact, you can delete a Quick Report from the DQL menu and a DQL procedure from the QBE—Quick Reports menu.

❏ *Printing a definition*. The Print option on each of the respective menus prints the report or procedure definition currently in RAM.

❏ *Running a report or procedure*. Select the Run menu option to begin execution of a procedure or report. DataEase runs the report or procedure currently in RAM.

Defining a Data-Entry Form

The DQL menu lists **3. Define Data-entry Form** as the third option, in place of **3. Define Record Selection** on the QBE—Quick Reports menu. However, no counterpart to a data-entry form exists in a Quick Report. A DataEase data-entry form also is not the same as a record-entry form, despite the similar names. Unlike a record-entry form, a data-entry form does not add data directly to the database.

A data-entry form is an optional input form that enables you to enter data during the running of a DQL procedure. The procedure then can use the data as it processes the database. For example, you may design a procedure that displays a data-entry form prompting you to enter a particular customer number. When you enter the customer number and press F2 (SAVE), the DQL procedure continues and uses the customer number to select records for processing. Without this data-entry form, you have to modify the procedure to change the record selection criteria each time you want to use a different customer number.

By contrast, when you define a Quick Report, you can use the Record Selection screen to include particular records in the report, but you have no opportunity to change the selection criteria while the Quick Report is running. If you want to generate a report from a different group of records, you have to make an appropriate change on the Record Selection screen and then run the report again. This procedure is often referred to as batch processing because you specify all the data at the beginning of the procedure in a "batch." A data-entry form, on the other hand, enables you to interactively provide data to a procedure at run-time. You can even design the procedure so that it runs an indefinite number of times, returning to the data-entry screen for more data each time it completes the procedure.

Chapter 8 describes the steps for creating and using data-entry forms.

Defining a Query

The other DQL menu option that does not correspond to a choice on the QBE—Quick Reports menu is **4. Define Query**. This selection in effect performs the functions of the **3. Define Record Selection** and **4. Define List Fields** options in Quick Reports.

In general usage, a *query* is a question or a request for information. When your spouse asks you, "What time is it?," that is a query. Your spouse has made a specific request for information.

A valid response or answer to a query should be as specific as the question. When your spouse requests the time, you don't respond with the date, or even the day of the week. You look at your watch and announce the current time of day.

In DataEase, when you build a query, you in essence are asking a question requesting specific information from your database. Using DataEase Query Language commands, you can ask DataEase to retrieve data that meets criteria you specify. For example, you can create a DataEase query that retrieves the values from the Order Number, Customer Number, and Date fields in Widget Order for every order in June, 1989 (see fig. 7.2). Figures 7.3 and 7.4 show the Quick Report Record Selection and Field Selection screens that this query replaces.

Fig. 7.2.

A DataEase query that selects Order Number, Customer Number, and Date fields for widget orders placed between June 1, 1989, and June 30, 1989 (inclusive).

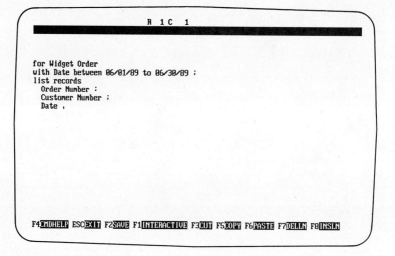

Fig. 7.3.

A Record Selection screen that selects orders placed between June 1, 1989, and June 30, 1989 (inclusive).

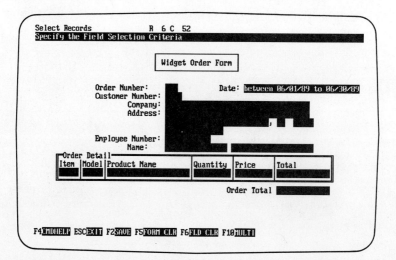

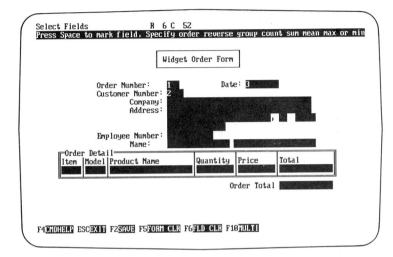

Fig. 7.4.

A Field Selection screen that selects the fields Order Number, Customer Number, and Date.

Using a DataEase query, you can do more than just retrieve data. DQL has a full complement of commands, operators, and functions that enable you to manipulate data from your database for use in a report. You can even use DQL commands to add, modify, or delete existing records.

Using Low-Level Interactive Mode

To begin defining a query, select **4. Define Query** from the DQL menu. DataEase displays the Query Definition screen shown in figure 7.5.

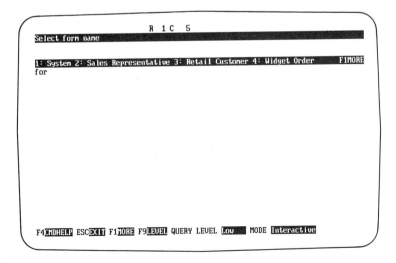

Fig. 7.5.

The Query Definition screen.

A message in the lower right corner indicates that you are in Interactive mode. To the left of this message, another message says that the screen is in low level. DataEase has two modes for defining a query: Interactive and Edit modes. The Query Definition screen always starts in Interactive mode.

Interactive mode has two levels: low and high. The Query Definition screen starts out in low level.

The low-level Interactive mode is better for learning how to create queries because it enables you to build a query by choosing options from relatively short line menus. The Interactive mode is, however, a bit cumbersome to use. You are required to make all selections from what sometimes seems to be an endless succession of menus. For this reason, when you are familiar with building queries, you may want to use the Edit mode to type the query directly. This chapter discusses the Interactive mode.

Tip: One of the most common mistakes made by new users of any program is reading screen messages too hastily, if at all. When using DataEase in the Interactive mode, observing and reading carefully are particularly important. DataEase makes full use of the screen, displaying pertinent information in several lines of the screen at once. Unless you keep a close eye on the prompt lines and think carefully before you make a choice from a line menu, you may quickly get lost.

If you find yourself in what appears to be an endless loop of menus and cannot figure out what to do, press Backspace or the left-arrow key to move the cursor to the last position where you understood what was going on. You will be in the Edit mode at this point, so press F1 (INTERACTIVE) to return to the Interactive mode. DataEase then reads the query at the cursor, and you can pick up again where you got lost.

Selecting the Primary Form

Just as is true with Quick Reports, each DataEase procedure is associated with a DataEase form. This form is referred to as the *primary* form. You can access any related forms from your database in the procedure, but you must define one form as the starting point. Other forms, referred to as *secondary* forms, are then accessed according to how they are related to the primary form.

The first command in a DataEase query, defined in the low-level Interactive mode, always defines the primary form.

This Query Definition screen is subtly different from the others that have been described in preceding chapters (see fig. 7.5). The top line of the screen still contains the title area, the mode/cursor position area, and the message area. In the other screens (for example, the Form Definition screen), the second line of the screen is the prompt line, which DataEase normally uses for instructions and line menus. But, in the Query Definition screen, DataEase uses lines 2 through 4 for instructions and line 5 for line menus. Line 5 also is occasionally used for prompts when a line menu is not appropriate.

For convenience, this book refers to lines 2, 3, and 4 as the *prompt lines*. When DataEase displays more than one prompt line, it draws your attention to the most specific instruction by highlighting it (in red on color screens). Line 5, the line that usually contains line menus, is referred to as the *menu line*. The menu line also is highlighted (in green and blue on color screens) whenever it contains a line menu.

Caution: If you press Esc while building a query, DataEase displays the question Do you want to abandon the procedure? in a message window. Be careful to respond 1: no to this question. If you respond 2: yes, DataEase erases the procedure from RAM. Unless you have already saved the procedure to disk, you will have to start defining it from the beginning again.

When DataEase first displays the Query Definition screen, it types the word for just below the menu line, on the first line (or row) of the query, and leaves the cursor at R1C5. The word for is a DQL command used to define the primary form for the query; it is always the first command in a query defined in the low-level Interactive mode.

The Query Definition screen is in the low-level Interactive mode. The LEVEL and MODE indicators at the bottom of the screen display Low and Interactive respectively.

DataEase instructs you in the first prompt line to Select form name. The menu line displays a list of all forms in the database. As shown in figure 7.5, the entire list of forms often does not fit on the menu line, and DataEase displays F1MORE at the right end of the menu. As with all line menus, pressing F1 (MORE) enables you to see the complete list of forms in a window menu.

To select the primary form, choose a form name from the line menu. DataEase types the form name to the right of the for command, on the first line of the query, and moves the cursor to the beginning of the second line of the query, position R2C1. The first prompt line now says Any record selection criteria?

Suppose that you want to generate a list of all your orders in May and June, 1989. You want the sales grouped by sales representative and by customer, and then in order by the Order Number. You also want to see the date of each order. So that you can compare their performance, the Order Total field should be totaled for Sales Representative. Finally, you also would like to see a grand total of all May and June orders.

All of this information is contained in the Widget Order Multiform data, so you choose the Widget Order form as the primary form for the query. You select 4: Widget Order from the line menu shown in figure 7.5. DataEase then types the form name Widget Order to the right of the for command and moves the cursor to row 2, ready for you to specify record selection criteria.

> **Tip:** Without a doubt, when you first begin building low level queries, you will make a few mistakes. Often, you will realize the error immediately and want to fix it on the spot. The Interactive mode does not appear to have a "back-up" feature, but you can easily correct any mistake you make and then continue with building the query.
>
> As soon as you notice you have made an incorrect menu choice, press Backspace or the left-arrow key until the cursor is at the position where you made the error. When you press Backspace or the left-arrow key, DataEase switches from the Interactive mode to the Edit mode. You don't really have to delete the erroneous choice from the line because DataEase will overwrite it, but the query may be less confusing if you do. Just press Del until the invalid choice is gone. To switch back to the Interactive mode, press F1 (INTERACTIVE). DataEase reads the query up to the cursor, displays the message This is a Processing procedure, and displays the appropriate prompt and line menu. You're back in business and can continue building the query.

Specifying Record Selection Criteria

In addition to specifying a primary form, you also must indicate which of the primary form's records are to be processed by the procedure. This specification is very similar in concept to specifying search criteria when searching for records to view in Record Entry (discussed in Chapter 4). It is virtually identical in purpose to the Record Selection screen in Quick Reports (covered in Chapter 5).

Selecting All Records

In Quick Reports, you type record selection criteria in the Record Selection screen. While in the low-level Interactive mode, after you select a primary form, DataEase moves the cursor down to the beginning of row 2. This second line begins record selection criteria. DataEase displays the prompt Any record selection criteria? in the first prompt line and displays two choices in the menu line: 0: NONE, and 1: with.

When you create a Quick Report, you can skip the record selection step, and DataEase assumes that you want to include all records from the primary form. Similarly, when building a low-level query in the Interactive mode, you can skip record selection by choosing 0: NONE from the line menu. DataEase places a semicolon (;) in the record selection line to indicate that the procedure you are building will process *all* records in the primary form. DataEase then types the command list records in row 3 and moves the cursor to row 4, position R4C3, where you can begin specifying the fields to be included.

Tip: Although the menus don't list it as an option, you can always use the Tab key to skip a menu instead of choosing 0: NONE (use Esc in DataEase 2.53). When the prompt instructs you to enter a number, the only way to skip to the next menu is to press Tab because DataEase would interpret *0* as a number rather than a menu choice. You may, therefore, find using Tab to skip a menu to be more consistent even when you can use *0*. However, reading each menu and/or prompt carefully before using either method to skip is much more important. If you follow this advice, you will always know which key you should press.

Selecting a Comparison Field, Operator, and Value

Queries created in low-level Interactive mode are used to list or retrieve records (instead of entering, modifying, or deleting records). You don't often want the query to retrieve all records. Using low-level Interactive mode, you specify a selection criterion by indicating a *comparison field*, a *comparison operator*, and a *comparison value*. To begin specifying a record selection criterion that will limit the records retrieved by the query, select 1: with from the line menu. DataEase types the operator *with* and stops the cursor one space to the right, at position R2C6. The *with* operator is always the first word in the record selection criteria.

With the cursor at position R2C6, DataEase still displays the question Any record selection criteria? in the first prompt line and displays the prompt Select field name in the second prompt line (the third line of the screen). This third line is highlighted. The prompt is instructing you to select a *comparison field*. This field is used to select records. The menu line (line 5 of the screen) contains the option 0: NONE followed by a list of all the field names in the primary form.

When you want to use a comparison field, select the comparison field name from the line menu. DataEase types the field name, moves the cursor one space to the right, and displays the prompt Select a comparison operator or 'not' in the second prompt line. The line menu now contains these options:

    1: = 2: › 3: ‹ 4: ‹= 5: ›= 6: between 7: not

To specify a selection criterion, you first choose a *comparison operator* from this menu. These comparison operators work as described in Chapter 5 (see table 5.4 and accompanying text). The *equal to* operator (=) retrieves records that exactly match the value that follows the operator (you will specify the match value in the next step). All the other operators indicate that a match can occur within a range of values.

After you choose a comparison operator, you must specify a *comparison value*. A comparison value (referred to as a match value in the discussion of the Record Selection screen in Chapter 5) can be another field value, a current system-supplied value (date, time, page number, item number, user name, user level, computer name, or status), a field value from another related form, a statistical computation from a related form (see "Using Relational Operators" later in this chapter), a constant value, or a combination of any of these values. The Interactive mode presents these options to you in a succession of line menus.

After you complete one selection criterion by selecting a field name, a comparison operator, and a comparison value, DataEase asks Any more criteria? and displays these options:

    0: NONE 1: and 2: or

The *and* and *or* operators are used to combine two selection criteria. When you use the *and* operator to connect two criteria, the procedure selects a record only if both criteria are met. But when you use the *or* operator, the procedure retrieves a record if either criterion is true. If you choose either operator, DataEase moves the cursor to the next line in the query and takes you through another round of menus to create the second criterion.

When you finally complete the record selection criteria by choosing 0: NONE at the Any more criteria? prompt, DataEase types a semicolon (;) at the end of the last criterion to indicate the end of the record selection criteria. DataEase then types list records in the next query line, moves the cursor to the next line, and indents to column 3. You can now begin specifying the fields to be listed from the selected records. Field selection is covered in the "Specifying Fields" section.

Looking at an Example

The following example continues the one begun in the preceding section. You want to generate a list of all widget orders in May and June, 1989. You already have selected the Widget Order form as the main form and need to indicate the records from Widget Order that should be retrieved by the query. This example demonstrates the use of low-level Interactive mode to specify record selection criteria.

In the Widget Order example, after you select Widget Order as the primary form, DataEase displays the choices 0: NONE and 1: with in the line menu. You don't want to include all orders in the list, just those from May and June, so you select 1: with. DataEase types the command with and displays a list of the fields from Widget Order in the menu line.

Because the Date field contains the information that should be used to select records, you choose it from this list. DataEase types the field name Date to the right of the command with.

Next, you must select a comparison operator. DataEase displays the list of comparison operators in the line menu. You select 6: between because you want the query to retrieve only records with dates between May 1, 1989, and June 30, 1989 (including the beginning and ending dates). DataEase types the word between to the right of the Date field name. The criterion now reads as follows:

    with Date between.

DataEase then prompts you to Define lower value for the comparison range in the second prompt line and to Select field name in the third prompt line. DataEase once again lists the field names in the line menu, this time as potential comparison values. In this example you don't want to compare the values in the Date field to the value of another field, so you choose 0: NONE from the line menu.

DataEase then displays a second comparison value menu:

    0: NONE 1: current

This menu accesses system-supplied values, including the current date, but it still does not list the comparison value you are looking for, so you select 0: NONE again.

DataEase then prompts you, in the third prompt line, to Select a relational operator. Relational operators can be used to match field values and statistical summary values in related forms (see "Using Relational Operators" later in this chapter). Again, this is not the menu you need, so you choose 0: NONE.

Finally, DataEase prompts you to Specify a constant value in the third prompt line. The menu line contains the prompt Enter a number. To skip hit TAB (there is no line menu). Type the date *05/01/89*. Press the space bar to indicate that you have finished typing the date.

DataEase types the word to and prompts you to Define higher value for the comparison range. You again press 0: NONE (or Tab) three times, but this time you type the date *06/30/89* and press the space bar.

DataEase recognizes that you have completed a record selection criterion and asks Any more criteria? in the first prompt line. You don't need to specify another criterion, so you select 0: NONE. DataEase types a semicolon (;) at the end of the line, types list records on line 3, and moves the cursor to line 4. Figure 7.6 shows the query to this point.

Fig. 7.6.

A partially completed query to retrieve orders for widgets placed during May and June, 1989.

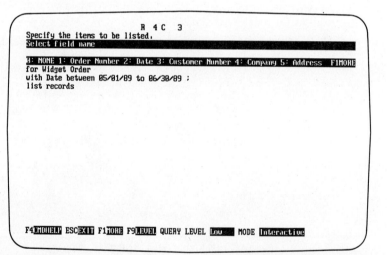

Specifying Fields

The third specification in a query created in low-level Interactive mode indicates the fields that should be processed. This portion of the query performs the same function as the Field Selection screen in Quick Reports. After DataEase places a semicolon (;) at the end of the last record selection criteria line, it moves the cursor to the first column in the next line, types list records, and moves the cursor to column 3 in the next line. The top prompt line says Specify the items to be listed, and the second prompt line instructs you to Select field name. The menu line displays a list of the primary form's fields (see fig. 7.6).

You select fields one at a time from this list, along with an optional *sorting operator*. Sorting operators indicate whether you want the records to be sorted by the specified field in ascending or reverse (descending) order and whether you want the records grouped with or without group totals.

For number, date, and time fields, you also can specify optional statistical operators discussed in "Selecting Statistical Operators" later in this chapter.

Selecting Sorting Operators

To select the first field, choose its name from the line menu. DataEase types the field name in row 4, beginning in column 3. It then displays the question Select records in groups or in a specific order? in the second prompt line and lists the following sorting operators in the line menu:

❑ 0: NONE. Select this option when you don't want to specify a sorting operator.

❑ 1: in order. This operator has the same effect as its counterpart in the Quick Reports Field Selection screen—the keyword *order*. Choose it when you want DataEase to sort records in ascending order by the selected field. For text fields, ascending order is in alphabetical order, and for number, time, and date fields, ascending order is from the lowest value to the highest. Choice fields, however, are sorted in order by the choice number, not the choice value.

❑ 2: in reverse. You can sort records by the selected field in descending order by choosing this option from the line menu. Descending order is the opposite of ascending order: reverse alphabetical order for text fields and highest value to lowest value for other field types.

❑ 3: in groups. This operator groups records by the values in this field. DataEase also sorts the grouped records in ascending order and displays the *group identifier*, the value from the specified field, only at the beginning of each group. Using the *in group* operator also enables you to create group headers and trailers for placement in the procedure's output before and after each grouping. Frequently, a procedure's output is easier to understand when the data is separated into discernible groups, preceded by a group header that includes the group identifier. For example, instead of creating a phone list that includes only sales department employees, you can include all employees, grouping them by department and including a group header in the output that identifies each group by department name. Refer to Chapters 5 and 8 for a discussion of how to create group headers and trailers in the report format.

❑ 4: in groups with group totals. This choice is most like the *group* keyword in the Quick Reports Field Selection screen. Select it when you want DataEase to group records and include group statistical subtotals in any group trailer in the report format.

The order in which you select the fields is important. The first field listed below the List Records command is equivalent to list number 1 in the Quick Reports Record Selection screen. The second field listed is equivalent to list number 2, and so on (see the "Grouping and Sorting Records" section of Chapter 5).

When you use the sorting operators, the field order determines the order of sorting precedence. The first field listed with the *in groups* or *in groups with group-totals* operators is the *primary sort* field and enjoys highest precedence when DataEase sorts on multiple fields. When neither of these operators is used in a query, the first field with the *in order* or *in reverse* operator is the primary sort field. Fields assigned to either of the two grouping operators sort before fields with the *in order* or *in reverse* operator.

For example, you want to see the list of widget orders grouped by sales representative and then by company name. You also want to be able to produce a subtotal for each sales representative. To accomplish this result, you select the Sales Rep ID field first, assigning it the *in groups with group-totals* operator (you don't group by the Last Name field because more than one sales representative can have the same last name).

After you select the sorting operator, DataEase asks, Any more items to be listed? in the first prompt line and displays the following menu in the menu line:

    0: NONE 1: ;

You certainly want the query to retrieve several other fields so you choose 1: ;. This selection is equivalent to answering, "Yes, I want to list more items." DataEase types a semicolon (;) and moves the cursor to column 3 in the next line, position R5C3. Again, DataEase displays a line menu containing a list of the fields from Widget Order.

Because you also want to see each sales representative's name in the report, select the First Name and Last Name fields without sorting operators.

So that the records will be sorted by company name and then by order number, you next choose the Company field and then the Order Number field, assigning each the *in order* operator. Figure 7.7 shows the query with Sales Rep ID, First Name, Last Name, Company, and Order Number fields selected.

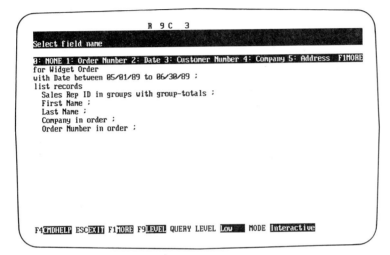

R 9 C 3

Select field name

0: NONE 1: Order Number 2: Date 3: Customer Number 4: Company 5: Address F1MORE
for Widget Order
with Date between 05/01/89 to 06/30/89 ;
list records
  Sales Rep ID in groups with group-totals ;
  First Name ;
  Last Name ;
  Company in order ;
  Order Number in order ;

F4CMDHELP ESCEXIT F1MORE F9LEVEL QUERY LEVEL Low MODE Interactive

Fig. 7.7.

A partially completed query that groups records by Sales Rep ID and sorts records by Company and Order Number.

Selecting Statistical Operators

Whenever you include a number, date, or time field in the *list records* section of a query, DataEase gives you a chance to assign a statistical operator. These operators have the same effect as their counterparts in Quick Reports, explained in Chapter 5. When you select the field and skip or choose a sorting operator, DataEase displays a menu containing the following options.

Note: Only the *NONE, item, count, mean, max,* and *min* options appear when you select date or time fields. The other statistics are available only with number fields—integer, fixed point, floating point, and dollar.

❏ 0: NONE. Select this choice when you don't want to assign any statistical operators.

❏ 1: item. When you assign a statistical operator to a selected field, DataEase by default does not include the field values in the procedure output. It only computes the statistic at the end of the report and in group trailers if the *in groups with group-totals* operator is used. Select this menu option to cause DataEase to list the value of this field in every record.

❏ 2: count. This option counts the number of records that meet the record selection criteria.

❏ 3: sum. This option computes a total of the values in the selected field from among the records that meet the record selection criteria.

❏ 4: mean. Use this operator to calculate the average of values in the specified field from the selected records.

❏ 5: max. Choose this option to compute the highest value in the target field from among the selected records.

❏ 6: min. Select this choice to return the lowest value in the specified field from the records that meet the record selection criteria.

❏ 7: variance. This operator calculates the sample variance statistic (the standard deviation squared), using the values from the specified field in the selected records as the sample data.

❏ 8: std.dev. Choose this operator to calculate the standard deviation (the square root of the variance) statistic for the target field values in the selected records.

❏ 9: std.err. This statistical operator computes the standard error (standard deviation divided by the square root of the count) of the values in the specified field for the records that meet the record selection criteria.

You can choose one or more of these operators with a single item. DataEase produces each statistic at the end of the procedure output. When you have chosen the sorting operator *in groups with group-totals*, DataEase also places each statistic in each group trailer. Most of the above statistics are most meaningful in a group trailer.

Tip: If you don't choose any statistical operator for a field listed in the *list records* section of the query, DataEase includes the field values themselves in the procedure output along with the respective records. But whenever you assign a statistical operator to a field, DataEase only displays the statistic, not the underlying values, unless you also choose 1: item. Without the *item* operator, DataEase only lists the chosen statistic(s) at the end of the report (and in group trailers whenever you assign the *in groups with group-totals* sorting operator).

Again, the Widget Order query can be used as an example to demonstrate the use of statistical operators. You want this query to generate a list of widget orders from May and June. You also want the list to show the total for each order, subtotals for each sales representative, and a grand total at the end. Figure 7.7 shows the query as it is so far. The fields Sales Rep ID (in groups with group-totals), First Name, Last Name, Company (in order), and Order Number (in order) already have been included in the *list records* section of the query.

To include the date that each order was placed in the widget orders list, you first select the Date field from the line menu. You needn't sort by the Date field because you are already sorting by the Order Number field; therefore, you skip the sorting operator menu by selecting 0: NONE.

DataEase then asks, Any statistics desired on this item? in the second prompt line and displays the following menu:

    0: NONE 1: ;

To indicate that you do not want to specify a statistic for the Date field, choose 0: NONE. Then choose 1: ; to complete this list item. DataEase types the semicolon (;) and moves to the next line, indented to column 3.

The last field you need to include is the Order Total field. You want the total for each order to appear in the procedure output, but you also want DataEase to compute the sum of these totals for each sales representative as well as at the end of the report.

First, you select the Order Total field from the line menu and skip the sorting order menu. DataEase asks, Any statistics on this item? in the second prompt line. You select 1: : from the line menu to indicate that you do want to specify a statistic. DataEase types the colon (:) and moves one space to the right.

Next, you choose 3: sum from the line menu that lists the available statistical operators. DataEase types sum to the right of the colon. However, to include the actual order totals with each Widget Order record in the output, you also select 1: item from the line menu. DataEase types item to the right of sum.

Finally, to indicate that you have no more statistical operators for this item, select 0: NONE. DataEase asks one more time, Any more items to be listed?. To show that you're finished with this *list records* item and that you do not want to select any more fields, you choose 0: NONE to complete the query definition. DataEase types a period (.) to the right of the last character in the last item, saves the query to RAM, and returns to the DQL menu. Figure 7.8 shows the completed query.

Fig. 7.8.

*A completed query
to retrieve records
from Widget Order
for May and June,
1989.*

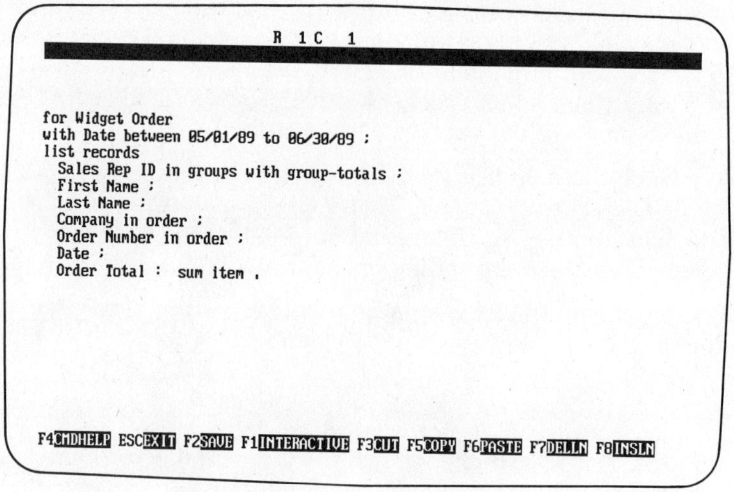

```
                           R  1 C  1


for Widget Order
with Date between 05/01/89 to 06/30/89 :
list records
   Sales Rep ID in groups with group-totals :
   First Name :
   Last Name :
   Company in order :
   Order Number in order :
   Date :
   Order Total :  sum item .




F4 CMDHELP  ESC EXIT  F2 SAVE  F1 INTERACTIVE  F3 CUT  F5 COPY  F6 PASTE  F7 DELLN  F8 INSLN
```

Using Relational Operators

Chapter 3 introduces you to the *lookup* operator in field definition
derivation formulas, and Chapter 6 discusses derivation formulas that use
relational statistical operators. The First Name and Last Name fields in the
Widget Order Multiform are *lookup* fields, and the Order Total field in the
Widget Order Multiform is a field derived through use of a relational
statistical operator, *sum of*.

Although creating derived fields in forms and Multiforms that perform
lookups and compute relational statistics is often most convenient, in some
situations, you may determine the need for such fields at the time you
design a procedure. Instead of going to the trouble of adding a field to the
form or Multiform definition, you can derive these values using DQL
relational operators in a query.

When defining an item in the *list records* section of a query, you can look
up a field value or values from a related form. You specify a *relational
operator* and then specify a relationship and a field in the related form.

Instead of choosing a field name from the line menu, choose 0: NONE twice.
DataEase then displays the prompts Specify the items to be listed in the
first prompt line and Select a relational operator in the second prompt
line. The menu line contains the following options:

❑ 0: NONE—skips the relational operator menu.

❑ 1: all—retrieves matching values from multiple matching related
   records. This operator is useful when the related form is on the
   many-side of a one-to-many relationship with the primary form.

❑ 2: any—selects the first matching record in a related form. This operator is equivalent to a lookup derivation formula in form definition. Use this operator to look up a value on the one-side of a many-to-one relationship (for example, when there is only one matching record to lookup).

❑ 3: count of—counts the number of matching records in a related form for each record in the primary form.

❑ 4: highest of—returns the highest value in the specified field from among the matching records in the related form.

❑ 5: lowest of—selects the lowest value in the specified field from the matching related records.

❑ 6: sum of—calculates the arithmetic sum of the field's values in the matching related records.

❑ 7: mean of—produces the arithmetic mean (average) of the values in the specified field in the matching related records.

When you select a relational operator, DataEase displays the question Select a predefined relationship?. Select the relationship that defines the link from the primary form to the field you want to look up. (The relationship usually has the same name as the form that contains the data.)

DataEase then gives you a chance to specify selection criteria that would apply in addition to the record selection criteria. This criteria would further limit the records looked up, selecting some rather than all matching records in the related form. Specify criteria in the same way that you would create record selection criteria. Choose 0: NONE to skip the menu.

Next, DataEase instructs you to Select field name. The line menu contains a list of fields from the related form. Choose the name of the target field from this menu. The target field is the field whose value will be retrieved or on which the procedure will perform the statistical computation.

After you select a field, you can assign a sorting operator—in order, in reverse, in groups, or in groups with group-totals. You should avoid using *in groups* or *in groups with group-totals* with relational operators. This method does not consistently produce the intended results.

Finally, DataEase asks, Any more items to be listed?. Choose 1: ; if you want to specify more list items, or select 0: NONE to indicate that you are finished.

For example, you may want to see the widget orders grouped first by sales region and then by sales representative. But the Region field is in the Sales Representative form, and the primary form for the procedure is the Multiform Widget Order. You can go back and add a lookup field to the

Multiform, or you can use a relational operator to retrieve the value in the Region field from Sales Representative. This field should be the first one listed in the *list records* section, so that it will be the primary sort field. Records are displayed in the report in order by the values in the Region field. (Refer to "Modifying a Query" later in this chapter for help in adding a line to a query without having to start from scratch after you have completed the first draft.)

In the line below the List Records command and at the prompt Select field name, skip the menu that lists the field names by pressing 0: NONE. Also skip the next menu. DataEase then prompts you to Select a relational operator. Because the Sales Representative form is on the one-side of a many-to-one relationship, you select 2: any as the relational operator. (If it were a one-to-many relationship, you would select the relational operator 1: all.) DataEase types the operator any. After you have selected a relational operator, DataEase displays a list of relationships and prompts you to select one. You choose Sales Representative from the line menu. DataEase types Sales Representative to the right of any and asks whether you want to Specify any additional relationship criteria?. You do not want to specify any other criteria, so you respond with 0: NONE.

DataEase next prompts you to Select field name. You have to select the field you want the procedure to look up from the Sales Representative form. Choose the Region field from the line menu; DataEase types Region to the right of Sales Representative and asks for a sorting operator. You want the records sorted by the sales region, so you select 4: in groups with group totals. DataEase types this operator to the right of the field name Region.

At this point, DataEase is ready to define more list items. It asks, Any more items to be listed?. You then can go on to define other items in the query. Figure 7.9 shows the query with the Region field as the first item in the *list records* section of the query.

Displaying the Result

As you know, a query is only part of a procedure. In addition to the query, a procedure also must have a procedure format and a print style. By default, however, DataEase chooses a format and print style for you. As in Quick Reports, the default format sends output to the screen in the *columnar* format. You will rarely create a procedure without modifying one or both of these default settings.

Figure 7.10 shows the widget orders list displayed on-screen in the default columnar format. Notice that the records are grouped by the values in the Region field and then by Sales Rep ID. However, because of the number of

```
for Widget Order
with Date between 05/01/89 to 06/30/89 ;
list records
  any Sales Representative Region in groups with group-totals ;
  Sales Rep ID in groups with group-totals ;
  First Name ;
  Last Name ;
  Company in order ;
  Order Number in order ;
  Date ;
  Order Total :  sum item .




F4CMDHELP ESCEXIT F2SAVE F1INTERACTIVE F3CUT F5COPY F6PASTE F7DELLN F8INSLN
```

Fig. 7.9.

A completed query that groups orders by sales region.

fields, not all the columns can be viewed on-screen at once, and the data is difficult to understand. Figure 7.11 shows the same query after the format has been modified somewhat. Refer to Chapter 8 for a complete discussion of customizing procedure/report formats.

```
                                 Running procedure
SPACE or PgDn: More  EXIT: Abort PgUp Home LEFT RIGHT Arrows: Scroll

================================================================================
 any Sales    Sales Rep       First              Last                     Com
Representati     ID           Name               Name
    ve
  Region
--------------------------------------------------------------------------------
Northern     329-76-2219 Sharon            Kellogs          Ace Airplanes
                         Sharon            Kellogs          Hidden Resorts
--------------------------------------------------------------------------------
sum
================================================================================
             921-65-1234 Gertrude          English          Ace Airplanes
                         Gertrude          English          Ace Airplanes
--------------------------------------------------------------------------------
sum
================================================================================
--------------------------------------------------------------------------------
sum
================================================================================
Southern     448-09-6721 Samantha          Green            Alpha Freight Lin
                         Samantha          Green            Alpha Freight Lin
F4 CMDHELP ESC EXIT C:\DEDATA\             ORDER TRACKING   06/05/89  11 19 am
```

Fig. 7.10.

The widget orders query displayed in default columnar format.

Fig. 7.11.

The widget orders query displayed in a modified columnar format.

```
                                    Running procedure
SPACEorPgDn: Continue procedure EXIT: Abort procedure PgUp: Scroll
==================================================================
            Company              Order  Date   Order Total
------------------------------------------------------------------
Northern Sales Region

Sales Rep 329-76-2219 - Sharon Kellogs

            Ace Airplanes        101  05/08/89    1,798.25
            Hidden Resorts       105  05/16/89    1,798.50
                                                 ----------
Sales Rep Total                                   3,596.75

Sales Rep 921-65-1234 - Gertrude English

            Ace Airplanes        100  05/02/09    6,043.25
            Ace Airplanes        100  06/05/89      899.00
                                                 ----------
Sales Rep Total                                   6,942.25

                                                 ==========
Region Total                                     10,539.00

F4 CMDHELP ESC EXIT C:\DEDATA\        ORDER TRACKING    06/05/89  12 17 pm
```

The print style settings for DQL procedures are identical to the settings for Quick Reports. To make changes to print style, select the **6. Define Print Style** option on the DQL menu. Refer to Chapter 5 for more information about assigning an output device on the Print Style Specification screen.

To run the procedure, you select **1. Run Procedure** from the DQL menu. DataEase sends the procedure's output to the device designated on the Print Style Specification screen.

Modifying a Low-Level Query

If life were perfect, Perrier would flow from every tap, no one would ever accidentally format a PC's hard disk, and you would create every DataEase query exactly the way you want it the first time. At least where DataEase is concerned, making changes to a query is easy.

Using the Edit Mode

After you finish defining the query initially and return to the DQL menu, DataEase changes the menu option from **4. Define Query** to **4. Modify Query**. Select this choice whenever you want to make a change to a query.

DataEase does not activate the Interactive mode when modifying a query; instead, the screen is in the Edit mode. If you feel comfortable with the DQL command syntax, you can edit the screen, making the modifications you desire. The cursor-movement keys listed in table 7.1 are available for moving around the screen. The function-key commands listed in table 7.2 also are available to assist you in editing the query.

Table 7.1
Query Definition
Edit Mode
Cursor-Movement Keys

Key	Moves Cursor to
↑	Previous line
↓	Next line
←	One position (space) to the left
Backspace	One position to the left
→	One position to the right
Home	Position R1C1
End	Column 1 in last line containing any text or field
Tab	Six positions to the right
Shift-Tab	Six positions to the left
Ctrl-→	Column 81, same row; column 121; 161; 201; and so on
Ctrl-←	Column 1, same row
Enter	Column 1, next row
PgDn	Bottom row of screen, same column
PgUp	Top row of screen, same column

Table 7.2
Query Definition
Edit Mode
Function-Key Commands

Function Key (KEY NAME)	Function
Esc (EXIT)	Abandons the procedure (requires confirmation by 2: yes or 1: no)
F1 (INTERACTIVE)	Activates the Interactive mode
Alt-F1 (HELP)	Provides help on current operation

Table 7.2—*continued*

Function Key (KEY NAME)	Function
F2 (SAVE)	Returns to DQL menu after saving all changes to RAM (not to disk)
F3 (CUT)	*Cuts* a block of text
F4 (CMDHELP)	Displays pull-down menus
F5 (COPY)	*Copies* a block of text
F6 (PASTE)	*Pastes* a *cut* or *copied* block of text
F7 (DELLN)	Deletes a complete line (blank or text)
F8 (INSLN)	Inserts a new line above the cursor
F9 (LEVEL)	Toggles between low and high level
F10 (FIELD)	Activates the Interactive mode (same as F1)

Using the Interactive Mode

In addition to using the Edit mode, you also can modify a query in the Interactive mode. In fact, you may prefer this method until you get your "DQL-legs" and begin to feel comfortable with DQL syntax. The Interactive mode is not without its drawbacks, however. Accidentally overwriting a portion of the query that you do not want to delete is fairly easy, but you will not have a problem if you develop a clear understanding of how the Interactive mode works.

When you activate the Interactive mode by pressing F1 (INTERACTIVE), DataEase reads the query from the beginning up to the space just to the left of the cursor, checking for correct syntax. If you have introduced a mistake when editing the query in the Edit mode, DataEase beeps and places the cursor at the beginning of the word containing the error. DataEase switches to the Interactive mode and displays the appropriate menu at the point of the error. You then can respond to the prompts and menus as needed to correct the mistake.

When DataEase finds no errors, it begins the interactive query building process at the position the cursor is in when you press F1 (INTERACTIVE). Be aware, however, that DataEase ignores anything to the right of or below the cursor on-screen and overwrites text beyond the cursor as it rebuilds the query.

To return to the Edit mode, you usually can press the Backspace key. If pressing Backspace doesn't work (for instance, when the cursor is already in column 1), press the up-arrow key.

In the Interactive mode or the Edit mode, you can press F2 (SAVE) to save the changes to RAM and return to the DQL menu.

Tip: The most practical method of inserting a new series of DQL commands using the Interactive mode is to insert enough blank lines to accommodate any additions before activating the Interactive mode. For example, the only difference in the queries shown in figures 7.8 and 7.9 is the following line:

any Sales Representative Region in groups with group-totals;

You can add this line to the query in figure 7.8 using the Interactive mode. First, you access the query in the Edit mode and insert a blank line at row 4. Then, with the cursor in column 3 in the new blank row, you press F1 (INTERACTIVE). DataEase reads the query to this point and, finding no errors, picks up with the Interactive mode menus and prompts. You then can add the Region field by responding as described in the preceding section. At the end of the item, DataEase types a semicolon (;) and moves the cursor to row 5, completing the addition of the Region field. You press the F2 (SAVE) to save the changes.

Saving and Loading a Procedure Definition

A DQL query created in low-level Interactive mode is not difficult to create, but you certainly don't want to start over again each time you need to use the procedure. Just as with Quick Reports, DataEase enables you to save a DQL procedure definition to disk for use at a later time.

When you have completed a query, you should save the definition. Then, as you add a custom format and print style, you can save it again. From the DQL menu, select **7. Save Procedure**. DataEase displays the prompt Please enter the procedure name:. Type a procedure name up to 20 characters long and press Enter. If this is the first time you have saved the procedure, DataEase saves to the specified disk file all the procedure settings and selections currently in RAM and displays the message New procedure created in the message area at the top of the screen. It also adds the new procedure name to the prompt line, to the right of the words Current report:.

Note: If you have run the procedure and then select **7. Save Procedure** from the DQL menu, DataEase takes you first to the Query Definition screen. To continue the same process, press F2 (SAVE). Then, DataEase asks you to specify a procedure name as described above.

Tip: When you name the procedure, make the name descriptive. You can say a lot in 20 characters. For example, you might name the widget orders list procedure developed in this chapter *May-June Orders* to remind you that it produces a list of the orders placed in May and June.

When you have previously saved the procedure definition and want to save it again in its modified form, DataEase asks, Do you want to save modified procedure under another name?(y/n): To replace the old version with the modified settings, answer this prompt 1: no. When you want to create a new procedure file, leaving the original unchanged, respond 2: yes. DataEase then asks for a new name. Type a unique procedure name up to 20 characters long and press Enter. DataEase saves the new version of the procedure with the new name.

Of course, the purpose of saving a procedure definition to disk is to be able to use it again at a later time. To load a previously saved procedure definition, choose 8: Load Procedure from the DQL menu. DataEase displays the available Quick Reports and DQL procedures in a window menu on the right side of the screen. Move the highlighted selection bar to the procedure you want to use and press Enter. DataEase loads the procedure settings to RAM and displays the message Procedure *p* Read *where p* is the name of the procedure definition you selected. DataEase also shows the name of the procedure definition in the prompt line. You can now run the procedure or use it as a starting point to create a different procedure.

Deleting a Procedure Definition

Occasionally, you may need to clear old procedure definitions from the data disk to make more room or just to clear away obsolete files. To delete a procedure definition, select **9. Delete Procedure** from the DQL menu. Choose the name of the procedure to be deleted from the window menu that lists all available Quick Report definitions and DQL procedures and press Enter. DataEase asks you to confirm the deletion. Answer 2: yes. DataEase deletes the procedure definition and displays the message procedure deleted in the message area.

Printing a Procedure Definition

DataEase provides two ways to print a hard copy of the DQL procedure definition (also called the procedure *specification*). From the DQL menu, select **10. Print Procedure Definition**, or from the Format Definition screen, press Shift-F9 (PRINT). Both methods print a listing that includes the query definition, procedure format, field descriptions, and the memory required by the procedure definition when in use. You should make it a habit to print a copy of every procedure definition. File the copy away with the printouts that you have made of the record-entry form definitions. Both types of printed definitions will come in handy later when you have to start making significant changes to your system. Without the hard copies to jog your memory, you may have to start designing the system from scratch again.

Chapter Summary

This chapter has introduced you to the most fundamental DQL concepts and terminology. It explained the terms *query* and *procedure* and then went into detail about how to define a simple DQL query created using low-level Interactive mode that can retrieve information, sort records, group data, and use relational operators. The chapter also explained how to modify a query, save a query to RAM, save a procedure to disk, and print a hard copy of a procedure's definition. Now that you have a good grasp on how to build a query, take a look at Chapter 8 for specifics on how to create custom procedure/report formats and at Chapter 10 for help in creating menus that can tie all your DQL procedures and Quick Reports together into one easy-to-use system. Then, you will be ready to turn to Chapter 11 for information about creating full-blown DQL queries and procedures.

8

Customizing
DataEase Reports

This chapter expands on discussions begun in Chapters 5, 6, and 7. In Chapters 5 and 6 you learn how to present information from your database on-screen or on paper using the DataEase Quick Reports capability. Chapter 7 then explains how to use the DataEase Query Language to create simple DQL procedures.

This chapter describes how to create more powerful and easier-to-use reports and procedures by using data-entry forms, custom report formats, and predefined template formats. Data-entry forms are available only in procedures, but custom report formats and template formats can be used in Quick Reports and in procedures that create output.

In this chapter, unless specifically stated otherwise, the term *report* refers to a procedure that produces displayable or printable output as well as to a Quick Report. Although you can design procedures that perform some other function (for example, procedures that modify your database without creating visible output, such as procedures for deleting records or reorganizing a form—see Chapter 12), all procedures you have seen so far in this book do create displayable output. The term *report* most accurately describes the output itself, and the term *procedure* refers to the steps that DataEase must take to produce the output. But the two terms are commonly used almost interchangeably.

Creating a Data-Entry Form

As you have learned, DataEase enables you to create reports that include selected records and fields. In Quick Reports, you use the Record Selection and Field Selection screens to specify the records and fields to be displayed in the report. Similarly, a DQL query retrieves records and fields for processing. Both methods, however, require you to specify the selection criteria before running the report. You process the data in a *batch*; that is, after you start the report or procedure, it runs without further input or instructions from you and then quits. Whenever you want to select a different group of records or fields, you have to modify the appropriate selection screen or query and run the report again.

This batch processing method is fine for anyone who understands how to modify Quick Reports selection screens or DQL queries. If you design a report to be run by someone who is not very familiar with DataEase, however, the capability of changing the selection criteria *interactively* while the report is running is desirable. DataEase provides this convenience through *data-entry* forms, available in DQL procedures but not in Quick Reports.

Despite their similarity in name, a data-entry form is not the same as a DataEase record-entry form. The sole purpose of a data-entry form is to provide data to a procedure. As you know, a record-entry form is used to place data into your database as well as to view and modify the data. In contrast, data entered into a data-entry form is not placed directly into the database. Instead, data typed into a data-entry form is available to be processed by the DQL procedure.

Data-entry forms have two major benefits: they enable you to input different selection criteria each time you run a procedure without having to modify the query and to interactively change the selection criteria and process the data again without returning to the DQL menu.

The first portion of this chapter discusses creating and using data-entry forms, beginning with a look at factors to help you determine whether you need to create one at all.

Determining the Need for a Data-Entry Form

Whenever you create a DataEase procedure, creating a data-entry form is optional. To help you decide when you should exercise this option, ask yourself the following questions:

❏ *Are you designing the procedure for use by someone else?* When you are the only person using a database system, you can add or alter the parameters used by a procedure as often as you need to by modifying the query. But, if the system is for someone not familiar with building DataEase queries, consider using a data-entry form. A data-entry form provides a convenient way for you to elicit information from a user to be processed by the procedure.

❏ *Do you frequently change the selection criteria?* Although designing a DQL query in the Interactive mode is fairly easy, the capability of changing a value in a selection criteria without having to modify a query definition is more convenient. Data-entry forms enable you to change selection criteria each time you run the procedure without making a single modification to the query itself. For example, you can run the same report several times using a different ZIP code each time to create a mailing list for that ZIP code.

❏ *Do you want to provide variable information to a procedure not already in the database?* Sometimes you may want to provide to the procedure a value from outside the database that can vary from time to time—an interest rate, for example. A data-entry form enables you to provide the value each time you run the procedure.

❏ *Do you want to run the procedure more than once before returning to the DQL menu?* Normally, when you run a procedure, it produces its output and returns to the DQL menu. If you want to run the procedure again, you have to choose **1. Run Procedure** from the menu. A procedure can be designed, however, so that it returns to a data-entry form when it is finished. You can then choose to provide further data and run the procedure again without first returning to the DQL menu.

If you answer "yes" to one or more of these questions, you should consider using data-entry forms.

Building a Data-Entry Form

To create a data-entry form, you first access the DQL menu. Refer to Chapter 7 for a description of the methods available for displaying this menu. As you are defining the procedure that will use the data-entry form, select **3. Define Data-entry Form** from the DQL menu. If you have previously defined the procedure, load it into memory (RAM) before selecting this menu option. DataEase adds a window below the DQL menu containing the question, After running the procedure, display data-entry form again?

Respond 2: yes to this question when you want the procedure to return, after running, to the data-entry form instead of the DQL menu. When the data-entry form reappears, enter data and run the procedure again or press Esc to return to the DQL menu.

When you only want the procedure to run once, select 1: no at this question. You can use the data-entry form to enter data for the procedure to use, but when the procedure finishes, it will return directly to the DQL menu.

When you make a choice at the first prompt, DataEase displays the Data-Entry Form Definition screen, identical in appearance to the Form Definition screen. In fact, the mechanics of designing a data-entry form and a record-entry form are nearly identical. The cursor-movement keys and function-key commands available in the Form Definition screen are also available here, except F9 (SUBFORM). Subject to the following limitations, you place text and fields on a data-entry form in the same manner as in a record-entry form. The following field definition characteristics are not available in the definition of a data-entry form:

❏ Field indexing

❏ Unique fields

❏ Field sequencing

❏ Virtual fields

❏ View or write security

Oddly enough, all of these characteristics, except the virtual field feature (the 3: yes and do not save (virtual) option at the Prevent Data-entry? prompt), appear as options on the Field Definition screen. They have no effect if you choose them.

Subforms also are not available in a data-entry form. You can, however, use derivation formulas including lookup formulas to retrieve values from matching records in another form in the database. As with record-entry forms, you also must create a predefined relationship between a data-entry form and the related form before you can successfully perform the lookup, as described in the next section.

When you finish designing the form, you need to save it. Press F2 (SAVE), and DataEase saves the form definition to memory and returns to the DQL menu. The third menu option now reads **3. Modify Data-entry Form**.

Looking at an Example

An example will help explain how useful a data-entry form can be. Assume that you have created the May-June Orders procedure described in Chapter 7. This procedure prints a list of widget orders for the months May and June, 1989. You want to use this report, however, to print reports for other time periods. You could, of course, define a different report for each month, each quarter, and so on. But a more efficient solution is to design a data-entry form that enables you to enter start and end dates for the report. You can then modify the May-June Orders procedure so that it uses the dates that you provide through the data-entry form when the procedure runs. (This procedure modification is explained later in this chapter.)

Before you create the data-entry form, you must first load the May-June Orders procedure by selecting **8. Load Procedure** from the DQL menu and then choosing the form name from the window menu. DataEase displays the message Procedure May-June Orders Read in the message area. It also shows the message Current procedure: May-June Orders in the prompt line. Now you're ready to begin creating the form.

To create the data-entry form, choose **3. Define Data-entry Form** from the DQL menu. DataEase displays the question, After running the procedure, display data-entry form again? Respond 2: yes so that you can use the procedure more than once without returning to the DQL menu. DataEase displays the Data-Entry Form Definition screen, which contains the message Form: May-June Orders in the title area.

The purpose of this data-entry form is to supply the start and end dates for the report. You therefore need to define two date fields, one for each date. Position the cursor where you want the prompt for the first field to begin and type *Start Date:*. Then, press F10 (FIELD) to display the Field Definition screen. Define this field as a date field with the *required* characteristic. Similarly, define a date field named *End Date*, again assigning the *required* characteristic. Then, to make the form easy to understand and nicer to look at, add some instructions and a border. The result is shown in figure 8.1.

To save the form, press F2 (SAVE). DataEase saves the data-entry form to memory and returns to the DQL menu. See "Using a Data-Entry Field in a Query" later in this chapter for a description of the modifications you must now make to the query in order to use the data entered in the two date fields.

Fig. 8.1.

The data-entry form for the May-June Orders procedure.

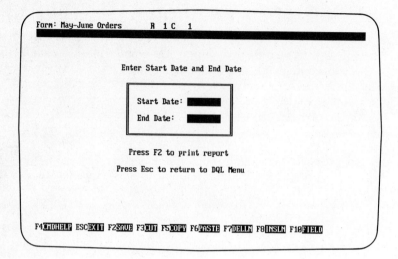

```
Form: May-June Orders        R 1 C  1



                    Enter Start Date and End Date


                  ┌─────────────────────────────┐
                  │  Start Date: ▉▉▉▉▉▉▉         │
                  │                              │
                  │  End Date:   ▉▉▉▉▉▉▉         │
                  └─────────────────────────────┘


                    Press F2 to print report

                  Press Esc to return to DQL Menu




    F4 CMDHELP  ESC EXIT  F2 SAVE  F3 CUT  F5 COPY  F6 PASTE  F7 DELLN  F8 INSLN  F10 FIELD
```

Creating a Lookup Field

Creating one or more lookup fields in a data-entry form may sometimes be convenient. You create a lookup field for a data-entry form in the same way as you create a lookup field for a record-entry form, using a *lookup formula* in a derived field. Before the lookup field can actually accomplish its purpose, you also must define a relationship between the data-entry form and the related form.

To define a relationship between a data-entry form and a record-entry form, select **1. Form Definition and Relationship** and then **3. Define Relationships** from the DataEase Main menu. DataEase displays the Form Relationship screen with the cursor in the Form 1 field. Notice that all the record-entry forms from your database are listed in a line menu in the prompt line, but the data-entry form is not listed.

Tip: When you plan to define a relationship between a data-entry form and a record-entry form, you must save the procedure that contains the data-entry form with a name that is different from any existing record-entry form. Using a unique name is a good practice anyway: avoid using the same name for any two DataEase objects (forms, procedures, Quick Reports). DataEase enables you to use up to 20 characters to define form names and procedure names, and you should take full advantage of this feature. Longer, more descriptive names are easier to understand and to distinguish from one another.

Press Esc, and DataEase removes the line menu from the prompt line. Then, at the Form 1: prompt, type the name of the DQL procedure containing the data-entry form and press Enter or Tab. DataEase moves the cursor to the next field, to the right of the prompt And 2:. Select the name of the related form from the line menu. DataEase moves the cursor to the field to the left of the first equal sign (=).

DataEase does not list the names of the data-entry form fields in a line menu, so you must type the name of the match field from the data-entry form and press Enter or Tab again. DataEase then moves to the right of the equal sign (=) and lists the field names from the related form in a line menu. Select the match field from the list, and DataEase moves to the next line, to the left of the second equal sign (=). When multiple match fields exist, use the remaining rows of the Form Relationship screen.

When you have defined the relationship, press F2 (SAVE) to save it to memory. Then, press Esc (EXIT) to return to the Form Definition menu. Press Esc (EXIT) again to return to the DataEase Main menu.

Using a Data-Entry Form

Adding a data-entry form to a procedure is really a two-step process. After you define the data-entry form, you must then include its fields in the procedure's query. This section of the chapter describes the ways you can use a data-entry field in a query.

When you run a procedure for which you have defined a data-entry form, you are immediately presented with the data-entry form so that you can enter data. This part of the chapter also describes how entering data in a data-entry form differs from entering data in a normal record-entry form.

Using a Data-Entry Field

Fields from a data-entry form can be used in a DQL query or a DQL procedure format just as you would any field from the primary record-entry form. You must precede the field name, however, with the keyword *data-entry* to indicate that the field is from the data-entry form. These data-entry fields are most typically used to specify record or field selection criteria or to provide some constant value needed by the procedure.

After you have defined the data-entry form for a procedure, you can even use the Interactive mode to add the data-entry fields to the query. For example, you can use the Interactive mode to add data-entry fields to the May-June Orders query. The data-entry form developed in the preceding section contains two fields: Begin Date and End Date. You need to add these fields to the *with* line in the query in place of the dates 05/01/89 and 06/03/89.

To make this change, you first choose **4. Modify Query** on the DQL menu. DataEase displays the existing query (developed in Chapter 7) shown in figure 8.2.

Fig. 8.2.

The May-June Orders query, before adding data-entry fields.

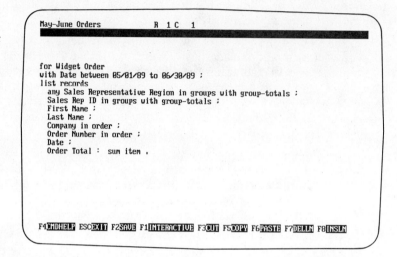

```
May-June Orders            R 1 C  1


for Widget Order
with Date between 05/01/89 to 06/30/89 ;
list records
   any Sales Representative Region in groups with group-totals ;
   Sales Rep ID in groups with group-totals ;
   First Name ;
   Last Name ;
   Company in order ;
   Order Number in order ;
   Date ;
   Order Total :  sum item .




F4 CMDHELP ESC EXIT F2 SAVE F1 INTERACTIVE F3 CUT F5 COPY F6 PASTE F7 DELLN F8 INSLN
```

Before attempting to make any additions to the query, delete the existing record selection criterion. Move the cursor to the 0 in the first date (05/01/89), and press Del until both dates are deleted and the line reads

    with Date between

The cursor is still on line 2 of the query. To be sure that you have allowed enough room for the data-entry fields, move the cursor to line 3 and press F8 (INSLN) to add a blank line below the current with line. Then move the cursor back to the position one space to the right of the keyword between, position R2C19.

To invoke the Interactive mode, press F1 (INTERACTIVE). DataEase reads the query to this point and determines that you are in the middle of defining record selection criteria. It displays the prompts Any record selection criteria? in the first prompt line, Define lower value for the comparison range in the second prompt line, and Select field name in the third prompt line. The menu line contains a list of field names from the primary form but no data-entry fields. The screen is in low query level and in the Interactive mode.

Bypass this first menu by pressing 0: NONE or Tab. DataEase displays the following menu:

    0: NONE 1: current 2: data-entry

Before you created the data-entry form, this menu did not include the 2: data-entry option. Choose this option, and DataEase types data-entry to the right of the keyword between. It now lists the two data-entry fields, Start Date and End Date, in the menu line.

You want the new record selection criterion to range between the dates you enter in the Start Date and End Date fields. The with line in the query now reads

    with Date between data-entry

Select 1: Start Date from the menu, and DataEase types Start Date to in the query, so that the entire line reads as follows:

    with Date between data-entry Start Date to

Again, DataEase lists the primary form fields as line menu options. Skip this menu by pressing 0: NONE or Tab. Just as before, select 2: data-entry from the next menu. DataEase types data-entry, just as before, and displays the two data-entry field names in the menu line. Finally, choose 2: End Date from the line menu. DataEase types End Date in the query and the message Any more criteria? in the second prompt line. Because you only want to specify this one criterion, select 0: NONE or press Tab to skip the menu. DataEase types a semicolon (;) at the end of the line in the query, types list records on line 3 of the query, and moves the cursor to position R4C3. The new with line in the query is now

    with Date between data-entry Start Date to data-entry End Date;

Even with the additions, it still fits on one line, and you can press F7 (DELLN) to delete the extra *list records* line. Deleting the line also returns the screen to the Edit mode. Figure 8.3 shows the completed query. Finally, press F2 (SAVE) to save the modified query to memory (RAM). If you don't need to delete a line, press F2 (SAVE).

Now that you have made this change to the query, you decide that the report itself (the output) should indicate the range of dates that it covers. To modify the format, select **5. Modify Format** from the DQL menu. DataEase asks, Do you want to keep the existing procedure format? Because you want to modify the format, not delete it, you respond 2: yes. DataEase displays the current format, shown in figure 8.4.

You decide to add the data-entry fields to the report header at the top of the format, above the column heading labels. Place the cursor on line 2 and press F8 (INSLN) twice. Then, add the text *Widget Orders for the period* to line 2. Because you want to place the Start Field from the data-entry form in the report header, press F10 (FIELD). DataEase displays the Report Field Definition screen.

Fig. 8.3.

The May-June Orders procedure query, after adding the data-entry fields, data-entry Start Date and data-entry End Date.

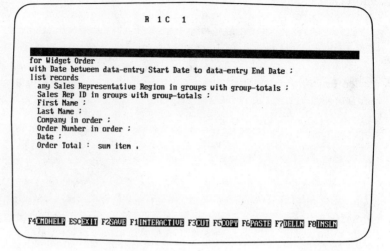

```
                         R  1 C   1


for Widget Order
with Date between data-entry Start Date to data-entry End Date ;
list records
   any Sales Representative Region in groups with group-totals ;
   Sales Rep ID in groups with group-totals ;
   First Name ;
   Last Name ;
   Company in order ;
   Order Number in order ;
   Date ;
   Order Total :  sum item .




      F4 CMDHELP ESC EXIT F2 SAVE F1 INTERACTIVE F3 CUT F5 COPY F6 PASTE F7 DELLN F8 INSLN
```

Fig. 8.4.

The May-June Orders procedure format before adding data-entry fields.

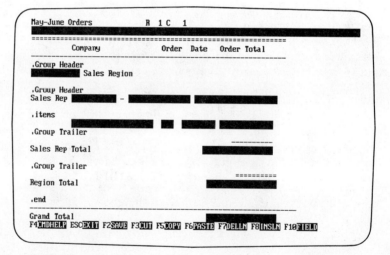

```
May-June Orders          R  1 C   1
================================================================
          Company              Order  Date   Order Total
----------------------------------------------------------------
,Group Header
            Sales Region

,Group Header
Sales Rep            -

,items

,Group Trailer

Sales Rep Total

,Group Trailer

Region Total

,end
----------------------------------------------------------------
Grand Total
F4 CMDHELP ESC EXIT F2 SAVE F3 CUT F5 COPY F6 PASTE F7 DELLN F8 INSLN F10 FIELD
```

The cursor is in the field to the right of the prompt Field Name. DataEase displays a line menu containing a list of all field names from the *list records* section of the query. It does not, however, list the data-entry fields. A message below the field reads (for new field, leave blank and press RETURN). Because you need to specify a data-entry field, press Return.

Tip: If you define the format for the first time after defining the data-entry form and after adding the data-entry fields to the query, the data-entry fields will be listed in the line menu so that you don't have to define them as new fields.

DataEase opens a small window with the title REPORT FIELD FORMULA (see fig. 8.5). Type *data-entry Start Date* and press F2 (SAVE). DataEase types this formula in the Field Name field and enters Date in the Field Type field. The cursor rests in the field to the right of the prompt Supress Spaces. Again, press F2 (SAVE) to save the field definition. DataEase places the data-entry Start Date on the Format Definition screen.

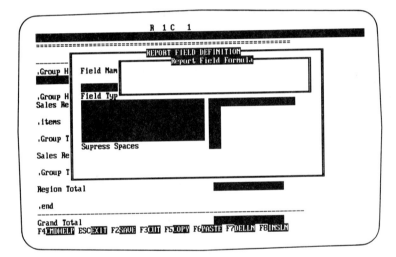

Fig. 8.5.

The Report Field Definition screen.

Next, type the word *to* to the right of the data-entry Start Date field and press F10. Again, DataEase displays the Report Field Definition screen. Again, press Enter to define a new field. In the Report Field Formula window, type *data-entry End Date*, and then press F2 (SAVE) two times. DataEase places the data-entry End Date field on the format. The modified procedure format is shown in figure 8.6. Finally, press F2 (SAVE) to save the format to memory (RAM).

Tip: When you want to use a data-entry form in a procedure, you must define the data-entry form before you try to add the data-entry field(s) to the procedure's query.

Fig. 8.6.

Fig. 8.6.

The May-June Orders procedure format after adding data-entry fields.

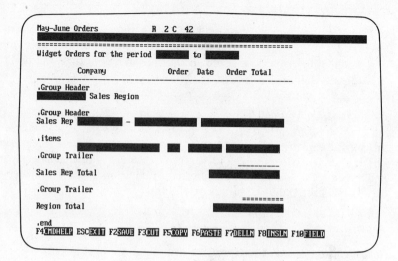

With these modifications made, the name of the procedure, May-June Orders, is no longer appropriate. To change the name, save the procedure again to disk, this time with the name *Widget Orders List*. Select **7. Save Procedure** from the DQL menu. DataEase asks, Do you want to save modified procedure under another name(y/n):. Type the letter *y*. When DataEase prompts you to enter the new procedure name, type *Widget Orders List* and press Enter. DataEase displays the message New procedure created in the message area and Current procedure: Widget Orders List in the prompt line.

At this point, you have two versions of this procedure: the original May-June Orders procedure and the new Widget Orders List.

Tip: It is a good idea to save a modified procedure with a different name. You then have an opportunity to test the new version and still return to the old version if you don't like the results. After you are satisfied that the modified procedure is better, you can delete the old version.

Entering Data into a Data-Entry Form

Entering data into a data-entry form is similar to entering data into a record-entry form. When you run the procedure, DataEase displays the data-entry field with the cursor in the first field. The cursor-movement keys listed in table 8.1 enable you to move from field to field. The function-key commands listed in table 8.2 are also available.

Table 8.1
Data-Entry Form
Cursor-Movement Keys

Key	Moves cursor to
↑	Field above
↓	Field below
←	One space to the left; from left end of field, moves to preceding field
Backspace	One space to the left, erasing preceding character
→	One position to the right; from right end of field, moves to next field
Ctrl-←	Start of long:text line
Ctrl-→	End of long:text line
Home	First (top left) field of first page
End	Last (bottom right) field of last page
Tab	Next field
Shift-Tab	Preceding field
*Enter	Next field
PgDn	First field of next page (multipage forms only)
PgUp	First field of preceding page on multipage forms; first field of current page on single-page forms

*The DataEase documentation refers to the Enter key as the Return key because earlier versions of DataEase referred to F2 as the Enter key.

After you enter data into the data-entry form, press F2 (SAVE) to continue with the procedure. The procedure takes the values you entered in the form, inserts them in the query and/or format, and completes its processing.

When the procedure is finished, it displays the data-entry form again if you so requested in the data-entry form definition. Next, you have the option of entering new field values, pressing Shift-F5 (DEFAULT FORM) to use the values from the previous data-entry screen, or pressing Shift-F6 (DEFAULT FIELD) to use the value of a corresponding field in the previous data-entry screen. Again, press F2 (SAVE) to continue executing the procedure.

At any time while the data-entry form is displayed, you can return to the DQL menu by pressing Esc (EXIT).

Table 8.2
Data-Entry Form
Function-Key Commands

Function Key (KEY NAME)	Function
Esc (EXIT)	Returns to DQL menu
F1 (MORE)	Displays a window menu
Alt-F1 (HELP)	Provides help on current operation
F2 (SAVE)	Continues with procedure
*F4 (CMDHELP)	Displays pull-down command menus
F5 (FORM CLEAR)	Clears values from all fields on-screen
Shift-F5 (DEFAULT FORM)	Fills in all data-entry values just used by procedure
F6 (FIELD CLEAR)	Clears value from current field on-screen
Shift-F6 (DEFAULT FIELD)	Fills in value from corresponding data-entry field value just used by procedure
Shift-F7 (DELLN)	Deletes a line from a long:text field
Shift-F8 (INSLN)	Inserts a blank line in a long:text field
Alt-F9 (SUSPEND CALC)	Suspends calculation
*Ctrl-F9 (RECALCULATE)	Recalculates

*New in DataEase 4.0.

Again, the Widget Orders List procedure serves as an example. Suppose that you want to print two reports, one for May and another for June. First, you must load the procedure into memory, unless the current procedure already is Widget Orders List. Choose **8. Load Procedure** and select the Widget Orders List procedure from the window menu. DataEase indicates that the Current Procedure is Widget Orders List.

Then, to run the procedure, select **1. Run Procedure** from the DQL menu. DataEase displays the data-entry screen shown in figure 8.7. The instructions you placed on-screen remind you what to do. To print a report that includes orders for the period May 1 to May 31, 1989, type *05/01/89* in the Start Date field and *05/31/89* in the End Date field. Then, press F2 (SAVE) to continue with the procedure and to print the report. The resulting report (printed to screen) is shown in figure 8.8.

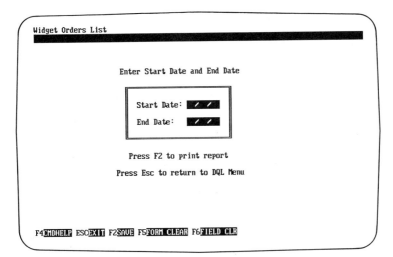

Fig. 8.7.

Using the Widget Orders List data-entry form.

Fig. 8.8.

Widget Orders for the period 05/01/89 to 05/31/89.

When the report is finished, DataEase returns to the data-entry screen. To generate a separate report for June, type *06/01/89* in the Start Date field and *06/30/89* in the End Date field. To continue processing the procedure, press F2 (SAVE). Again, DataEase prints the report, but this time for the period 06/01/89 to 06/30/89. When the second report finishes, DataEase displays the data-entry screen for a third time. You press Esc (EXIT) to return to the DQL menu.

This example illustrates the added flexibility that you have with data-entry forms. By adding a data-entry form to the May-June Orders procedure, you have created a procedure that can print a report for any date range that you specify. You do not have to modify the procedure's query at all; you just need to enter different dates in the data-entry form. Converting a Quick Report to a DQL procedure is often worthwhile just to take advantage of the data-entry form feature.

Modifying and Deleting a Data-Entry Form

You usually need to make a few adjustments to a data-entry form after testing it out, and at times you may want to delete it completely. In either case, you must first load into memory (RAM) the procedure containing the data-entry form. From the DQL menu, select **8. Load Procedure**. DataEase displays a window menu with a list of all the DQL procedures and Quick Reports. Choose the procedure containing the data-entry form you want to modify.

Whether you want to modify or delete the procedure's data-entry form, select **3. Modify Data-entry Form** from the DQL menu. DataEase displays, in a window below the menu, the question Delete the Data-entry Form?

When you want to delete the form, answer 2: yes. DataEase then adds a second question to the screen, Are you sure? Again, answer 2: yes. DataEase deletes the data-entry form from the procedure definition in memory (RAM).

Tip: DataEase does not provide an "undo" capability to undo deletion of a data-entry form, but you can undo a deletion in many cases if you take the correct action. Assuming that you loaded a previously saved procedure definition into memory (RAM) from the disk and then accidentally deleted the data-entry form, the data-entry form is really not gone until you save the procedure definition again. That is, the data-entry form still exists in the procedure definition on disk. Just load the definition again *without* saving it in memory. This method restores the procedure definition including the data-entry form as it was before you made any changes. Unfortunately, it also wipes out other changes that you may have made to other parts of the procedure (for example, to the query or to the format).

To modify the data-entry form, answer 1: no to the prompt, Delete the Data-entry Form? DataEase then displays a second question in the window below the menu, After running the procedure, display form again? Respond 2: yes when you want to be able to use the procedure more than once without returning to the DQL menu. Answer 2: no if the procedure should run once and then quit. After you respond to this second question, DataEase displays the Data-Entry Form Definition screen.

When DataEase displays the data-entry form, you can add or delete fields and text as desired. When you finish making changes, press F2 (SAVE) to save them to memory (RAM). They are not saved to disk until you save the procedure again to disk.

Creating a Custom Report Format

In Chapter 5, you learned how to create DataEase Quick Reports. You briefly examined the several predefined report format types available for use with Quick Reports: *columnar, field per line, record entry, GrafTalk chart, export,* and *mailing labels.* Each of these format types is also available for use in controlling the layout of DQL procedure output. Of these predefined formats, all but the GrafTalk chart and export formats produce output that can be printed or displayed to screen. The GrafTalk chart and export formats produce files that can be used with other software packages.

Two additional format types are not predefined: *custom* and *template.* With the custom format, you define the report layout completely from scratch, positioning fields and text exactly where you want them. A template, on the other hand, is a "canned" format that you define. You use the Form Definition screen to define a sort of "do-it-yourself" predefined format—a template. You can then use this template to generate reports using data from any database.

This section of Chapter 8 discusses how to create a custom format from scratch using the basic DataEase report format elements. However, starting with one of the predefined formats and then modifying it to suit your requirements is often easier. In the final analysis though, all DataEase format types that produce displayable/printable reports are built from the same set of report format elements. Whether you are using a predefined format or a format that you have designed from scratch, you need to develop an understanding of DataEase report format fundamentals. This portion of the chapter will help you to do so.

Starting from Scratch

Whether you are defining a format for a Quick Report or for a procedure, when you create a *custom* format you must design the format from scratch. Choose **5. Define Format** from the DQL menu or the QBE—Quick Reports menu. DataEase displays the message

```
Minimum line length for a columnar report is n
What type of report format do you want? :
```

where *n* is a positive integer. The prompt line contains a list of the available format types. Select **6. Custom** from the menu. DataEase displays the Format Definition screen, which is completely blank between the prompt line and the function key line. It looks much like the Form Definition screen.

Adding text and fields to this screen is similar to adding text and fields to the Form Definition screen. The cursor-movement keys listed in table 8.3 and the function-key commands listed in table 8.4 are available in the Format Definition screen.

Table 8.3
Format Definition Screen
Cursor-Movement Keys

Key	Moves cursor to:
↑	Preceding line
↓	Next line
←	One position (space) to the left
Backspace	One position to the left
→	One position to the right
Home	Move to position R1C1
End	Column 1 in last line containing any text or field
Tab	Six positions to the right
Shift-Tab	Six positions to the left
Ctrl-→	Column 81, same row; column 121; 161; 201; and so on
Ctrl-←	Column 1, same row
Enter	Column 1, next row
PgDn	Bottom row of screen, same column
PgUp	Top row of screen, same column

Table 8.4
Format Definition Screen
Function-Key Commands

Function Key (KEY NAME)	Function
Esc (EXIT)	Returns to QBE—Quick Reports menu or DQL menu after saving all changes—same as F2 (SAVE)
Alt-F1 (HELP)	Provides help on current operation
F2 (SAVE)	Returns to QBE—Quick Reports menu or DQL menu after saving all changes—same as Esc (EXIT)
F3 (CUT)	*Cuts* a block of text or fields
*F4 (CMDHELP)	Displays pull-down menus
F5 (COPY)	*Copies* a block of text or fields
F6 (PASTE)	Pastes a *cut* or *copied* block of text or fields
F7 (DELLN)	Deletes a complete line (blank, text, or fields)
F8 (INSLN)	Inserts a new line at the cursor
F10 (FIELD)	Defines a field
Alt-F10 (BORDERS)	Draws borders; ASCII character set

*New in DataEase 4.0.

Understanding Report Format Elements

A report format essentially defines how the fields from a single record in the primary form are to be laid out in the report. When DataEase actually generates the report, it repeats the format you have designed one time for each record selected from the primary form. These primary form records drive the report, and everything else defined in the format is ancillary to their output.

The elements used to define a DataEase report can be conveniently grouped into three categories: formatting commands, format text, and fields. Format text and fields are analogous to text and fields in a record-entry form; that is, you use format text to describe and enhance the report data in the same way you use text in a record-entry form to describe the field entries. Each field in the format represents the data from the corresponding field in a single record in the form data. Both format text and report fields appear in the final output in precisely the positions defined in the report format.

Defining a Field

To define a field in a report format, press F10 (FIELD). DataEase displays the Report Field Definition screen, shown in figure 8.9. DataEase places the cursor in the field to the right of the prompt Field Name and displays in the prompt line a list of all the fields that you have selected for inclusion in the report. When you want to select one of these fields, choose it from the line menu. DataEase reads the field definition from the record-entry form definition and fills in the Field Type area of the Report Field Definition screen.

Fig. 8.9.

The Report Field Definition screen for Widget Orders List.

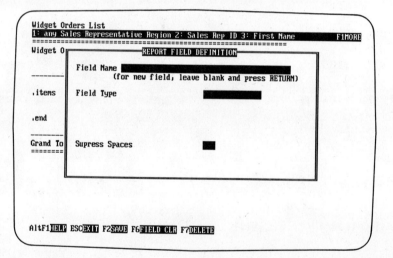

For text fields, a third prompt on the Report Field Definition screen (not shown in fig. 8.9) asks for field length. DataEase initially reads the field length from the record- or data-entry form definition and displays it on-screen, but you can increase or decrease this number. Any change made to the length does not affect the field's actual definition.

The last prompt on the Report Field Definition screen for text fields asks whether you want to Supress Spaces between fields. You often may place fields side by side in the report format that should have no more than one space separating them. However, by default, DataEase displays field values in the position where you placed the field in the format. For example, if you place one field in the format at R8C20 and the next field at R8C40, the first field prints starting at column 20 and the second field at column 40. The actual values of these fields may vary in length from one record to the next. Whenever the value of the first field is less than 19 spaces long, extra spaces are left between the two fields.

To suppress extra spaces between fields, (in other words, to have DataEase adjust the positions of the fields as it creates the report output), select 2: yes at the Supress Spaces prompt on the Report Field Definition screen. DataEase then maintains the spacing you define between the fields on that line in the format instead of maintaining the starting position of the fields.

For example, you usually want a person's first and last names to be displayed together with only one space separating them. Therefore, when you place the First Name field on the format, you indicate that spaces should be suppressed by selecting 2: yes at the Supress Spaces prompt in the Report Field Definition screen. You then place the Last Name field just one space beyond the end of the First Name field. After you have made any necessary changes to the Report Field Definition characteristics, press F2 (SAVE) to save the definition to memory.

When you use the F10 (FIELD) command to place a number field on the Report Format Definition screen, the Report Field Definition screen displays several more options than it does for text fields. When you have specified more than one statistical function for this field in the query, DataEase prompts you to choose a Statistical Function. You also can specify field type, maximum number of digits to the left of the decimal point, and number of digits to the right of the decimal. Additionally, you can choose to suppress the decimal point, commas, and spaces.

In addition to placing fields from the query in the format, you also can use DQL formulas to add other fields. When you want to add a field to the format that is not listed in the *list records* section of the query, position the cursor where you want the field to start and press F10 (FIELD). DataEase displays the Report Field Definition. At the Field Name prompt, press Enter, and DataEase displays a small window with the title Report Field Formula. Type a DQL formula that would be valid in the *list records* section of the query. You cannot use the *all* relational operator or any sorting, grouping, or statistical operators. However, you can use relational statistical operators. The data-entry fields discussed earlier in the chapter are examples of fields that you may sometimes have to define in this manner. In addition, the Page Number field, discussed in "Using Page Level Formatting Commands" later in this chapter, is another example of using the Report Field Definition screen.

> **Tip:** You should refrain from defining new fields in the format. A better practice is to specify all the fields that are to be included in the report in the *list records* section of the query so that the query includes a complete list of fields. Then, when you define list fields in the Query Definition screen, DataEase provides the Interactive mode with its extensive prompting. You do not have the benefit of this help in the Report Field Definition screen.

Placing Formatting Commands

Formatting commands control when and how often text and fields are printed in the report. They control what prints at the beginning and end of the report and at the top and bottom of each page, as well as what prints along with each record from the selected data. Because each formatting command begins with a period or dot (.), these commands are sometimes called *dot commands*. Each formatting command must be on a line by itself and must begin in column 1.

DataEase makes it easy to enter formatting commands on the Format Definition screen. With the cursor in column 1, type a dot (.). DataEase displays the dot in column 1 and then displays a window menu containing all the available formatting commands (see fig. 8.10). It also displays the message Select a Command in the prompt line. To enter a command, you simply select it from the window menu. DataEase then types the command on the screen immediately to the right of the dot.

Fig. 8.10.

Entering a formatting command.

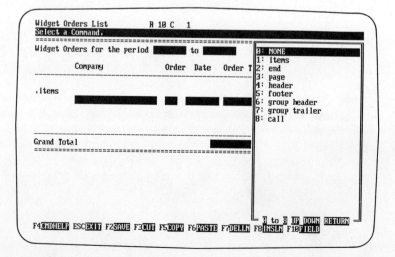

When you use one of the predefined formats, DataEase inserts all the necessary formatting commands for you. But, if you create a custom format, you position the commands where you want them. Therefore, you have to know where formatting commands should be placed in order to create the report you want. The eight available formatting commands are listed in figure 8.10. These formatting commands can be divided into four groups: required commands, group-level commands, page-level commands, and the *.call* command. The two required formatting commands, *.items* and *.end*, must appear in every format. Group level commands, *.group header*, and *.group trailer*, are used only when you specify *in groups* or *in groups with group-totals* in the query. The page level commands are the *.page*, *.header*, and *.footer* commands. The *.page* command causes the report to begin a new page, and the commands *.header* and *.footer* determine which text or fields print at the beginning and end of the report. Finally, the *.call* command can be used at the end of a report format to run another program, such as GrafTalk or Lotus 1-2-3. The discussions that follow explain in more detail how to create custom formats using these formatting commands.

Understanding Report Format Areas

If you have not already grown accustomed to the terminology that is peculiar to database report formats, you need to get your bearings before continuing. The basic areas of a DataEase report format are the report header, page header, group header, items area, group trailer, page footer, and report end. When the DQL query (or Quick Reports Field Selection screen) defines more than one grouping, you can define a corresponding number of group header/group trailer pairs. These areas control the order in which text and fields are printed in the report. You can place format text and fields in any area, but you need to know the print sequence and frequency of each area. The following paragraphs summarize how DataEase uses each report format area to determine print sequence and frequency:

❏ The *report header* area prints only once at the beginning of the report after the first page header. The *report end area* prints only once at the end of the report before the last page footer.

❏ The *page header* area prints at the top of each page (screen page or printer page) and the *page footer* at the bottom of each page (screen or printer).

❏ A *group header* area prints above its grouping, whereas a *group trailer* area prints below its grouping. You typically locate the group field in the group header area and locate summary statistics for a grouping in its group trailer area.

❑ When you have multiple groupings, all *group header* areas print at the beginning of the report just before the first record is printed in the order listed in the report format definition.

❑ The *items* area prints once for each record selected by the query.

❑ When you have multiple groupings, each *group trailer* area prints whenever the value of its grouping field changes just after the last record in the group is printed. It also prints when a higher level trailer prints.

❑ When you have multiple groupings, all *group trailer* areas print at the end of the report just after the last record prints in the order listed in the report format definition.

❑ Each *group header* area prints after its corresponding group trailer and when a higher level header prints.

Figure 8.11 shows a format from the Sales Representative form labeled to show the various report format areas. It demonstrates many of the available formatting commands. A derived field containing the current page number also appears to the right of the word Page. Figure 8.12 shows the first page (printed to screen) of the report resulting from the format in figure 8.11, and figure 8.13 shows the second (and last) page of the report. These three figures should help you understand the print order of the various parts a DataEase report format.

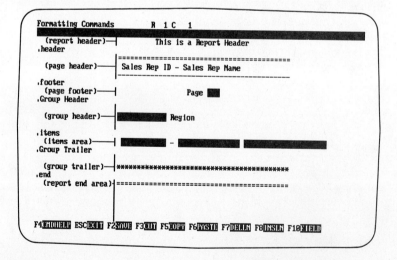

Fig. 8.11.

A sample report format showing the various format sections.

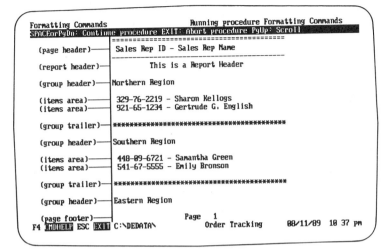

Fig. 8.12.

The first page of the report resulting from the format in fig. 8.11.

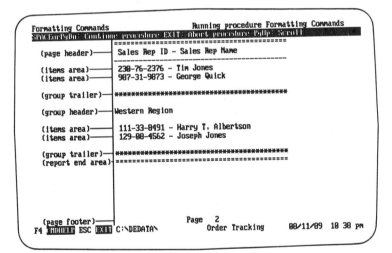

Fig. 8.13.

The second and last page of the report resulting from the format in fig. 8.11.

Using Required Formatting Commands

Every DataEase report format should always contain at least two formatting commands, the so-called required commands: *.items* and *.end*. These commands clearly distinguish the items area of the format from other format areas.

The area between the *.items* command and the *.end* command is the items area and prints once for each record selected by the query. When you place no other formatting commands in the format, the area of the format above the *.items* command is the report header area, and the area below the *.end* command is the report end area.

Figure 8.14 shows a simple version of the Widget Orders List procedure format. The two required commands, *.items* and *.end*, are the only formatting commands included in the format. As shown in figure 8.15, the text and fields above the *.items* command in the format become a report header area and appear at the beginning of the report. The text and field below the *.end* formatting command become the report end area and appear at the end of the report. The fields between the two formatting commands are in the items area, so they print once for each record in the Widget Order form.

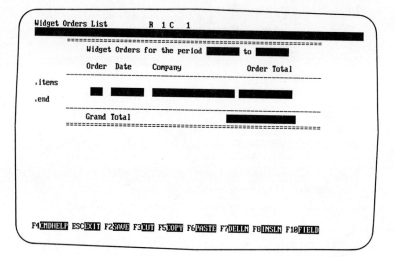

Fig. 8.14.

A report format using the required formatting commands, .items and .end.

Fig. 8.15.

The report resulting from the format in fig. 8.14.

Whenever the items area of the report extends over several lines, you run the risk of splitting the output for one particular record at the end of a page. To prevent this from happening, you can add the keyword *nosplit* to the *.items* formatting command. When you use the *.items nosplit* command, DataEase begins a new page when a record does not completely fit on the current page. If each record is more than a page in length, then each begins on a new page and continues for as many pages as necessary to print the data in the record.

Chapter 5 explained another type of *.items* command. The command *.items across n wide m* is used in the mailing labels format, where *n* is the number of labels in each row and *m* is the width of a single label. More generally, this command causes DataEase to print *n* records across the page, each record taking up *m* spaces in width, where *n* and *m* are positive whole numbers, and *n* times *m* is not greater than the report width in characters.

You also can use the *across* and *wide* keywords separately. The command *.items across n* causes DataEase to print *n* records across the page horizontally. DataEase adjusts the width of the fields so that *n* records will fit on each line of the items area. The command *.items wide m* causes DataEase to print as many records of *m* width side by side as will fit across the page.

You set the report width in the Print Style Specification screen, introduced in Chapter 5, by specifying the page size in inches and then indicating the left and right margins, also in inches. For example, if you specify 8.5-inch paper with 1-inch margins left and right, the report width is 6.5 inches.

You also use the Print Style Specification screen to set the number of characters that print per horizontal inch in the report. Ten characters per inch is the most common setting. DataEase then multiplies this number by the page width to determine the report width in characters—the number of characters that will fit on each line of the report. Thus, if the report width is 6.5 inches and you print the report at 10 characters per inch, then the report width in characters is 65. DataEase uses this number to determine where subsequent records should begin.

Using Group-Level Formatting Commands

Chapter 7 explained that two DQL grouping operators cause DataEase to group records according to the value in a specified field—the *in groups* and *in groups with group-totals* operators. The group-level formatting commands enable you to take full advantage of these DataEase grouping features.

As a prerequisite to using the group-level formatting commands, you first use one of the two grouping operators in the query to establish each group field (or use the *group* keyword in the Quick Reports Field Selection screen). For example, in the Widget Order List query developed in Chapter 7 and earlier in this chapter, you used the following two lines:

> *any Sales Representative Region in groups with group-totals*
> *Sales Rep ID in groups with group-totals.*

These lines in the query establish the Region and Sales Rep ID fields as group fields. When DataEase produces the report, the program first groups records by sales region (Northern, Eastern, Western, Southern) and then by Sales Rep ID.

Record grouping enables you to label blocks of data for clearer understanding and to summarize group data through group statistics. This labeling and summarizing is done in group header and trailer areas.

As explained previously in this chapter, a group header area prints above its grouping. To define a group header area in a report format, place the formatting command *.group header* at the beginning of the area. The group header area then extends down to the next formatting command in the format.

You can place text or fields in a group header area in the same manner as any other area of the format. Typically, you place the group field itself in the group header area rather than in the items area so that DataEase prints the group field value for each grouping in the header just above the grouping, rather than once for each item.

In the Widget Orders List example, you want the name of the sales region to appear at the beginning of each grouping of records from that region, but you do not need to repeat the region name with every record. You simply place the *any Sales Representative Region* field (the Region field, looked up from Sales Representative with the *any* relational operator, described in Chapter 7) in the group header area.

When you are grouping by more than one field, one group field usually creates subgroupings of the other. In the Widget Orders List example, each Sales Rep ID grouping is a subgrouping of a Region field value. In other words, each sales region is made up of a number of sales representatives. You want to see widget orders grouped by region. Within each region, however, you want the orders grouped by the sales representative who handled them.

DataEase enables you to group records within larger groups. This procedure is often referred to as *nesting* groups. When nesting groups, you must first be particular about the order in which the fields are listed in the *list records* section of the query. The higher precedence group field (Region in this example) must be listed above the lower precedence group field (Sales Rep ID).

You can then define one group header area in the report format per group field in the query. The group header areas must be defined in the same order as the group fields are listed in the query. Thus, the first *.group header* formatting command in the Widget Orders List format screen defines the beginning of the group header area for the Region field. The next formatting command, again *.group header*, defines the end of the first group header area and the beginning of the group header area for the Sales Rep ID group field. You place the Region field in the first group header area and the Sales Rep ID, First Name, and Last Name in the second group header area (see fig. 8.16).

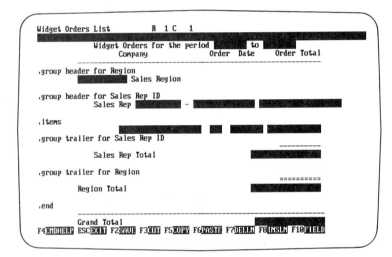

Fig. 8.16.

The Widget Orders List format with nested group header areas.

Tip: Although this capability is undocumented, DataEase enables you to label the group level commands. For example, you can use the command *.group header for Region* and *.group trailer for Region* at the beginning of the respective group header and group trailer areas for the Region group field. Similarly, you can label the group level commands for the Sales Rep ID field with the words *for Sales Rep ID*. Following this convention, demonstrated in figure 8.16, helps you see clearly which header goes with which group field and helps you match header area to trailer area.

Every *.group header* command has an alter ego, a *.group trailer* command marking the beginning of a group trailer area. The *.group header* and *.group trailer* commands always travel in pairs.

Whereas a group header area prints above its grouping, a group trailer area prints below its grouping. You generally locate summary statistics for a grouping in a group trailer area. For example, the Order Total : *sum* field in the *list records* section of the Widget Orders List query is included in the group trailer area for the Region field. This field generates a subtotal of all Order Total values from the same Region.

Like group header areas, group trailer areas also can be nested. Group trailer areas, however, are listed in the format in reverse order of precedence. The *.group trailer* command for the Sales Rep ID group field must be listed before the *.group trailer* command for the Region group field. Figure 8.16 shows the Widget Orders List report with group header areas and group trailer areas. Both group trailer areas contain the Order Total : *sum* field. The statistical operator *sum* computes a subtotal for each respective grouping in the corresponding group trailer area. (As suggested in the preceding tip, figure 8.16 labels each *.group trailer* command with the group field name.) Figure 8.17 shows the resulting report.

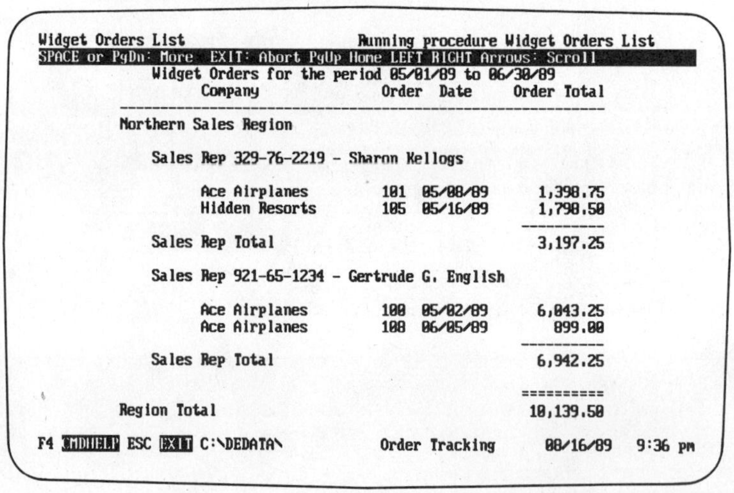

Fig. 8.17.

The report resulting from the Widget Orders format shown in fig. 8.16.

```
Widget Orders List                    Running procedure Widget Orders List
SPACE or PgDn: More  EXIT: Abort PgUp Home LEFT RIGHT Arrows: Scroll
           Widget Orders for the period 05/01/89 to 06/30/89
              Company              Order  Date    Order Total
        ------------------------------------------------------------------
        Northern Sales Region

           Sales Rep 329-76-2219 - Sharon Kellogs

                 Ace Airplanes      101  05/08/89     1,398.75
                 Hidden Resorts     105  05/16/89     1,798.50
                                                     ----------
           Sales Rep Total                            3,197.25

           Sales Rep 921-65-1234 - Gertrude G. English

                 Ace Airplanes      100  05/02/89     6,043.25
                 Ace Airplanes      108  06/05/89       899.00
                                                     ----------
           Sales Rep Total                            6,942.25

                                                     ==========
        Region Total                                 10,139.50

F4 CMDHELP ESC EXIT C:\DEDATA\        Order Tracking     08/16/89    9:36 pm
```

You easily can create a report that displays only the summary statistics. Create the report format as described in the preceding paragraphs but delete any fields or text between the *.items* command and the first *.group trailer* command. Then, move each group field from its group header area to its group trailer area and delete any remaining lines from the group header areas. Do not delete the *.items* command or any *.group header* command. Figure 8.18 shows a summary report format for the Widget Orders List in which only the group trailer areas contain fields and text. The summary report that results from this format is shown in figure 8.19.

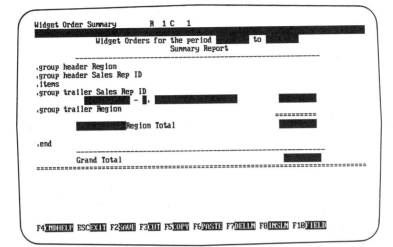

Fig. 8.18.

A report format to generate a summary report.

Fig. 8.19.

The summary report resulting from the format in fig. 8.18.

Using Page-Level Formatting Commands

Database reports are commonly many pages in length; therefore, clearly marking the top of each page with information that identifies it with the report and numbering each page at the top or bottom is often helpful. Labeling and numbering pages are the two most frequent uses of the page header and page footer.

The *.header* formatting command specifies the beginning of the page header area of a report format, which extends to the next formatting command. Any text or fields placed in the page header area print at the top of every page in the report.

To begin a page header for the first time on a specific page other than page 1, just follow the *.header* command with a positive whole number. For example, *.header 2*, shown in figure 8.20, instructs DataEase to start the page header on page 2 of the report. This feature is particularly useful for suppressing the page header on the first page of the report. Otherwise, the page header would print at the top of the first page above the report header. In figure 8.20, the column headings appear in the report header and the page header. The report header prints at the top of the first page, including the column headings. Then, the page header prints at the top of page 2 and all following pages.

Fig. 8.20.

Using the .header *command to create a page header that starts on page 2.*

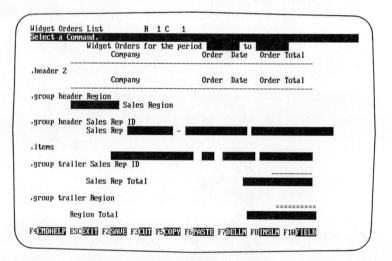

The counterpart to the *.header* command is the *.footer* command, which begins the page footer area. Unlike *.group header* and *.group trailer*, *.header* and *.footer* do not have to occur in a pair. In addition, each of these page-level commands may be used only once in the report format.

The page footer area prints at the bottom of each page. You can start it on a particular page by including a number in the command. The command *.footer 2* instructs DataEase to start printing the footer on page 2. However, the footer command should be placed at the beginning of the report, right after the *.header* command.

You can place statistical summary fields in the page footer area as well as in group trailer areas. A summary field in the page footer area computes the chosen statistic using all records processed up to the end of the page on which it appears. The Order Total: *sum* field, for example, can be used in the page footer area to accumulate a running total of the orders at the end of each page of the report. Contrast this to a statistic computed in a group trailer that computes for only its group.

The third and last page-level command is *.page*. This command causes DataEase to process any page footer area and begin a new page. You can place the *.page* command anywhere in the report, as often as you want, but it is usually placed at the beginning of the group header area or at the end of the group trailer area of the highest precedence group field. In either location, the group header starts on a new page.

You also can place a *.page* command at the end of the report format so that DataEase ejects the last page of the report, leaving the printer set to print the next report at the beginning of a clean piece of paper.

Another way to ensure that DataEase ejects the last page of the report is to include a page footer. To print the page number, for example, you can type the word *Page* in the footer area. Then, to define the field that will print the actual number, press F10 (FIELD) to display the Report Field Definition screen. Press Enter so that you can define a new field. Type the following formula:

>   *current page number*

Press F2 (SAVE). DataEase fills in the Report Field Definition screen with field type, number type, maximum digits, and so on. Press F2 (SAVE) again to save the page number field definition.

Using the *.call* Command

One of the most interesting DataEase formatting commands is the *.call* command, which enables you to run another program from within DataEase.

Whenever it is used, the *.call* command always should be placed on the last line of the report format after the *.end* command. It is most useful in passing data to another program or immediately running another program. For example, you can generate a data file in a format compatible with GrafTalk and then run the graphics program in order to see an immediate graphic representation of your data. When you are finished with GrafTalk, you return to DataEase.

Using Printer Control Commands

You learned in Chapter 3 how to apply special highlighting and color to the record-entry form. These colors do not carry through to the printer, but you can use a similar procedure to apply special print effects to the report printout. The commands that you use to apply these special effects are referred to as printer control commands.

For any printer control command to have the desired effect, the stage has to be properly set. First, you must modify the System Configuration form (see fig. 8.21) and select the printer definition matching the printer connected to your system as well as the port type and port number to which your printer is connected. Second, the Printer Definition screen (see fig. 8.22) must contain the correct control strings for your printer. Refer to Appendix B for a discussion of how to use both screens. This chapter assumes that you have selected the correct printer definition and printer port on the System Configuration screen and that the printer definition contains the correct control strings for your printer.

Tip: The link between computer and printer is notoriously weak regardless of the program you are using. Problems with printing are usually mechanical in nature: the ribbon is out, the paper is out, the paper is jammed, the printer cable is disconnected from the printer or the computer, the printer cable is connected to the wrong printer port, or the printer isn't turned on. When your printer doesn't do what you expect, first check each of these common troublespots before assuming that you have made a mistake in DataEase. Many printer problems also mysteriously disappear when you turn the printer off and then back on.

Applying print special effects to the report format is similar to applying color attributes to the record-entry form. You insert special commands at the beginning and end of the area to which DataEase should apply the special effect. The command at the beginning turns on the special effect and thus can be called a *turn-on command*. The command at the end turns off the special effect and can be referred to as the *turn-off* command. These commands are listed in table 8.5.

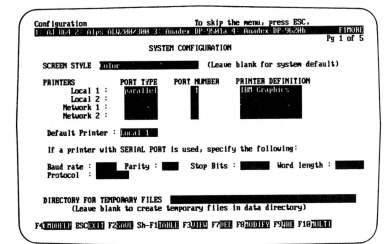

Fig. 8.21.

The System
Configuration screen.

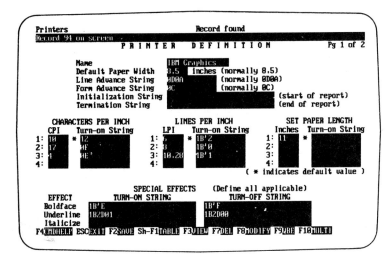

Fig. 8.22.

The Printer
Definition screen.

You can custom define the nine special effects on the Printer Definition screen (see Appendix B). For example, you may define double-strike print as Special 1, Near Letter Quality mode as Special 2, and so on.

To apply one of these special effects, first toggle on the Insert mode and then type the turn-on command to the left of or above the point where the special effect should be applied. You must type the command in the Insert mode because the turn-on command takes up space in the format, although it does not print. The format appears to be out of alignment but straightens out when the report prints. Type the turn-off command to the

Table 8.5
Printer Control Commands

Print special effect	Turn-on command	Turn-off command
Underline	@u	@nu
Boldface	@b	@nb
Italics	@i	@ni
Special 1	@s1	@ns1
Special 2	@s2	@ns2
Special 3	@s3	@ns3
Special 4	@s4	@ns4
Special 5	@s5	@ns5
Special 6	@s6	@ns6
Special 7	@s7	@ns7
Special 8	@s8	@ns8
Special 9	@s9	@ns9

right of or below the point where the special effect should no longer be applied. After you turn a print special effect on, it continues to be in effect until you turn it off. Any text or fields to the right and below the turn-on command up to the turn-off command will be printed with the designated special printing effect.

For example, suppose that you want to spruce up the Widget Orders report a bit by adding a few print enhancements. You decide that you want to emphasize the report header with boldface print. To apply the boldface special effect, you type the turn-on command @b to the left of the first word in the first line of the report header. You also type the turn-off command @nb to the right of the last word in the report header. You also decide that you want the page header to be printed in italics, so you type the command @i to the left of the first word in the page header and the command @ni to the right of the last word of the header.

For the underline, boldface, and italics special effects, you can use a second way to insert the printer control commands. Table 8.6 lists Alt-key combinations for this purpose. To apply the underline special effect to the items area of the Widget Orders List format, for example, you position the cursor on the first character in the area and press Alt-U. You then move the cursor to the end of the area that you want underlined and press Alt-E. DataEase inserts @u to the left of the fields in the items area and @nu at the end.

Table 8.6
Printer Control
Keystroke Commands

Keystroke combination	Function
Alt-U	Turn on underline
Alt-B	Turn on boldface
Alt-I	Turn on italics
Alt-E	Turn off printer special effect

DataEase enables you to insert commands in the format to change the number of characters per inch (CPI) that print horizontally and the number of lines per inch (LPI) that print vertically. You can define up to four different CPI settings and up to four LPI settings for each printer in the Printer Definition screen (see Appendix B). You then apply these spacing settings by typing an appropriate turn-on command.

Both the CPI and LPI settings in the Printer Definition screen are numbered 1 through 4. To turn on a CPI setting, type *@c* followed by the number of the CPI setting (2 to 4). To return to the default setting, the first CPI setting in the Printer Definition screen, type *@c1*. Similarly, *@l* followed by a number between 2 and 4 switches the line spacing to a new setting. The command *@l1* returns to the default setting, the first LPI setting in the Printer Definition screen.

You also can apply the underline, boldface, and italics special effects and the CPI and LPI settings through the Highlight pull-down menu. Press F4 (CMDHELP), and DataEase displays the first pull-down menu. Press the left-arrow key once or the right-arrow key three times to display the Highlight menu, shown in figure 8.23. Use the down-arrow key to move the menu selection bar to the special effect or setting that you want to apply and press Enter. Then, move the cursor to the end of the area to which this printer control command should apply and press Alt-E. DataEase types the appropriate commands at the beginning and end of the area you designated.

Tip: You also can use the Print Style Specification screen to set the CPI and LPI settings as well as up to three special effects. Normally, these settings apply to the entire report. Be aware, however, that settings applied through the Print Style Specification screen can be overridden by printer control commands applied in the report format. Refer to Chapter 5 for further discussion of the Print Style Specification screen.

Fig. 8.23.

The Highlight pull-down menu.

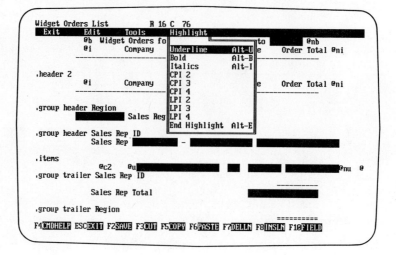

Caution: Although DataEase enables you to use printer control commands to change the number of lines per inch (LPI) and characters per inch (CPI) printed, it does not take these changes into account when it calculates page length for automatic page breaks and line length for automatic line wrap. It calculates the physical space available for printing based on the page size, margin settings, LPI setting, and CPI setting established in the Print Style Specification screen. If you want to use CPI or LPI commands in a report format, you may have to adjust line length and page length manually.

Saving a Format

When you finish building a report format, you have to save it to memory (RAM) and then save it to disk as a part of the procedure. While displaying the format on the screen, press F2 (SAVE) to save it to memory. DataEase saves the format and returns to the DQL menu.

Then, to save the entire procedure to disk, select **7. Save Procedure** from the DQL menu. DataEase asks, Do you want to save modified procedure under another name(y/n):. To save the procedure with the same name, type *n*. DataEase saves the procedure, including the report format, to disk and displays the message procedure modified in the message area.

Modifying a Format

Whenever you want to make a change to a format that has already been saved, you must first load it into memory (RAM). When the procedure containing the format is not the current procedure listed at the top of the screen, load the procedure using the **8. Load Procedure** option on the DQL menu.

When the procedure containing the format is in memory, choose **5. Modify Format** from the DQL menu to display the format for modification. DataEase asks, Do you want to keep the existing procedure format? Respond 2: yes and DataEase displays the format in the Report Format Definition screen.

When the format is displayed, you can add or remove text, fields, and formatting commands using the procedures described in this chapter. Of course, don't forget to save the changes by pressing F2 (SAVE) and then choosing **7. Save Procedure** from the DQL menu.

Creating a Template Format

Even though DataEase makes defining a report format fairly easy, fine-tuning a format can become a tedious process. If you find that you are repeatedly designing the same type of report format for several different databases, consider designing a *template* format.

A DataEase template format is a special form definition that you can use as a report format. You define the template format in the Form Definition screen as if it were a record-entry form. You then use the template format to define a report format in Quick Reports or while defining a DQL procedure.

A template format is not intended for Record Entry, so you should not confuse it with a normal record-entry form. Its sole purpose is to provide a predefined report format that you design yourself. You can store the template format on any disk or directory; it does not have to be stored in the same database in which you will use it. Indeed, creating all your template formats in an exclusive template format database is advisable so that you don't accidentally confuse them with normal record-entry forms.

Perhaps the greatest benefit of a template format is its portability. You can create a template format on one computer and use copies of it to generate standardized reports on many other computers.

Defining a Template Format

To define a template format, start at the DataEase Main menu and select **1. Form Definition and Relationships** to display the Form Definition menu. Then, select **1. Define a Form** and type a form name. Again, you have 20 available spaces, so be descriptive in the template name. Then, press Enter, and DataEase displays the Form Definition screen.

Even though you are working in the Form Definition screen, you design the template as if you were in the Report Format Definition screen. Two significant differences exist between the two definition screens. First, the special field characteristics available in the Field Definition screen have no effect in a template format, and the special field features such as *suppress spaces* that are normally found in the Report Format Definition screen are not available in the Form Definition screen. Second, you have to know how to spell the formatting commands because the Form Definition screen does not display a list of formatting commands when you type a dot (.). Except for these differences, you can use the Form Definition screen in the same way as the Report Format definition screen.

When you create a template format, you are designing a generic format. You use this format to create actual report formats from record-entry forms that are usually in another database. For this procedure to work, however, the field names you define in the template format must match the field names in the target forms that will use the format.

If you are designing a template format for a particular database or family of databases and you know the exact names of the fields to be used in the format, then use those field names here. However, you often don't know in advance the names of fields that will ultimately be used in the target forms. You may find that you routinely use the same field names in database after database, especially if you make frequent use of DataEase Dictionary Fields. But, to improve your odds of being able to match field names, DataEase enables you to define field names using *wildcard* characters. You can use the asterisk (*) to take the place of multiple characters and the question mark (?) to stand for a single character.

When you have designed the format in the Form Definition screen, press F2 (SAVE) to save it to memory. Then, return to the point in the database where you intend to use the format.

Using a Template Format

A short example will help to explain how to use a template format and show the benefits of this feature.

Suppose that you frequently generate lists of names and telephone numbers from various databases. You decide to create a template format named

Telephone List, shown in figure 8.24. This format has a page header area,
an items area and a page footer area. The fields, Company and Telephone,
are all copied from the DataEase Dictionary form, but to be more flexible,
you rename the Telephone field to *phone* so that it matches names such
as Phone, Telephone, Telephone No., and Phone #. This form is defined in
a database named Templates, not in the Order Tracking database.

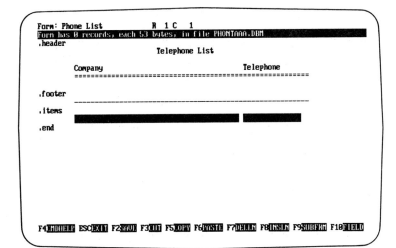

Fig. 8.24.

A template report
format named
Telephone List.

When you create the form, you need to make note of its file name. To see
the file name on screen, save the format and then choose **2. View or
Modify a Form** from the Form Definition menu. Select the name of the
template format from the window menu. When DataEase displays the form,
it displays the file name in the prompt line, as shown in figure 8.24. The
file name in this example is PHONTAAA.DBM, which is, however, the name of
the records file. Because the form definition has the extension DBA, the
file name of the template format is PHONTAAA.DBA.

After you have noted the file name, save the form again and return to the
Order Tracking database. You want to use the Phone List template format
to create a telephone list from the Retail Customer data.

Next, you must define a query or a Quick Report to use the template with.
Suppose that you decide to define a DQL query. You select **4. DQL
Advanced Processing** from the DataEase Main menu and **4. Define
Query** from the DQL menu. Then, you define the query shown in
figure 8.25.

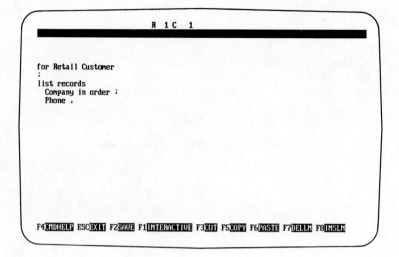

Fig. 8.25.

A query to be used with the Telephone List template format shown in fig. 8.24.

```
                                R  1 C  1
████████████████████████████████████████████████████████████████


for Retail Customer
;
list records
  Company in order ;
  Phone .
```

```
F4 CMDHELP ESC EXIT F2 SAVE F1 INTERACTIVE F3 CUT F5 COPY F6 PASTE F7 DELLN F8 INSLN
```

When you have defined the query, you are ready to use the template. From the DQL menu, select **5. Define Format**. DataEase asks, What type of procedure format do you want? and displays a line menu in the prompt line containing the list of available format types. You choose 4: Template, and DataEase prompts you to enter the Name of the Template file :. In the field provided, type *PHONTAAA.DBA* and press Enter. DataEase reads the template format, matches Company from the template with Company from Retail Customer, and matches *phone* from the template with Phone from Retail Customer. It then displays the new format on the Report Format Definition screen. You can then continue defining the procedure as usual. The report generated by the format is shown in figure 8.26.

Fig. 8.26.

The report resulting from the template format shown in fig. 8.24 and the query shown in fig. 8.25.

```
                              Running procedure
SPACEorPgDn: Continue procedure EXIT: Abort procedure PgUp: Scroll
                              Telephone List

        Company                              Telephone
        =======================================================

        Ace Airplanes                        (301)-555-2777
        Alpha Freight Lines                  (703)-555-1119
        Eastern Enterprises                  (703)-555-2355
        Hidden Resorts                       (703)-555-9662
        Sangster Insurance                   (703)-555-9995
        Signal Plumbing                      (301)-555-8379
```

```
F4 CMDHELP ESC EXIT C:\DEDATA\        ORDER TRACKING    06/16/89 12:03 am
```

Tip: You still can modify a format created from a template in the same way as any other report format. However, if the purpose of the template format is to generate standardized reports, you probably should refrain from making major changes unless you coordinate the modifications with the others who are using the format.

Chapter Summary

This chapter has expanded on discussions begun in Chapters 5, 6, and 7. It has described how to create more powerful and easier-to-use reports and procedures using data-entry forms, custom report formats, and predefined template formats. You should now have a good understanding of how to create and use a data-entry form, how to design a report format from scratch using fields, how to format text, how to use formatting commands, and how to create and use a template format to generate standardized report formats.

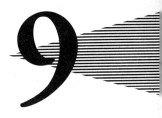

Maintaining Your Database

The preceding chapters have explained how to perform the major tasks of a database management system—creating a database; entering, viewing, modifying, and deleting data, and creating reports. However, many other chores must be performed in your day-to-day use of DataEase. This chapter addresses these chores, describing them collectively as *maintenance* of your database. The chapter actually discusses options from three different DataEase menus: the Maintenance menu, the Administration menu, and the Utilities menu.

In this chapter, you learn how to obtain status information about your DataEase forms, procedures, and import specifications; how to back up and restore your database; how to perform DOS functions; how to lock and unlock a database on a local area network (LAN); how to define user names and passwords; how to set security levels, screen styles, and help levels; how to import data from other programs; how to transfer data between forms; how to install forms; how to change a database name, and how to delete a database.

Obtaining Database Status Information

The overall approach of DataEase pointedly avoids references to DOS file names, permitting you to give databases, forms, reports, and procedures names up to 20 characters in length. Ultimately, however, you cannot escape the fact that DataEase is a DOS program that must create and store files using DOS file names. You sometimes need to know the actual DOS file names DataEase uses to store an object, such as a form definition. Table 9.1 lists the general file name conventions used by DataEase when storing DataEase objects to disk, but you may need the actual file name of a particular object. The DataEase status option on the Maintenance menu can provide this information as well as other information about the files.

Table 9.1
DataEase Data Files

File type	DOS filename*
Form definition	*formdaaa*.DBA
Form records	*formdaaa*.DBM
Form index	*formdaaa*.Inn
Form error	*formdaaa*.Enn
Procedure definition	*procdaaa*.DBR
Data-entry form	*procdaaa*.DBF
Forms directory	RDRR*daaa*.DBM
Procedure directory	REPO*daaa*.DBM
Users	USER*daaa*.DBM
Configuration	CONF*daaa*.DBM
Printers	PRIN*daaa*.DBM
Screen style	SCRE*daaa*.DBM
Relationships	RELA*daaa*.DBM
Menus	MENU*daaa*.DBM
Import specifications	*specname*.DBI

*Filename conventions: *form* represents the first four letters of the form name, *proc* the first four letters of the procedure name, *d* the database letter, *aaa* three letters assigned by DataEase, *nn* a hexadecimal (base 16) number assigned by DataEase, and *specname* the import specification name.

DataEase enables you to create separate status reports for forms, procedures, and import specifications. Forms and procedures have been covered extensively in the preceding chapters of this book. Import specifications, used to import data from other programs, are discussed in a later section of this chapter.

To generate any of the three status reports, you first must display the Maintenance menu. From the DataEase Main menu, select **6. Database Maintenance**. DataEase displays the menu shown in figure 9.1. Then, select **1. Database Status**, and DataEase displays the Database Status screen shown in figure 9.2. Each of the three reports is generated from this screen.

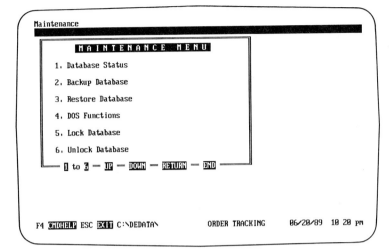

Fig. 9.1.

The Maintenance menu.

Fig. 9.2.

The Database Status screen.

Obtaining a Forms Status Report

When DataEase displays the Database Status screen (see fig. 9.2), it types the words Status of: in the top left corner of the screen (below the prompt line) and displays a line menu listing the options 1: Forms, 2: Procedures, and 3: Import Specifications. To obtain a report listing the forms in your database, choose 1: Forms from this line menu.

DataEase types the word Forms to the right of Status of: and displays the message, Press PRINT key to print status, else press any other key. This message indicates that you can display the report on-screen and print the report on your printer at the same time by pressing Shift-F9 (PRINT). Alternatively, you can press any other key to display the forms status report only to the screen. When the screen is full, the report pauses, and DataEase prompts you to press the space bar or PgDn to continue the report or Esc (EXIT) to abort (see fig. 9.3). Each time this happens, press the space bar or PgDn until the report is complete. When the report is finished, DataEase returns the screen to the Maintenance menu.

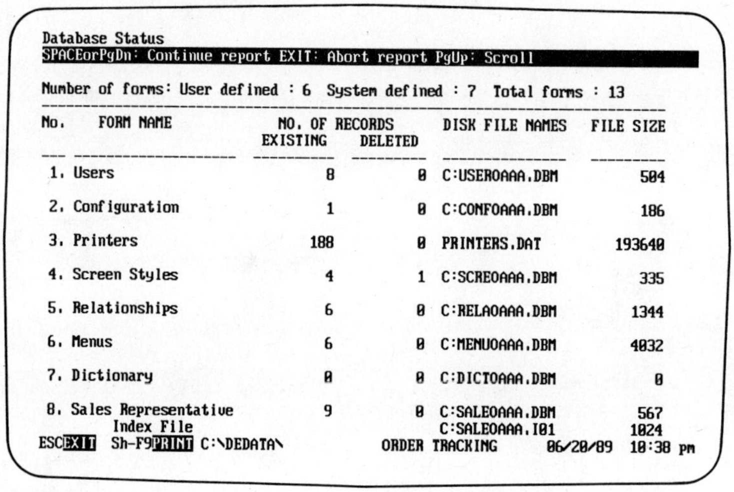

Fig. 9.3.

The first page of the forms status report.

```
Database Status
SPACEorPgDn: Continue report EXIT: Abort report PgUp: Scroll

Number of forms: User defined : 6  System defined : 7  Total forms : 13
----------------------------------------------------------------------
No.    FORM NAME           NO. OF RECORDS        DISK FILE NAMES   FILE SIZE
                           EXISTING   DELETED
---    ------------        --------   -------     ---------------   ---------
 1. Users                      8          0      C:USEROAAA.DBM        504

 2. Configuration             1          0      C:CONFOAAA.DBM        186

 3. Printers                 188          0      PRINTERS.DAT       193640

 4. Screen Styles             4          1      C:SCREOAAA.DBM        335

 5. Relationships             6          0      C:RELAOAAA.DBM       1344

 6. Menus                     6          0      C:MENUOAAA.DBM       4032

 7. Dictionary                0          0      C:DICTOAAA.DBM          0

 8. Sales Representative       9          0      C:SALEOAAA.DBM        567
    Index File                              C:SALEOAAA.I01       1024
ESCEXIT  Sh-F9PRINT C:\DEDATA\        ORDER TRACKING    06/20/89  10:38 pm
```

In the first line of the forms status report, DataEase states the total number of user- and system-defined forms in the database. DataEase routinely supplies seven system forms for each database: Users, Configuration, Printers, Screen Styles, Relationships, Menus, and Dictionary. Figure 9.3 indicates that the database has six user-defined forms.

The bulk of the report consists of six columns of information about the forms in your database with the following column headings: No., FORM NAME, NO. OF RECORDS EXISTING, NO. OF RECORDS DELETED, DISK FILE NAMES, and FILE SIZE. Each numbered row in the report contains data about one form in the database. The first column numbers the forms in the order they were created. System forms are listed first because DataEase created these forms when you started the database. The report then lists the forms you defined in the order you defined them. The second column includes the form name. The third column indicates the number of existing (active) records, and the fourth column lists the number of records marked as deleted but not yet removed from the file.

The last two columns list the two pieces of information that are often of interest when you want to perform a DOS function on the Database—file name and file size (in bytes). Whenever you need to know the DOS file name for database files, just display the forms status report.

DataEase lists only one file for each system-supplied form in the status report. These files contain the actual data. DataEase lists at least two files for each of the user-defined forms—the form definition file (DBA file name extension) and the form records file (DBM file name extension). When you have defined any indexed field(s) for a form, DataEase also lists the index file(s) in the status report.

> **Tip:** This report is another piece of database documentation that you should file away along with the form definition, Quick Report, and procedure definition printouts. It will give you a permanent record of the DOS file names that contain the various building blocks making up your database.

Obtaining a Procedures Status Report

To generate a status report listing the procedures and Quick Reports that you have defined in the database, choose 2: Procedures from the line menu in the prompt line of the Database Status screen.

DataEase types the word Procedures to the right of Status of: and displays the message, Press PRINT key to print status, else press any other key. Press Shift-F9 (PRINT) to print and display the report or press any other key to display the procedures status report to the screen without printing. When the screen is full, the report pauses, and DataEase prompts you to press the space bar or PgDn to continue the report or Esc (EXIT) to abort (see fig. 9.4). Each time this happens, press the space bar or PgDn until the report is complete. When the report is finished, DataEase returns the screen to the Maintenance menu.

In the first line of the procedures status report, DataEase states the total number of procedures and Quick Reports defined for the database. This count lumps procedures and Quick Reports together to arrive at the total number. Figure 9.4 indicates that the sample database has a total of 17 procedures currently defined and saved to disk.

The main portion of the procedures status report consists of four columns of information about the DQL procedures and Quick Reports in your database. The column headings are No., PROCEDURE NAME, DISK FILE NAME, and FILE SIZE Bytes. Each numbered row in the report contains data about

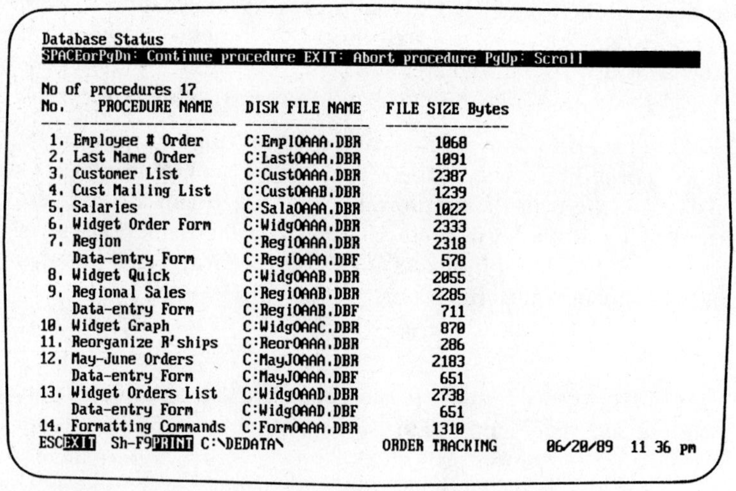

Fig. 9.4.

*The first page of the
procedures status
report.*

```
Database Status
SPACEorPgDn: Continue procedure EXIT: Abort procedure PgUp: Scroll

No of procedures 17
No,     PROCEDURE NAME       DISK FILE NAME    FILE SIZE Bytes
        ─────────────────    ──────────────    ──────────────
  1, Employee # Order        C:Empl0AAA.DBR          1068
  2, Last Name Order         C:Last0AAA.DBR          1091
  3, Customer List           C:Cust0AAA.DBR          2387
  4, Cust Mailing List       C:Cust0AAB.DBR          1239
  5, Salaries                C:Sala0AAA.DBR          1022
  6, Widget Order Form       C:Widg0AAA.DBR          2333
  7, Region                  C:Regi0AAA.DBR          2318
     Data-entry Form         C:Regi0AAA.DBF           578
  8, Widget Quick            C:Widg0AAA.DBR          2855
  9, Regional Sales          C:Regi0AAB.DBR          2285
     Data-entry Form         C:Regi0AAB.DBF           711
 10, Widget Graph            C:Widg0AAC.DBR           870
 11, Reorganize R'ships      C:Reor0AAA.DBR           286
 12, May-June Orders         C:MayJ0AAA.DBR          2183
     Data-entry Form         C:MayJ0AAA.DBF           651
 13, Widget Orders List      C:Widg0AAD.DBR          2738
     Data-entry Form         C:Widg0AAD.DBF           651
 14, Formatting Commands     C:Form0AAA.DBR          1310
ESCEXIT  Sh-F9PRINT C:\DEDATA\           ORDER TRACKING    06/20/89  11 36 pm
```

one procedure in the database. The first column simply numbers the
procedures in the order you created them; the second column lists the
DataEase name for each procedure or report, and the third and fourth
columns list the respective DOS file name and file size (in bytes) of each
procedure or Quick Report.

Obtaining an Import Specifications Status Report

DataEase import specifications, discussed later in this chapter, enable you
to import data generated by other programs into a DataEase record-entry
form. When you find you are continually doing the same import operation,
you can save the import specification to a file on disk. You also can
generate a list of the available import specification files using the Database
Status screen.

To obtain an import specifications status report, choose 3: Import
Specifications from the line menu in the prompt line of the Database
Status screen. DataEase types the word Import Specifications to the right
of Status of: and displays a window containing the prompt Import Spec
File Directory:. DataEase then completes this field with the current data
directory name and enables you to modify it. If you have stored import
specification files in a directory different from your DataEase data
directory, you must enter the proper path in the field.

After you indicate the import specifications file directory, press Shift-F9 (PRINT) to print and display the report or Enter to send the report to the screen only. DataEase begins displaying the report. When the screen is full, the report pauses, and DataEase prompts you to press the space bar or PgDn to continue the report or Esc (EXIT) to abort. Each time this happens, press the space bar or PgDn until the report is complete. When the report is finished, DataEase returns the screen to the Maintenance menu.

The import specification status report consists of four columns of information with the headings No., IMPORT NAME, DISK FILE NAME, and FILE SIZE Bytes. Each numbered row in the report contains data about one import specification. The first column numbers the specifications in the order you created them; the second column lists the specification names, and the third and fourth columns list the respective DOS file name and file size (in bytes) of each procedure or Quick Report. The DOS file name is the import specification name with the file name extension DBI added on.

Backing Up Your Database

Regardless of all the safeguards you may construct to protect your database from inadvertent errors or malicious mischief, it is only as safe as your last backup copy. The importance of routinely making a complete copy of your database cannot be overemphasized. Any number of catastrophic events may be lurking in the shadows just waiting for an opportunity to gobble up your most irreplaceable files. If you use your PC to store important business or personal data, you owe it to yourself and anyone else who depends on the security of that data to make frequent, complete backup copies of your database. Fortunately, the DataEase backup feature makes this task painless.

When you want to make a complete copy of your database using the DataEase backup feature, you should have available enough blank formatted floppy disks to hold all the database files. You can estimate the amount of disk space required by adding the file sizes listed in the database status reports described in the previous "Obtaining Database Status Information" section of this chapter. DataEase backup compresses some files, however, so that the backup files may be smaller than the originals.

To begin the backup operation, select **6. Database Maintenance** from the DataEase Main menu to display the Maintenance menu. Then, choose **2. Backup Database**. DataEase opens a window in the bottom portion of the screen and displays the prompt Specify the Path Name to use for backup

> **Tip:** DataEase provides two completely different methods of creating a backup copy of your database. This discussion covers the DataEase method referred to as *DataEase backup*. Files created by DataEase backup can be used only if restored using *DataEase restore*. As an alternative, DataEase lists the operating system functions, DOS BACKUP and DOS RESTORE on its DOS Functions menu, described later in this chapter.
>
> Each of these methods has its advantages and disadvantages. DataEase backup is faster than DOS BACKUP because it copies only data files, not index files or deleted records. However, DOS RESTORE is faster than DataEase restore because the DataEase version has to recreate all index files. The major benefit of the DataEase backup/restore combination is that it permanently removes all deleted records from every form in the database.
>
> Experiment with both backup methods to see which one you like better. But, by all means, back up your database!

and press RETURN:. You can specify any valid disk drive and directory at this prompt, but you should not back up a database to the disk containing the original—you don't want to lose both copies to the same disk crash. Specify the drive letter, usually a floppy disk drive, and directory (if any) and press Enter.

DataEase then presents the question, If a backup Error occurs, what do you want to do ?. The prompt line contains a line menu with the following options:

1: Ignore Error and Continue   2: Cancel   3: Decide upon Error

Select either of the first two options when you are not going to be present during the backup (for example, if you are designing the system for someone else to use). If you select 1: Ignore Error and Continue, DataEase continues with the backup even when an error occurs. Option 2 aborts the backup when an error occurs. If you will be present, select 3: Decide upon Error. You then can decide whether to cancel or continue with the backup at the time an error actually arises.

DataEase next displays a nearly blank screen with the title Backup Database. Below the prompt line, DataEase displays

STARTING BACKUP
PLEASE INSERT FIRST BACKUP DISK IN DRIVE *D*:
PRESS 'RETURN' WHEN READY OR 'ESC' TO ABORT

where *D:* is the drive you specified for the backup copy. Place a blank formatted disk in the designated drive and press Enter.

DataEase begins the backup process, indicating that the backup is in progress, and then lists on-screen the name of each form, procedure, and import specification as it is copied. If your database is too large to fit on one floppy disk, DataEase prompts you to remove the first disk and label it as follows:

```
BACKUP DISK NUMBER: 1
DATABASE NAME: name of your database
DATE: mm/dd/yy TIME: hh:mm:ss
```

DataEase substitutes the name of your database and the system date and time in the appropriate places. The program also instructs you to insert a new disk in the drive and press Enter (RETURN). In a similar manner, it prompts you to remove, label, and replace second and subsequent disks until the database is completely copied. You must follow these instructions carefully, labeling the disks in the correct sequence, or you will not be able to restore the database later.

When DataEase finishes, it instructs you to remove and label the disk currently in the drive and then to press Enter (RETURN). When you press Enter, if no errors have occurred, DataEase displays the following message:

```
**BACKUP COMPLETED - NO ERRORS**
PRESS 'RETURN' TO EXIT BACKUP.
```

Store the backup copy of your database in a safe place.

The next time you want to back up the database, you can use the same set of disks. If you do, DataEase displays a screen similar to figure 9.5 asking whether you want to erase the existing files and replace them with the new backup copy of the database. To re-use the disk, respond by typing *y*. DataEase requires you to confirm this answer, asking ARE YOU SURE ? (y/n) :. Again, type *y*. DataEase first deletes the files on the disk and then begins the backup procedure.

Restoring Your Database

The DataEase restore feature is a companion to the DataEase backup feature; it will only restore files originally backed up by the DataEase backup command (that is, NOT the DOS BACKUP command). You use it in two different circumstances:

❑ Some or all of the database files are deleted, damaged, or destroyed, and you want to restore them to usable condition.

❑ Many records have been deleted, and you want to recover lost space by removing the deleted records from the data files.

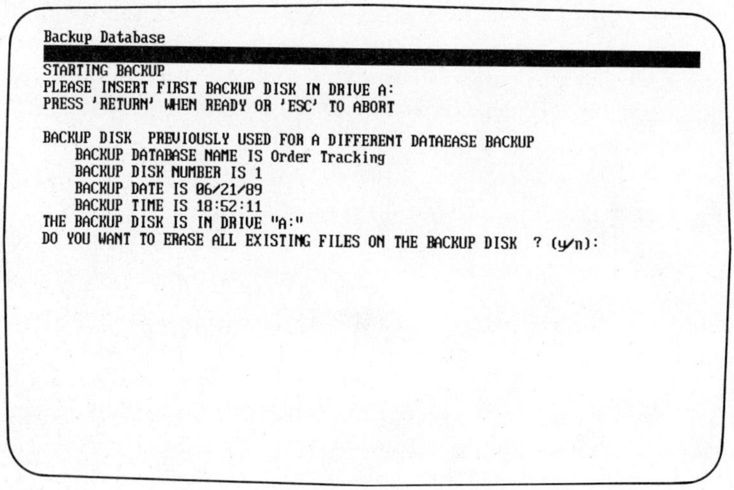

Fig. 9.5.

Re-using a backup disk.

```
Backup Database

STARTING BACKUP
PLEASE INSERT FIRST BACKUP DISK IN DRIVE A:
PRESS 'RETURN' WHEN READY OR 'ESC' TO ABORT

BACKUP DISK  PREVIOUSLY USED FOR A DIFFERENT DATAEASE BACKUP
     BACKUP DATABASE NAME IS Order Tracking
     BACKUP DISK NUMBER IS 1
     BACKUP DATE IS 06/21/89
     BACKUP TIME IS 18:52:11
THE BACKUP DISK IS IN DRIVE "A:"
DO YOU WANT TO ERASE ALL EXISTING FILES ON THE BACKUP DISK  ? (y/n):
```

To begin restoring a database from a backup copy created by the DataEase backup feature, place the first backup disk in a floppy disk drive and select **6. Database Maintenance** from the DataEase Main menu to display the Maintenance menu. Then, choose **3. Restore Database**. DataEase instructs you to indicate the Path Name—that is, the disk drive (and directory, if appropriate) containing the backup disk. Type the name of the drive (and directory, if appropriate) and press Enter.

DataEase then asks, If a Restore Error occurs, what do you want to do?. The prompt line contains a line menu listing these options:

    1: Ignore Error and Continue 2: Cancel 3: Decide upon Error

Select either of the first two options when you are not going to be present during the restore (for example, you are designing the system for someone else to use). If you select 1: Ignore Error and Continue, DataEase continues with the restore even when an error occurs. Option 2 aborts the restoration when an error occurs. If you will be present, select 3: Decide upon Error. You then can decide whether to cancel or continue with the restoration at the time an error actually occurs.

Next, DataEase instructs you to insert the first backup disk in the floppy drive and press Enter (RETURN). Before DataEase actually begins the restore process, it asks you to confirm that the database on the backup disk is actually the one that you want to restore. Read the message on-screen to reassure yourself that you are using the correct backup copy, and then type the letter *y* to continue (or *n* to abort the process). DataEase then displays restore in progress.... As it reads the backup disk, DataEase lists the forms, procedures, and import specifications. When it finishes reading data, DataEase rebuilds any index files required by the various forms.

When the backup copy is on multiple disks, DataEase instructs you when to remove and replace each disk. Make sure that you insert them in the same sequence as they were created. DataEase does alert you, however, if you get them out of order.

When DataEase finishes the restoration of your database, it announces, if no errors have occurred,

```
**RESTORE COMPLETED - NO ERRORS**
PRESS 'RETURN' TO EXIT RESTORE.
```

When you press Enter (RETURN), DataEase informs you that it is exiting the program and that you must sign on again in order to use the newly restored database.

Using DOS Functions

For better or for worse, DataEase is an MS-DOS/PC-DOS program, and you may occasionally find that you need to perform DOS functions while working with DataEase. For your convenience, DataEase enables you to perform several DOS tasks without leaving DataEase at all. In addition, it enables you to execute other DOS commands in what often is referred to as a DOS *shell*, by swapping itself out to disk (or EMS memory) and loading another copy of the DOS command interpreter. This section of the chapter explains how to use these special DOS-related features.

Viewing the Data Disk Directory

The DataEase status reports described earlier in this chapter generate lists of forms, procedures, and import specifications that include DOS file names and file sizes. When you are looking for any of this information, the status reports are the place to turn.

However, you may want to see a complete list of files in the data directory. The directory may, for example, contain a spreadsheet file produced by another program. You intend to import the data from the spreadsheet into a DataEase form, but you cannot remember the spreadsheet's file name. The status reports cannot help because the file is not a form, procedure, or import specification.

To view a complete list of all DOS files in the data directory, display the Maintenance menu and then select **4. DOS Functions** to display the DOS Functions full-screen menu. Choose **1. Data Disk Directory**. DataEase begins to scroll the DOS Functions menu up, off the screen, and displays the DOS command

    Dir *D*:*datadir*\\/P

where *D* is the data drive and *datadir* is the data directory. DataEase then scrolls this command up and off the screen to display the DOS directory listing. When the files cannot fit on one screen, as is often the case, DataEase stops scrolling the screen when it fills and displays the message, Strike a key when ready . . . at the bottom of the screen, as shown in figure 9.6. To continue scrolling, press any key. Each time the screen stops, press any key again until all files have been displayed.

Fig. 9.6.

The first screen in a data disk directory listing.

```
.                <DIR>      3-22-89    1:57p
..               <DIR>      3-22-89    1:57p
RDRROAAA DBM        808      6-21-89   10:57p
REPOOAAA DBM        663      6-21-89    9:28p
RELAOAAA DBM       1568      6-21-89    9:28p
USEROAAA DBM        504      6-21-89    9:28p
CONFOAAA DBM        186      6-21-89    9:28p
PRINOAAA DBM          0      6-21-89    9:28p
SCREOAAA DBM        268      6-21-89    9:28p
MENUOAAA DBM       4032      6-21-89    9:28p
DICTOAAA DBM          0      6-21-89    9:28p
DICTOAAA DBA       3268      6-21-89    9:28p
SALEOAAA DBM        567      6-21-89    9:28p
SALEOAAA DBA        961      6-21-89    9:28p
CONFIGUR DAT       1208      3-30-89   11:24a
RETAOAAA DBM       1770      6-21-89    9:28p
RETAOAAA DBA        943      6-21-89    9:28p
WIDGOAAA DBM        364      6-21-89    9:28p
WIDGOAAA DBA       2267      6-21-89    9:28p
PRODOAAA DBM        352      6-21-89    9:28p
OLD              <DIR>      4-05-89   11:36a
PRODOAAA DBA        404      6-21-89    9:28p
ORDEOAAA DBM       1023      6-21-89    9:28p
Strike a key when ready . . .
```

After DataEase has displayed all files from the data disk, it instructs you to press any key to return to the menu. Press a key, and DataEase returns to the DOS Functions menu.

Checking the Data Disk

At various times while you are using DataEase, you may be interested in knowing how many files are on the data disk and how much space and memory (RAM) remain. DataEase enables you to obtain all of this information without quitting DataEase by performing the DOS CHKDSK command.

First, display the Maintenance menu and select **4. DOS Functions** to display the DOS Functions menu. Choose **2. Check Data Disk**. DataEase begins to scroll the DOS menu up, off the screen, and displays the DOS command

Chkdsk *D*:

where *D* is the data drive. DataEase then scrolls this command up the
screen to display information similar to figure 9.7. This DOS command tells
you the size of the disk, the total size and number of hidden files, the total
size and number of directories, the total size and number of user files, and
the amount of space left on the disk. In addition to this file information,
the CHKDSK command also lists the total amount of memory (RAM) in
your computer and the amount of memory still available for DataEase to
use.

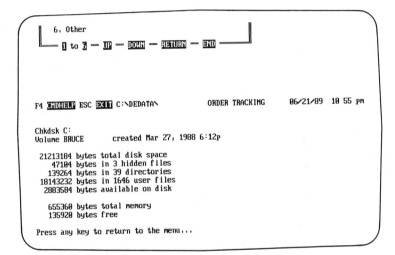

Fig. 9.7.

Output from the
CHKDSK command.

Tip: The DOS CHKDSK function does not work on local area
networks.

Formatting a Disk

If you use a PC, you must format a disk before you use it. The DOS
FORMAT command performs this chore for you.

You probably find that you most often need a formatted disk when you are
right in the middle of an application program such as DataEase. To quit
from DataEase, format a disk, and then restart DataEase just to obtain a
formatted disk is not very convenient. To avoid this inconvenience,
DataEase includes the FORMAT command on its DOS Functions menu.

To format a disk from within DataEase, display the Maintenance menu and
select **4. DOS Functions** to display the DOS Functions menu. Then, place
a new disk in the floppy disk drive and choose **3. Format New Disk**.

DataEase prompts you to specify the drive containing the disk to be formatted. Type the drive letter followed by a colon and press Enter. DataEase then executes the DOS command

Format *D:*

where *D:* is the floppy disk drive containing the disk to be formatted. When DOS finishes formatting the disk, it displays the total disk size as well as space available and asks, Format another (Y/N)?. If you have more disks to format, type *y* and press Enter. Otherwise, to get back to DataEase, type *n* and press Enter.

Finally, DataEase displays a prompt instructing you to press any key to return to the menu. Press any key, and DataEase displays the DOS Functions menu. The floppy disk is formatted and ready to use.

Caution: Because formatting a disk destroys all data on the disk, you should use this command with extreme care. ALWAYS specify a drive letter, and NEVER specify a drive letter designating a hard disk, especially one containing data. Many versions of DOS format the current drive whenever you fail to specify a particular drive letter. This practice could be disastrous when the current drive contains your DataEase data and is a hard disk with a great deal of other data you would hate to lose! On most systems, drive A is a floppy disk drive, and you would normally format a new disk in this drive.

Using DOS BACKUP and RESTORE

As mentioned earlier in this chapter, DataEase provides an alternate method for making a backup copy of your DataEase database. This DOS BACKUP feature is discussed in the next several paragraphs.

To back up your database using the DOS BACKUP command, display the Maintenance menu and select **4. DOS Functions** to display the DOS Functions menu. Then, place a blank formatted disk in the floppy disk drive and choose **4. DOS Backup**. DataEase prompts you to specify the drive (and directory, if appropriate) that you want to receive the backup copy. Type the drive letter, followed by a colon (and directory, if appropriate), and press Enter. DataEase then executes the DOS command

Backup *C:*????*x*A??.* *D:*

where *C:* is the current data disk drive; *x* is the database letter, and *D* is the destination disk drive. DOS then prompts you through the backup process, instructing you to insert and remove disks as necessary. When the backup process is complete, DataEase displays the prompt, Press any key to return to the menu.... Press a key and DataEase returns to the DOS Functions menu.

This DOS BACKUP function copies all files associated with the database, including index files and error files ignored by the DataEase backup function. It also copies the entire form records file for each form, whereas the DataEase backup leaves deleted records behind. For these reasons, DOS BACKUP may take significantly longer to complete than its DataEase counterpart.

If you ever need to use the backup created by the DOS Backup function to restore lost files, you must use DOS RESTORE, not DataEase restore.

Caution: Make sure that you use the same version of DOS to restore the database that you used to make the backup copy. If DOS RESTORE doesn't seem to work, check to see that you're using the same version.

To restore your database using the DOS RESTORE command, display the Maintenance menu and select **4. DOS Functions** to display the DOS Functions menu. Then, place the first backup disk created by DOS backup in the floppy disk drive and choose **5. DOS Restore**. DataEase prompts you to specify the drive (and directory, if appropriate) containing the backup copy. Type the drive letter followed by a colon (and directory, if appropriate) and press Enter. DataEase then executes the DOS command

Restore D: C:????xA??.*

where C: is the current data disk drive; x is the database letter, and D is the disk drive containing the backup disk. DOS then prompts you through the restore process, instructing you to insert and remove disks as necessary. When the restore process is complete, DataEase displays the prompt, Press any key to return to the menu.... Press a key, and DataEase returns to the DOS Functions menu.

This DOS RESTORE function copies all files associated with the database, including index and error files, back to the data directory, but it does not rebuild index files. For this reason, DOS RESTORE may be somewhat faster to complete than its DataEase counterpart.

> **Tip:** Carefully read the documentation for your network software before attempting DOS BACKUP or DOS RESTORE on a local area network (LAN). The network operating system may have a different program that accomplishes the same end. For example, users of Novell Netware can use the programs LARCHIVE and LRESTORE in place of BACKUP and RESTORE.

Using the DOS Shell

As explained in the preceding paragraphs, DataEase enables you to perform a number of DOS commands from within DataEase. However, several of these DOS commands take parameters, often called switches, that cannot be used from within DataEase. For instance, you can use the **3. Format New Disk** option on the DOS Functions menu to format a disk, but you cannot use the FORMAT command's special /S switch to create a DOS system disk. In addition, many DOS commands are not available at all from the DataEase DOS Functions menu. Fortunately, DataEase provides an easy way to access DOS directly so that you can perform any DOS command and still return quickly to DataEase. Accessing DOS in this way is often referred to as accessing a *DOS shell*.

To access a DOS shell from DataEase, first display the Maintenance menu and select **4. DOS Functions** to display the DOS Functions full-screen window. Then, choose **6. Other**. DataEase clears the screen and displays the following message:

```
*** Type 'exit' to return to DataEase ***
Swapping DataEase to disk ...
```

This message indicates that you return to DataEase by typing *exit* and pressing Enter and that DataEase is freeing up memory (RAM) by copying the contents of memory to disk. (DataEase swaps itself to EMS expanded memory, if your system has it, instead of to disk—see Appendix A.) DataEase then loads a second copy of the DOS command interpreter into memory, and you are greeted with the DOS prompt,

> *D:\datadir>*

where *D* is the drive, and *datadir* is the directory from which you started DataEase.

If your system has 640K total conventional memory, you now have approximately 500K to work with. You are free to use most DOS commands and run other programs with the following limitations:

❏ Never run a memory resident (also called TSR) program from the DOS shell, including the DOS commands MODE, PRINT, and GRAPHICS. Sidekick and ProKey are examples of commercially available memory resident programs.

❏ Do not delete DataEase data files. Or, better yet, do not delete any file from the data directory. You may accidentally delete the file into which DataEase copied the contents of memory.

To return to DataEase, type *exit* and press Enter. DataEase reloads itself into memory and returns to the DOS Functions menu. You should always return to DataEase and exit the program using Esc (EXIT) before turning off the computer system.

Locking and Unlocking a Database

If you use DataEase on a local area network (LAN), you often work with a shared database in a shared data directory. DataEase therefore provides various tools enabling you to work around the inevitable competition for data resources that occurs when multiple network users attempt to access the same data at the same time. One of these tools is found on the Maintenance menu.

Chapter 4 describes the restrictions DataEase places on simultaneous access to database records by multiple network users, referred to generically as *locking rules*. To override these locking rules and obtain exclusive use of the entire database, select **5. Lock Database** on the Maintenance menu. DataEase displays the message Database Locked in the message area of the screen. This type of lock completely prohibits other users from even signing on to the database. No other user can use the database at all until you unlock it. Users who attempt to sign on are greeted with the message, Access not allowed—Database locked.

You can apply this all-inclusive lock only if no other users are currently using the database. If you try to apply the lock while another user is still signed on, DataEase displays the message, Not allowed—other users active.

Because this lock is so restrictive, you should use it sparingly, only when you intend to perform major maintenance, such as copying, renaming, or deleting forms. DataEase applies this lock when you perform a backup operation or use restore; you don't want any additions, changes, or deletions made to any file in the database while a backup or restore operation is taking place.

Locking the database before running a procedure or Quick Report that draws data from multiple forms is also advisable so that the data in the entire database is *frozen* while you are generating the report.

When you finish the task that prompted you to lock the database, unlock it by choosing **6. Unlock Database** from the Maintenance menu. DataEase displays the message Database unlocked in the message area of the screen to indicate that other network users can now sign on to the database. In addition, DataEase automatically unlocks the database after performing backup or restore.

Defining Users

When you first create a new database, DataEase asks for your name. The name you provide becomes the *system administrator* name (also called *database administrator*) for the new database. In a sense, the system administrator is the owner of the database with the right to grant or deny access to other potential users. The system administrator also can assign and modify each user's password, security level, screen style, start-up menu, and help level. This portion of the chapter describes how to define and modify this user information.

Caution: Be aware that any user with a High security level also can modify this user information, even to the point of locking you out by changing your password. Because users are assigned a High security level if you don't assign a lower level, you should add users and assign security levels with some degree of caution.

All user names, passwords, and so on are stored in the Users form, one of the forms that DataEase supplies when you first create the database. DataEase fills in the first record in this form with the user name and password that you supply the first time you sign on to the new database. DataEase also grants you a High security level.

You can choose to leave both name and password blank. DataEase will create a record in the Users form with blank Name and Password fields. Later, you can add a user name and password to the first record in the form, but after you add a name, you can no longer save the record without a name. In other words, you only get one chance to create the database so that it can be accessed with no name and no password. After you add a name to the first record in the Users form, DataEase requires that you always use a name to sign on to the database.

You can access the Users form to add users and user information in two ways. The first method is to choose **7. System Administration** from the DataEase Main menu to display the Administration menu (see fig. 9.8) and then **1. Define Users**. The alternate method is to select **2. Record Entry** from the DataEase Main menu, 1: System, and then 1: Users at the Records menu. In either case, DataEase displays a blank record from the Users form, as figure 9.9 illustrates.

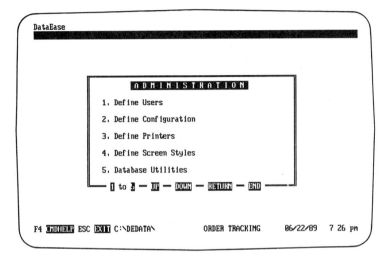

Fig. 9.8.

The Administration menu.

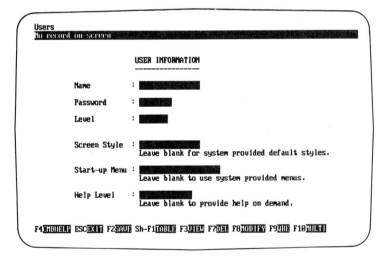

Fig. 9.9.

A blank record from the Users form.

The first three fields in the Users form are Name, Password, and Level. The primary purpose of these three fields is to maintain data security. When you are the only user of a database, you may not need to be concerned with limiting or preventing access by others. In most business environments, however, many users need access to the system, so security is an important consideration.

DataEase also enables you to customize screen colors for each user. The system-generated Screens form contains a number of predefined screen styles, and you can design even more (see Appendix B). You can then use the Screen Style field to assign a particular screen style to each user.

You can use the next field, Start-up Menu, to have DataEase display a specified menu in place of the usual DataEase Main menu when the user signs on to DataEase. Chapter 10, "Creating Custom DataEase Menus," covers this feature.

Help Level is the last field on the User form. This field determines whether the DataEase context-sensitive help facility provides help automatically or on demand.

The paragraphs that follow discuss in more detail how and when to assign user names, passwords, security levels, screen styles, and help levels. Start-up menus are explained fully in Chapter 10.

Keep in mind that the Users form is a record-entry form. You enter, edit, modify, and delete records in this form using the same procedures as any other record-entry form (see Chapter 4). Also remember that any entries or changes you make to your own Users form record do not go into effect until you quit DataEase and start a new session.

Assigning a User Name

Each time a user signs on to a particular database in DataEase, the user must enter a *user name*, the name the system administrator assigns to the user and adds to the Users form. DataEase only permits authorized users to access the database.

A *user* is not necessarily one individual. Several individuals could use the same user name and would therefore appear to DataEase as one entity. For the purpose of the discussions in this book, the term *user* is singular.

You (as the system administrator) enter each DataEase user name in the Name field of the Users form. This value can consist of up to 15 characters including letters, spaces, numbers, symbols, and ASCII extended characters. Each user name must be unique (that is, not repeated in the Users form for this database).

Tip: Avoid assigning user names that are difficult to type. Remember that the name must be entered by the user each time he or she signs on to DataEase. ASCII extended characters have to be entered by holding down the Alt key and typing the decimal code for the character on the number pad. They are therefore not recommended for use in a user name.

The Name field is a required field. The only way to create a Users form record with a blank Name field is at the time you initially create the database, as explained in the preceding section.

Assigning a Password

DataEase enables you to assign an optional, separate password for each named user of a DataEase database. Type the password for each user into the Password field of the user's record in the Users form. The password can be up to 8 characters in length and can include letters, spaces, numbers, symbols, and ASCII extended characters.

At sign-on, after the user enters the user name, DataEase prompts the user to type a password. The user must then type the password, but DataEase does not display the characters being typed. When the user presses Enter, DataEase looks for a record in the Users form that matches the name entered and then checks the value in the Password field. They must be an exact match before the user is given access to the database. DataEase gives the user three tries to enter both the user name and password correctly. If the user cannot successfully enter the proper combination, DataEase quits and returns to the DOS prompt.

DataEase does not differentiate between upper- and lowercase characters when checking for the proper user password.

Assigning Security Levels

DataEase enables you to assign one of seven levels of security to each user you authorize to access your database: High, Medium1, Medium2, Medium3, Low1, Low2, and Low3. Each of these security levels carries certain default rights and restrictions regarding access to the forms, reports, and procedures that make up the database. If you don't assign a security level, DataEase assigns the default High security level.

To assign a security level, move the cursor to the Level field in the Users form. DataEase displays a line menu containing a list of the seven available security levels. Select the appropriate security level from the menu.

The Low security level is actually made up of three sublevels: Low1, Low2, and Low3—Low3 being the lowest level. Users assigned one of these security sublevels can do the following:

❑ View records in record-entry forms

❑ Load and run previously defined Quick Reports and DQL procedures

❑ Use the **1. Database Status** and **2. Backup Database** options on the Maintenance menu

The Medium security level also consists of three sublevels: Medium1, Medium2, and Medium3. Medium1 is the highest, and Medium3 is the lowest Medium security sublevel. By default, all users assigned one of these Medium security sublevels can perform all the Low-level tasks as well as the following:

❑ Enter, modify, and delete records in record-entry forms

❑ Define but not save Quick Reports or DQL procedures

❑ Use the Maintenance menu options

❑ Use the Utilities menu options

The High security level, the highest level available, has no sublevels. Users with this security level can access all DataEase facilities and can enter, modify, and delete records from all system-supplied forms, including the Users form. The system administrator should always be assigned the High security level in order to be able to perform system maintenance.

The Form Properties screen, accessed from the Form Definition screen and described in Chapter 3, overrides these default restrictions and enables you to control precisely which users are permitted to view, enter, modify, or delete records in Record Entry. For example, you can use the Form Properties screen shown in figure 9.10 to permit users with Low3 and higher security levels to view records in the Widget Order form, users with Medium3 and higher security levels to enter new form records, Medium2 and higher level users to modify records, and Medium1 and higher level users to delete Widget Order records.

Fig. 9.10.

A Form Properties screen with different security levels.

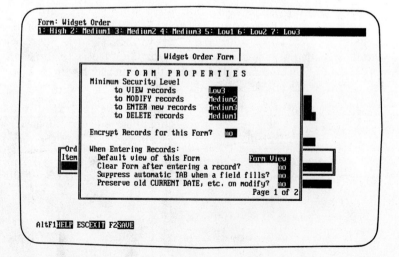

```
Form: Widget Order
1: High 2: Medium1 3: Medium2 4: Medium3 5: Low1 6: Low2 7: Low3

                        ┌ Widget Order Form ┐

                     F O R M   P R O P E R T I E S
              Minimum Security Level
                      to VIEW records        Low3
                      to MODIFY records      Medium2
                      to ENTER new records   Medium3
                      to DELETE records      Medium1

              Encrypt Records for this Form?     no

      ┌Ord   When Entering Records:
      │Item     Default view of this Form          Form View
               Clear Form after entering a record?       no
               Suppress automatic TAB when a field fills?  no
               Preserve old CURRENT DATE, etc. on modify?  no
                                              Page 1 of 2

      AltF1 HELP ESC EXIT F2 SAVE
```

Refer also to Chapter 3 for an explanation of how to use the View Security and Write Security field characteristics on the Field Definition screen to further restrict the security level required to view, enter, or modify data in a particular form field.

Defining a User's Screen Style

Each time you create a database, DataEase installs a Screen Styles form. The Screen Styles form is accessed through the Administration menu and is discussed in Appendix B. Each record in this form, referred to as a screen style, defines the colors DataEase uses when it displays each of 11 different areas of the screen: the title area, the cursor/mode area, the prompt line, regular fields, highlight 1, highlight 2, highlight 3, menu highlighting, key names, and other.

When you first install DataEase, the Screen Styles form contains three screen styles: color, monochrome, and color-mono. You can design custom screen styles, giving each a unique name. Each time you sign on to a database, DataEase uses the screen style specified in the Configuration form (see Appendix B) unless the user's record in the Users form specifies a different screen style.

To use a screen style tailored to a particular user's preferences, move the cursor to the Screen Style field of the user's Users form record and type the name of a screen style. DataEase does not present a line menu containing all valid choices, so you need to know exactly how the particular screen style you want to use is spelled in the Screen Styles form. When the user signs on to the database, DataEase provides the user's screen style rather than the one specified in the Configuration form.

Defining a User's Help Level

As explained in the first chapter of this book, DataEase provides excellent built-in context-sensitive help messages. Chapter 3 also explains that DataEase enables you to create your own form-level help messages and field-level help messages for each Record Entry form.

By default, DataEase displays help messages on demand—that is, only when the user presses Alt-F1 (HELP). Additional help then is summoned by pressing F1 (MORE). In a record-entry form for which you have defined form-level help and field-level help, DataEase displays the help messages in the following order: field-level help message, form-level help message, and built-in help message. The field-level help displays when the user presses Alt-F1; the form-level help message displays when the user presses F1 (MORE), and the system-supplied when the user presses F1 (MORE) again.

The last field on the Users form enables you to have DataEase display help automatically whenever a particular user is signed on to DataEase. Move the cursor to the Help Level field in the Users form. DataEase displays a line menu containing the choices 1: On Demand and 2: Automatically. Choose 2: Automatically from the menu.

When the Help Level field is set to *Automatically*, DataEase displays context-sensitive help in all system screens containing fields to be filled in. For example, when the user displays the Field Definition screen while defining a record-entry form, DataEase displays a help message explaining what the user should enter into the Field Name field, without the user having to press Alt-F1 (HELP) (see fig. 9.11).

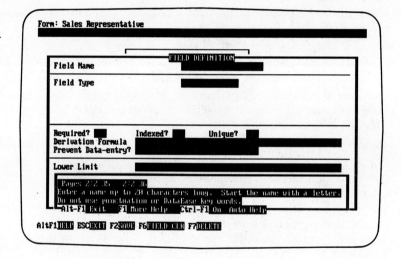

Fig. 9.11.

A context-sensitive help message for the Field Name field of the Field Definition screen.

During Record Entry, however, DataEase displays only field-level help messages. In addition, when you have defined a form-level help message but no field-level message for a particular field, DataEase displays the form-level help message. The system-supplied context-sensitive help messages do not automatically display during Record Entry.

Using DataEase Utilities

One of the primary reasons for using a computer is to avoid repeating work. You certainly don't want to design the same form or procedure more than once or enter the same data repeatedly. Ideally, you would like to make use of forms, procedures, or data that have already been entered. The DataEase Utilities menu provides a number of options that can help you avoid unnecessary repetition. Options on this menu help you make use of existing data, forms, or procedures from other DataEase databases and even other programs.

To display the Utilities menu, choose **7. System Administration** from the DataEase Main menu. DataEase displays the Administration menu. Select **5. Database Utilities**, and DataEase displays the Utilities menu, shown in figure 9.12.

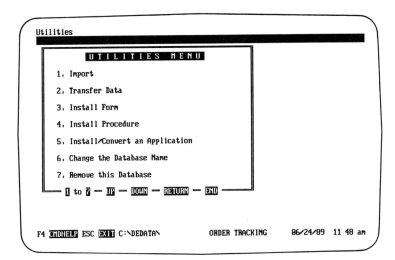

Fig. 9.12.

The Utilities menu.

The first four options on the Utilities menu enable you to do the following:

- ❏ **1. Import**. Imports data from other popular database and spreadsheet programs.

- ❏ **2. Transfer Data**. Transfers data between DataEase forms.

- ❏ **3. Install Form**. Copies form definitions from other DataEase databases.

- ❏ **4. Install Procedure**. Copies procedures or Quick Reports from other DataEase databases.

The last two Utilities menu choices are **6. Change the Database Name** and **7. Remove this Database**. This portion of the chapter describes how to get the most out of these six utilities.

The fifth option on the Utilities menu, **5. Install/Convert an Application** is a utility that copies complete DataEase applications and converts complete applications from other programs into DataEase applications. This utility is of primary interest to professional application developers and is therefore beyond the scope of this book.

Importing Data

Although DataEase is a popular relational database program, it is not by any means the only database program around. In fact, PC-based database programs are becoming more and more common. Even though these programs may run on your computer, each program usually saves data files using its own file format, making it difficult for you to use data created by another program.

Fortunately, the DataEase Data Import capability enables you to convert many popular file formats to the DataEase format. Using this facility, you can import data created in any of the following formats: Lotus 1-2-3, dBASE II, dBASE III/IV, DIF (Data Interchange Format), Mail-Merge (WordStar), Variable Length ASCII, or Fixed Length ASCII. You also can use Data Import to copy records from a form in another DataEase database to a form in the current database. This portion of the chapter describes how to import data from each of these formats.

To use the Data Import facility, first display the Data Import menu. From the Utilities menu, select **1. Import**. DataEase displays the Data Import menu, shown in figure 9.13.

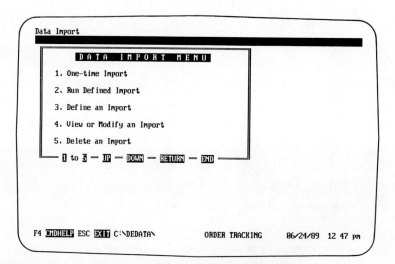

Fig. 9.13.

The Data Import menu.

You can take two approaches to importing data from another file format:

❑ **1. One-time Import**. Use this menu option when you don't expect to import data from the same file or file format again. You have to answer a number of questions that specify the file and file format to be imported and the destination DataEase form. Then, you press F2

(SAVE), and DataEase executes the import. It does not, however, save the answers that you provide. If you want to perform the same import again, you have to answer all the questions again.

❏ **3. Define an Import**. Select this choice on the Data Import menu when you think you may want to run the same import operation more than once. DataEase asks essentially the same questions as during one-time import, but when you press F2 (SAVE), it saves your answers to disk as an *import specification*.

The other three options on the Data Import menu enable you to run, modify, or delete an import specification.

Defining an Import Specification

When you expect to perform the same or a similar import operation more than once, begin defining an import specification by selecting
3. Define an Import from the Data Import menu. DataEase displays the following message in a small window below the menu

```
Import Spec File Directory:
    D:\DATADIR\
Import Specification Name:
```

where *D:\DATADIR* is the current data directory. The cursor is in a field to the right of the Import Specification prompt.

Type a unique name of up to eight characters and press Enter. You can use letters, numbers, and these characters:

```
! @ # $ % ^ & ( ) - { } `
```

Do not include any spaces. Unlike other DataEase object names, an import specification name is the same as its DOS file name. DataEase adds the extension DBI to the import specification name to create the DOS file name.

For example, suppose that one of your sales representatives, Sharon Kellogs, uses Lotus 1-2-3 to maintain a list of her customers on her own laptop computer. She keeps the data in a worksheet file named RETCUST.WK1. From time to time, you want to merge her list with the master list, adding new customers and updating the information on existing customers. You therefore begin defining an import specification and assign it the name *CUST_123* because you will use it to import data into the Retail Customer form from a 1-2-3 format file.

After you type the import specification name and press Enter, DataEase displays the Data Import Facility screen with the prompt Please select the destination form name as well as a window menu containing a list of available record-entry forms. Select the name of the form that is to receive the imported data—the *destination* form. In the CUST_123 example, the destination form is Retail Customer.

When you select a destination form, DataEase instructs you to enter the *source data* file name. In the space provided, enter the complete path (drive, directory, and file name) of the file containing the data you want to import. For example, assuming that the 1-2-3 file RETCUST.WK1 is on a floppy disk in drive A, you type *A:RETCUST.WK1* as the source data file and press Enter.

After you specify the source file name, DataEase asks, What is the data file format ? and displays a line menu listing eight options: 1: DATAEASE, 2: DIF, 3: dBASE II, 4: MAIL MERGE, 5: VARIABLE LENGTH, 6: FIXED LENGTH, 7: LOTUS 1-2-3, and 8: dBASE III/IV. Select the format that matches the source data file. For the CUST_123 example, choose 7: LOTUS 1-2-3.

Because each data file format is different, the remaining import specification questions depend on the format you choose. Each of the formats and the corresponding import specification questions are discussed in the sections that follow. Figure 9.14 shows the screen as it appears after selecting 7: LOTUS 1-2-3 as the data file format.

Fig. 9.14.

Using the DataEase Data Import facility to import data from a Lotus 1-2-3 file.

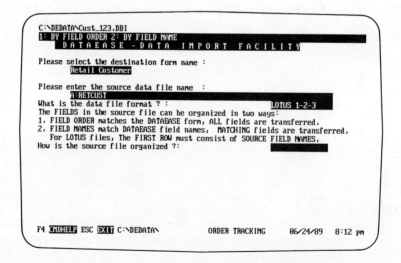

```
C:\DEDATA\Cust_123.DBI
1: BY FIELD ORDER 2: BY FIELD NAME
         D A T A E A S E  -  D A T A    I M P O R T    F A C I L I T Y

Please select the destination form name :
         Retail Customer

Please enter the source data file name   :
         A:RETCUST
What is the data file format ? :                       LOTUS 1-2-3
The FIELDS in the source file can be organized in two ways:
1. FIELD ORDER matches the DATAEASE form, ALL fields are transferred.
2. FIELD NAMES match DATAEASE field names, MATCHING fields are transferred.
   For LOTUS files, The FIRST ROW must consist of SOURCE FIELD NAMES.
How is the source file organized ?:

F4 CMDHELP ESC EXIT C:\DEDATA\          ORDER TRACKING      06/24/89  8:12 pm
```

Using the DataEase Data File Format

Sometimes, you need to copy data from a DataEase form in another database to a DataEase form in the current database. (See "Transferring Data Between Forms" later in this chapter for a discussion of how to copy data between forms in the same database.) Even if your sales representative, Sharon Kellogs, used DataEase to keep track of her customers on her laptop PC, the data wouldn't be in the same DataEase database as your master Retail Customer form. The DataEase data file format enables you to combine data from DataEase forms in separate databases.

When you choose 1: DATAEASE at the data file format on the Data Import Facility screen, DataEase asks, Is the source form same as the destination form ?. This question is asking whether the form definition for the source file and the form definition for the destination form are the same (that is, same field name, same field definitions, same field sequence, etc.). If the form definitions are identical, answer 2: yes. Otherwise, respond 1: no.

If the form definitions are not identical, DataEase instructs you to enter the source form file name. Again, this instruction is a bit vague, but it is telling you to type the name of the DOS file containing the source form definition (the DBA file). Because you have already entered the source data file name at the second prompt on the Data Import Facility screen (the DBM file), just type the same file name, changing the file name extension from *DBM* to *DBA*. Then, press Enter.

Tip: If the source form definition and the destination form definition are not identical, only data from fields with the same field names copy from the source file to the destination form. The fields don't have to be in the same order or defined in exactly the same way. Fields in the source file that don't have a counterpart in the destination form are not copied. Fields in the destination form that don't have a counterpart in the source file are left blank.

Whether or not the form definitions are identical, DataEase also asks how it should handle a record from the source data that matches an existing record in the destination form. In this sense, *match* means that all fields with the unique field characteristic are exactly the same in both the source record and the existing record. For example, how do you want DataEase to use a customer record from Sharon Kellogs's customer list that already exists in the master copy of the customer list? What about customers in her list that are not in the destination form? The choices are as follows:

❏ 1: ADD NON-MATCHING. Choose this option when you want DataEase to add only records that don't already exist in the destination form. DataEase notes all matching records in an exception file but doesn't add them to the destination form. Use this choice when you want the source file to provide new records but never change the value of existing records in the destination form.

❏ 2: UPDATE MATCHING. Select this choice when you intend for DataEase to update (overwrite) field values in existing destination form records, but not add new records. Any new records from the source—that is, records without a match in the destination form—are not added to the destination file but are noted in an exception file.

❏ 3: ADD OR UPDATE. Use this selection to add all records from the source file to the destination form. DataEase adds new records (records that don't match) and updates existing records (matching records).

❏ 4: DO NOT MATCH. This option adds all records to the end of the destination form data whether or not fields with the unique field characteristic match.

When you import Sharon Kellogs's customer list, you want any new customers she has added to be in your updated list. In addition, you want to update your customer list with any changes she has made to addresses, phone numbers, and so on. The appropriate choice in the Data Import Facility screen is therefore 3: ADD OR UPDATE.

Finally, DataEase instructs you to Press F2 to Save, Esc to EXIT, or F8 to Modify Specification, as shown in figure 9.15. Read over the screen. If all answers are correct, press F2 (SAVE) to save them to memory. DataEase returns to the Data Import menu. If you see any errors, press F8 (MODIFY). DataEase goes back to the destination form prompt so that you can go through the questions again. You have to select the destination form name again, and then press Enter until you reach the answer that you need to change. Make the correction and press Enter until you are back at the last prompt. Press F2 (SAVE) to save the import specification.

Fig. 9.15.

An import specification, CUST_DE.DBI, to copy data from a DataEase data file in another database to a DataEase form in the current database.

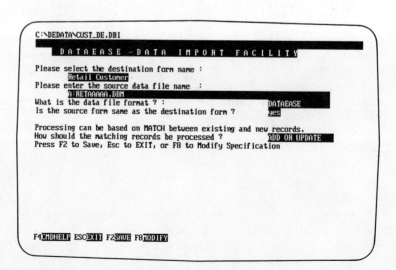

Tip: Refrain from pressing Esc (EXIT) while you are working on the Data Import Facility screen. It completely clears the import specification from memory, requiring you to start over. Whenever you realize you have made a mistake, go back to the beginning by pressing F8 (MODIFY). You then go through each question again until you get to the one that needs correcting. You don't have to wait until you get to the last question to press F8 (MODIFY).

Using the Lotus 1-2-3 Data File Format

Lotus 1-2-3 has from its first release in 1983 been the most popular PC-based program of any kind. Even though it is not primarily a database management program, many people have used it for that purpose, so you will likely need to be able to use data stored in a Lotus 1-2-3 data file format.

When you choose 7: Lotus 1-2-3 at the data file format prompt on the Data Import Facility screen, DataEase displays a five-line prompt asking how the source worksheet file is organized. It explains that you can organize the source file in two ways and displays a line menu listing your options:

❑ 1: BY FIELD ORDER. Specify this choice when the field names in the first row of the source worksheet file are not the same as the field names of the destination form. DataEase then imports values from the first column in the worksheet to the first field in the destination form, from the second source column to the second destination field, and so on. Each column represents a field, and each row represents a record. Field names must be in row 1, and data must start in the first column and second row of the worksheet (cell A2). When more columns exist in the worksheet than fields in the destination form, the excess worksheet columns (fields) are ignored. If more destination fields exist than worksheet columns, the excess fields are left blank.

❑ 2: BY FIELD NAME. Select this option when the worksheet does contain field names. The field names must be in row 1, starting in column A, one per column. Actual data must start in row 2, each record in a separate row. DataEase imports data from worksheet fields with names that match destination form fields. Field order in the worksheet file does not have to be the same as field order in the DataEase destination form. Fields in the source file that do not have a counterpart in the destination form are not copied. Fields in the destination form without a counterpart in the source file are left blank.

Assume, for example, that Sharon Kellogs keeps her customer list in the worksheet RETCUST.WK1 shown in figure 9.16. Row 1 of the worksheet contains field names matching those in the DataEase form Retail Customer. You therefore select 2: BY FIELD NAME when asked how the source file is organized.

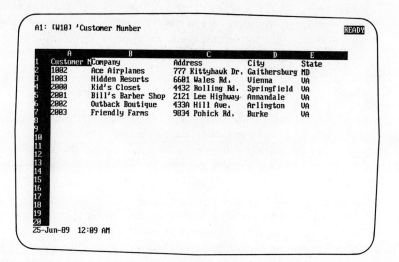

After you indicate how the source file is organized, DataEase asks how it should handle a record from the source data that matches an existing record in the destination form. Refer to the discussion of this situation in "Using the DataEase Data File Format." The appropriate response to import Sharon Kellogs's worksheet is 3: ADD OR UPDATE. Figure 9.17 shows the completed import specification CUST_123.DBI.

Finally, press F2 (SAVE) to save the import specification to disk and return to the Data Import menu, press Esc (EXIT) to quit without saving or press F8 (MODIFY) to return to the top of the screen to correct errors.

Using dBASE, DIF, and Mail-Merge Data File Formats

Several other data file formats have become popular because of the successful programs that introduced them: dBASE II, dBASE III, dBASE IV, DIF (Data Interchange Format—VisiCalc), and Mail-Merge (Wordstar). Many other software products have adopted these formats for convenience or compatibility. Even if a particular database program has its own proprietary data file format, it almost certainly can convert the format to one of these five popular formats. Likewise, DataEase can import data from any of these formats.

```
 C:\DEDATA\CUST_123.DBI
    D A T A E A S E  - D A T A  I M P O R T  F A C I L I T Y
 Please select the destination form name :
              Retail Customer
 Please enter the source data file name  :
              A:RETCUST.WK1
 What is the data file format ? :                   LOTUS 1-2-3
 The FIELDS in the source file can be organized in two ways:
 1. FIELD ORDER matches the DATAEASE form, ALL fields are transferred.
 2. FIELD NAMES match DATAEASE field names, MATCHING fields are transferred.
    For LOTUS files, The FIRST ROW must consist of SOURCE FIELD NAMES.
 How is the source file organized ?:               BY FIELD NAME
 Processing can be based on MATCH between existing and new records.
 How should the matching records be processed ?    ADD OR UPDATE
 Press F2 to Save, Esc to EXIT, or F8 to Modify Specification




 F4 CMDHELP  ESC EXIT  F2 SAVE  F8 MODIFY
```

Fig. 9.17.

An import specification, CUST_123.DBI, to import data from the Lotus 1-2-3 worksheet file RETCUST.WK1 to the DataEase form Retail Customer.

When you choose 3: dBASE II or 8: dBASE III/IV data file format (dBASE III/IV includes dBASE III, dBASE III Plus, and dBASE IV) on the Data Import Facility screen, DataEase displays a five-line prompt asking how the source file is organized. It explains that you can organize the source file in two ways and displays a line menu listing your options:

❏ 1: BY FIELD ORDER. Specify this choice when the dBASE file's field names are not the same as the destination form's field names. The fields have to be arranged in the same order in both files for the data to be properly imported. When more fields exist in the source file than fields in the destination form, the excess source fields are ignored. If more destination fields exist than source fields, the excess fields are left blank.

❏ 2: BY FIELD NAME. Select this option when the dBASE file's field names and the destination form's field names are the same. Field order in the source file does not have to be the same as field order in the destination DataEase form. DataEase does not copy fields in the source file that do not have a counterpart in the destination form, and it leaves blank fields in the destination form without a counterpart in the source file.

If you choose 2: DIF or 3: MAIL-MERGE as the data file format, DataEase greets you with the same five-line prompt with the same choices:

❏ 1: BY FIELD ORDER. Specify this choice when the field names in the DIF or Mail-Merge file are not the same as the field names in the destination form. The field names still must be the first row in the file, and the fields have to be arranged in the same order in the source file as the corresponding fields in the destination form. When more fields exist in the source file than in the destination form, DataEase ignores the excess source fields. If more destination fields exist than source fields, it leaves the excess fields blank.

❑ 2: BY FIELD NAME. Select this option when the DIF or Mail-Merge file's field names and the destination form's field names are the same. Field names must be located in the first row of the file. Field order in the source file does not have to be the same as field order in the destination DataEase form. Fields in the source file that do not have a counterpart in the destination form are not copied, and fields in the destination form without counterpart in the source file are left blank.

After you indicate how the source file is organized, DataEase asks how it should handle a record from the source data that *matches* an existing record in the destination form. Refer to the discussion of this question in "Using the DataEase Data File Format."

Finally, press F2 (SAVE) to save the import specification to disk and return to the Data Import menu, Esc (EXIT) to quit without saving, or F8 (MODIFY) to return to the top of the screen to correct errors.

Using Variable Length and Fixed Length ASCII Data File Formats

Many older database programs as well as programs on bigger computers (minicomputers and mainframe computers) create files in a generic format known as variable length ASCII (American Standard Code for Information Interchange), in which the file is stored as a continuous stream of ASCII characters. A specific ASCII character is designated to separate records and another character is used to separate fields. These characters are often referred to as *delimiters* or *separators*. Not all variable length ASCII formats are the same. When you import data from a file in this format, you have to inform DataEase what the field and record separator characters are.

A significant number of programs also can create files in fixed length ASCII format. Instead of using delimiters to separate fields and records, each record is a separate row and each field has a fixed length. To import a file stored in fixed length ASCII format successfully, the destination form must be defined with fields in exactly the same order and with exactly the same lengths as the fields in the source file. You should obtain a printout of the source data and physically count characters to determine proper field sizes.

Running an Import Specification

When you have defined and saved an import specification, it is available for use. To run the import operation, select **2. Run Defined Import** from the Data Import menu. DataEase prompts you to specify the import specification name and displays a window menu containing a list of all available import specifications. Select the one you want to use, and DataEase displays the message, Press RETURN to start transfer, or press EXIT to abort. Press Enter, and DataEase displays the message, Transferring data. When the import operation is completed, DataEase returns the screen to the Data Import menu and displays a status report in the message area indicating the number of records added, the number updated, and the number discarded (that is, neither added nor updated).

For example, to update the Retail Customer form with Sharon Kellogs's customer list, you run the CUST_123.DBI import specification (see fig. 9.17). The data shown in the worksheet in figure 9.16 is imported into the Retail Customer form. Because four of the customers are new, they are added to the Retail Customer data. The records of the two customers already in the Retail Customer form data are updated with the most current information contained in the source data file. No records are discarded.

Modifying an Import Specification

After you have saved an import specification to disk, you can still return to it to make changes if necessary. For example, you may want to change the name of the source file but leave all the other settings the same.

Whenever you want to modify an import specification, select **4. View or Modify an Import** from the Data Import menu. Select the name of the import specification you want to modify from the window menu. DataEase then displays the completed specification. The cursor blinks at the last prompt, instructing you to press F8 to modify the specification. Press F8 (MODIFY), and DataEase moves the cursor back to the top of the screen to the destination form prompt so that you can go through the questions again. All answers will already be filled in. You have to select the destination form name again, and then press Enter until you reach the answer that you need to change. Make the correction and press Enter until you are back at the last prompt. Press F2 (SAVE) to save the import specification and return to the Data Import menu.

Deleting an Import Specification

You also can delete a previously defined import specification. Select **5. Delete an Import** from the Data Import menu. Then, select the name of the import specification that you want to delete from the window menu. DataEase asks,

```
Are you sure you want to delete it ?
```

Respond 2: yes, and DataEase deletes the specification from the disk and displays the message Import Specification deleted in the message area.

Using One-Time Import

When you will not re-use an import specification, you don't have to save it to disk. You can use the One-time Import feature instead. From the Data Import menu select **1. One-time Import**. Then, follow the steps for creating an import specification, just as if you were defining one to be saved. When you finish answering all the questions on the Data Import Facility screen, DataEase prompts you,

```
Press F2 to Run, Esc to EXIT, or F8 Modify Specification
```

To run the import without saving the specification to disk, press F2 (RUN). DataEase displays the message, Transferring data. When it finishes executing the import specification, it returns to the Data Import menu and displays a status report in the message area.

Transferring Data Between Forms

Occasionally, you may need to copy data from one DataEase form to another in the same database. This situation shouldn't arise very often when your database is properly designed. When it does, DataEase makes transferring data between forms in the same database easy.

To copy data from one DataEase form to another in the same database, select **2. Transfer Data** from the Utilities menu. DataEase clears the menu from the screen and displays the Form Transfer screen.

The first prompt in this screen instructs you to select the *source form* and displays a line menu containing a list of available record-entry forms. Choose the form containing the data you want to copy.

DataEase displays a second prompt instructing you to select the *destination form*. From the line menu, choose the form to which DataEase should copy the data. As soon as you make this selection, DataEase adds all records from the source form to the end of the destination form data and returns to the Utilities menu.

This Transfer Data feature only copies data between fields with exactly the same name. Fields in the source form that do not have a counterpart in the destination form are not copied. Fields in the destination form without a counterpart in the source form are left blank in the new records created by the transfer.

DataEase also does not enforce any unique field characteristics during the data transfer. It adds all records to the destination form, even if duplicates—records with identical values in all unique fields—already exist.

Tip: Refer to "Using the DataEase Data File Format" earlier in this chapter for a description of how to use the Data Import facility to copy data from one form to another. The Data Import facility enables you to copy data between forms in different DataEase databases, but it also can be used to copy records between forms in the same database. Use this facility instead of the Transfer Data feature to copy records when you want DataEase to check for duplicates.

Installing a Form

The overall design and implementation of DataEase prevents you from inadvertently mixing databases together. Each form you create is explicitly associated with a single database, and, to sign on to another database, you have to quit from DataEase and start again. However, you may want to use a form definition and maybe even the data from a form in more than one database. For this reason, DataEase provides the Install Form utility that enables you to copy a form definition and, optionally, its data from one DataEase database to another.

To *install* (copy) a form definition from another database into the current database, select **3. Install Form** on the Utilities menu. DataEase displays the Form Installation screen and prompts you to enter the name of the new form you are defining. Type a form name that hasn't already been used in the current database and press Enter.

Next, DataEase instructs you to enter the Form (DBA) file name. Type the DOS file name of the source form definition you want to copy and press Enter. If the file is in a different data directory, you must include the full DOS path (drive and/or directory followed by the file name). You don't have to type the file name extension DBA because DataEase adds it automatically.

DataEase then asks you to enter an optional data (DBM) file name. When you want to copy all data from the source form into the new form, type the DOS file name of the source form data file and press Enter. This file name is almost always the same as the form definition file name, but with the extension DBM. You can leave this extension off because DataEase automatically adds it. When you don't want any data to be copied into the new form, just leave the line blank and press Enter.

When you press Enter at the data file name line, DataEase performs the installation, copying the form definition and, optionally, the form data into the current database.

Assume, for example, that you are designing a payroll database named Payroll for your company. One of the forms you must design contains data about your employees. The Sales Representative form in the Order Tracking database contains just such information but only about your sales representatives. Instead of starting from scratch, you decide to use the Install Form facility to copy both the definition and data for the Sales Representative form from the Order Tracking database into the Payroll database. You then can modify the definition of the new form as needed.

First, of course, you have to create and sign on to the Payroll database. Then, with this new database current, you access the Utilities menu and select **3. Install Form**. DataEase displays the Form Installation screen.

At the first prompt, type the name of the new form *Employee* and press Enter. Next, type the DOS file name of the Sales Representative form definition file, *SALEOAAA* (DataEase adds the DBA file name extension), and press Enter. Finally, type *SALEOAAA* again, this time the name of the Sales Representative form data file (minus the DBM file name extension), and press Enter. Figure 9.18 shows the Form Installation screen with all the lines filled in before you press Enter.

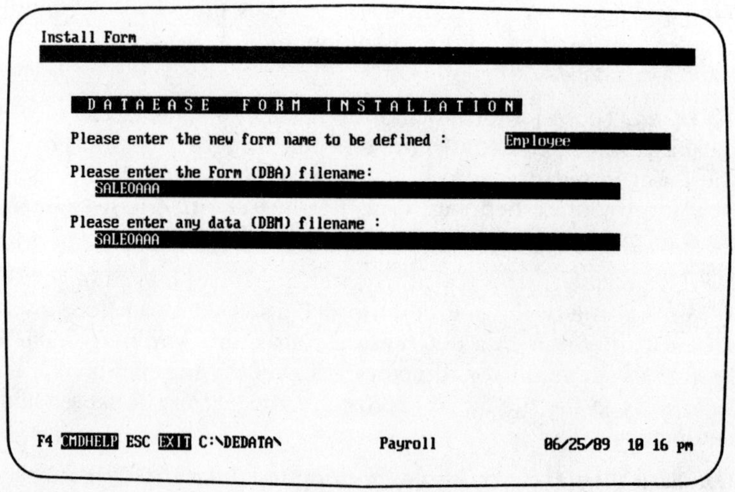

Fig. 9.18.

The Form Installation screen completed for installing the new Employee form using form definition and data from the Sales Representative form.

```
Install Form


        D A T A E A S E   F O R M   I N S T A L L A T I O N

    Please enter the new form name to be defined :        Employee

    Please enter the Form (DBA) filename:
        SALEOAAA

    Please enter any data (DBM) filename :
        SALEOAAA







    F4 CMDHELP ESC EXIT C:\DEDATA\          Payroll          06/25/89  10 16 pm
```

When you press Enter at the data file name line, DataEase uses the definition found in SALEOAAA.DBA to install the new Employee form into the Payroll database. It also adds to Employee all the records found in the data file SALEOAAA.DBM.

At this point, Employee in Payroll is identical to Sales Representative in Order Tracking, but they are two separate forms in different databases. You can now modify Employee to the needs of your new payroll application.

Installing Reports and Procedures

Just as you occasionally may need to copy forms between DataEase databases, you also may need to use DataEase Quick Reports or DQL procedures in several databases. They probably cannot be used in multiple databases without at least some modification, but at least you don't always have to start from scratch. DataEase enables you to copy Quick Reports or DQL procedures using the Install Procedure facility.

To install (copy) a Quick Report or DQL procedure from another database into the current database, select **4. Install Procedure** from the Utilities menu. DataEase displays the Procedure Installation screen and prompts you to enter the name of the new Quick Report or procedure that you are defining. Type a name that hasn't already been used for a procedure or Quick Report in the current database and press Enter.

Next, DataEase instructs you to enter the Procedure (DBR) file name. Type the DOS file name of the source procedure or Quick Report definition you want to copy and press Enter. If the file is in a different data directory, you must include the full DOS path (drive and/or directory followed by the file name). DataEase adds the file name extension, DBR, so that you don't have to type it.

Finally, DataEase asks, Does the Procedure have a Data-entry Form? Respond 2: yes if it does or 1: no if it doesn't (a Quick Report never has a data-entry form). DataEase then installs the new Quick Report or procedure in the current database.

At this point, you have two copies of the same Quick Report or procedure, but each is in a different database. You may need to modify the new procedure or Quick Report definition so that the form and field names are the same as the ones in the current database.

Changing the Database Name

DataEase enables you to change the name of your database easily. However, in order to initiate this operation, you must have a High security level. Ideally, only the system administrator should change the database name.

To rename the current database, access the Utilities menu and choose **6. Change the Database Name**. Because this operation is important, DataEase requests your user name with the prompt, What is your name?. Type your user name and press Enter.

DataEase next asks for your password. Type it and press Enter again. If you don't have a High security level or enter an invalid user name/password combination, DataEase aborts the operation and returns to the Utilities menu.

Assuming that you have the proper security level, DataEase then reminds you of the current database name, displaying it on-screen, and asks, What is the new database name ?. Type the new name and press Enter.

Before DataEase completes the operation, it asks for confirmation. Respond 2: yes, and DataEase renames the database.

> **Tip:** Even though DataEase changes the name of the database, it does not change the database letter used as the fifth character in most database DOS file names. No DOS file names are changed in any way.

Deleting the Database

Whenever your hard disk becomes cluttered, you may decide to get rid of a database or two. But, the data directory listing with its myriad similar file names may be disconcerting. You are justifiably reluctant to start deleting files for fear you may delete the wrong ones. DataEase, as you may suspect, comes to the rescue again by providing a utility to delete an entire database in one step. However, you can use this utility only if you have a High security level.

> **Tip:** Before deleting a database, by all means make a backup copy (discussed earlier in this chapter). DataEase does not supply a utility to "undo" an erroneous database deletion, but you can restore a backup copy if you realize that you have deleted the database prematurely.

To delete the current database, access the Utilities menu and select **7. Remove this Database**. DataEase displays the Remove the Database screen and warns you,

```
*** ALL the data base information will be Removed from the disk***
```

DataEase then asks for your name. Type your user name and press Enter. At the prompt, What is your password?, type your password and press Enter. If you don't have a High security level or you enter an invalid user name/password combination, DataEase aborts the operation and returns to the Utilities menu. Otherwise, it asks,

```
Are you sure you want to remove the ENTIRE DATA BASE ?
```

If you are sure that you want to delete the database (presumedly you have a backup copy), respond 2: yes. (Respond 1: no to abort the deletion.) DataEase deletes the database and quits DataEase, returning you to DOS.

Chapter Summary

You are equipped now with a full complement of DataEase tools. You already knew how to create a database, define forms, enter data, modify data, and produce sophisticated reports. This chapter has explained how to perform all the database maintenance and system administration tasks and use the general utilities necessary to keep your database fine-tuned.

You have learned how to obtain status information about your DataEase forms, procedures, and import specifications. You have seen two methods for making backup copies and then restoring your database. You can perform DOS functions without leaving DataEase as well as lock and unlock a shared database on a LAN. You also learned how to define a user name, password, security level, screen style, and help level for each user of your database; import data from other programs; transfer data between forms; install forms; change the database name, and delete a database.

Now that you know how to build a powerful database system, you are ready to examine the DataEase facility for dressing it up with a complete, menu-driven user interface. Turn to Chapter 10 to learn how to bind DataEase forms, reports, and procedures into a cohesive, easy-to-use database application using the DataEase menu design facility.

10

Creating Custom
DataEase Menus

DataEase is a remarkably powerful program considering how easy it is to use. This chapter discusses the DataEase features that enable you to design easy-to-use database systems. This chapter also describes how to use DataEase Menu Definition to create complete menu-driven database applications. You can create custom menus that provide easy access to otherwise complex features while preventing access to features you want placed off limits.

This chapter explains how to name a menu, define security levels, assign a menu title, create menu choice descriptions, and select a function for each menu choice. The chapter also explains how to create a chain menu and how to assign a start-up menu.

Understanding DataEase Menus

DataEase menus can be divided into two categories: system menus and user menus.

System menus are defined by DataEase and include the eight full-screen menus listed in table 10.1. You cannot change the content of these menus.

Table 10.1
Full-Screen Menus

Menu	Called from
DataEase Main	Sign On screen
Form Definition	Main menu
Records	Main menu
QBE—Quick Reports	Main menu
DQL	Main menu
Administration	Main menu
Utilities	Administration menu
Maintenance	Main menu

User menus also are full-screen menus, but you design and create them. These menus can have up to nine choices, each of which can perform one of the following functions:

❑ Display the DataEase Main menu

❑ Display another user menu

❑ Display a record-entry form for entering, viewing, modifying, or deleting records

❑ Display the DQL menu

❑ Run a DQL procedure or Quick Report

❑ View the Database Status menu to create a status report on the forms, procedures, or import specifications currently in the database

❑ Begin backup database process

❑ Begin the restore database process

❑ Display the Utilities menu

❑ Execute an import specification

❑ Execute a DOS command or program

❑ Reorganize a form

❑ Lock a database (LAN use only)

❑ Unlock a database (LAN use only)

❑ Install an application using an Installation command file

When a user selects an option from a user menu, the specified function executes transparently. That is, the user does not see intermediate steps that DataEase may take but sees only the result. You might, for example, define a menu choice to display the Widget Order form in Record Entry. To perform that operation manually, you would select **2. Record Entry** from the DataEase Main menu and then choose the Widget Order form from the window menu at the Records menu screen. Only then does DataEase display the form in Record Entry. But when you select an option from a user menu to perform the same function, DataEase immediately displays the Widget Order form in Record Entry and does not display the DataEase Main or Records menus.

For each user name in the Users form you can define a *start-up* menu, which can be one of the system menus, or a user menu. Whenever someone signs on to a database, DataEase checks whether a start-up menu is assigned to that user. If so, DataEase displays that menu. When no start-up menu is designated for a user, DataEase displays the DataEase Main menu.

A complete menu system, often referred to as a *database application*, can insulate novice or infrequent users from the more difficult tasks such as form design and report generation. You can design the application so that the user never sees the DataEase Main menu, Records menu, QBE—Quick Reports menu, DQL menu, or any of the other full-screen system menus, but still provide all the necessary database functions through the 15 functions available in user menus. Because each user name can be assigned a start-up menu, you also can permit more advanced users full access to the program by assigning them the DataEase Main menu or by not assigning a start-up menu for them at all.

The DataEase menu definition feature also enables you to control access to sensitive records in your database. You can define multiple start-up menus for a database, each providing access to different forms and reports. The access of each user to a particular form or report then depends on the start-up menu you assign in the User Information form.

Before you begin creating menus, you should map them out on paper. An example of such a menu map is shown inside the front cover of each of the DataEase Reference Manuals. The map shows the DataEase Main menu and each of the other seven full-screen system menus. Lines show how the menus are related. For example, when you select **1. Form Definition and Relationships** on the DataEase Main menu, the Form Definition menu is displayed; accordingly, the menu map shows a line connecting this first menu option on the DataEase Main menu to the top of the Form Definition menu.

DataEase permits you to create up to nine options on each menu. If you need to define more menu choices than will fit on a particular menu, define the last choice so that it displays a second user menu. You can then place the remaining options on the second menu.

If possible, it is best not to "nest" menus more than two levels deep. Users can get lost quickly when they have to navigate too far into the menu structure. Remember that you want to make your database system easier to use; you are not designing a "Dungeons and Dragons" game.

Assume, for example, that you want to design a menu system to enable a user to access the Widget Order forms or Retail Customer forms in Record Entry, run the Widget Orders List procedure, or run a Quick Report named Labels 2-Up that produces customer mailing labels, and back up or restore the database.

After you have the menu structure designed on paper, you are ready to create it on-screen. Starting at the DataEase Main menu, select **5. Menu Definition**, and DataEase displays the Menus form (see fig. 10.1).

Fig. 10.1.

The Menus form.

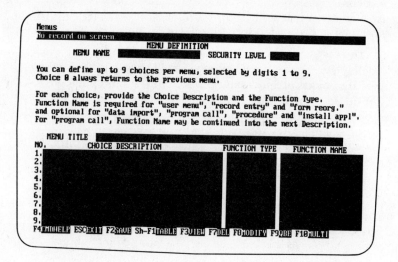

The Menus form is actually a DataEase record-entry form. In fact, you also can display it by selecting **2. Record Entry** from the DataEase Main menu, and then choosing 1: System and 6: Menus from the Records menu.

The Menus form is one of the system forms automatically created by DataEase for each database. (The others are the Users form, the Configuration form, the Screen Styles form, and the Relationships form.) Each record in the Menus form represents one menu in the database. Because the Menus form is a DataEase form, all the Record Entry features described in Chapter 4 for entering, viewing, deleting, modifying, and saving a form record apply. When you finish defining a menu, press F2 (SAVE) to save it to memory. If you later make a change to the definition, save the modification by pressing F8 (MODIFY). To clear the screen to define another menu, press F5 (FORM CLEAR). To quit and return to the DataEase Main menu, press Esc (EXIT).

Naming a Menu

The first field on the Menus form is the Menu Name field. You must give
each menu in your database a unique name in the Menu Name field. A
menu name can be as many as 20 characters long. Any particular menu
name can be used only once in a database. This is a required field; every
menu must have a name.

A menu name never appears on-screen in the menu itsclf but is intended
only to provide a way to reference each menu. When you define a menu
choice that displays another menu, you refer to the other menu by its
menu name. You also specify start-up menus by their menu name.

Menu names should be descriptive, especially if you plan to create many of
them. Because the top-level menu is often called the *main* menu, you may
want to include the word "Main" in the name of your top-level menu. The
top-level system menu is the DataEase Main menu. In the example, the top-
level menu is called "Widget Order Main."

To define the menu name, type the name in the Menu Name field and
press Enter or Tab. DataEase moves the cursor to the next field, the
Security Level field.

Setting Security Levels

After you name the menu, you have the option of establishing a security
level for the menu. After you enter the menu name, DataEase moves the
cursor to the Security Level field and displays the security level options as
a line menu in the prompt line. To assign a higher security level, choose
the appropriate line menu option. DataEase enters the security level in the
field and moves to the Menu Title field.

As explained in Chapter 9, DataEase enables you to assign, on the Users
form, any one of seven levels of security to each user you authorize to
access your database: High, Medium1, Medium2, Medium3, Low1, Low2,
and Low3. By default, a user need have only a Low3 security level to be
able to display a menu.

Each security level carries with it certain default rights and restrictions to
do such things as view, enter, modify, and delete fields. For example, by
default, users with the lowest security level can view any record in any
form in the database but cannot modify or delete a record (refer to
Chapter 9 for a complete list of these default settings). Assigning a security
level to a menu does not change any of these defaults. It simply
determines whether or not the user is allowed to see the menu in
question.

Tip: Keep in mind that you also can control each user's access to each menu through your assignment of start-up menus. Assignment of start-up menus is discussed near the end of this chapter. When you have only a small number of users who may need to access your system, you can control menu access precisely by assigning each user a particular start-up menu that has been tailored specifically for his needs and requirements. When there are many users, however, you may want to assign nearly everyone the same start-up menu and control access to specific menus through the use of security levels.

Be aware that you can completely lock a user out of a database by assigning a start-up menu that requires a security level higher than the user's security level.

When a user attempts to access a menu that is above his or her security level, DataEase displays the message, This menu does not exist.

Giving the Menu a Title

Although they sound alike, the *menu title* is not the same as the *menu name*. The menu name is used in the Users form and in other menus to refer to a menu but never appears on the menu screen itself. A menu name can be used only once in a database. It is a unique field in the Menus form.

By contrast, the menu title always appears on the menu screen, in reverse video, centered below the top edge of the menu border (in the same position as the title of a system menu). The menu title does not have to be a unique value in the database. You can design slightly different versions of the same menu for different users without changing the menu title, so long as each menu has a different menu name.

With the cursor in the Menu Title field, type the title and press Enter or Tab. The menu title can be up to 60 characters long, including characters, numbers, or punctuation. After you enter the title, DataEase moves the cursor to the first Choice Description column.

In the Widget Order Main menu example, you might use the title "Widget Order Main Menu."

Describing a Menu Choice

The Menus form enables you to define up to nine menu options for each user menu. For each option you can define a Choice Description, a Function Type, and a Function Name. The cursor moves to the Choice Description column first.

The Choice Description column for the first choice is actually the field d1 in the Menus form. The second Choice Description column is field d2, and so on. If you switch the Menus form to Table View (by pressing Shift-F1 (TABLE)), you see these actual field names listed as column headings.

In field d1 (the first Choice Description column), type the text that you want to appear as the first option on the menu screen. DataEase provides 44 spaces for a description. When you have finished typing the description, press Enter or Tab to move to the Function Type column.

In the Widget Order Main menu example, you want the first choice to access Record Entry for entering, viewing, or modifying data in Widget Order or Retail Customer. You therefore enter the description *Record Entry* and press Enter to move to the Function Type column.

Choosing a Function

Each menu choice must specify a Function Type—the action that you want DataEase to perform when you choose the option. The Function Type column for the first menu choice is the dt1 field in the Menus form. The Function Type column for the second menu choice is field dt2, and so on.

When the cursor is resting in the first Function Type column, DataEase displays a list of available functions in the prompt line. (Actually, 18 functions are listed, but 3 are for future use, so that only 15 are available function types.) Choose one of these functions. DataEase enters the Function Type in the column and moves to the Function Name column.

Several of the function types also require that you fill in a name in the Function Name column. For example, when you want a menu option to display another user menu, you must type the other menu's name in the Function Name column. The sections that follow explain when you need to provide this information.

Calling the Main Menu

DataEase lists 1: MAIN menu as the first function type available. The purpose of this function is to display the DataEase Main menu. Indeed, it is the only function that provides access to all the DataEase system menus.

When the user selects a Main menu option from a user menu, DataEase displays the normal DataEase Main menu. The user can then use all the DataEase system menus almost as if he or she had not started from a user menu at all. The only distinction is when the user presses Esc (EXIT) at the DataEase Main menu, DataEase returns to the original user menu instead of exiting from DataEase.

Tip: When you are designing a complete "turn-key" database application where everyone will have a start-up menu assigned, make sure that you place the Main menu option on the start-up menu of at least the system administrator. The system administrator should always have access to all DataEase system menus to perform system maintenance.

To indicate a Main menu function type, select 1: Main menu in the Function Type column. DataEase moves the cursor to the Function Name column. Because you don't enter a value in the Function Name column for this function type, just press Enter or Tab to move the cursor down to the next menu choice.

Calling a User Menu

When you want one menu choice to display another user menu, select the User Menu function type. This procedure is often referred to as *calling* another menu. The called menu is sometimes referred to as a *submenu*.

A submenu can contain choices that display still other user menus. DataEase permits you to "nest" user menus many levels deep. The only limitation to the number of user menus that you can use this way is the amount of memory (RAM) available in your computer. DataEase loads all user menus for the database into memory whenever a user of the database signs on. Each menu uses 672 bytes of memory.

Tip: DataEase automatically loads user menus into expanded memory if your system has it.

Caution: Never design a user menu choice that calls the menu which called the current menu. With DataEase, the user can press Esc (EXIT) to return to the calling menu, so that there is no need for such an option.

To indicate that a menu choice should display another user menu, select 2: user menu from the line menu. DataEase enters user menu in the Function Type column and moves to the Function Name column.

When the cursor is resting in the Function Name column, DataEase displays a list of previously defined user menus as a line menu in the prompt line. Choose the appropriate user menu from this list. If you haven't yet defined the menu, press Esc and then type the name you plan to give the menu.

For example, in the Widget Order Main menu, all three menu choices should display other user menus. The first choice should display the user menu named Record Entry; the second choice should call a user menu named Reports, and the third menu option on the Widget Order Main menu should display a user menu named Maintenance. None of these submenus has yet been defined.

First, fill in the Choice Description column, as described in the preceding section. For the first menu option, type the words *Record Entry* as the Choice Description, and DataEase moves the cursor to the Function Type column. Because you want this menu option to display the Record Entry menu, a user menu, choose 2: user menu as the Function Type, and DataEase moves the cursor to the Function Name column.

Next, you must indicate the name of the menu in the Function Name column. But, because you have not yet defined the Record Entry menu, it does not appear as a choice in the line menu. Instead of selecting a user menu from the prompt line, you press the Esc key. DataEase removes the line menu, and you can type a menu name in the field. Type the menu name *Record Entry* and press Enter. DataEase moves the cursor to the left end of the row for the second menu choice. You use a similar procedure to define the second and third menu choices for the Widget Order Main menu. Figure 10.2 shows the completed user menu definition.

Tip: You also can use the user menu function type to call the Administration system menu. Choose 2: user menu in the Function Type column of the Menus form and type *$$ADMIN* as the function name. Then, when the user selects this option from the user menu, the Administration menu is displayed. This capability is peculiar to the Administration menu and does not work for other system menus.

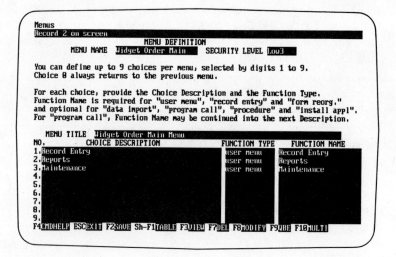

Accessing Record Entry

Often, you will want a user menu to provide access to the DataEase Record Entry facility. This is the purpose of the *record-entry* function type.

When the user selects a record-entry type user menu choice, DataEase immediately displays a particular form in Record Entry. The user never sees the Records menu. The user can enter, edit, modify, or delete records (subject to any security-level restrictions you have placed on the form).

To indicate a record-entry function type, select 3: record entry in the Function Type column. DataEase then moves the cursor to the Function Name column where you must specify a form name. DataEase displays a line menu of all available record-entry forms. Select the form that you want the menu choice to access. DataEase places the form name in the Function Name column and moves the cursor to the next menu choice. When you have not yet defined the form, you can press Esc and type the name you intend to use for the form in the Function Name column. Then, press Enter or Tab to move to the next line.

In the Widget Orders application example, the Record Entry menu contains two menu choices. The first, Widget Order, displays the Widget Order form in Record Entry. The second choice, Customers, accesses the Retail Customer form in Record Entry.

To define the Record Entry menu for this example application, you must start with a blank Menus form. Press F5 (FORM CLEAR) to clear any previously defined user menu definition from the screen. You type the menu name *Record Entry* in the Menu Name field and press Enter or Tab.

(*Note:* You do not have to use this particular menu name every time you intend to use a record-entry function type. It is used in this example because it best describes the purpose of the user menu.) DataEase moves the cursor to the Security Level field. You press Enter or Tab again to accept the default security level, and DataEase moves the cursor to the Menu Title field. Again, you type *Record Entry* and press Enter or Tab. (*Note:* The menu name and the menu title don't have to be the same, but there is no reason why they must be different, so long as the menu name is unique.) DataEase moves the cursor to the first line in the Choice Description column.

Using your design (see "Understanding DataEase Menus" earlier in this chapter), type *Widget Order* in the Choice Description column and press Enter or Tab to move to the Function Type column. Next, select 3: record entry from the line menu, and DataEase moves the cursor to the Function Name column. Finally, type the name of the form that you want displayed, *Widget Order*, and press Enter or Tab. DataEase moves the cursor to the second line of the Choice Description column. You use a similar procedure to define the second menu choice so that it will display the Retail Customer form in Record Entry. The completed Record Entry user menu is shown in figure 10.3.

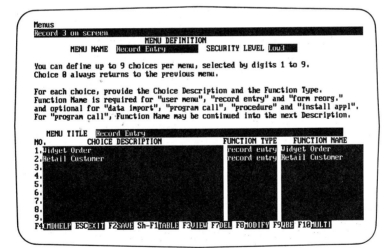

Fig. 10.3.

The completed Record Entry user menu definition including two choices that use the record-entry function type.

Calling the DQL Menu

Occasionally, you may want to create a user menu choice that displays the DQL Menu so that the user can access any of the DQL options. Use the *query* function type for this purpose.

To define a menu choice with the query function, choose 4: query from the line menu when the cursor is in the Function Type column. Press Enter or Tab to skip the Function Name column. You don't specify a Function Name value for this type of menu choice function.

Running a Procedure or Quick Report

Frequently you will need to provide one or more menu choices that generate output from the database—reports. The *procedure* function type is used to run both DQL procedures and Quick Reports. You also can use this function type to run any DQL procedure, even when it doesn't generate displayable or printable output.

To use the *procedure* type function, select 5: procedure from the line menu when the cursor is in the Function Type column. In the prompt line, DataEase displays a line menu containing a list of all available DQL procedures and Quick Reports. Choose from this menu the one you want the menu option to run.

Again, following your design, you want to define a submenu in the Widget Orders application named *Reports*. This menu should enable a user to run either a Quick Report named Labels 2-Up that generates mailing labels from the Retail Customer form data or run the Widget Orders List report (a DQL procedure developed in Chapters 7 and 8). You therefore need to define two menu choices, both using the procedure function type.

Starting in a blank Menus form, type *Reports* in the Menu Name field. Press Enter or Tab twice to move the cursor to the Menu Title field and type *Reports* again. Press Enter or Tab once more to move to the first line of the Choice Description column.

Type *Customer Mailing Labels* as the first choice description, and press Enter or Tab to move to the Function Type column. Select 5: procedure from the line menu. DataEase moves the cursor to the Function Name column and displays a line menu containing the available procedures and Quick Reports. Select the Quick Report named Labels 2-Up. Following a similar procedure, you also define the second menu option. The completed Reports user menu is shown in figure 10.4.

Tip: You also can use this option to access any DataEase system menu directly. First, define a DQL Control Procedure (discussed in Chapter 11) that calls the system menu. Then, use the procedure function type in a user menu to run the procedure.

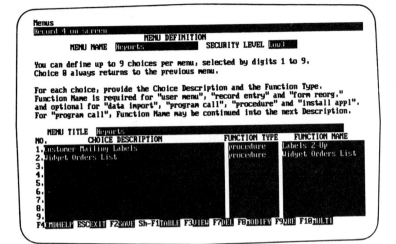

Fig. 10.4.

The Reports user menu definition containing two procedure function type menu choices.

Choosing Database Maintenance Functions

Six user menu function types enable the user to perform database maintenance tasks such as status, backup, restore, program call, lock db, and unlock db.

The status function type has the same effect as selecting **1. Database Status** from the Maintenance menu. The backup function duplicates the **2. Backup Database** choice on the Maintenance menu. The function restore is the same as choosing **3. Restore Database** from the Maintenance menu. None of these functions requires an entry in the Function Name column.

The function type program call is the same as choosing DOS Functions on the DataEase Maintenance menu. Refer to the next section in this chapter for more about the program call function.

Both the lock db and unlock db function types have no effect unless you are using DataEase on a local area network (LAN). Assuming that you are using a LAN, the lock db function type is the same as choosing **5. Lock Database** on the Maintenance menu, and the unlock db function type is equivalent to choosing **6. Unlock Database** on the Maintenance menu. Neither lock db nor unlock db require a Function Name value.

Refer to Chapter 9 for a complete discussion of the Maintenance menu and these database maintenance operations.

The last menu that you need to design in the Widget Order example is the Maintenance user menu (which is different from the system provided Maintenance menu). According to your original design, this menu has two options—Backup and Restore.

Starting in a blank Menus form, type *Maintenance* in the Menu Name field. Press Enter or Tab twice to move the cursor to the Menu Title field and type *Maintenance* again. Press Enter or Tab once more to move to the first line of the Choice Description column.

Type *Backup the database* as the first choice description and press Enter or Tab to move to the Function Type column. Select 7: backup from the line menu. DataEase moves the cursor to the Function Name column. Press Enter or Tab to skip the Function Name column, and move to the next line.

To define the second menu choice, type *Restore the database* in the Choice Description column and choose 8: restore in the Function Type column. Again, you enter no value in the Function Name column. The completed Maintenance user menu is shown in figure 10.5.

Fig. 10.5.

The Maintenance user menu definition containing a backup function type menu choice and a restore function type menu choice.

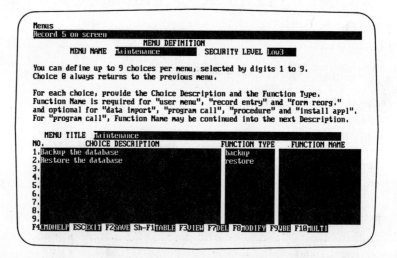

Calling Another DOS Program

As versatile as computers are, it is likely that users of your database application will from time to time want to use other programs for such tasks as word processing, spreadsheet, business presentation graphics, or telecommunications. DataEase provides the program call function type that enables you to add to a user menu the capability to call other DOS programs from within DataEase. This function type is equivalent to choosing **4. DOS Functions** from the Maintenance menu and **6. Other** from the DOS Functions.

To define a user menu choice that can call a specific DOS program, select the 11: program call in the Function Type column and specify a DOS program name in the Function Name column. When you want the user to be able to type DOS commands directly at the DOS prompt, just leave the Function Name column blank.

In use, when a program call function menu choice is selected by the user, DataEase swaps itself out to either EMS memory (if your computer has this type of expanded memory) or to disk and runs the DOS program specified in the Function Name column. If you left the Function Name value blank, DataEase sets up a DOS shell and displays the following message:

```
*** Type 'exit' to return to DataEase ***
```

The user then sees the DOS prompt.

> **Caution:** Never execute a memory-resident program from within DataEase. It may damage your system.

To be able to call another DOS program from within DataEase, you must add a parameter to a special configuration file named PROGCALL.DAT. This parameter must inform DataEase of the memory requirements of the DOS program you want to call from within DataEase. This file is found in the DataEase program directory. Use a text editor or word processor that can read and write ASCII text files to modify the file. When you first install DataEase, the PROGCALL.DAT file contains the following lines:

```
convert     350000
graftalk    350000
command     350000
prexvu      350000
```

You should add to the left column the name of any DOS program you want to use (the name of the .EXE, .COM or .BAT file that starts the program, for example). Follow the name with the minimum number of bytes of memory required to run the program. DataEase uses this number to clear a sufficient amount of memory before it attempts to call the program. DataEase uses the command 350000 parameter when you create a program call menu option and leave the Function Name column blank.

Many DOS programs require that you provide certain information along with the start-up command. This might be a file name, a directory name, or certain other start-up parameters. For this reason, DataEase permits you to type parameters after the DOS program name in the Function Name column. For example, you might want to call a program named SUPERAPP from within DataEase. Assume that this hypothetical program requires that you type the path of its data directory immediately after the program name. If the program's data is in the directory C:\SUPDATA, the proper start-up command would look like the following:

SUPERAPP C:\SUPDATA

You therefore would type this start-up command in the Function Name column in order to use a program call menu option to start the DOS program.

Sometimes you want the user to provide the value of a program parameter at the time the choice is made on the user menu. Taking the preceding example a step further, assume that you can instruct the SUPERAPP program to load a specific file when it starts by including the path for a data file after the program name. To load a file named MYFILE.DAT, the complete start-up command would look like the following:

SUPERAPP C:\SUPDATA\MYFILE.DAT

The DataEase program call function type can be used with a number of special keywords that enable you to substitute start-up parameters supplied by the user or by DataEase itself. This feature is referred to as *parameter substitution*. The keywords used to specify parameter substitution all start with the percent sign (%). Table 10.2 lists the available parameter substitution keywords and the parameter that is substituted. The table also indicates whether DataEase or the user will supply the information, and what (if any) prompt is displayed to inform the user what information is needed. Two of the keywords enable you to add an optional prompt, denoted by the word Message in the table. These parameter substitution keywords can be used alone, following the program name, or in combination with other parameters or other keywords.

Table 10.2
Program Call Parameters

Keyword	Parameter Substituted	Information provided by	Prompt
%a	DataEase Program Directory	DataEase	None
%b	DataEase Data Directory	DataEase	None
%d	Current Database Name	DataEase	None
%f	Filename	User	File Name
%f"Message"	Filename	User	Message File Name
%"Message"	Any parameter	User	Message

In the SUPERAPP example, the following command can be used:

SUPERAPP C:\SUPDATA\%f'Enter the"

When the user chooses the menu choice that contains this command, the message Enter the File Name: appears at the bottom of the screen. The user types the file name and presses Enter. DataEase executes the start-up command for SUPERAPP, replacing the keyword with the file name that has been provided by the user.

Choosing Utilities

Occasionally, you may want to create a user menu choice that displays the Utilities menu, which is fully covered in Chapter 9. The user can then access any of the Utilities options. You can use the utilities function type for this purpose.

You also can access two of the Utilities menu options directly without first displaying the Utilities menu. The data import function type enables the user to run an import specification to import data from another program; the install appl function type can be used to install an application into the DataEase database.

To define a menu choice with the utilities function, choose 9: utilities from the line menu when the cursor is in the Function Type column. Press Enter or Tab to skip the Function Name column. You do not specify a Function Name value for this type of menu choice function.

When you want to add a user menu option that will run an import specification, select 10: data import in the Function type column. You then normally specify the name of the import specification in the Function Name column. If you leave the Function Name column blank, DataEase enables the user to define a one-time report. Refer to Chapter 9 for a description of how to create and use import specifications.

To create a user menu choice that will install an application, choose **18. install appl** at the Function Type column. When you want the option to always install the same application, specify an Installation Command file in the Function Name column. If you want the user to specify an installation file at run time, leave the Function Name column blank. Creations and use of Installation Command files, however, are beyond the scope of this book.

Reorganizing a Form

When you create a DataEase application that permits users to delete records from a database form, you should provide the capability to reorganize the form. Otherwise, the form's records file may grow large. The form reorg. function type is used for this purpose. This function has the same effect as selecting **1. Form Definition and Relationships** from the DataEase Main menu, choosing **5. Reorganize a Form** from the Form Definition menu, and then selecting the form name.

To define a menu choice that will reorganize a form, choose 12: form reorg from the line menu when the cursor is in the Function Type column. DataEase moves the cursor to the Function Name column and displays a line menu containing a list of the forms in the database. Select the form to be reorganized from the line menu. When the user chooses this menu option from the user menu, DataEase reorganizes the form, removing all records that are marked as deleted, recovering lost space, and rebuilding indexes. The resulting file takes less space on the disk and is quicker for DataEase to sort or search.

Creating Chain Menus

This chapter has discussed defining menu choices that perform one function each. DataEase also has a special type of menu choice called a *chain menu* that can perform a virtually unlimited number of functions.

You define a chain menu as a separate user menu, but it is really a list of functions that you want performed in sequence. When the menu is called, DataEase performs all the menu's functions, one after the other but never displays the menu itself.

To create a chain menu, start a new record in the Menus form and type a unique name in the Menu Name field. After selecting or accepting a security level, type the word *CHAIN* in the Menu Title field. Every chain menu has this same menu title. Use the menu choice lines to list the functions that DataEase should perform whenever a user menu calls this chain menu. Because the Choice Description column has no effect on the operation of the chain menu, it can be left blank. You should, however, use this column to document for future reference the purpose of each link in the chain. Entries in The Function Type column and the Function Name column have the same effect as when called one at a time.

You can call a chain menu using a user menu function in another user menu, or you can make it the start-up menu for a user. When it is called from another menu, DataEase performs the functions listed in the chain menu, and then returns to the calling menu. If you use a chain menu as a start-up menu, then one of the lines of the chain menu should call another user menu. Otherwise, DataEase executes the chain of functions and then returns to DOS. A chain menu can contain up to nine functions. If you need a chain menu that performs more than nine operations, define the last choice of the first chain menu to call a second chain menu. You can perform an unlimited number of functions by chaining menus together in this fashion.

Assigning a Start-Up Menu

Normally, when you start DataEase, it displays the DataEase Main menu. This is fine for someone who has the time to learn a powerful relational database program but may be daunting for many users. The whole subject of this chapter is how to design an alternative set of menus that enable users to perform sophisticated database tasks without having to learn all the ins and outs of DataEase.

So far, this chapter has discussed how to create user menus that perform various database functions to include calling other user menus. But, we have not discussed how to get the first user menu to display. Ideally, you want the menu to display when the user signs on to the database. This is the purpose of the *start-up* menu.

> **Tip:** The only other way to call the first menu in a DataEase application is with the *call menu* command in a DQL control procedure, discussed in Chapter 11.

Chapter 9 discusses how to add authorized users of your database. It also explains how to assign each of these users a password, security level, screen style, and help level. To assign a start-up menu for a user, access the Users form and enter, in the Start-up Menu field, the name of the menu that you want displayed first in the application. This should be the top-level menu in your application design. All other menus are then called from the start-up menu. After you have filled in the Start-up Menu field, press F8 (MODIFY) to save the modified Users record.

To complete the menu-driven application developed in this chapter, assign the Widget Order Main menu as the start-up menu for each user. Then, when the users sign on to DataEase, they are greeted with the Widget Order Main menu shown in figure 10.6.

When a user selects **1. Record Entry**, DataEase displays the Record Entry user menu shown in figure 10.7. The user can then access the Widget Order form in Record Entry by selecting **1. Widget Order** or the Retail Customer form by selecting **2. Retail Customer**. When the user presses Esc (EXIT) to quit from either record-entry form, DataEase returns the screen to the Record Entry user menu. The user then presses Esc (EXIT) again to return to the Widget Order Main menu.

Fig. 10.6.

The Widget Order Main menu, the top-level menu in the application.

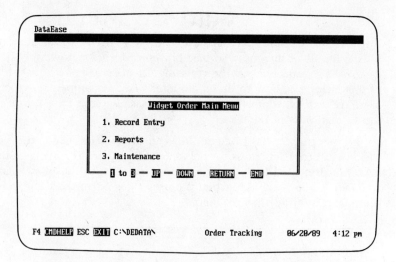

Fig. 10.7.

The Record Entry menu, providing access to the Widget Order and Retail Customer record-entry forms.

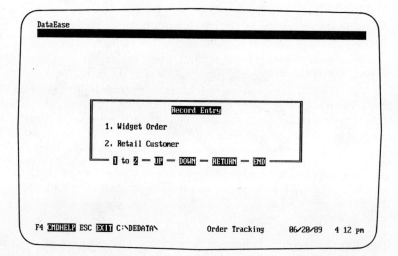

Any time a user wants to generate a report, he chooses **2. Reports** from the Widget Order Main menu. DataEase then displays the Reports menu, shown in figure 10.8. To print a batch of customer mailing labels, the user selects **1. Customer Mailing Labels** from the Reports user menu. Whenever the user wants to print a Widget Orders List report, he chooses **2. Widget Orders List** from this same menu. Each time DataEase finishes running one of these reports, it returns the screen to the Reports menu. To return to the Widget Order Main menu, the user presses Esc (EXIT).

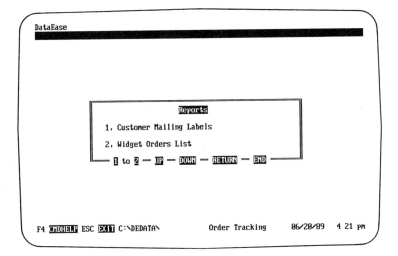

Fig. 10.8.

The Reports menu, with options to print customer mailing labels, and to run the Widget Orders List procedure.

When the user wants to back up the database or restore the database from a backup copy, he selects **3. Maintenance** from the Widget Order Main menu. DataEase displays the Maintenance user menu shown in figure 10.9. To back up the database, the user chooses **1. Backup the database** from the menu. If the user's data disk is damaged or lost and he needs to restore the data from a previous backup, the user should use the **2. Restore the database** option on the menu. To return to the start-up menu from the Maintenance menu, the user presses Esc (EXIT).

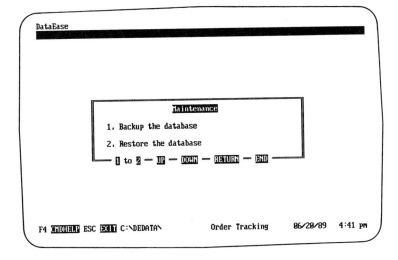

Fig. 10.9.

The Maintenance user menu, providing access to the database backup and restore maintenance functions.

To leave DataEase altogether, the user presses Esc (EXIT) from the start-up menu, the Widget Order Main user menu.

Chapter Summary

This chapter has addressed the DataEase menu-building facility that enables you to design database systems that are easy for anyone to use. You have learned how to use this menu generator to create complete, menu-driven database applications. You have learned how to create custom menus that provide easy access to otherwise complex features while preventing access to features you want placed off limits. This chapter explained how to name a menu, define security levels, assign a menu title, create menu choice descriptions, and select a function for each menu choice. You also have learned how to create a chain menu and assign a start-up menu.

Chapter 11 presents an overview of the powerful capabilities of DQL procedures. This last chapter will be of particular interest to system developers who want to build additional controls and safeguards into DataEase applications.

Part III

Advanced DataEase Processing: Using DQL

Includes

Building Full-Powered
Procedures with DQL

11

Building Full-Powered Procedures with DQL

This chapter gives you an overview of the fully programmable capabilities of DataEase available through the DataEase Query Language (DQL). In Chapter 7, "Building Simple Procedures with DQL," you learn how to use DQL to create simple procedures that retrieve information, sort records, group data, and use relational operators using low-level Interactive mode. This chapter takes you a step up to DQL *high-level* queries that can perform virtually any DataEase task, from entering and printing records to backing up and restoring the database.

The DataEase Query Language is a high-level database programming language suitable for use in developing full-featured database applications. Although extensive coverage of this programmable side of DataEase is beyond the scope of this book, this chapter helps you develop a good feel for the overall capabilities of DQL and gives you a good start at learning to program with DQL.

Understanding DataEase Query Language

The DataEase Query Language (DQL) is a highly structured language that enables you to perform simple data manipulation or to control complete accounting, billing, or other complex database applications. You have already used DQL to create simple queries using low-level Interactive mode. This chapter describes how you can use high-level Interactive mode to realize the full potential of DQL.

Creating Full-Powered Queries

You can use all the available DQL commands to tap the full power of DataEase when you create a query in high-level Interactive mode or Edit mode. However, a query is only one element of a DQL procedure. You arrange a query's output using a report format definition; you should specify the report destination in the Print Style Specification screen. You also still have the option of using a data-entry form to accept additional information for use by the query.

High-level Interactive mode enables you to create complex queries without typing a command (see chapter 7). You respond to prompts and select options from a series of line menus. You never have to worry about proper spelling or command syntax, because DataEase enters everything for you. When you are comfortable with the DQL commands and structure, however, the Interactive mode may seem slow and tedious. If this happens, you can create full-powered queries by typing commands directly on-screen while in Edit mode.

Note: DQL enables you to place commands anywhere on the line. You do not have to precede these commands with a period (.), and you do not have to place them in column 1 as you do with formatting commands. Many users like to use indenting to show the structure of the query. This chapter presents queries with commands indented exactly as they would be if you used the Interactive mode to create them. When you create a query in Interactive mode, however, the first command should begin in the first column and first row (R1C1).

When you use high-level Interactive mode or Edit mode, you can use all DQL commands. The complete complement of DQL commands can accomplish the following tasks, not available in low-level Interactive mode:

❑ Add, modify, and delete records

❑ Process records that meet different selection criteria in different ways—referred to as *conditional processing*

❑ Queries can use variables to hold information in memory for use in processing actual records. These queries can even use these variables to pass information from one procedure to another.

❑ A query can call other procedures.

You easily can start a new query in high-level Interactive mode, but it does take a few steps. From the DataEase Main menu, select **4. DQL Advanced Processing** to display the DQL menu. Then, choose **4. Define Query**. DataEase displays the Query Definition screen and types the command for in the first row of the query. All queries created in low-level Interactive mode start with the *for* command.

At this point, the level is still low, as shown by the level indicator in the bottom line of the screen and the mode indicator, which says Interactive. To switch to high level, press F9 (LEVEL). Now, the level indicator shows that the level is high. The mode is still Interactive.

Queries created in high-level Interactive mode don't have to start with the *for* command. Press the Home key to move the cursor back to the first column of the first row. The screen is still in high level, but no longer displays the level indicator. (It is replaced by the list of available function-key commands.) Now, the screen is in Edit Mode. You can type DQL commands on-screen, but you get no help from DataEase as you create the query. When you try to save the query, however, DataEase does a syntax check and finds your mistakes. DataEase does not save the query until you correct all typos and syntax errors.

To return to Interactive mode, so that you can take advantage of the prompts and menus and let DataEase do all the typing and checking syntax, press F1 (INTERACTIVE). You are now ready to create a query in high-level Interactive mode. DataEase displays a partial list of DQL commands as a line menu in the prompt line. To see a complete list of DQL commands as a window menu, press F1 (MORE). You see the screen shown in figure 11.1. It lists 19 of the 35 available DQL commands. Press PgDn to see the remaining 14 commands, shown in figure 11.2.

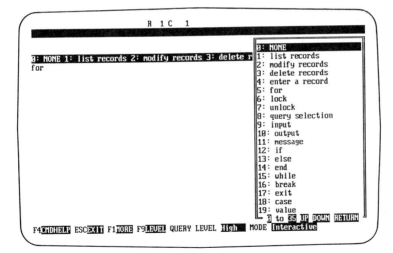

Fig. 11.1.

Listing the first 19 DQL commands available for use in a high-level query.

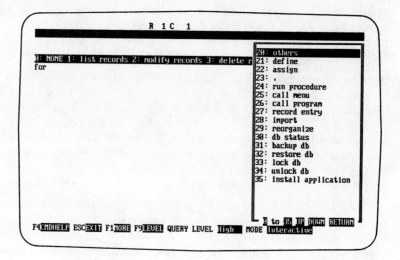

Fig. 11.2.

*Listing the last 14
DQL commands
available for use in
a high-level query.*

Note: For convenience, this chapter uses the term *low-level query* to refer
to queries created in low-level Interactive mode. It also uses the term
high-level query to mean any query created using high-level Interactive
mode. Keep in mind that all DQL commands always are available when
you use Edit mode to create a query.

Procedure Types

There are two types of DQL procedures: *processing procedures* and
control procedures. All procedures based on low-level queries fall into the
former category.

Processing procedures directly use or manipulate data in your database.
Processing procedures can sort and list record, and add, modify, and delete
records.

Control procedures, on the other hand, do not directly use or affect data.
Instead, these procedures call other processing or control procedures,
menus, or programs. They also can invoke Record Entry or perform
database maintenance functions. For example, you can create a control
procedure that duplicates the effect of a menu system designed with the
DataEase Menu Definition facility (see chapter 10).

You create queries for control procedures and processing procedures in
the same way. They are distinguished implicitly by the type of DQL
commands you use.

DQL Command Types

DQL commands fall into three categories: *processing commands*, *procedural commands*, and *control commands*. The commands you use determine whether the procedure is a control procedure or a processing procedure.

The first nine commands listed in figure 11.1 are *processing commands*. The two commands used in low-level queries—*for*, and *list records*—are in this group. You can use all nine of these commands to manipulate records. As soon as you use one of these commands, the procedure that contains the query becomes a processing procedure. At that point, you can no longer use the commands numbered 24 through 35 in figure 11.2.

The last eleven commands shown in figure 11.2 are *control commands*. This group of commands enables you to run other procedures, call menus, call programs, and so on. When you use one of these commands, the procedure that contains the query becomes a control procedure, and you cannot use the commands numbered 1 through 9 in figure 11.1 (the processing commands).

You can use the *procedural commands*, the third category, in either type of procedure. The DQL commands numbered 10 through 23 in figures 11.1 and 11.2 make up this group.

DataEase automatically recognizes whether you are defining a query for a processing procedure or for a control procedure. When appropriate, the program displays the following message in the message area of the screen:

This is a Processing procedure

or

This is a Control procedure

When you use Interactive mode to define a query, DataEase lists only eligible commands in the menus, so that you cannot accidentally use a processing command in a control procedure or a control command in a processing procedure. The remainder of the chapter describes how and when you use each of the available commands in all three categories.

Design Considerations

Every good programmer develops and continually refines his or her approach to programming, with the goal of consistently generating the best solution in the least amount of time. Any programmer will agree that programming is an art; no two programmers ever solve the same problem in precisely the same way. Only you can come up with an approach to programming that is most effective for your needs, but as you approach programming with DQL, consider the following suggestions:

❑ Just as your database consists of a collection of related forms tied together by defined relationships, a DQL program should usually consist of a collection of related processing procedures, tied together by a menu system or control procedures.

❑ Analyze the problem from the top downward. Define the primary goal in general terms first. Next, list the major steps required to reach the goal. Then, refine the subordinate steps needed to accomplish each of the major steps. Continue this analysis of the problem until you determine precisely how to solve it, using the smallest steps you can define.

❑ Write the program from the bottom upward. Create processing procedures to accomplish each of the lowest level steps in your solution. Be alert for multiple steps that can use the same procedure. Then, use one or more control procedures or the DataEase Menu Definition facility to tie the processing procedures together.

As with any other "art form," the only way to become really proficient at programming is to practice. The cleanly structured nature of DQL and its unique Interactive mode make the language an easy one to play around with. Don't be afraid. Try it, you'll like it!

Using Processing Commands

You use processing commands to do all of the real "work" (the manipulation of data in the database) done by a processing procedure query. Procedural commands merely determine if, when, and how many times DataEase does the work. Subject to the effect of any procedural commands that you may use, DataEase executes processing commands in the query from left to right and from top to bottom.

Selecting Records for Processing

The most common DQL command is the *for* command. It is always the first command in every low-level query and is often the first command in high-level queries. You use *for* to select a form for use in a query. Often, you use *for* with the operator *with*, which specifies record selection criteria. The following command, for example, selects all records from the Sales Representative form with the Salary field value greater than 25000 and makes Sales Representative the primary form:

```
for Sales Representative
with Salary › = 25000;
```

The following properties distinguish the use of the *for* command in a high-level query from its use in a low-level query:

❑ You use the *for* command once in each low-level query to define the primary form, as explained in Chapter 7. However, you can use it any number of times in a high-level query to select one or more primary forms and to select form relationships.

❑ You can nest *for* commands in a high-level query. The outermost *for* command specifies a primary form and must end with a semicolon (;). Each nested for command must have a corresponding *end* command. Each nested *for* command selects a relationship rather than a form and does not end with a semicolon.

❑ All commands listed between a *for* command and its corresponding *end* command execute once for each record selected from the form or relationship.

For example, you may want to see a list of your customers that shows the orders they have placed, including order totals. The query shown in figure 11.3 uses nested *for* commands to produce this list.

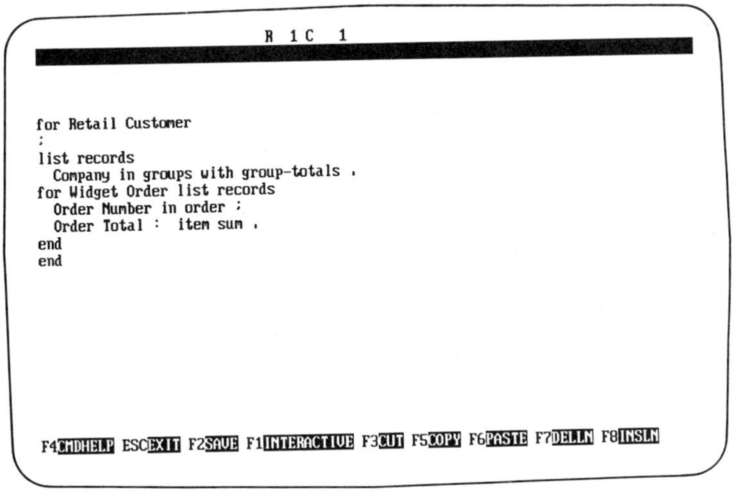

```
                          R  1 C   1


    for Retail Customer
    ;
    list records
      Company in groups with group-totals .
    for Widget Order list records
      Order Number in order ;
      Order Total :  item sum .
    end
    end




    F4CMDHELP ESCEXIT F2SAVE F1INTERACTIVE F3CUT F5COPY F6PASTE F7DELLN F8INSLN
```

Fig. 11.3.

A high-level query to produce a customer list with orders placed and order totals.

The first *for* command

    for Retail Customer

    ;

selects the Retail Customer form as the primary form. Notice that this command ends with a semicolon (;). All commands listed between this command and the last *end* command execute once for every record in

Retail Customer. For each Retail Customer record, the *list records* command lists the Company field, and DataEase then executes the nested *for* command.

The second *for* command

```
for Widget Order
```

selects the predefined relationship between Retail Customer and Widget Order. All commands listed between this command and the first *end* command execute once for each record in Widget Order that matches the Retail Customer record currently being processed from Retail Customer. Figure 11.4 shows the report output generated by this query (and an appropriate report format).

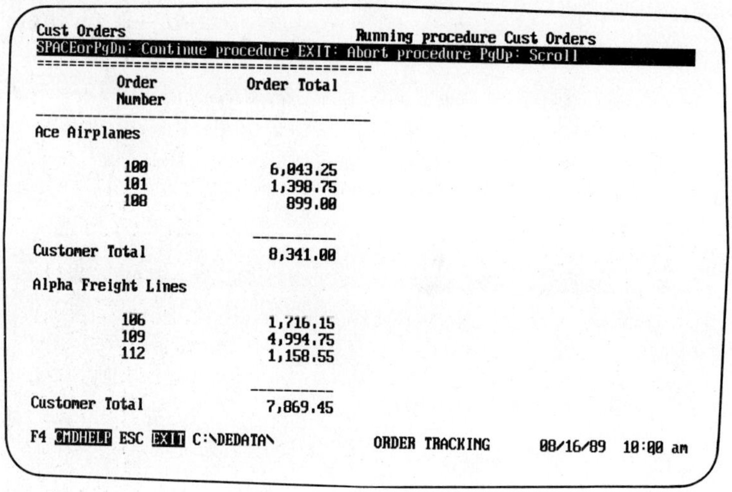

Fig. 11.4.

A customer list with orders placed and order totals.

```
Cust Orders                           Running procedure Cust Orders
SPACEorPgDn: Continue procedure EXIT: Abort procedure PgUp: Scroll
==============================================
        Order          Order Total
        Number
----------------------------------------------
Ace Airplanes

        100             6,043.25
        101             1,398.75
        108               899.00
                        ----------
Customer Total          8,341.00

Alpha Freight Lines

        106             1,716.15
        109             4,994.75
        112             1,158.55
                        ----------
Customer Total          7,869.45

F4 CMDHELP ESC EXIT C:\DEDATA\        ORDER TRACKING    08/16/89  10:00 am
```

Listing and Sorting Records

When you want to display data in a report, you use the *list records* command. This command is used in every low-level query to select items for display in the report.

Whether in a low-level query or a high-level query, the *list records* command usually follows a *for* command. Refer to the "Specifying Fields" section of Chapter 7 for a discussion of the *list records* command and a look at how to group and sort records using the sorting operators.

Adding Records

One of the major advantages of creating a query in high-level Interactive mode over creating a query in low-level Interactive mode is the capability to add data to the database. The *enter a record* DQL command accomplishes this task.

The syntax for this command is as follows:

enter a record *Formname*

where *Formname* is the name of the target record-entry form or relationship. You then use the assignment operator (: =) to assign a value to each field in the target.

Suppose, for example, that you want to extract from the Sales Representative form a list of all sales representatives from the Northern sales region and place that list in a new form that you have defined, named Northern Region. Figure 11.5 shows the query to perform this extraction.

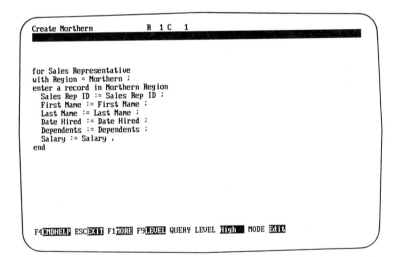

```
Create Northern         R  1 C   1




  for Sales Representative
  with Region = Northern ;
  enter a record in Northern Region
    Sales Rep ID := Sales Rep ID ;
    First Name := First Name ;
    Last Name := Last Name ;
    Date Hired := Date Hired ;
    Dependents := Dependents ;
    Salary := Salary ,
  end








  F4 CMDHELP  ESC EXIT  F1 MORE  F9 LEVEL  QUERY LEVEL  High  MODE Edit
```

Fig. 11.5.

Using the enter a record command to add records to the Northern Region form.

The field names on the left side of each assignment operator (: =) are from the Northern Region form. The field names on the right side of each assignment operator (: =) are from the primary form in the query, the Sales Representative form. In this particular case, the field names in both forms are the same.

You can accomplish the same result as the query in figure 11.5 with fewer lines by using the *copy all from* command. You can use this command only when it follows the *enter a record* command or the *modify records* command. Figure 11.6. shows the same query, using the *copy all from* command. You also can use this command or the assignment operator (;=) to transfer data from a data-entry form to a record-entry form.

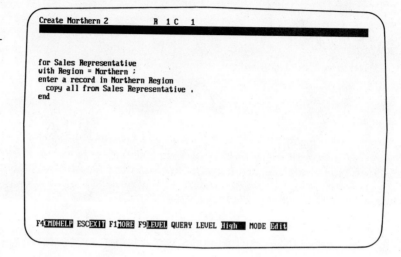

Fig. 11.6.

Using the copy all from command to add records to the Northern Region form.

```
Create Northern 2          R  1 C   1


for Sales Representative
  with Region = Northern ;
enter a record in Northern Region
   copy all from Sales Representative .
end
```

F4 CMDHELP ESC EXIT F1 MORE F9 LEVEL QUERY LEVEL High MODE Edit

Modifying Records

Perhaps even more important than the capability to add records, a query created in high-level Interactive mode or in Edit mode also can modify existing records in the database. You use the *modify records* command for this purpose.

In a query, the *modify records* command looks much like the *enter a record* command. The syntax for this command is as follows:

   modify records in *Formname*

where *Formname* is the name of the target record-entry form or relationship. When you are modifying records in the primary form, you can leave off the *in Formname* portion of the command syntax. Similar to the *enter a record* command, the assignment operator (:=) assigns a value to each field in the target form. The difference between the *modify records* command and the *enter a record* command is that the former changes the field values of existing records, rather than adding new records.

At some time, for example, you may decide to grant an across-the-board four percent raise to all your sales representatives. You can use the *modify records* command with the assignment operator (;=) to calculate the new salary and then substitute it for the old salary. The query is as follows:

```
for Sales Representative
;
modify records
Salary : = Salary * 1.04 .
end
```

When you run the procedure that contains this query, DataEase replaces the old salary value in each Sales Representative record with a new one that is four percent higher.

Deleting Records

In any database, information eventually becomes obsolete. This is especially true when you have a great deal of data, and you are about to run out of disk space; you need to be able to remove easily unwanted information from the database. DataEase provides a DQL processing command to help you do this—the *delete records* command.

When you want to delete *all* the selected records from the primary form, use the following command:

```
delete records
```

For example, you can use the following query to purge the Widget Order form of all orders prior to January 1, 1989:

```
for Widget Order
with Date < 01/01/89 ;
delete records
  end
```

Often, you need to delete records from related forms as well. When you delete a record from Widget Order, for example, you should also delete all related records from the Order Detail form. The following query deletes related records from both forms for orders placed before 1989:

```
for Widget Order
with Date < 01/01/89 ;
delete records
  delete records in Order Detail
  end
```

The first delete command in this query deletes all records from Widget Order where the value of the Date field is less than January 1, 1989. The second delete command deletes all records in Order Detail related to the selected records in Widget Order.

Tip: Similar to the F7 (Delete) key in Record Entry, the *delete records* command doesn't permanently remove records from the form. Instead, this command marks deleted records in the form so that DataEase doesn't display them or use them in processing. They are, however, still stored in the form until the next time the form is reorganized. See the "Maintaining the Database" section of this chapter for information on the Reorganize DQL control command. Remember that you don't recover disk space by simply deleting records; you also must reorganize the form.

The only way to undelete a record is to use the method described in the "Recovering Deleted Records" section in Chapter 4; you must do this *before* you reorganize the form, however. After you reorganize the form, you cannot recover deleted data; you must retype all of your data.

Controlling Input

One of the strongest features of DataEase is the degree of control you have over its Record Entry facility. With derivation fields, prevent data-entry, automatic sequencing, security levels, help messages, Multiforms, Multiview, ad-hoc Multiforms, dynamic lookup, and more, you can often design nearly idiot-proof forms. However, at times you still may not want data entered directly into a form without further screening or processing by the query first. DataEase now provides the Input command for this purpose.

Tip: The Input command is an advanced feature that gives you complete control of the processing of all data entered and/or viewed on-screen. The added layer of protection, however, can significantly add to the complexity of the DQL procedure. Use this feature only as a last resort if you feel that DataEase's built-in safeguards are not adequate to protect your database.

The Input command, available in DataEase 4.0, provides the capability to accept data from the user into a form on-screen that looks and acts, from the user's perspective, like a record-entry form. Any data entered or changes made, however, go into a temporary form, rather than in the record-entry form so that the data can be processed by the query before being added to the form.

The syntax for the Input command is as follows:

input using *Formname* into *"Tempform"*

where *Formname* is the name of a record-entry form in the database, and *Tempform* is any valid form name that was not used in the database or the query. The second form name is for the temporary form that exists only in memory and only while the procedure executes. It can hold just one record at a time. You must enclose the name of the temporary form in double quotation marks in the Input command.

When DataEase executes the Input command, it displays the record-entry screen. The user can view records and use Multiview just as in Record Entry. To the user, records appear on-screen exactly as they would in Record Entry. However, when the user presses a processing key—Esc (Exit), F2 (Save), F7 (Delete), or F8 (Modify)—DataEase copies the data in the current record to the temporary form in memory, rather than to the actual record-entry form.

Caution: When you use the *input* command with a Multiform, F2 (SAVE) and F8 (MODIFY) have their normal effects on subform records, including enforcement of referential integrity (if one of the referential integrity options is specified for the subform in the Relationships form record). These commands, however, have no direct effect on the main form records. In order to avoid creating orphan subform records, the query must include DQL commands that properly update main form records. When you use the *input* command with a Multiform, F7 (DELETE) has no effect on either main form records or subform records. The best policy is to avoid using the *input* command with Multiforms.

When the user presses one of the four processing keys listed in table 11.1, DataEase does not perform the normal function. Instead, it assigns a value of 1, 2, 3 or 4 to a special system-supplied variable named *current status*. The value assigned depends on which key the user presses. The value of the current status variable therefore indicates what the user wants done with the data. You normally use conditional processing commands (discussed later in this chapter) in the query to test for the value of this variable. You then include DQL commands to process the data accordingly.

Depending on the value of the current status variable, the query can do the additional screening or processing that you want and then can perform the action requested by the user. It can enter a new record using the *enter a record* command, modify an existing record using the *modify records* command, or delete a record using the *delete records* command.

Table 11.1
Current Status

Value of current status	When user presses
1	Esc (Exit)
2	F2 (Save)
4	F7 (Delete)
3	F8 (Modify)

Network Related Commands

The *lock*, *unlock*, and *query selection* commands are effective on a local area network (LAN) only. Each of these commands overrides the default Multi-User Locking options (discussed in Appendix B) assigned by the system administrator.

The *lock* command is actually several commands, *lock all files, lock file*, and *lock selected record*:

❏ The *lock all files* command locks all record-entry forms used in the query. You normally place it at the beginning of the query when you want to override default locking rules for the duration of the query. This command prevents other users from adding, deleting, or modifying data in any of the locked forms. Other network users can, however, still view records in these forms.

❏ When you want to lock a particular form, but not necessarily all forms referenced by the query, use the *lock file* command. The syntax is as follows:

    lock file *Formname* shared
or
    lock file *Formname* exclusive

where *Formname* is the name of the form that you want to lock. Use the *shared* keyword with the Lock File command to permit others to view records in the locked form, but prevent them from entering, modifying, and deleting of records. When you use the *exclusive* keyword, DataEase prevents even viewing of the locked form's records.

❏ The *lock selected record* command is the least restrictive of the three lock commands. It locks only the record currently being processed, and automatically releases the lock when the record is no longer being processed. You must include either the *shared* keyword or the *exclusive* keyword with this command to indicate whether other users can view a record while your query is processing it. Always use this command inside a *for* command loop (between the *for* command and its corresponding *end* command).

DataEase automatically terminates all three of these commands at the end of the query.

The *unlock* command is the reverse of the *lock* command. It also has three variations: *unlock all files, unlock file,* and *unlock selected records.* You can use these commands to explicitly remove a lock placed by a *lock* command, or to override an unnecessarily restrictive default locking option.

The *query selection* command is highly technical and potentially injurious to data integrity. Discussion of this command is beyond the scope of this chapter. Refer to the DQL Lexicon in the *DataEase Query Language Guide*, Volume 3 of the DataEase documentation for information on this topic.

Fine Tuning DQL Commands

The various DQL commands control how the query uses or processes data. DataEase uses a number of words, characters, and symbols to fine tune these commands. These tools fall into two broad groups: *symbols* and *operators*. The next two sections briefly summarize the uses of these tools.

DQL Symbols

DQL symbols divide neatly into three groups: *punctuation symbols, math symbols*, and *wildcard symbols*.

❑ *Punctuation symbols* are used in DataEase much as they are used in English sentences. A colon (:) indicates that a list of statistical operators follows; semicolons (;) separate lists of items in processing commands, and a period (.) denotes the end of a list of items. If you want to add a nonprinting comment (sometimes called internal documentation) to a query, precede the comment with two hyphens (--).

❑ *Math symbols* perform standard arithmetic operations. The plus sign (+) denotes addition. The minus sign (−) means subtract. An asterisk (*) denotes multiplication, and a slash character (/) represents division.

❏ *Wildcard symbols* are used in record selection criteria. The asterisk (*) stands for any number of characters in an alphanumeric search criterion. The question mark (?) takes the place of a single character in an alphanumeric search criterion. The tilde (˜) performs a *soundex* or "sounds like" search, when you include it in an alphanumeric search criteria. Refer to the "Using Wildcards in Search Criteria" and "Performing a Soundex (Sounds Like) Search" sections of Chapter 4 for further details.

DQL Operators

You can divide DQL operators into seven categories. You have already seen most of the following operators in earlier chapters of this book:

❏ *Comparison operators* in a selection criterion specify which records from a form or relationship are processed. Refer to Chapter 5 for a table of the comparison operators as well as examples of how you can use each one. Look also at the "Selecting a Comparison Field, Operator, and Value" section of Chapter 7 for a description of using comparison operators in a query. You also can use these operators to compute a *conditional statistic* (discussed below). The following operators are in this group:

> =
> <
> >
> <=
> >=
> between
> not

❏ *Logical operators* combine two selection criteria. The operators in this category are the following:

> and
> or

When you use the *and* operator to connect two criteria, the query selects a record only if it meets both criteria. When you use the *or* operator, however, the query retrieves a record if either criterion is true.

❏ *Grouping and sorting operators* determine the order in which DataEase processes records from a particular form. Refer to the "Selecting Sorting Operators" section of Chapter 7 for a discussion of these operators. The grouping and sorting operators include:

in groups
in groups with group totals
in order
in reverse

❑ *Relational operators* enable you to select fields from records in related forms. Refer to the "Using Relational Operators" section of Chapter 7 for a discussion of these operators. The operators in this category include the following:

all
any

❑ *Statistical operators* perform summary computations on the values in a particular field for all records processed. Refer to "Selecting Statistical Operators" in Chapter 7 for a discussion of these operators. They include:

item
count
max
min
std.dev.
std.err.
sum
variance

❑ *Conditional statistical operators* enable you to compute conditional statistics. You use these operators with a comparison operator to generate statistics on a subset of the selected records. The operators in this category follow:

item
count
percent

The *item* operator returns a value of yes for each record that meets the condition and no for each record that doesn't. The *count* operator returns the total number of records that meet the specified condition. The *percent* operator computes the percentage of the total number of selected records that meet the condition.

Suppose, for example, that you want to see the salary of all sales representatives, particularly those of $25,000 or more. The following query lists sales representatives' names and salaries. The last item, before the end command, computes three conditional statistics for the subset of records where the salary is equal to or greater than 25000.

```
        for Sales Representative
    ;
list records
    First Name ;
    Last Name in order ;
    Salary : item sum ;
    Salary >= 25000 : item count percent.
end
```

Figure 11.7 shows the report that results from this query, using the standard columnar report format. Six out of nine of the salaries are equal to or greater than $25,000, or 66.67% of the total number of sales representatives.

Fig. 11.7.

A report showing item, count, and percent conditional statistics for sales representatives' salaries equal to or greater than $25,000.

```
Conditional Stats                          Running procedure Conditional Stats
END OF PROCEDURE, SPACE: Return to Menu    PgUp: Scroll

==============================================================================
      First                Last                  Salary      Salary >=
      Name                 Name                                 25000
------------------------------------------------------------------------------
    Harry            Albertson              33,540.00      yes
    Emily            Bronson                24,830.00      no
    Susan            Carson                 22,800.00      no
    Gertrude         English                38,220.00      yes
    Samantha         Green                  51,312.56      yes
    Tim              Jones                  43,056.00      yes
    Joseph           Jones                  78,936.00      yes
    Sharon           Kellogs                22,744.00      no
    George           Quick                  55,120.00      yes
------------------------------------------------------------------------------
sum                                        370,639.36
percent                                                     66.67
count                                                           6
==============================================================================

F4 CMDHELP ESC EXIT C:\DEDATA\          ORDER TRACKING      07/06/89   9 46 pm
```

❏ *Relational statistical operators* are discussed in "Creating Relational Statistical Derived Fields" in Chapter 6 and "Using Relational Operators" in Chapter 7. This category contains the following operators:

    count of
    highest of
    lowest of
    mean of
    sum of

DQL Functions

The examples used in this book have dealt with a simple order processing scenario that hasn't required any heavy duty textual manipulation or numeric computation. It is likely, however, that your application of DataEase may require more complex processing. Whatever your needs, however, DataEase probably has several built-in functions that will make life easier for you.

DataEase offers 58 built-in functions, many of which can perform complicated computations or difficult textual manipulation. You can group these functions as follows:

❏ The *if function* enables you to create an expression that has two possible values. DataEase determines the value the query actually uses when the procedure runs, based on whether a condition specified with the *if* function is true or false.

❏ *Date functions* convert a date, month, year, day of the week, or day of the year into a number that it can use in calculations. Date functions include:

> month
> day
> year
> yearday
> weekday
> yearweek
> date
> julian

❏ *Spell functions* convert date or numerical values into a text value. The functions that fall into this category are as follows:

> spellmonth
> spellweekday
> spelldate
> spellnumber
> spellcurrency

❏ *Time functions* convert 24-hour (military) time to 12-hour (am/pm) time or extracts an integer from the time value for use in calculations. This group includes:

> hours
> minutes
> seconds
> timeampm
> ampm

❑ *Text functions* manipulate text values and enable you to join text values, trim off portions of a text value, extract portions of a text value, put last names first or first names first, capitalize all characters, make all characters lowercase, or capitalize the first character of proper names. Text functions include:

firstc
lastc
midc
firstw
lastw
midw
jointext
length
*textpos
*upper
*lower
*proper
lastfirst
firstlast

*The functions marked with an asterisk in this and subsequent lists are new in DataEase 4.0.

❑ *Financial functions* can calculate values relating to term loans, installment loans, and annuities. When the query has values for four out of five of the variables (*beginning value, end value, interest rate, installment amount,* and *number of payment periods*), it can use a financial function to solve for the fifth value. The functions in this category correspond to the five financial variables:

presentvalue
futurevalue
installment
rate
periods

❑ *Scientific functions* appear most often in scientific and engineering applications. The following functions are in this group:

exp
log
log 10
power
sqrt

❑ *Trigonometric functions* perform trigonometric computations. They include:

sin
cos
tan
asin
acos
atan
*atan2
sinh
cosh
tanh

❑ *Math functions* round numbers, generate absolute value, and generate a pseudo random number. These functions are as follows:

random
abs
ceil
floor
mod

Controlling a Procedure with Procedural Commands

Procedural commands, the DQL commands numbered 10 through 23 in figures 11.1 and 11.2, unlike processing commands, have no direct effect on data in the database. Rather, you use procedural DQL commands to control output to the screen and other devices during the processing, to control which commands execute and how many times, and to create variables for use by a procedure. The following commands are in this category:

output
message
if
else
end
while
break
exit
case

value
others
define
assign

DQL procedural commands operate in a similar manner to procedural commands commonly found in most other high-level programming languages. You can use these commands in a processing procedure or a control procedure. The discussions that follow demonstrate briefly how to use some of these procedural commands.

Controlling Output

The DataEase Report Format design facility is a powerful report writing feature that enables you to create sophisticated results but sometimes may not give you the flexibility you need. Probably the biggest drawback of the Report Format is that there can be only one per procedure and that it always prints at the end. When you run a procedure, the query retrieves and processes data, and then prints the data or displays it according to the report format. In some cases you may want to display or print data in several formats and at various points in the procedure. You can use the Output command, newly available in DataEase 4.0, for this purpose.

When DataEase encounters the Output command in a query, it sends directly to the current output device the text and/or fields specified with the command. The command syntax is as follows:

output:

The command must appear on a line by itself, followed by the colon (:), and terminated by a period (.) in column 1 of a subsequent line of the query. Any text in the query that occurs between the *output* command and the period goes to the output device.

You also can place fields in this output section of the query using F10 (FIELD) as on the Report Format definition screen. Position the cursor where you want the field to appear in the output and press F10 (FIELD). DataEase displays a Report Field Definition screen for you to define a field. Refer to "Defining a Field" in Chapter 8 for an explanation of how to define a field using this screen.

You can use the *output* command as often as you want in a query. When you want to display fields, use the *output* command immediately after you specify the fields with a *list records* command.

Tip: The Output command is an advanced feature that gives you complete control of the output, rather than relying on and taking advantage of the built-in capabilities of DataEase report formats. There are limits to its use, however, due to its inability to send output to a particular device; it always sends output to the device indicated on the Print Specification screen. Use this command to generate output only as a last resort, when you are certain you cannot get the result you are looking for with a report format. If you find you would like to generate two different formats in sequence, define two procedures, each with a different report format, and then use a control procedure or a chain menu to link them together.

Displaying Messages

DataEase often uses messages to prompt you for actions and to explain what the program is doing. The *message* procedural command enables you to provide the same sort of prompting and/or explanations to a user of a database application that you design.

The syntax of the *message* command is as follows:

message "*message text*".

where *message text* is the message that you want to display. The command ends with a period (.) on the same line. DataEase displays a message of up to 40 characters in the message area of the screen.

For example, you might have created a query that does a great deal of time-consuming processing before it generates any output. To keep the user informed during the processing, you include the following *message* command at the beginning of the query:

message "Report is being generated. Please wait.".

To clear this message before it prints the report, you also place the following *message* command immediately before the first command that generates output (the first *list records* command, for example):

message " ".

DataEase also provides several options for use with the *message* command. You can cause processing to pause until the user presses a key, and you can cause DataEase to display a message of up to 4,000 characters in a window.

When you want DataEase to pause processing after it displays the message, and until the user presses a key, add the keyword *pause* to the end of the command, after the message text and before the terminating period. For example, you may want to warn users that they should prepare the printer for output. The following *message* command would accomplish this goal:

message "Prepare the printer." pause.

Place this command above the first *for* command loop that contains a *list records* command that generates output. Then, when DataEase reaches this command during execution of the procedure, it suspends processing, "beeps," and displays the prompt Press any key to acknowledge. You can resume processing by pressing a key.

To display the message in its own window, follow the message text with the keyword *window*. DataEase sizes the window to fit a message of up to 4,000 characters. You can also specify the exact size of the window. Begin the message text (inside the double quotation marks) with four numbers indicating: (1) number of columns; (2) the starting row; (3) the starting column; and (4) the number of rows. You can specify where a new line of the message starts by using the pipe character (|). DataEase always "beeps" and pauses processing while it displays the message window. It also adds the text Press any key to acknowledge. to the message. It removes the window and continues processing after the user presses any key.

To further enhance a message displayed in its own window, you can apply color/highlighting to the message text. The standard color used for windowed message text is the menu highlighting color specified in the current Screen Style (see Appendix B). To cause message text to be displayed in the regular field color, enclose it in braces ({}). Enclose text in angle brackets (<>) that should display in the key name color. Text enclosed in regular brackets ([]) is displayed in regular text color (listed in the Screen Style form as All Other). See Appendix B for more information on Screen Styles and colors.

Using Conditional Processing

Often life is not as cut-and-dry as you might like, forcing you instead to make decisions and choices before you can proceed. It would be convenient if you could build a query that also makes choices as it processes data. If the query can "decide" how it should process data by examining a criterion you have set up, you will not have to create multiple procedures to take care of all the possible contingencies. DataEase provides just such a capability through a number of DQL procedural commands:

if
else
end
case
value
others

These commands are fairly typical programming commands. Several examples will show you how useful they can be.

Suppose that you want to pay a commission to your sales representatives for each sale made. To encourage larger sales, you want to use a graduated scale to compute the commission. Order totals of less than $1,000 generate a 10% commission. Order totals between $1,000 and $1,999 produce 10% on the first $1,000 and 20% on the amount over $1,000. Order totals between $2,000 and $2,999 produce 10% on the first $1,000, 20% on the second $1,000 (or a total of $300) plus 30% on the amount over $2,000. The scale goes up 10% for each $1,000 with a maximum commission rate at 50% for the portion of the order total over $4,000.

This is the type of complicated formula that computers were invented to solve. The following query uses the *if* and *else* commands to do just that. This query assumes that you have added a field to the Widget Order form named Commission to store the computed commission. It also demonstrates use of the Define and Assign commands to create a temporary variable to hold the calculated commission. DataEase then uses the variable to modify the value of the Commission field in Widget Order:

```
define temp ''Commission'' Number.
for Widget Order
;
if Order Total ‹ 1000 then
   assign temp Commission : = Order Total * 0.1.
   else
   if Order Total ‹ 2000 then
      assign temp Commission : = 100+((Order Total-1000) *0.2) .
      else
      if Order Total ‹ 3000 then
         assign temp Commission : = 300+((Order Total-2000) *0.3) .
         else
         if Order Total ‹ 4000 then
            assign temp Commission : = 600+((Order Total-3000) *0.4) .
            else
            assign temp Commission : = 1000+((Order Total-4000) *0.5) .
         end
      end
   end
end
modify records
   Commission : = temp Commission .
end
```

The *case* command provides an often clearer way to accomplish processing that would otherwise require multiple *if* commands. The following query achieves the same result as the preceding query:

```
define temp ''Commission'' Number.
for Widget Order
;
case (Order Total)
   value < 1000 :
      assign temp Commission : = Order Total * 0.1
   value < 2000 :
      assign temp Commission : = 100+((Order Total-1000)*0.2).
   value < 3000 :
      assign temp Commission : = 300+((Order Total-2000)*0.3).
   value < 4000 :
      assign temp Commission : = 600+((Order Total-3000)*0.4).
   others:
      assign temp Commission : = 1000+((Order Total-4000)*0.5).
modify records
   Commission : = temp Commission .
end
```

Creating a Loop

One of the things that computers do very well is perform repetitive tasks quickly. Programming languages always provide some method of causing a given command or group of commands to execute over and over until they reach a specific goal. DataEase is no exception. The DQL *while* procedural command enables you to create sections of the query that execute multiple times until a specified condition is true. Sections of the query that execute repeatedly are often referred to as *loops*. A loop created by a *while* command is therefore a *while* loop.

You might, for example, want to print 10 copies of a series of customer mailing labels. You could, of course, build a procedure that prints the labels onceand then manually run it 10 times, but the name of the game is to get the computer to do as much of the work as possible. The following query uses a *while* loop to cause the set of labels to print 10 times. Notice the use of the *Define* and *assign* commands to increment the variable temp Copy Count. When temp Copy Count reaches a value of 10, the loop terminates:

```
define temp ''Copy Count'' Number.
assign temp Copy Count : = 0 .
while temp Copy Count < 10 do
   for Retail Customer
```

```
  ;
  list records
     Company;
     Address;
     City;
     State;
     Zip in order.
  end
  assign temp Copy Count : = temp Copy Count + 1 .
end
```

Controlling an Application through a Control Procedure

After you design all the procedures necessary to run your database, you can use one or more DQL control procedures to tie them together. A control procedure can also call system-supplied menus, and menus you have designed with the DataEase Menu Definition facility, as well as perform a number of database management functions. The commands available for use exclusively in control procedures are the following:

run procedure
call menu
call program
record entry
import
reorganize
db status
backup db
restore db
lock db
unlock db
install application

If the purpose of a control procedure sounds familiar, that is because it is nearly identical to the purpose of a chain menu, discussed in Chapter 10. The primary differences between chain menus and control procedures are as follows:

❑ DataEase executes chain menu options in sequence, regardless of the surrounding circumstances when the menu is invoked. In a control procedure, however, you can include DQL procedural commands that execute given commands only when specified conditions are met. For example, you can define a control procedure that performs different actions depending on the day of the week that you run it.

❏ A control procedure can use the *call menu* command to call any user-defined menu and any of the system menus listed in table 11.2. Chain menus can call any user-defined menu. But, of the system menus, a chain menu can call only the DataEase Main menu, the DQL menu, or the Utilities menu.

Table 11.2
Names Used to Call System Menus

System menu	Name used in a Call Menu command in a control procedure
DataEase Main	MAIN
Form Definition	FORMS
Records	RECORDS
QBE—Quick Reports	QUICK REPORTS
DQL	DQL PROCEDURES
Maintenance	MAINTENANCE
Administration	ADMINISTRATION
Utilities	UTILITIES

Otherwise, the capabilities of control procedures and chain menus are the same. Both methods of tying your application together can perform the following tasks:

Call a user menu
Call another program
Invoke Record Entry
Import data
Reorganize a form
Display database status
Backup the database
Restore a backed-up database
Lock the database (LAN only)
Unlock the database (LAN only)
Install an application

Control procedures are really best suited for programmers and application developers. The DataEase Menu Definition facility is a much more "user-friendly" method of chaining operations together as long as its few limitations do not get in your way. A good approach might be to develop the forms, procedures, and reports necessary to manage your database, and then use the Menu Definition facility to pull them all together into an application. If you need a menu option to execute a series of functions, develop an appropriate chain menu. Then, define a DQL control procedure that simply calls the top-level user menu in the menu system you have designed.

For example, the top-level menu developed in Chapter 10, "Creating Custom DataEase Menus," is named *Widget Order Main*. A control procedure to call this menu, thus starting your menu system, is as follows:

call menu "Widget Order Main".

You can then run this one-line control procedure any time you want to invoke the menu system for testing, or just to use it. Without this procedure, the only way to start your menu-driven application is by assigning a start-up menu and then restarting DataEase.

After you have used your system, you may decide that you need more control over the action than the chain menu provides. At that point you can define a control procedure to replace the chain menu.

Chapter Summary

This last chapter of the book gave you an overview of the fully programmable capabilities of DataEase available through the DataEase Query Language (DQL). The chapter described the basics of advance processing with DQL queries which can perform virtually any DataEase task, from entering and printing records to backing up and restoring the database. The DataEase Query Language is a high-level database programming language suitable for use in developing full-featured database applications. This chapter helped you to develop a general understanding of the overall capabilities of DQL. It is now up to you to give it a try. Although DQL is not as easy and quick to learn as the more interactive features of DataEase, if you use it just to fine tune your applications, you will find that the database management capabilities of DataEase are virtually unlimited.

DataEase Installation
and Start Up

This appendix explains how to install DataEase 4.2 and begin using the program. Installation of DataEase on a local area network is not covered in this appendix. Network administrators should see the *Installation and New Features Guide*, supplied with the program, for help.

Understanding System Requirements

Before installing DataEase 4.2, make sure that your system meets the minimum requirements to run DataEase 4.2. To run DataEase 640K as a single-user program, your system must be an IBM PC, XT, AT, PS/2, or compatible. The system must have at least 640K of system memory (RAM) and DOS 3.1 or higher. DataEase 4.2 can be run only from a hard disk.

The requirements for running DataEase 16M as a single-user program are more stringent than requirements for DataEase 640K. Your system must be an IBM Personal Computer AT, PS/2, or compatible equipped with an Intel 80286 or 80386 CPU (central processing unit). Your system must have at least 640K of conventional memory, at least 384K of extended memory (above one megabyte), a hard disk, and DOS 3.1 or higher.

Performance and capacity will be improved if your system includes expanded memory (LIM/EMS or EEMS).

Installing DataEase

DataEase is distributed on five 5 1/4-inch 360K disks and three 3 1/2-inch 720K disks. The installation process is similar for either disk size, but the 3 1/2-inch disks require less disk swapping.

Before installing DataEase, you should make a working copy of the distribution disks and use the copy to perform the installation. If you have only one floppy disk drive (drive A), copy each disk using the DOS command

    DISKCOPY A: A:

If your drive isn't drive A, substitute the appropriate letter for A in the command. When you have two floppy disk drives, place the distribution disk in drive *A* and a blank disk in drive *B*. Then use the following command to make each copy:

    DISKCOPY A: B:

As you make each working copy, label the disk with the same name as the distribution disk. Store the original disks in a safe, dry location away from extreme heat, cold, and magnetic fields.

If you are upgrading from a previous version of DataEase, you should use the old software to create a DataEase backup of each database before you install DataEase. (This step is unnecessary if you are upgrading from DataEase 4.0 or DataEase 4.01 to DataEase 4.2.) After you install the new software, you will use the DataEase *restore* operation (described in Chapter 9) and these backup copies to install each old database as a DataEase database.

To begin installation, you must be at the DOS prompt. The current drive should be the drive on which you want to install DataEase. Usually, you will be installing the program on a hard disk, on drive C. In this case, you are at the C› prompt. (C› is the default prompt, but many systems are set up to display C:\›.)

Tip: You must use the Install program to install DataEase. The program files on the distributed disks are in a compressed format. The Install program decompresses these files as it copies them to your hard disk.

Place the working disk marked DISK 1 in a floppy disk drive, usually drive A, type

    A:INSTALL

and press Enter. Install displays a copyright notice and asks

    Is your computer's screen Color [C] or Monochrome [M]?

In response, type a *C* for a color system or *M* if you have monochrome system. Install displays the Main menu screen.

If you are installing DataEase for the first time, the menu is entitled Install Main menu. Select the first menu option **Install DataEase** (by pressing Enter) to begin the installation process. If you are installing an upgrade package to upgrade a previous version of DataEase, the menu is entitled Upgrade Main menu. Select the first menu option **Upgrade a previous DataEase version** by pressing U.

Install displays a second menu, entitled Software Version that lists three options: **DataEase (640K version)**, **DataEase 16M (Extended memory version)**, and **Both versions**. Use the arrow keys to highlight the DataEase version your system will support and press Enter. If your system has adequate configuration to run DataEase 16M, consider installing both versions.

Tip: You need at least 1.4M of free hard disk space to install DataEase 640K, at least 1.5M of free hard disk space to install DataEase 16M, and at least 2.2M of free hard disk space to install both versions on your system.

Install then displays a third menu, Networks, that lists a number of network related options. Press Enter to select **No network (standalone)**.

Install asks which floppy drive will contain the master disks (the working copy of the installation disks). The default is drive A. Press Enter if this is correct or change it to the appropriate letter, and press Enter.

This screen also asks you for the DataEase System file directory, which is the directory to which you want the DataEase program files copied. When you are upgrading, make sure that the drive and directory at this prompt designate the location of the old DataEase program files. For a new installation, specify the drive and directory where you want the files installed. The default is C:\DEASE. To accept the default, don't make any changes.

After you have assured yourself that both the floppy drive letter and system files directory are correctly specified, press F2 (SAVE) to proceed with installation. Remove and replace disks only when instructed to do so.

When Install finishes installing the DataEase program, it automatically displays a file from the disk named README.TXT. This file contains important information that was not included in your documentation. Press Esc (EXIT) to return to DOS.

Tip: DOS reads a file named CONFIG.SYS each time you restart the computer. For DataEase to work properly, the following line must appear in this file:

FILES = 60

Ensure that this line exists in the CONFIG.SYS file. If it doesn't, then use any text editor that produces ASCII text to add this line. This file is located on the root (main) directory of the disk containing the DOS system files. If you don't find such a file, then create one containing only the single line.

If you change or add this file, you have to restart the computer for the modification or addition to take effect.

Follow a similar procedure to install the tutorial or the DataEase demonstration program, if you want.

Starting DataEase

Now that your program is installed, you are ready to start DataEase. The simplest way is to change to the directory in which DataEase is installed (which is C:\DEASE if you used the default directory). Type *DEASE* (to start DataEase 640K) or *DE16M* (to start DataEase 16M). First, you see DataEase as the program is loaded and then you see the DataEase Sign On screen shown in figure A.1. You can now sign on and begin to use DataEase. This method is the easiest but is not the best way to start DataEase.

Fig. A.1.

The DataEase Sign On screen.

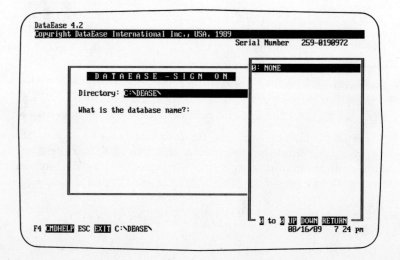

As you build a database with DataEase, the program normally places files in the DOS directory from which you started the program. It is a good practice not to mix data files and program files in the same directory. You should therefore create a separate directory for your DataEase database files. You might, for example, create a directory named DEDATA. To do this, access the root directory on the hard disk that contains DataEase. From the DOS prompt, (probably C›), type

MD \DEDATA

and press Enter. DOS creates the new directory but returns to the same prompt. If you see the message Unable to create directory, you have probably already used the directory name. Choose a different name and try the MD command again.

After you have created a directory for your database files, there are two ways to use this directory with DataEase. The first method involves switching to the directory on your hard disk that contains the DataEase program files. If that directory is named DEASE, from the DOS prompt, type

CD \DEASE

and press Enter. To start DataEase 640K and tell it where to store database files during your DataEase session, type

DEASE C:\DEDATA

and press Enter.

To give the same commands for DataEase 16M, type

DE16M C:\DEDATA

and press Enter.

As DataEase loads, you see the DataEase Sign On screen, similar to figure A.1. Database files are created in the C:\DEDATA directory. This method works fine for most purposes. Certain DataEase utilities don't work as you might expect, however, because the current DOS directory is the same as the current data directory. Specifically, the **4. DOS Backup** option found on the DOS Functions menu (discussed in Chapter 9) cannot find the proper files to back up when you start the program using this method.

The second method is a bit more complicated, but it is the preferred method. Essentially, you have to draw a map for DOS defining the path to the directory that contains the DataEase programs. You then can start DataEase from any directory on the disk, including the directory that you want to use for DataEase data. You draw this map by adding the name of the DataEase directory to the PATH command found in a special file on your disk.

Each time you start the computer, DOS looks for a file named AUTOEXEC.BAT on the root (main) directory of the boot (start-up) disk. If this file exists, DOS executes any DOS commands that it contains. One of the commands normally placed in AUTOEXEC.BAT is the PATH command.

Using a text editor program that can read and write ASCII files, you must add the name of the DataEase program directory to the PATH command. For example, if you find that the current PATH command is as follows:

    PATH=C:\;C:\DOS;C:\LOTUS

add *;C:\DEASE* to the end of the command, creating the new PATH command:

    PATH=C:\;C:\DOS;C:\LOTUS;C:\DEASE

If you find that there is no such command in AUTOEXEC.BAT, use the ASCII text editor to add the PATH command:

    PATH=C:\;C:\DOS;C:\DEASE

Replace C:\DOS in the above PATH command with the name of the directory that actually contains the DOS files on your system's hard disk. If there is no AUTOEXEC.BAT file at all, create one.

After you have made the required modification to the PATH command, restart the computer. DOS read the new PATH command in the AUTOEXEC.BAT file and "knows" how to find the DataEase program files from any directory on the disk.

Now, whenever you want to start DataEase, change to any directory in which you want to include data, type *DEASE* (or *DE16M* if using DataEase 16M), and press Enter. DataEase starts and displays the DataEase Sign On screen; all DataEase features will work as expected.

Using Start-Up Parameters and a Batch File

Note: This section describes the start-up parameters for DataEase 640K. The same parameters can be used to start DataEase 16M by substituting *DE16M* for *DEASE*.

In addition to the data directory path, you can specify several other parameters in the start-up command. To see a list of these options, type the following command at the DOS prompt:

    DEASE -HELP

Instead of starting DataEase, this command displays the following help message:

    DataEase 4.2
    Copyright DataEase International Inc., USA. 1989

```
DERUN [datadir] dbname username password [-NOEMS]
   Parameters: (all are optional)
      datadir    DOS path name, including drive
      dbname     Database name, or a single letter
      username
      password   Use "" for a blank password
      -NOEMS     Disables use of EMS
      -Llanguage Loads specific language
```

Leaving a space between each parameter, you can include the data directory, the database name, your user name, and your password. By including all this information in the start-up command, you don't have to answer these questions on the Sign On screen. The following command, for example, starts DataEase in the C:\DEDATA data directory, using the Order Tracking database. The user's name is Dave Short and his password is AR123:

```
DEASE C:\DEDATA "Order Tracking" "Dave Short" AR123
```

Notice that because the database name and user name both contain a space, they had to be enclosed in double quotation marks. Assuming that the current directory is already C:\DEDATA and that you have included the DataEase program directory in the PATH command, you could use the following start-up command instead:

```
DEASE "Order Tracking" "Dave Short" AR123
```

Both of these commands require a significant amount of typing on the DOS command line. Fortunately, there is a way to automate this command with a DOS *batch* file.

A batch file is an ASCII file that contains a list of DOS commands. You type the name of the batch file at the DOS prompt, and DOS executes the commands contained in the file. The advantage of this capability, at least when it comes to starting a program like DataEase, is that the batch file name can be as short as one letter. Most often, however, you use a batch file name that is more meaningful and easier to remember.

You can create a batch file with a text editor or word processor that produces ASCII text files. You must use the file name extension BAT in naming the batch file.

The easiest way to create a short batch file is by using the DOS COPY command. To create a batch file named ORDERS.BAT that will start DataEase and load the Order Tracking database, type the following commands, pressing Enter at the end of each line:

```
copy con orders.bat
echo off
cls
```

```
cd \dedata
dease "Order Tracking" "Dave Short"
cd \
```

Press F6, and DOS types ^Z on-screen. Press Enter and DOS displays the message 1 File(s) copied. This creates a file named ORDERS.BAT on the disk. Notice that for security reasons the password is not included in the batch file.

To start DataEase and access the Order Tracking database, type *orders* at the DOS command line prompt and press Enter (assuming that the batch file is in the current directory, or is in a directory that is listed in the PATH command). DataEase starts, types the database name and user name in the Sign On screen, and waits for you to type your password.

The last two start-up parameters that you can include are of more specialized use. The first, -NOEMS, is of interest to you only if you have installed an *expanded memory* board in your computer. This is a special type of memory (RAM) device that enables DataEase to run faster. By default, DataEase uses all available expanded memory configured in compliance with the Lotus/Intel/Microsoft Expanded Memory Specification (EMS version 3.2 or 4.0). If you plan to load another program while you are using DataEase (from within DataEase using one of DataEase's *call program* features) and the program will need to use EMS, include the -NOEMS parameter in the start-up command.

When you have more than one language version of DataEase loaded onto your computer, you can use the last parameter listed in the help message to indicate which version you want to use. The following command starts the German language version:

```
dease -lGerman
```

This parameter has no effect if you have only one language version of the program loaded. The various language versions available are:

Danish
Dutch
English
Finnish
French
German
Icelandic
Italian
Japanese
Norwegian
Portuguese
Russian
Spanish
Swedish

Configuring DataEase

This appendix describes how to use the System Configuration form to customize many DataEase features. Default settings for screen style, printers, the directory for temporary files, country configuration, beep, starting year, compatibility with DataEase 2.12, and multiuser locking options can all be set or modified on the System Configuration form. This appendix also explains how to design a printer definition using the Printers form and how to adjust screen colors using the Screen Styles form.

Using the System Configuration Form To Change Defaults

The Configuration form is added to each database automatically by DataEase. It contains information about your system's hardware configuration and certain other default settings. You easily can modify these settings, but you must do so for each database.

There are two ways to access the Configuration form. The most direct method is through the Administration menu. From the DataEase Main menu, select **5. System Administration**. Then, choose **2. Define Configuration**. DataEase displays the Configuration form, similar to the screen shown in figure B.1. Notice that a message in the top right corner of the form indicates that this is Pg 1 of 5.

The second method of displaying the Configuration form is through the Records menu. Select **2. Record Entry** from the DataEase Main menu and choose : System from the list of forms on the right side of the Records menu. DataEase displays a second list of forms, this time including only the system-supplied forms. Choose 2: Configuration from this list. Again, DataEase displays the first page of the Configuration form, shown in figure B.1.

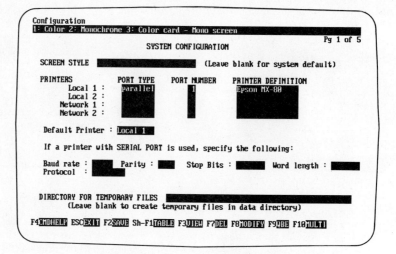

Fig. B.1.

The first page of the Configuration form.

Selecting Screen Style

You use the first field on page 1 of the Configuration form to indicate the type of display adapter and screen that your computer is using. When you first display the form, the cursor is resting in this field. DataEase displays a line menu containing the choices:

❑ 1: Color. Select this option when you are using a color monitor attached to an IBM Color Graphics Adapter (CGA), IBM Enhanced Graphics Adapter, IBM Video Graphics Array (PS/2), or other graphics adapter that is compatible with one of these standards. Refer to the "Customizing Screen Style" section in this appendix.

❑ 2: Monochrome. Choose this selection when you are using a monochrome screen with an IBM Monochrome Display Adapter (MDA) or other nongraphics monochrome adapter.

❑ 3: Color card-Mono screen. Use this choice when you are using a monochrome monitor attached to an adapter capable of displaying graphics. Typical examples are most laptop and portable computers.

Choosing a Printer

Before sending output to your printer, you should make sure that DataEase is using the correct printer definition (refer to the "Customizing a Printer Definition" section in this appendix). The section of the Configuration that begins with the prompt PRINTERS is used to specify up to four printers for each database—two local (connected to your computer) and two connected to a local area network (LAN) server.

Move the cursor to the Local 1: prompt beneath the column heading PORT TYPE. This line defines the first printer connected to your computer. DataEase displays the choices:

❏ 1: parallel. This is the default selection when you first create a new database and is the appropriate choice for most printers. Check your computer's documentation as well as any label next to the connection to which the printer is attached to determine whether your printer is connected to a *parallel* port. Use this choice also when you have mapped parallel output to a serial port using the DOS MODE command.

❏ 2: serial. Choose this option if your printer uses a serial interface. Many older laser printers connect to a serial port on your computer. Your computer manual will usually refer to the first serial port as *COM1* and the second serial port as *COM2*.

After you have selected the port type, the cursor moves to the column headed PORT NUMBER. Enter the number of the port in the space provided (*1* for the first parallel port or first serial port, *2* for the second parallel port or second serial port, and so on). DataEase moves the cursor to the PRINTER DEFINITION column.

When the cursor first moves into the PRINTER DEFINITION column, DataEase indicates that it is building the list of printers and then displays a line menu containing a list of available printer definitions. The default printer definition is for an Epson MX-80 dot-matrix printer. Press F1 (MORE) to display a window menu listing nearly 200 printer definitions. Use the down-arrow or PgDn keys to find the name of your printer in the list (or one with which yours is compatible). When you have highlighted the correct printer name, press Enter.

Following a similar procedure, you can select a printer definition for more printers.

Next, move the cursor to the space to the right of the prompt Default Printer. This is the printer definition that is selected when you press F3 (DEFAULT VIEW) at the Printer Name prompt on the Print Style Specification screen while defining a Quick Report or a DQL procedure. The default value in this field is Local 1, which is the printer you have defined in the Local 1 line in the preceding section of the Configuration form. If you want to change this setting, select 2: Local 2, 3: Network 1, or 4: Network 2 from the line menu.

When you have selected serial as the port type of the default printer, you must also specify baud rate, parity, stop bits, word length, and protocol. Consult your printer manual for the correct values to enter in each of these spaces.

Setting a Directory for Temporary Files

By default, DataEase stores in the data directory any temporary files that it creates. When you want to store these files on a different disk or directory, enter the complete DOS path of the new storage area at the DIRECTORY FOR TEMPORARY FILES prompt. You might do this, for example, to send temporary files to a RAM disk.

Country Customization

The second page of the Configuration form enables you to select the language used in screen messages, the date format, and special currency format settings.

To display the second page of the Configuration form, display the first page and press PgDn. DataEase displays a screen similar to figure B.2. As indicated in an on-screen message, these settings are established by the software manufacturer to match the language version of the software you have licensed. You rarely, if ever, make changes to these settings.

Fig. B.2.

The second page of the Configuration form.

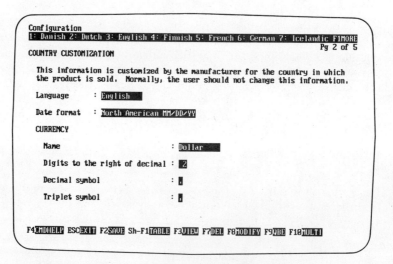

If you have more than one language version installed on your system, you can choose the language you want to use in this database at the Language prompt.

The Date format field enables you to choose between the default North American format MM/DD/YY, the international format (DD/MM/YY), or the metric format (YY/MM/DD).

You use the second half of the COUNTRY CUSTOMIZATION screen to define the format you want to use for currency fields in record-entry forms. Enter the name of the standard currency unit at the Name prompt (this name appears as a field type in the Field Definition screen when you define a record-entry field in the Form Definition screen). In the next space, indicate the number of digits that should appear to the right of the decimal point and then indicate the symbol to be used as the decimal point (some countries use the comma; some use the period). Finally, in the last field on this page, specify the symbol that should be inserted after every third whole-number digit (countries that use the comma for the decimal point usually use a period to separate every third whole-number digit).

Disabling the Beep

The third page of the Configuration form, shown in figure B.3, contains three settings. The first enables you to disable the beep that occurs whenever DataEase detects an error in processing. The beep is intended to draw your attention to the error and any resulting error message so that you can take corrective action.

To disable this beep, display the third page of the Configuration form and respond 2: yes to the prompt Stop the Beep upon Error.

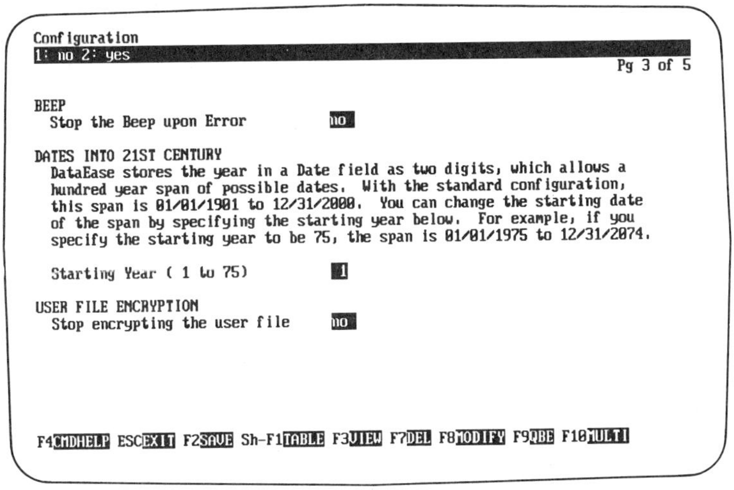

Fig. B.3.

The third page of the Configuration form.

Setting the Starting Year

DataEase enables you to create and use date fields in your database. By default, you can enter dates that fall in the range 01/01/1901 to 12/31/2000. DataEase can, however, handle any 100-year span beginning on the first day of any year from 1901 to 1975.

To indicate a 100-year span that starts on January 1 of a year between 1901 and 1975, display the third page of the Configuration form. At the Starting Year (1 to 75) prompt, enter the last two digits of the starting year. Using this feature, you can configure DataEase to accept dates up to 12/31/2074.

Toggling User File Encryption

For each database that you create, DataEase builds a Users form. Because this form contains user names, passwords, and security levels, DataEase normally encrypts the entries in this file when it saves each to disk. The only way to read the file's contents is from within DataEase, providing you have a High security level.

If you want to turn off the encryption feature (defeating this built-in security feature), access the third page of the Configuration form (see fig. B.3) and select 2: yes at the Stop encrypting the user file prompt. You also must use F8 (MODIFY) to resave each user's record in the Users form (see Chapter 9). With the encryption feature disabled, DataEase saves the Users form as an ASCII file that can be viewed with any text editor or word processor capable of using ASCII files. You also can display the file using the DOS TYPE command. After you remove the encryption, you can reinstate it by changing to 2: no the response at the Stop encrypting the user file prompt, on page 2 of the Configuration form.

Maintaining Compatibility with DataEase 2.12 Files

The fourth page of the Configuration form (see fig. B.4) provides two options to help you maintain the compatibility of data files created with DataEase 2.12.

To be able to use files created with DataEase 2.12, respond 2: yes to both questions on this screen.

```
Configuration
1: no 2: yes
                                                              Pg 4 of 5

COMPATIBILITY WITH DATABASE VERSION 2.12

  Suppress Automatic Checks and Derivations
             in Batch Updates and Imports?   no

  Suppress Zero padding in Numeric Strings?  no




      F4 CMDHELP  ESC EXIT  F2 SAVE  Sh-F1 TABLE  F3 VIEW  F7 DEL  F8 MODIFY  F9 QBE  F10 MULTI
```

Fig. B.4.

The fourth page of the Configuration form.

Default Multiuser Locking Options

When you use DataEase on a network, DataEase places certain restrictions on simultaneous access by multiple network users to data, form definitions, and report definitions. These restrictions are referred to as *locking rules*. The minimum locks automatically placed by DataEase are referred to as *default minimum* locks. On the last page of the Configuration form, you can add more restrictive locks, but you cannot remove these minimum locks. This is a technical topic and is of primary interest to application developers creating forms and procedures for use on a LAN.

While you are creating, deleting, backing up, or restoring a database, or installing an application, you always have exclusive access to the database. This default minimum lock cannot be changed.

Any time that you are viewing or modifying a form definition, DataEase automatically locks it. The first field on the last page of the Configuration form (see fig. B.5) enables you to select one of the following types of locks:

❑ 1: Shared access. Shared access means that multiple users can view the form definition at the same time. When a form definition is locked in this manner and more than one user is viewing the form definition, neither is allowed to save any changes to the definition under the same name. Instead, DataEase displays a resource conflict message.

❑ 2: Exclusive access. This option is the default lock. Only one user can view the form definition at a time. You therefore always are able to save any changes to the definition, but no other user can use a form in Record Entry to enter, modify, or view the form's records until you release the definition.

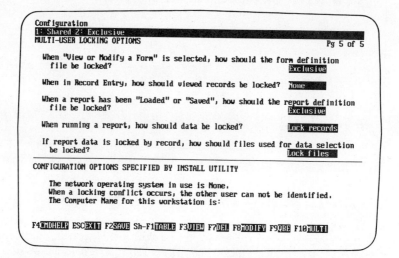

Fig. B.5.

The fifth page of the Configuration form.

Any time that you are updating a shared database by adding records, modifying existing records, or deleting records, DataEase places a lock on the record or records you are working with to prevent other users from reading or changing the record(s). The user updating the record has exclusive access. This lock applies to only records that you are updating. It does not prevent other users from accessing other records in the same form.

When you are viewing a shared record (making no changes, additions, or deletions), DataEase prevents other users from making changes to the record(s) you are viewing for the time it takes your computer to read the data from the disk, but otherwise gives users complete access to the data. The second option on the fifth page of the Configuration form enables you to place a more restrictive lock on multiuser access to records in Record Entry. You have the following choices:

❑ 1: None. This is the default selection. With this lock option selected, multiple users can view, modify, or delete records at the same time. When one user has changed a record, however, others that were viewing the record are no longer permitted to save further modifications.

Suppose, for example, that you are updating the address of a customer in the Retail Customer form. DataEase will not permit another user to display the same customer's record until you have finished making the modification. DataEase displays a conflict message indicating that the resource (record) is in use.

If, however, the record that you are changing was already on another user's screen when you called it, their copy will not be correct. They might try to modify their version of the record and save it. When they save it, DataEase displays the message Record modified since it was read and prevents them from saving their changes. They must first find out what changes you made. This is done through the refresh option explained in Chapter 4.

❑ 2: Shared. Select this option to permit multiple users to view the same record at once. While one user is viewing a record, however, another user cannot modify it in any way.

❑ 3: Exclusive. This option is the most restrictive access type, and it prevents more than one user from viewing the same record at a time. Normally, restricting access to records to this extent is not necessary to protect the integrity of the data. In most cases, shared access or even the default minimum lock is sufficient.

Any time that you are viewing or modifying a report or procedure definition, DataEase automatically locks it. The third question on the last page of the Configuration form enables you to select one of the following locks:

❑ 1: Shared access. Shared access means that multiple users can view the definition at the same time. When a report or procedure definition is locked in this manner, and more than one user is viewing the definition, neither is allowed to save changes to the definition under the same name. Instead, DataEase displays a resource conflict message. If one user tries to load a definition while another user is in the process of saving a modification to the definition or deleting the definition, DataEase refuses access, displaying a resource conflict message instead.

❑ 2: Exclusive access. The default lock is exclusive, which means that only one user can view the report or procedure definition at a time. You therefore are always able to save any changes to the definition, but no other user is able to run the report or procedure until you release the definition.

Whenever you are running a Quick Report or DQL procedure, DataEase prevents other users from deleting or making changes to the selected records the report or procedure is processing, but otherwise gives all users complete access to the other records in the form. The fourth option on the fifth page of the Configuration form enables you to place a more restrictive lock on multiuser access to files that are being processed. You have the following choices:

❏ 2: Lock records. This is the default condition. DataEase locks records one at a time as each is processed by the report/procedure. Other network users can still view all records that are not being processed and records that are being listed (with list records) by the report/ procedure. Other users cannot change or delete a record while it is being processed.

❏ 3: Lock Files. Choose this option to lock all records in every form used by the report/procedure. Other network users can still view all records that are being listed (with list records) by the report/ procedure. Other users cannot change or delete any record in any of the forms while the report/procedure is running.

When you give DataEase the command to run a DQL procedure or Quick Report, it determines which records are needed for the query. If the report/procedure will select or sort these records by an indexed field, then DataEase can place certain locks on these records while the report/ procedure prevents a change or deletion from being made to a record already selected for processing. The fifth and last option on the fifth page of the Configuration form determines whether you want to place these locks and how restrictive they should be. The options are as follows:

❏ **1. Lock nothing**. Select this choice when you want to maintain maximum availability of the data to all users. This can, however, result in erroneous reports if a user changes the value in an indexed field after the record has been selected but before it has been processed by the report/procedure.

❏ **2. Lock records**. This option locks only the records that have been selected for the query. Use this option sparingly and never if more than a few records will be selected by the report/procedure. Most LANs cannot handle the number of locks that would be required to lock many individual records.

❏ **3. Lock files**. This option is the default selection. It locks all the records in any form that will be selected or sorted on an indexed field. The form is locked until the report/procedure is finished.

Customizing a Printer Definition

The "Choosing a Printer" section of this chapter explains how to use the Configuration form to assign up to four printer definitions. The printer definitions chosen by the Configuration form are stored in the Printers form. DataEase enables you to customize each printer definition through this form.

To display the Printers form, select **7. System Administration** from the DataEase Main menu to display the Administration menu and then select **3. Define Printers**. DataEase displays the Printers form, shown in figure B.6.

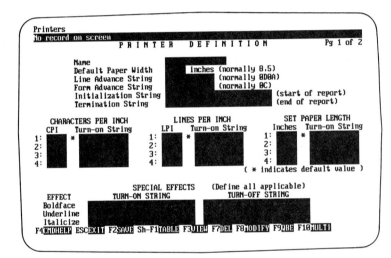

Fig. B.6.

The Printers form.

Each time you create a database with DataEase, it installs a copy of the Printers form into the database. This form contains nearly 200 records, each one representing a separate printer driver. Most likely, you can find your printer in this list. They are stored in alphabetical order by the Name field.

You can view records in the Printers form just as you do any other DataEase record-entry form. Press F3 (VIEW) at the initial blank record to see the first printer definition. Each time you press F3 (VIEW) again, DataEase displays the next printer definition in the list. You also can press Shift-F1 (TABLE) to view the form in Table View.

To go directly to the definition of a particular printer, press Alt-F5 (UNCHECKED) and type the name of the printer in the Name field. Then, press F3 (VIEW). To see the printer definition for an IBM Proprinter, for

example, you press Alt-F5 (UNCHECKED), type *IBM Proprinter* in the
Name field, and press F3 (VIEW). DataEase displays the screen shown in
figure B.7. This is the first of two pages. The second page of the form is
shown in figure B.8. Consult your printer manual to determine whether
you should modify any of the turn-on or turn-off strings (expressed in
hexadecimal). If you make any changes to a record, press F8 (MODIFY) to
save the modifications.

Fig. B.7.

*The first page of the
Printers form record
for an IBM
Proprinter.*

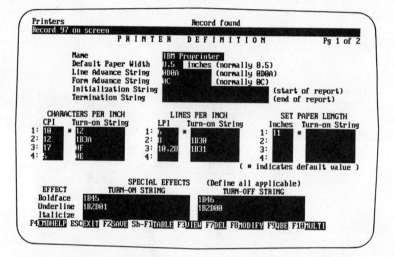

Fig. B.8.

*The second page of
the Printers form
record for an IBM
Proprinter.*

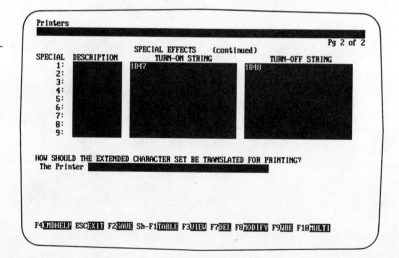

If you cannot find your printer among the available built-in printer definitions, check your printer manual to determine whether it emulates a popular printer. Most dot-matrix printers, for example, can emulate certain models of Epson printers or IBM printers. Many daisy-wheel printers can emulate certain Diablo printer models. Most laser printers emulate a Hewlett Packard printer model. If your printer isn't listed and doesn't emulate a listed printer, you need to create a record in the Printers form.

To begin creating a printer definition, press F5 (FORM CLEAR) to clear any other record from the screen. Type the name of your printer in the Name field, up to 15 characters long. This must be a name that has not already been used. Refer to your printer manual to determine the proper entries in the various fields. Using the Printer form, you can specify the following:

Default paper width
Line advance string
Form advance string
Initialization string
Termination string
Characters per inch (up to four settings)
Lines per inch (up to four settings)
Paper length (up to four settings)
Boldface turn-on and turn-off strings
Underline turn-on and turn-off strings
Italicize turn-on and turn-off strings
Special Effects (up to nine) turn-on and turn-off strings

You also can specify whether your printer is capable of printing the extended ASCII character set. Refer to the "Using Printer Control Commands" discussion in Chapter 8 for instructions on how to apply these special printer control features to a report.

After you have filled in the record, press F2 (SAVE) to save the new definition. Press Esc (EXIT) to return to the Administration menu. You must enter the name of the new printer definition in the PRINTER DEFINITION column of the Configuration form before DataEase will use it to control your printer.

Customizing Screen Style

DataEase uses color to highlight and emphasize portions of the screen. Even if you aren't using a color screen, you will notice that DataEase uses inverse video characters to accent parts of the screen. It is possible, however, that the default color scheme chosen by DataEase is not to your liking. In that case, you can use the Screen Styles form to design your own color scheme.

To display the Screen Styles form, select **7. System Administration** from the DataEase Main menu to display the Administration menu and then select **4. Define Screen Styles**. DataEase displays the Screen Styles form, shown in figure B.9.

Fig. B.9.

The Screen Styles form.

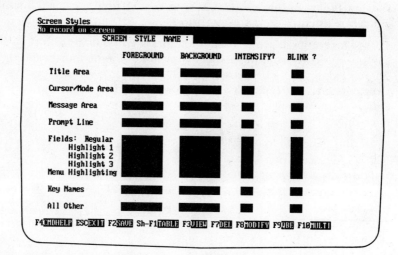

DataEase automatically installs the Screen Styles form in each database. When you first create a database, this form contains three records—one to match each of the standard choices for the Screen Style field in the Configuration form. The screen style named *color* corresponds to the *Color* Screen Style configuration choice; *monochrome* is the style selected when you choose 2: Monochrome in the Configuration form, and *color-mono* is chosen if you select 3: Color card-Mono screen on the Configuration form. To display one of these original three records, press F3 (VIEW). Figure B.10 shows the screen style record named *color*.

Each record in the Screen Styles form contains eleven rows of screen settings, one row for each of the following:

Title area
Cursor and mode area
Message area
Prompt line
Regular fields
Field Highlight 1
Field Highlight 2
Field Highlight 3
Menu highlighting
Key names
All other

```
 ╭─────────────────────────────────────────────────────────────────╮
 │ Screen Styles                      Record found                   │
 │ Record 1 on screen                                                │
 │             SCREEN  STYLE  NAME : color                           │
 │                                                                   │
 │                 FOREGROUND    BACKGROUND    INTENSIFY?   BLINK ?   │
 │                                                                   │
 │  Title Area     Brown         Black         yes          no       │
 │                                                                   │
 │  Cursor/Mode Area  Cyan        Black         yes          no      │
 │                                                                   │
 │  Message Area   Red           Black         yes          no       │
 │                                                                   │
 │  Prompt Line    Black         Green         no           no       │
 │                                                                   │
 │  Fields: Regular    Brown         Blue          yes          no   │
 │        Highlight 1  Light Gray    Red           yes          no   │
 │        Highlight 2  Brown         Black         yes          no   │
 │        Highlight 3  Black         Black         no           no   │
 │  Menu Highlighting  Light Gray    Blue          yes          no   │
 │                                                                   │
 │  Key Names      Light Gray    Red           yes          no       │
 │                                                                   │
 │  All Other      Brown         Black         yes          no       │
 │                                                                   │
 │ F4 CMDHELP  ESC EXIT  F2 SAVE  Sh-F1 TABLE  F3 VIEW  F7 DEL  F8 MODIFY  F9 UBF  F10 MULTI │
 ╰─────────────────────────────────────────────────────────────────╯
```

Fig. B10.

The screen style named color.

Each row of settings includes a selection for foreground color (the characters), background color, character intensity, and blink. Refer to Chapter 1 for a discussion of the various areas of the screen and to Chapter 3 for a discussion of how to apply these color combinations to fields and text in a record-entry form definition.

To customize one of the Screen Style form records, display the record and move the cursor to the setting you want to change. DataEase displays a line menu containing the available choices. In the FOREGROUND and BACKGROUND columns, you can choose between eight colors: 1: Black, 2: Blue, 3: Green, 4: Cyan, 5: Red, 6: Magenta, 7: Brown, and 8: Light Gray. Both INTENSITY and BLINK offer a choice between 1: no and 2: yes. When you have made the desired modification, press F8 (MODIFY) to update the record. Then, press Esc (EXIT) to return to the Administration menu.

When several people will be using DataEase on the same computer, you may find that they don't all agree on the color scheme. To accommodate the unique tastes of each user, create a different record in the Screen Styles form for each user and type the name of the user's screen style in the Screen Style field of their record in the Users form (discussed in Chapter 9).

Index

P

Q

Free Catalog!

Mail us this registration form today, and we'll send you a free catalog featuring Que's complete line of best-selling books.

Name of Book _____

Name _____

Title _____

Phone ( ) _____

Company _____

Address _____

City _____

State _____ ZIP _____

Please check the appropriate answers:

1. Where did you buy your Que book?
   - ☐ Bookstore (name: _____)
   - ☐ Computer store (name: _____)
   - ☐ Catalog (name: _____)
   - ☐ Direct from Que
   - ☐ Other: _____

2. How many computer books do you buy a year?
   - ☐ 1 or less
   - ☐ 2-5
   - ☐ 6-10
   - ☐ More than 10

3. How many Que books do you own?
   - ☐ 1
   - ☐ 2-5
   - ☐ 6-10
   - ☐ More than 10

4. How long have you been using this software?
   - ☐ Less than 6 months
   - ☐ 6 months to 1 year
   - ☐ 1-3 years
   - ☐ More than 3 years

5. What influenced your purchase of this Que book?
   - ☐ Personal recommendation
   - ☐ Advertisement
   - ☐ In-store display
   - ☐ Price
   - ☐ Que catalog
   - ☐ Que mailing
   - ☐ Que's reputation
   - ☐ Other: _____

6. How would you rate the overall content of the book?
   - ☐ Very good
   - ☐ Good
   - ☐ Satisfactory
   - ☐ Poor

7. What do you like *best* about this Que book?
   _____
   _____

8. What do you like *least* about this Que book?
   _____
   _____

9. Did you buy this book with your personal funds?
   - ☐ Yes   ☐ No

10. Please feel free to list any other comments you may have about this Que book.
   _____
   _____
   _____

Que

Order Your Que Books Today!

Name _____

Title _____

Company _____

City _____

State _____ ZIP _____

Phone No. ( ) _____

Method of Payment:

Check ☐ (Please enclose in envelope.)

Charge My: VISA ☐   MasterCard ☐

American Express ☐

Charge # _____

Expiration Date _____

Order No.	Title	Qty.	Price	Total

You can **FAX** your order to **1-317-573-2583**. Or call **1-800-428-5331, ext. ORDR** to order direct.
Please add $2.50 per title for shipping and handling.

Subtotal _____

Shipping & Handling _____

Total _____

Que

BUSINESS REPLY MAIL
First Class Permit No. 9918   Indianapolis, IN

Postage will be paid by addressee

11711 N. College
Carmel, IN 46032

BUSINESS REPLY MAIL
First Class Permit No. 9918   Indianapolis, IN

Postage will be paid by addressee

11711 N. College
Carmel, IN 46032